Apartheid's Festival

African Systems of Thought

GENERAL EDITOR
Ivan Karp

CONTRIBUTING EDITORS
James W. Fernandez
Luc de Heusch
John Middleton
Roy Willis

Leslie Witz

Apartheid's Festival

Contesting
South Africa's
National
Pasts

INDIANA
University Press
Bloomington & Indianapolis

davidphilip

Publication of this book is made possible in part with the
assistance of a Challenge Grant from the National Endowment
for the Humanities, a federal agency that supports research,
education, and public programming in the humanities.

This book is a publication of

Indiana University Press
601 North Morton Street
Bloomington, IN 47404-3797 USA

http://iupress.indiana.edu

Telephone orders	800-842-6796
Fax orders	812-855-7931
Orders by e-mail	iuporder@indiana.edu

The paper used in this publication meets the minimum
requirements of American National Standard for
Information Sciences—Permanence of Paper for Printed
Library Materials, ANSI Z39.48-1984.

Manufactured in the United States of America

Library of Congress Cataloging-in-Publication Data

Witz, Leslie.
    Apartheid's festival : contesting South Africa's national pasts / Leslie Witz.
        p.   cm. — (African systems of thought)
Includes bibliographical references (p.) and index.
    ISBN 0-253-34271-6 (cloth : alk. paper) — ISBN 0-253-21613-3 (pbk. : alk. paper)
    1. Cape Town (South Africa)—Anniversaries, etc. 2. Festivals—South Africa—History—20th century.
3. Public history—South Africa. 4. Apartheid—South Africa. 5. South Africa—Cultural policy. I. Title.
II. Series.
    DT2405.C3657 W58 2003
    968.73'55—dc21

                                                                    2002153778

1 2 3 4 5   08 07 06 05 04 03

Contents

Acknowledgments

In a book of this nature, which is primarily concerned with contests over the construction of public history, the range of people who have contributed to its production is very wide. It encompasses film and radio archivists, environmental activists, advertising agents, secretaries in government departments, curators at museums, sales assistants at secondhand bookshops, students in lectures, guests at dinner parties, and even passers-by in the street. While it is not feasible to acknowledge each of these contributions individually, they have enabled me to develop an understanding of how history is produced, contested, and received in different ways in the public terrain.

Historians tend to search for a beginning as a means to develop and sustain their arguments. Looking back over the more than ten years of research on the constructions of and contests over South Africa's public iconography, particularly the figure who came to represent apartheid history, Jan van Riebeeck—the commander of the Dutch East India Company's revictualing station at the Cape of Good Hope from 1652 to 1662—I find an originating moment difficult to pin down. Much like the subject matter of this book, which details the circuits of appearance and disappearance of historical events and figures in the public domain, I find it much more useful to try to locate many of the individuals who have given me, over the years and at different times, the support and encouragement to sustain this project. Without all their assistance this book would not have been possible.

One of the key moments was undoubtedly my move to Cape Town in 1990 to take up a lecturing post at the University of the Western Cape (UWC). Two people at UWC who encouraged and facilitated this move, Ciraj Rassool and Gary Minkley, have become my close friends and colleagues. We developed a common interest in public history and have worked and taught together on several projects that examine the construction of public images of the past in spheres ranging from festivals to museums, tourism, memorials, and heritage sites. This has allowed for an incredible cross-fertilization of ideas that, in turn, have fed into many of the formulations and arguments I develop here. A paper I co-authored with Ciraj in 1992, "The 1952 Jan van Riebeeck Tercentenary Festival: Constructing and Contesting Public National History in South Africa," informs many of the ideas in this book. The article was published in the *Journal of African History*, 34 (1993), and parts appear here with the permission of Cambridge University Press. An unpublished piece that Gary and I wrote for the History Workshop conference at the University of the Witwatersrand in July 1994, "Sir Harry Smith and His Imbongi: Local and National Identities in the Eastern Cape, 1952," forms a key component of the arguments developed in chapter 5. I am indebted to Ciraj and Gary for allowing me to draw on our collaborative work for this book.

A large portion of this book is based on my Ph.D. dissertation that I completed in 1997. The supervisor of my doctoral research, Nigel Worden at the University of Cape Town (UCT), gave me constant support and encouragement, directed me to certain material, and, most important, helped me to refine and cohere the ideas I presented. Many others made substantial contributions toward the research and writing of the dissertation. Andrew Meston, Carol Witz, Patricia Hayes, Uma Mesthrie, John Mason, Chris Saunders, William Frater, Rena Sherman, Andrew Ball, and Michele Pickover all helped in locating and providing source material and entered into sometimes lengthy discussions about my work and the directions it was taking. Ingrid Scholtz and Wayne Dooling assisted with the translation of Dutch documents. Anriette Esterhuysen and Ran Greenstein not only extended their hospitality to me during research trips to Johannesburg but also, through discussion, encouraged and supported the project. Carolyn Hamilton's comments and incisive questioning helped to provide direction at a stage when the dissertation threatened to become bogged down in the almost overwhelming mass of sources on the festival. Andrew Bank read chapters of an early draft and made very useful, detailed comments. Pat van der Spuy proofread the dissertation, picking up on my inconsistencies, incorrect usage of certain phrases, and various other grammatical errors.

Most of the work on the development of the manuscript of the book took place in 2002. I was most fortunate in being awarded a fellowship on the Institutions of Public Culture program at the Center for the Study of Public Scholarship (CSPS) at Emory University. This was one of the most intensive and comprehensive periods of study and research for me, which, in no small measure, was owing to the constant support and encouragement from the directors and staff at the CSPS. Anne Walker, the CSPS program coordinator, was absolutely amazing in facilitating the smooth running of the fellowship program. Cory Kratz, co-director of the CSPS, was not only one of the most astute critics of my work but someone who always managed to find time in a hectic schedule to ascertain how one's life, in general, and work, in particular, were progressing. Ivan Karp, also co-director of the CSPS, was a constant source of support. He promoted my work at every turn, read and reread drafts of chapters, engaged in ongoing discussion around the issues I was raising, and made immensely valuable suggestions as to the directions it could take. This fellowship was made possible by the University of the Western Cape, which granted me study leave, the institutions that provided the funds, the Rockefeller Foundation and Emory University, and my colleagues at UWC and UCT, who managed projects and taught various courses while I was at Emory. In the last category I am particularly grateful to Premesh Lalu, who not only took over many of my teaching and administrative responsibilities but also read my work and offered instructive critiques.

As the manuscript was nearing completion I was most fortunate to be able to call on the services of three most able research assistants, who located photographs, illustrations, and bibliographic references: Chrischené Julius and Jill Weintroub, students on the UWC, UCT, Robben Island Museum Postgraduate Diploma in Museum and Heritage Studies, and Mbulelo Mrubata, who had just completed his MA degree in history at UWC. Pete Stuckey at Graphco Processing and Matthew Cooke of Design Matters facilitated the reproduction of photographs and cartoons and the drawing of maps and diagrams. It was also a pleasure to work with a copy editor as meticulous as Rita Bernhard. Thanks also to Leonie Twentyman Jones who, at very short notice, compiled the index.

Lastly, thanks to my partner, Josi Frater. Josi, in addition to being my companion and friend, has also been one of my sternest critics, particularly in relation to language usage. She proofread parts of the work, attempting to eradicate some of the long sentences and tautologies. She was also incredibly helpful in collecting material, constantly being on the lookout for public images of Van Riebeeck and the festival. But, most of all, it was her encouragement and support that have sustained me in writing this book. Thank you, Josi.

Parts of this book are based on research conducted for the National Research Foundation (NRF)-funded Project on Public Pasts based in the Department of History at the University of the Western Cape. The financial support of the NRF toward this research is hereby acknowledged. Opinions expressed in this book and conclusions arrived at are those of the author and are not necessarily to be attributed to the NRF.

Parts of this book have appeared, in different form, as journal articles or as chapters in edited collections. An earlier version of chapter 4 appeared under the same title in *South African Historical Journal* 29 (November 1993). It is reproduced here by permission of the *South African Historical Journal*. Parts of this same chapter, in an adapted form, also appeared in a collection edited by Pippa Skotnes, *Miscast: Negotiating the Presence of the Bushmen*, published by UCT Press in 1996. The article "Fashioning the Bushman in Van Riebeeck's Cape Town, 1952 and 1993" was coauthored with Rob Gordon and Ciraj Rassool. Permission from UCT Press to reproduce parts of this article is hereby acknowledged. "From Langa Market Hall and Rhodes' Estate to the Grand Parade and the Foreshore: Contesting Van Riebeeck's Cape Town," a paper that was published in *Kronos* 25 (1998/99), takes up some of the issues dealt with in sections of chapter 3. Permission from *Kronos* to reproduce parts of this article is hereby acknowledged. A paper entitled "Beyond Van Riebeeck" was published in the collection *Senses of Culture,* edited by Sarah Nutall and Cheryl-Anne Michael. This paper, which examines the writing of school history textbooks, covers some of the aspects dealt with in chapter 1 and the postscript. Oxford University Press in Cape Town published the collection in 2000, and permission to use parts of the article is hereby acknowledged.

Abbreviations

Archives

ANV	Algemeen Nederlands Verbond Library, Cape Town
CA	State Archives, Cape Archives Depot, Cape Town
CAD	State Archives, Central Archives Depot, Pretoria
CORY	Rhodes University, Cory Library, Grahamstown
DPL	Durban Public Library
INCH	University of the Free State, Institute for Contemporary History, Bloemfontein
NFA	National Film and Video Archives, Pretoria
SABC	South African Broadcasting Corporation Sound Archives, Johannesburg
SAL	National Library of South Africa, Cape Town
UCT, ASL	University of Cape Town, African Studies Library
UCT, MA	University of Cape Town, Manuscripts and Archives
US	University of Stellenbosch Document Center
WITS (A)	University of Witwatersrand Archives
WITS (HP)	University of Witwatersrand, Historical Papers

Organizations and Institutions

AAC	All African Convention
ACVV	Afrikaanse Christelike Vroue Vereneging [Afrikaner Christian Women's Organization]
ANC	African National Congress
ANCYL	African National Congress Youth League
Anti-CAD	Anti-Coloured Affairs Department
ANV	Algemeen Nederlands Verbond
APO	African Political Organisation
ATKV	Afrikaans Taal en Kultuur Vereniging [Afrikaans Language and Cultural Association]
CATA	Cape African Teachers Association
CPNU	Coloured People's National Union
DRC	Dutch Reformed Church
FAK	Federasie van Afrikaanse Kultuurverenigings [Federation of Afrikaans Cultural Associations]

FRAC	Franchise Action Council
GRA	Genootskap van Regte Afrikaners [Fellowship of True Afrikaners]
NAD	Native Affairs Department
NEUM	Non-European Unity Movement
SAIC	South African Indian Congress
TEPA	Teachers Educational and Professional Association
TLSA	Teachers League of South Africa
TRC	Truth and Reconciliation Commission
UCT	University of Cape Town
WPBTL	Western Province Bantu Teachers League

Apartheid's Festival

Introduction

Journeys, Festivals, and the Making of National Pasts

The week of 26 to 31 October 1992 was a busy one for D. F. Malan Airport in Cape Town. Relegated for years to a minor air terminal, largely carrying domestic traffic, strong predictions of an imminent end to white rule in South Africa saw the doors of the airport being opened to the international world. Amid much fanfare and publicity, the first scheduled regular flights from Germany, France, and Holland landed on its runways, and the first weekly direct non-stop flight from Cape Town to London was inaugurated. The journey from Holland was accorded special symbolic significance, as Holland was the birthplace of Jan van Riebeeck, the man who officially had been proclaimed, in 1952, as the "founder [in 1652] of the white settlement at the then inhospitable southern tip of Africa." In acknowledgment of this, the official guest on board flight KL 593—specially renamed *Kaap De Goede Hoop*—was the mayor of Culemborg, the birthplace of Jan van Riebeeck. And, to the mayor's surprise, there to greet her when she landed and present her with a bunch of proteas was none other than the "son of Culemborg," Jan van Riebeeck, whose role was played by the director of the Cape Town Chamber of Commerce, Nick Malherbe.[1]

The arrival of *Kaap De Goede Hoop* at D. F. Malan Airport was not intended to celebrate the founding of white South Africa but its demise. Mayor Mieke Bloemendaal was representing a town which not only had borne Jan van Riebeeck but which, during the 1970s and 1980s, as the struggle against white rule intensified, had distanced itself from associations with the figure whom they labeled "the founder of apartheid land." Instead, Culemborg had played an increasingly active role in Local Authorities Against Apartheid [LOTA], a Dutch anti-apartheid group which supported civic organizations in South Africa's black townships. To cement this relationship Mayor Bloemendaal visited Villiersdorp, a small town in the western Cape, met members of the local civic structure, and, in what the *Culemborgse Courant* claimed was a "unique event" for a "white mayor," spent the night in the township of Nuwedorp, sharing a two-room house with its fifteen other inhabitants.[2]

But no matter what form of penance Mayor Bloemendaal took, she realized she could not easily discard the mantle of Jan van Riebeeck. "The arrival of Jan van Riebeeck in Cape Town is one moment in history which we cannot deny," she told members of the local business community. Nonetheless, she maintained, it was important to realize that Jan van Riebeeck had not intended to occupy the land "with all the consequences that flowed from that, such as slavery and so on." Culpability for the repercussions of this "meeting of countries" lay with those who had succeeded Jan van Riebeeck, settled in southern Africa, and introduced "terrible poverty, misery and oppression."[3]

Forty years before Mayor Bloemendaal ate and slept with the people of Villiersdorp, the town of Culemborg and its mayor, H. A. J. M. van Koningsbruggen, had no such qualms about their associations with the then Jan van Riebeeck. They participated with almost unbridled enthusiasm in a massive tercentenary festival, sponsored by D. F. Malan's National Party government which had come to power with the promise to implement apartheid, to commemorate with "the people of South Africa" the "establishment of the White settlement at the Cape of Good Hope by Jan van Riebeeck three hundred years ago." The central stage of the festival was the streets and Atlantic shore board of Cape Town. Pageants depicting South Africa's past and present paraded down Cape Town's main thoroughfare, Adderley Street; a festival fair was constructed on Cape Town's reclaimed foreshore, where "the city grew into the sea"; and, in a scene reminiscent of the famous mid-nineteenth-century painting by Charles Davidson Bell (a painting remarkable for its "blend of Dutch and English, with a touch of artistic licence thrown in"), Jan van Riebeeck (played by André Huguenet) made the short journey from Table Bay to Granger Bay onboard the *Dromedaris*, hoisted the flag, and took possession of the land "in the name of the Dutch East India Company" (Figure 1).[4]

A week later, from a replica of the Culemborg town hall at the festival fair, Jan van Riebeeck phoned home:

> This is Jan van Riebeeck here, a citizen of your town speaking to you from Culemborg in Cape Town. As the founder of this South African nation I want to express my pride at the achievement of my descendants. Their festival was a magnificent spectacle.[5]

Holland's response to Van Riebeeck was equally enthusiastic. The first of KLM's series of DC-6B airplanes was baptized *Jan van Riebeeck* at a ceremony at Schiphol Airport involving a "genuine ox-wagon" and "*volksdansen*" [folk/ national dances]. Culemborg sent the city of Cape Town a specially commissioned painting of the interior of the Barbara Church in Culemborg, where Van Riebeeck had been baptized, to adorn the mayor's parlor. Between 10 May and 2 June 1952, Jan van Riebeeck commemorative events were held in Culemborg, although on a much scaled-down version of the Cape Town celebrations. There were musical performances, sports tournaments, and a historical exhibition, "Jan van Riebeeck and His Times," in the town. Both the king and queen of the Netherlands paid special visits to Culemborg, and the latter was presented with a vase engraved with a depiction of the *Dromedaris*. At a gathering of Van Riebeeck's descendants, the South African ambassador unveiled

1. Landing of Jan, Maria, and Lambertus van Riebeeck at Granger Bay, 5 April 1952.
National Library of South Africa, Cape Division. Photo: *Cape Times.*

a present from the Cape Town City Council to Culemborg, a statue of Van Riebeeck. Culemborg's leading men were "delighted with the gift," "impressed"
with its appearance, and, along with "the inhabitants of South Africa," "proud
of what this Hollander did at the Cape."[6]

These journeys, from Schiphol Airport in Amsterdam to D. F. Malan, from
Table Bay to Granger Bay, from Culemborg to Cape Town and back again, were
passages through time and space, framed by a moment selected, in 1952, by the
South African government and a range of cultural organizations, to signify origins of nationhood: the establishment of a revictualing station at Table Bay in
April 1652 "to regularise the benefits which sailors [from Europe] had long derived from the Cape stopover." Embodying this moment was the official sent
by the Dutch East India Company to set up the station, Jan van Riebeeck. Indeed, far from merely representing Dutch/South African relations, Jan van Riebeeck and 6 April 1652 have come to frame South Africa, its History and its
future. This was no more evident than during South Africa's first "historic"
elections in April 1994, when the "dawn of freedom" always evoked the setting
of the sun some three hundred–odd years before. It was expressed most aptly

by one voter who, when asked for her feelings about "making history by standing in a queue" for hours, replied: " 'Have you heard the real meaning of Einstein's Theory of Relativity? . . . If you've waited 300 years for a vote, what's another five hours in the rain!' "[7]

But as much as South Africans and the rest of the world were constantly being reminded that History was being made in April 1994, history, as the interpretation and re-interpretation of changes in societies, was being replaced by a teleological progression from a distinct starting point to an ending. In this endocentric past, History now began, it was argued, when racial oppression started. "Ever since the first settlers from Europe appeared in South Africa in 1652, the country has been ruled by white people." It ended when "after nearly 350 years of white dominion" a "new South Africa" was born, "because the black people fought against" apartheid. In the intervening years, the government made "racist" laws to "keep whites in power . . . [and] black people poor and without power." Most "black people," in turn, "did not like apartheid," and through resistance organizations, like the African National Congress (ANC) which "held up the sun" in the three-hundred-year interregnum, they "made the white government change their mind." Out of this emerged the "new government" which "is going to stop apartheid and try to make the lives of our people better."[8]

This story might appear somewhat crude and simplistic—no one would really argue that the refreshment station established at Table Bay in 1652 was a country named South Africa—but it does point to the way that Van Riebeeck's landing in its role as an icon of whiteness helps to structure a framework of South African history built around repression and resistance. The "disembarking of Van Riebeeck at the Cape" has become the launching site of a story of racial domination, subjugation, and opposition in South Africa. In terms of this account, it was racial oppression that came into being in April 1652 and racial oppression that was discarded onto the garbage dump of History 342 years later, also in the month of April, when "Mandela lifted the hands of Deputy Presidents De Klerk and Mbeki skyward, like a referee proclaiming new title holders."[9]

These twin processes, the marking of 1652 and the flattening of South Africa's racial past around an originating moment and finite ending, owe more to the 1940s and 1950s, when apartheid was in its formative stages, than the events which followed the establishment of the revictualing station at Table Bay. As South African society, particularly after the coming to power of the National Party in 1948, was increasingly subject to regimes of racial hierarchies, political exclusion, and state repression, new forms and versions of South African history were created by the government, by cultural and political organizations, and by individual scholars. At times the historical narratives that were produced took a form that legitimated this "thoroughgoing system of racial engineering,"[10] often depicting the land as empty of people prior to European settlement. But, perhaps even more important, there were narratives that fundamentally questioned and contested apartheid histories. These largely emanated from individuals and organizations who were in some way challenging the increased racial ordering of society, many presenting the beginnings of the Dutch East India Company station at Table Bay as the dawn of an era of conquest, slavery, and dispossession. It was in these contests over new forms of South African history that Jan van Riebeeck was recoded in the image of South Africa as the shaper of its past.

This book deals with the moment when Van Riebeeck assumed this position of prominence—the National Party government–sponsored tercentenary festival of 1952. The festival was designed to commemorate a commonality of all people who were in the process of being racially classified as white—the Population Registration Act, promulgated in 1950, legislated that all inhabitants of the country had to be officially identified as belonging to a racial category: "white" or "Bantu" or "coloured" or "Asiatic"—as the distinct South African nation, with their joint past derived out of Europe and Van Riebeeck. These depictions of a South African nationhood based on whiteness and a European past, which were at the very core of the festival, were challenged by a range of political groups. The most sustained and vocal of these anti-celebratory campaigns came from the Non-European Unity Movement (NEUM), a broad front of political organizations fighting against racial domination through boycotts and non-collaboration. These organizations called for a massive boycott of the Van Riebeeck festival, labeling it a "festival of hate," an "orgy of *Herrenvolkism*," and a celebration of "the national oppression and exploitation of the Non-Whites." The ANC, although it did not primarily direct its attentions toward Van Riebeeck, deliberately chose 6 April, the day of his landing, to publicly launch its campaign of defiance against apartheid laws. In mass meetings across the country on 6 April 1952, speakers referred to the Van Riebeeck festival as mere "gilded hypocrisy and distorted history," with Van Riebeeck being depicted as a scoundrel, a thief, and the initiator of white domination.[11] Throughout the festival Van Riebeeck became the man who laid down the policy of apartheid, both for those in power and those excluded from it.

Productions of History and Culture

This abbreviated account of the emergence of Van Riebeeck on the historical stage in South Africa, where the early years of apartheid are treated as the explanatory device, resonates with two arguments, one presented within the field of heritage studies and the other dealing with the reading of cultural productions. In "the dominant ideology thesis in relation to heritage," where heritage is taken to refer to the representation of different histories to broad public audiences, the presentation of pastness is analyzed as a malleable instrument that is used by those holding the reins of state power (or alternatively those in opposition) to convey a particular political message to subordinate groups. Critics of such an approach point to the inconsistencies among the many different producers of meaning, the sometimes lack of a clear distinction between the dominant producer and subordinate receiver groups, and the ways the subordinate groups may construct their own meanings that are located outside the bounds of the dominant ideologies. Yet, in spite of these objections, these critics do accept the notion that the salient characteristics of these depictions are their political messages or their economic messages or both and that these need to be at the core of analytical inquiries into what they term "heritage products." [12]

Similarly, in relation to historical investigation of cultural productions, the methodology called on at times is to regard the search for, and analysis of, evidence of the past as a form of ethnographic fieldwork. Historians are enjoined to regard worlds of the past, as expressed in historical sources, as "other," which, like the words and actions of the "informant," need to be "captured" and read for meaning. Through a close reading, "alien system[s] of meaning" in the past are detected and then related back to "the surrounding world of significance" by "moving back and forth between the narrative and the surrounding documentation." In this manner the claim is made, a way is cleared "through a foreign mental world," and the "social dimension of meaning" is delineated. What this facilitates is a move beyond an empirically bound cause-and-effect analysis, where certain (usually Western) modes of thought and notions of person are taken as the norm, toward a re-imagining of societies where "seeing . . . experiences within the framework of [a society's] own idea of what selfhood is" is all-important. Ultimately this will lead to a more open-ended interpretation, in that participants and observers do not all extract the same meaning from an event, or even all its meaning. [13]

For both these approaches, it is the systems of significance that are at the core of investigation. In the "dominant ideology thesis," meanings are read through the operation of economic and political power and how these come to structure actions. In the interpretation of "cultural phenomena," performance and display are treated in textual terms and are read for meaning through their significance, modes of operation, and how they come to operate as an "activating dynamic." The metaphor used in cultural analysis is "webs of significance," with the aim being to describe, in sometimes very precise detail, the intimately connected processes of signification. It is the "webs, not the spinning; the culture, not the history; the text, not the process of textualizing" that are all-important.[14]

In examining a cultural event it is clearly important to investigate and describe the webs of signification. Most fruitfully, through interpretation, it enables complex readings and understandings of an event. An approach which purportedly seeks to present the world as accurately as possible through employing positivist methods—trying to keep an objective distance from the field of study and ensuring that the data are reliable, replicable, and representative—cannot accommodate multiple meanings and the researcher's intervention in imagining and re-constructing worlds of the past. What a deep reading at a very localized level may tend to lose sight of, at times, though, are the connections to broader trends in economy and society, the workings of relations of power, and the contests that emerge from and give shape to the makings of meanings. The danger here is that these intimate readings may neglect the different practices and histories of signs and texts, thereby "aestheticizing all domains." There is a need to go beyond the local case study, to analyze processes and contradictions that emerge when one begins "to extract the general from the unique, to move from the 'micro' to the 'macro.'"[15]

The key argument presented in this book is that to only examine portrayals, performances, and their representational forms in a world of the past overlooks many of the processes that go into the making and definition of cultural meanings. In order to go beyond the study of the 1952 tercentenary festival, to look at how different and contested meanings around the festival came to be defined, the starting point is the need to investigate the forms, practices, and social contexts that go into "the production of history." This notion takes history beyond the writings of the academy and recognizes that there are many producers, at various sites, who utilize different historical methodologies to process a range of pasts. These presentations of pastness, whether they are oral or written or visual, are not prior to history but are actual "historical practices within different genres characterized by different sociologies and modalities of historical production." Photographs, festivals, tourist spectacles, visual landscapes, dramatic performances, renderings of oral traditions, and museum exhibitions are domains of historical representation, "each informed by its own logic and generat[ing] its own particular images and insights." This opens up for exploration how these different sites of history making are constituted, what their various codes and conventions are, and how they articulate with one another.[16]

One major implication of asserting the existence of these "multiple locations of historical knowledge" is that there are constant "struggles for control of voices and texts in innumerable settings which often animate the processing of the past." Reading for meaning, although it does take into account some degree of conflicting interpretation and sub-texts, is ultimately always search-ing for an understanding of events, attempting to "map . . . with some preci-sion . . . an established range of meanings." The result is that once the signifi-cation has been found, defined, and limited, the contradictions and differences "which evoke and produce" histories often tend to be hidden, and a new veil is drawn over the text. Histories in the public domain are often sites of intense contestation and the products that emerge are the result of negotiations and conflicts between opposing groups over its constituent elements, what events and personalities should be included and excluded, and how they should be represented.[17]

Not only does a focus on the contemporary message reduce the numerous contests over historical representations to an analysis of their outcomes, it also tends to neglect histories of these portrayals. The importance of these pre-vious histories is that they facilitate and limit the ways in which new pasts may be created. At moments it is possible to recognize the contemporary circum-stances under which certain historical depictions acquire either a sense of pre-eminence or exclusion. But they cannot simply be inventions, especially if they are to be sustained and assume some forms of credibility for their respective audiences. This does not mean that it is impossible to make claims for and dis-tinguish moments of "new history" but that analysis of these public produc-tions requires much more than a search for an originating moment. It becomes necessary to track the circuits of appearance and disappearance of historical depictions, the specific contexts in which they come to assume particular forms and how traces of past representations can come to set the boundaries of pos-sibility for new histories.[18]

Third, in analyzing the meanings presented in displays of history, the public tends to be taken as undifferentiated, passive recipients of these historical rep-resentations. There is little cognizance of the distinctive nature of specific audi-ences, how they are conceived and how they may play a key role in shaping what may become the product. As has been noted with respect to displays in muse-ums, the response of audiences might be completely at variance with the inten-tions of the designers and curators of the exhibition. Many audience studies have taken this divergence as their starting point and suggested that the ways in which visitors make meanings in a museum encounter are almost unlimited and depend on their community and cultural backgrounds, the occasion of the visit, and the exhibitions they take in.[19] But this open-ended approach to audi-ences shifts the focus away from how and why institutions construct meanings toward a framework that delineates museums as spaces of education dependent on a series of cognitive interactions. Relations of power in the politics of rep-resentation in the public domain are often invariably sidelined. These politics "center on debates about how particular topics, perspectives, and images become prominent, how their depictions are formed and interpreted, and the social relations and inequalities reproduced through representational practices, including their institutional settings."[20] In much the same way as previous histories limit and facilitate the production of new pasts, the power and authority to represent histories through public display always "define boundaries for interpretive openness." If the politics of representation, and the limits they set, are brought into play, then a much more complex investigation emerges. Analysis of different visitors, in different settings, engaging and bringing their ideas to "bear on their understanding of what is shown," is firmly placed within the confines of the contests to author and authorize public histories.[21]

The problems involved in reading meaning into performance and display become particularly apparent when dealing with festivals. At one level festivals are usually rich in symbolism, emphasizing "consensus and oneness rather than distinction within the community," with "members of a whole community . . . sharing a world view" gathered in celebration of a particular event, day, or individual. Yet this richness in symbols and apparent unity is precisely why festivals are so difficult to read. Festivals are "multisensory, multifocus" moments when struggles over symbolism are increasingly evident, when signs become ambiguous and contests emerge over their adaptation, adoption, or rejection. Conflicts erupt over numerous issues: involvement and intention, organization and spontaneity, design and response, participation and exclusion. Searching for a unified meaning, or the norm, in these multiple confrontations would presuppose some "shared and unified symbolic universe." It would efface the conflicts over the social practices that went into constructing what appears to be a coherent and inter-dependent entity. Moments of most intense pressure and disturbance often occur when the intricate workings of social orders at micro and macro levels become more apparent.[22]

Not all festivals appear to have these conflicts, contradictions, and differences, particularly when the state plays a major role either in the festival's organization and production or in appropriating a local cultural event and transforming it into a national tradition. Such "deliberately engineered festivals" largely utilize singular and simplified narratives of history and tradition. The key objective of these festivals is to create a sense of belonging and identification to what is proclaimed to be a new nation, conveying a sense of pastness that is distinct and revelatory. The excessive power of those involved in the organization, through funding, authority, and media access, generally signifies that the meaning they confer to the festival triumphs "over the meaning experienced by the participants." But that does not erase the multiple conflicts inherent in the festivals. Indeed, when the state assumes the role of director of these cultural productions, tensions often heighten as "local factions, political parties, commercial interests, government, church, media, and tourism" compete to ascribe different meanings to events. Moreover, the ultimate success of a festival is in its ability to generate "festive excitement." This kind of excitement does not emerge when spectators and participants merely succumb to the official version of the event; rather, it is "the transgression of prohibitions, . . . the excess authorized by the festival" that exhilarates the participants and spectators. Paradoxically, these unofficial encounters and violations of the festival program are precisely what evoke the spontaneity the organizers desperately seek. No matter how much the festival is engineered or organized, in certain ways it is always an open forum, where everyone can derive "knowledge and skill" through "pleasurable, sensual experiences," a place that has the ability to generate festive excesses.[23]

But if one is then to accept that state-produced festivals are performances centering on contestation and conflict, events that cannot merely be reduced to cultural texts to be read for meaning, then the task of historical analysis becomes more complex. Clearly there is still a major responsibility both to investigate the intentions and strategies in the planning of the festival as well as the significance of the imagery of the festival and its historical depictions. It is useful in this regard to add festivals to the list of institutions that constitute the "public historical sphere," institutions that produce, circulate, and contain meanings about the past. The meanings of these institutions are best understood when the specific forms by which histories are created are located within a contemporary scenario, where the representational modes and genres are tied to "social, cultural and political preoccupations." These considerations are most apparent in constituting the spatial and temporal limits of nations being conceived as new or reborn. The past is aligned with the present, so that the nation appears to be the pre-determined outcome of a history usually seen as having begun in a "deep time" of "long ago." But this alignment of past and present does not end there. The alignment is projected into the future so that the trajectory of the nation is formulated as following the same historical path. Thus the nation and its history become a litany of struggles and achievements that demand replication in the future, manufacturing "a never-ending story of development."[24]

Although this formulation of the workings of public historical spheres, such as national festivals, provides the necessary framework to proceed with an examination of the Van Riebeeck festival, it tends to marginalize ambiguity and contradiction to "minority instances." As described above, discord, debate, and negotiations over historical representations, far from being peripheral issues in festivals and other cultural productions, are central to the content and form in which national pasts come to be presented. It is the urge to see order and meaning that "obscures the existence of conflict and struggle." Indeed, the significance of symbols often lies in their instability, mobility, and history, which make them "not always easily decipherable." This requires that we go beyond merely locating public historical representations in a past-present alignment but also search for disjunctions when this configuration is not so easily established. These fault lines, which occur in the process of construction, evocation, selection, presentation, and reception of public pasts, are integral to showing not only "how . . . multiple meanings are produced" but also how "the subtle ambiguities, . . . the layerings of history and context," come to be eliminated in the desire and search for a narrative of a national past. The past-present alignment thus enables a reading of the historical production, while an invocation of dissonance enables us to understand that attempting to establish this alignment is fraught with continual difficulty. The casting in 1952 of Van Riebeeck as the founder, and 1652 as the moment, of racial control in South Africa was made possible through the contests over the various processes that went into "nationing history while simultaneously historicizing the nation."[25]

Afrikaner Nationalism and the Apartheid State

A major impetus in attempting to establish a past-present alignment in the public historical sphere comes through the state. Decisions around material and other forms of support for heritage-type projects are grounded in the state constituting itself as the mechanism through which the spatial and temporal limits of a singular national unit are established. The state assigns a set of associations between selected moments to fix a national narrative, which moves in a specific direction toward an already determined future. This function of the state has been referred to as "curating the nation," where the nation, with its monuments, statues, memorials, museums, and so on, is equated with an open-air museum where the state, as curator, decides what to display and how.[26]

There can be little doubt in South Africa that the apartheid state, which took shape after the National Party's election victory in 1948, was a key curator in re-defining the nation. A major element in the emergence of the National Party as a political force had been the invocation of a series of cultural symbols that established and constantly re-affirmed an Afrikaner identity as autochthonous, that is, of Africa and the land, and as white. Most notable among these symbols was the construction of a monumental journey of nationhood, a great Afrikaner trek away from the tentacles of British colonial officialdom in the early nineteenth century and into the southern African interior, making it "inhabitable for a white race."[27] After coming to power, the party commissioned memorials dedicated to figures and events considered to represent the trials, tribulations, and triumphs of this Afrikaner national past. Public holidays were inscribed on the annual calendar to commemorate events invoking a predestined journey of occupation of the land and struggles for autonomy. Across the country, streets and towns with British imperial associations were renamed so they could be identified with events and people associated with a seemingly pre-ordained history of an Afrikaner nation. Commemorative days were seized on with alacrity for displays of pageantry, where, with high-ranking officials ever present, the narrative inevitably extolled the supposed progress and virtues of the Afrikaner nation and encouraged active participation in an apartheid future.

But the apartheid state was not an unchanging, monolithic entity. Several organizational structures existed within the ruling National Party as well as a series of strong relationships with a range of economic and cultural organizations, all claiming to represent the interests of Afrikaners. Although the interests of all these groups sometimes coalesced and found public expression in support of the party and the figure of the national leader, deep fractures were apparent between national and local structures, between the party and its leadership, and between the different regional power bases in the north and south of the country. Moreover, although the National Party had come to power on the election promise to implement apartheid, it lacked a "grand design" or "master plan" to put the system in place. Instead, starting in 1948 there followed a series of uneven, at times ad-hoc state responses to "the intensifying contradictions of industrialisation, urbanisation and popular struggles" taking place in South Africa after the Second World War. The primary concern of the apartheid state was to contrive strategies to counter a perceived threat against state power emerging from an increasingly militant, African working class. The various policies discussed and eventually implemented in this "battle to control African urbanisation" were both the source and result of this fracturing within the ruling National Party.[28]

Although a sense of Afrikanerization was most pervasive during the apartheid era, a sense promoted through the pre-eminence given to historical images supposedly symbolizing an Afrikaner *volk* [people/nation] and a policy of affirmative action favoring the recruitment of Afrikaans speakers, identified as white, into the civil service, the content and direction of this racially exclusive nationalism was not pre-determined. With the nature of the apartheid state shifting and fracturing as the economic, political, and cultural forces constituting it realigned themselves, it is difficult to claim that, over the course of almost half a century, South Africa was curated as a national entity following a singular, historical narrative with the same internal dynamism and direction. Furthermore, as indicated earlier, there are limits to the power of the state in institutionalizing a narrative of the nation, its past and prospective future. These may include previous histories in circulation, conflicts within the structures of the state and between elements of civil society as to what constitutes such a history, and the ability of unofficial pasts to be constructed, evoked, and distributed. There had always been deep discord as to how an Afrikaner nation and its past would be forged.

Afrikaner nationalism, from its beginnings in the late nineteenth century, was produced around a tension of asserting an anti-colonial political legacy while simultaneously claiming to be the bearers to Africa of "civilization" derived from Europe. This was resolved, in early Afrikaner nationalist versions of history, by portraying the Afrikaners as liberators of the land and rendering all other inhabitants as conquerors. Afrikaners were constructed as the exclusive bearers of the South Africa nation, its history and traditions, struggling for independence against the forces of imperialism—initially officials of the Dutch East India Company and later British colonial rule—and the power of imaginary armies of darkness, whereas the local inhabitants were cast as savage invaders of an empty land. In some ways this resembled nationalist projects emerging at the same time in the Indian sub-continent. Bengali writers of the time were suggesting that the anti-colonial struggle was against British and Muslim rule, with each depicted as foreign forces. An envisaged modern independent nation, with its own singular history, was presented as being based on Hindu civilization and excluded any sense of either a European-derived culture or a classical Islamic heritage.[29] This invocation of the anti-colonial was central to both Indian and Afrikaner nationalism.

But a fundamental difference existed between the two projects centering on their relationship to European culture. In India the political struggles against colonialism took on a material form, where the objectives were somehow to construct an independent modern state derived from models of states that had developed in Europe in the eighteenth and early nineteenth centuries. Simultaneously, and indeed prior to these contests, there was an assertion of a spiritual domain, where a cultural inner identity was proclaimed which was distinct from that of the colonizer. The project of anti-colonial nationalism, in this context, was "to fashion a 'modern' national culture that is nevertheless not western." In the case of Afrikaner nationalist writers, almost the opposite prevailed. In challenging British imperialism, Afrikaner nationalists asserted a culture based on belonging to the land and derived from a European lineage. So, for instance, when Afrikaans was codified in the late-nineteenth and early-twentieth centuries, words and phrases were selected not only to establish its uniqueness but to situate it as a European language. This and similar assertions were made in the face of continual claims by British colonial administrators and writers, throughout much of the nineteenth century, that the frontier farmers (Boers) had, at best, crude manners and, at worst, had become so like the "natives" that they were uncivilized.[30]

In the 1930s a far more virulent form of Afrikaner nationalism developed, with ideas of establishing an Afrikaner republic that eschewed any alliance with colonial forces or their remnants. Built on a dichotomy of a set of characteristics labeled as foreign—the city, Englishness, lack of moral values—and as one's own—rurally derived moral values, a sense of closeness to God, and the language of Afrikaans—this later form of Afrikaner nationalism, with its assertion of an inner spiritual domain, appears to be closer to other anti-colonial nationalist movements. Nonetheless, an even stronger assertion existed of a European heritage which moved beyond the realm of cultural affiliation into claims of racial ancestry. The basis of Afrikaner nationalism in the 1930s and 1940s was provided by the emergence of "poor-whites," mostly Afrikaans and Dutch-speaking inhabitants from rural areas who had lost their access to land and jobs with the increasing capitalization of agriculture and were moving to the cities in search of employment. Drawing on the insecurities of "poor-whites," especially their vulnerable position in the workplace where they faced competition for jobs from urbanized Africans, the Afrikaner nationalists increasingly campaigned against foreign imperialism (which they linked to capitalism of an exploitative nature) and for an extensive program of codified racial separation. In the invocation of an anti-imperialist struggle, which drew on symbols of a heroic Afrikaner past, there was not so much a dissociation from European-derived cultures but rather a claim to be almost the pre-ordained bearers to Africa of the untainted "virtues" of European civilization. This claim to moral and cultural purity was replicated in some of the racial ideas circulating in Afrikaner nationalist circles in the 1930s. One of these was that the Afrikaners constituted a specific racial type, combining Nordic and Alpine traits. This enabled the claim to a European racial ancestry as well as the assertion that these characteristics—a generally darker skin and a larger physical frame—made the Afrikaner uniquely suited to Africa. Yet this hybridization could not be extended to those categorized as African, as Africans were presented as biologically incompatible with Europeans and could potentially weaken a biologically defined Afrikaner race. The notion of Afrikaners as a hybrid was defined very much within the realm of European typologies, and, in terms of these biologically constructed categories, racial separation was to be actively pursued to ensure that whites—especially the poorer ones—remained white.[31]

These tensions between creating an anti-colonial nationalist project and at the same time situating it within a discourse of bringing civilization from Europe to Africa intensified as the National Party assumed office in 1948. The rhetoric of anti-colonialism and symbols of struggles for (Afrikaner) liberation had been key in mobilizing Afrikaans-speaking whites to the nationalist project. After 1948, though, it was increasingly seen as necessary to move beyond an Afrikaans-speaking political base. There were two reasons for this. First, although the National Party had won the general election (where the electorate was largely limited to people racially designated as white) by virtue of winning more constituencies than its opponents, it had not been able to garner the support of the majority of voters. In a very narrowly defined arena of South African parliamentary politics in the 1940s, the National Party clearly needed to widen its electoral support base in order to retain power. Second, within a much broader South African political context, the increasing numbers of Africans in the cities, coupled with a rise in outward displays of militancy in the form of strikes and boycotts, presented a perceived threat to "the preservation of white supremacy." Establishing a sense of legitimacy among people who racially designated themselves as white, and were in the process of becoming classified as such, was a major imperative of the apartheid state. One way of accomplishing this was to show that effectively the state was able to control the numbers and activities of people who lived in the townships constructed for African people in urban areas. The entire gamut of apartheid legislation, which set in place an increasing number of checks on the mobility of Africans, was partly designed to accomplish an increased sense of credibility among whites for the state and its operations.[32] Another way of establishing white legitimacy was to mobilize around a much more inclusive notion of a white identity and history. This would mean bringing onboard the very people, and their histories, who were cast as oppressors within the Afrikaner nationalist project of the 1930s and 1940s, thereby exacerbating the fissures between an anti-imperial narrative and one driven by the conceptualization of the metropole as the bearer of whiteness.

Over the past twenty years a great deal has been written about the processes and struggles that went into the making of the apartheid state. What has not been recognized in this body of work is the way that emblems of the past were crucial in developing a most "virulent form of racial ideology."[33] It was the coincidence of the three hundredth anniversary of Jan van Riebeeck's landing in 1952 that provided the National Party government an opportunity to construct a history and identity of whites as whites. Before 1952 Van Riebeeck had been depicted as the *volksvader* [father of the Afrikaner nation], the initiator of farming in South Africa, the bearer of Christianity to the sub-continent, and the [British] colonial founder. In many senses he was therefore ideally suited to be the figure around which a broader white history of South Africa could be constructed, where the nation was conceptualized as the coming together of two white races. But from the very moment the idea was broached to have a Van Riebeeck festival in 1952, the process of making such a nation and its history was racked with conflicting claims over what should be included and how the selected individuals and events should be represented. Within Afrikaner nationalist circles debates broke out over how (or indeed whether) the narrative of an anti-imperial struggle could fit into a past of whiteness devoid of conflict.

Some of the leading business and commercial enterprises expressed concerns over whether they would be cast, once again, as representatives of imperialism and hence enemies of the nation. Further, many pointed to the massive exclusions and distortions embedded in a project that centered on a history derived from establishing a moment of European founding. It was in these conflicts and negotiations over producing a scripted past for Van Riebeeck that a singular history for apartheid began to be constructed.

Festivals of Colonial Founding: Columbus and the Arrival of the First Fleet

The Van Riebeeck festival of 1952 was not unique on many counts. Colonial settler societies have sought to select a moment of colonial discovery or founding as the fount of a nation. Two of the most notable examples have been in Australia and the United States, where commemorative events in the nineteenth and twentieth centuries have singled out the arrival of the First Fleet and Christopher Columbus, respectively, as the beginning of a linear history in a nation's trajectory.[34] It is instructive to examine these commemorative events in some detail, as they were characterized by issues and struggles similar to those that beset Van Riebeeck and his past in 1952.

The disputes begin at the re-creation of the event intended to frame the festival: the moment of colonial settlement or European founding. The power of this moment lies in its seemingly natural occurrence, which merely has to be recovered and inserted into the time of the festival. The past of the festival is then constructed around this event. Yet, as was noted in the Australian bicentennial in 1988, the "decision had to be made that two hundred years since the arrival of the First Fleet was an event worth celebrating, and then the event itself had to be invented." In this founding it was the beginnings of settlement, marked by the arrival of Captain Arthur Phillip with a group of convicts, merchant seamen, and marines and their families at Sydney Cove on 26 January 1788, rather than the "discovery" of the east coast of Australia at Botany Bay by Captain Cook in 1770, which took the stage as the beginning of nationhood. Cook, the somewhat ambiguous figure of singular discovery, was "cast off" to be replaced by Phillip who, in 1988, marched "out of Myth into History," marking places, creating a "substantial history" of settlement, and emptying Botany Bay of a future.[35]

For the United States it is Christopher Columbus, the sailor from Genoa who made landfall at an as yet undisclosed island in the Bahamas on 12 October 1492, who came to be celebrated annually as the discoverer of America, the heralder of "a new age," and even the initiator of "The Modern Era [when] Man emerg[ed] from the Middle Ages."[36] In so doing he supplants other candidates such as Leif Eriksson, the Swede, who occupied Newfoundland from about 1000, or Amerigo Vespucci, who is presumed to have "discovered" mainland America in 1497.

These alternative moments of discovery, occupation, or settlement are not meant either as a corrective or a replacement for what may appear as the obvious date. They point out, however, how, from the beginning, the start of a "nation's journey" is open to contestation. At the same time, though, that beginning cannot merely be plucked from mid-air to suit a pre-determined political purpose and "the event itself . . . invented." Indeed, it is the history of that specific moment of origin that enables it to be shaped and transformed. For instance, in Australia, specifying the moment of settlement in 1988 was largely a formality. Cook had a long, undistinguished career in Australian public history well before 1988, and his apparent lack of enthusiasm, displayed by his inaccurate descriptions of the Australian coastline and the fact that he never returned, was regarded as damning evidence that he was not the founder. So despite opposition from South Australia, where it was argued that Phillip's landing was merely the founding of New South Wales rather than Australia, 26 January, since the beginning of the twentieth century, has been celebrated, albeit intermittently, as Australia Day, Anniversary Day, or Foundation Day in various Australian states. In 1938 the central event of the 150th anniversary celebrations of white settlement in Australia was the staging of Phillip's landing at Farm Cove (Sydney Cove was too small a venue to accommodate the spectators) to be met by a "'troupe of aborigines.'" By 1988, within a "new paradigm of national representation," the emphasis was placed on an Australian nation composed of many people, all having journeyed to Australia over *thousands* of years. A flotilla of Tall Ships was used to symbolize multiculturalism alongside a reproduction of the arrival of Phillip's First Fleet representing the "Australian heritage."[37]

A similar process has occurred with Christopher Columbus over the past five centuries. In the United States, where Columbus never set foot, Columbus Day became a national holiday, the centennials of his landing turned into massive extravaganzas, and more places are named after him than any other figure except George Washington. This explosion of Columbiana in the United States is largely associated with a shifting image of Columbus. Initially a barely commemorated symbol of exploration and heroism in the seventeenth century, from the inception of the United States in the late eighteenth century he became the personification of an essential patriotism of a "new nation" in a "new world" and a founder of an imagined American culture which claimed to champion personal freedoms and progress through science and commerce. One hundred years later, when tensions associated with industrial expansion, immigration, falling agricultural prices, and increasing debt were extremely apparent, the four hundredth anniversary became the vehicle on which to build the theme of progress and to commemorate the landing as a symbol of ongoing national success. In this way the populace of the United States could become public citizens instead of envisaging themselves as subjects of "forces that seemed to control their lives"; each citizen could follow Columbus's path, suffering at first but overcoming hardships in the end. Onto this image of Columbus as the initiator of national progress were added several "firsts." He was celebrated as the instigator of religious freedom, the bearer of Catholicism, a skillful navigator, and the embodiment of the American worker's supposed energy and fortitude. The Columbus quincentennial in 1992, although not confined to the United States, was planned to draw together selected elements of these public pasts to commemorate Columbus in different ways. He was, in 1992, the originator of the "first encounters between the Old and New Worlds," the man who "linked two old worlds . . . and made one," and the subject of extensive and "accurate" "historical and archaeological research" of "those earliest encounters" between Europeans and Native Americans. Echoing assertions made over the past two centuries, landfall in 1492 was proclaimed to be the beginning of a "process that eventually produced the United States of America," a country that was claimed to be, with somewhat exaggerated patriotic fervor, "a symbol and a haven of individual liberty for people throughout the world."[38]

While the previous public pasts have helped to shape the form these commemorations have taken, they have gained their authority by drawing on documents narrating the first moments of founding and subsequent events. These documents appear as original sources and enable a veracity that the previous accounts, considered secondhand, would not sustain. This follows a distinction many historians make between primary and secondary evidence, with the latter seeming to have only a superficial quality and the former apparently containing a deeper essence.[39] The journal of Christopher Columbus, which relates his travels, sometimes daily, is a clear example of such a "beginning text." Although the original of the diary was lost in the mid-sixteenth century (the only version we have is a summarized copy made by a Dominican priest), and the accuracy and authorship of some entries have been challenged, the journal remains the primary document of founding. Its time frames, descriptions, and motivations provide a key to any future histories and to the reconstruction of the moment of founding. It enabled 1992 to claim five hundred years with accuracy; it provides primary evidence of the first encounter; and it sustains a historical authenticity for Christopher Columbus, "a real person, whose story was known to every schoolchild and adult."[40]

But once the founder had landed, discovered, and established the first settlement, what was he to do with the country? This central question is of greatest concern to the organizers of festivals of founding as they plan their respective celebrations. In one sense the answer seems simple. They merely had to "renovate celebratory narratives of European superiority." " 'Australia's March to Nationhood' " in 1938, for instance, told a story about the "progress" of a land from the "backwardness" of the "aboriginal" state, a progression initiated by Phillip who planted " 'a fresh sprig of empire in this new and vast land.' " The Europeans then followed his example, crossing the Blue Mountains, discovering gold, developing industry, conquering the arts, and bringing into being the Commonwealth of Australia. Although aboriginal inhabitants were being cast in 1988 in a multicultural mosaic of Australians who had journeyed together, Phillip's tale was still a European one of "Discovery, Settlement, Convicts, Free Settlers [and] Gold." When Columbus set sail in the quincentenary celebration in 1992 the images evoked were also of European progression across a continent, leading toward a modern nation. Although Columbus was no longer considered the discoverer of America, his landing begins the story of America's "pioneer spirit" and marks the start of its "recorded history." It is a story of literal, material, and moral progress "all leading to the political progress that pointed toward resistance, revolution, and independence." Once independence had been gained and the mountains and prairies crossed (many other Columbuses having joined in the pioneering enterprise), democracy, liberty, progress, and History seemed to flow naturally until Columbus was able to assert himself, in 1992, with help from the U.S. army, as the guardian of "the new frontiers of democracy across the world."[41]

However, these narratives of Columbus and Phillip are missing a vital element. By assuming a straight, causal line between the organizers' intentions, images displayed, and meanings projected, they fail to answer an obvious crucial question: Which celebratory European narratives and their components should festival organizers select as most appropriate to renovate and elaborate? Although this decision, of course, does include selecting the moment of founding, that moment, while establishing a direction for the narrative, does not provide its contents. The Australian bicentennial celebrations in 1988 offer a clear example: although the year 1988 was not contested among the organizers, the contents of the program were heavily disputed. More conservative elements argued for a past that emphasized "tradition," the "Australian Achievement," the "British heritage," "the family," and "relative social harmony." Opposing elements called for depictions of Australia as a multicultural nation, benefiting from significant contributions from its aboriginal population. These elements envisioned a nation composed of people "living together," enjoying their own religions, cultures, and historic sites. After much bitterness, many battles, and resignations from committees, the result was a negotiated past. Although the arrival of the First Fleet remained central to this new nation, its entry into

Sydney Harbor in January 1988, in tune with its shifting paradigm, had to compete with a flotilla of Tall Ships, a fireworks display, and a reception hosted by Prince Charles and Princess Diana. Captain Phillip was also re-figured in a traveling exhibition in juxtaposition with an Aboriginal canoe as Australia was presented as embarking on a voyage "as a nation into the future."[42]

Giving Columbus and Phillip a country with a history not only required negotiating events of the past but also ensuring that these events fit the form of the festival. Three aspects are primary here. First, the events portrayed had to maintain a steady balance between evoking spontaneous reactions and keeping a semblance of order. The organizers of the festivals of founding did not wish to repeat the bizarre exaggerations of the popular European festivals between the sixteenth and eighteenth centuries, with their tumultuous scenes, confrontations through "theatrical and ritual gestures," "crowds obstructing the streets and public squares," and popular enthusiasm reaching fever pitch. Such excitement could not be tolerated as it "disconcerted or 'offended' reason" and could even lead to disunity. Order had to be continually asserted, public participation limited, and fantasy regulated to ensure that the selected "propitious . . . times, and [the] 'good' events" in the building of the nation could "ripen just like good fruit."[43]

The second formative aspect regarding historical content of concern to festival organizers was the weighing of spectacle and authenticity. Although many commemorative festivals tend to emphasize ritual, speeches, and a re-affirmation of an inner essence, the visual experience of the celebration is central to festivals of founding. There are elaborate historical journeys over sea and land, displays of pageantry in the streets, fairs and historical displays, and lavishly illustrated histories for schools and the general public. But this emphasis on spectacle is always in competition with the effort to achieve historical authenticity, and festival organizers can use this issue to motivate either for the exclusion or inclusion of historical events. Thus, in 1938, in an attempt to deny that Australia had a convict past, the arrival of convicts in Australia received little prominence in the pageantry, with the claim that "convicts were kept in the background in Phillip's time, and it would therefore be historically accurate to keep them in the background." Similarly, little-known events considered central to the visual spectacle had to be magnified. For instance, although no record testifies to Phillip delivering a speech when he landed at Sydney Cove in 1788, for the purposes of the 1938 landing at Farm Cove, a speech was made up inviting the crowd, almost literally, "to observe themselves from his perspective."[44] Important national events were therefore constituted by their ability to be made visually attractive.

Third, festival organizers had to make the commemorations national in spatial terms through organizing local events, constituting a journey to different places, or doing both as key components of the broader program. A distinctive feature about the journeys in these festivals of founding is the way they provided the route for returning inward to the place of (re)discovery and for local space to negotiate itself into a national past. The Columbus quincentennial celebration saw the *Niña, Pinta,* and *Santa Maria* take to the seas once again, calling at ports along the West and East Coasts of the United States. This provided an occasion for local dignitaries to greet the caravels and to organize their own displays in museums and art galleries around some of the issues the quincentenary raised. To coincide with their arrival in Miami on 15 February 1992, for instance, the Historical Museum of South Florida hosted "A Major Exhibition" entitled "First Encounters: Spanish Exploration in the Caribbean and the United States, 1492–1570," which focused on the encounters between the "Native Americans" and the Europeans at the Spanish settlement of La Florida. A few kilometers away, at the Miami Space Transit Planetarium, the "showtime schedule" included "The Explorers," a thirty-minute journey in the footsteps of Columbus, Marco Polo, and Captain Cook, exploring "the routes to the New World and beyond." An adjacent exhibition, "The Noble Savage: The New World in the Eyes of the Explorers," displayed images depicting "naïve" European perspectives of sixteenth- and seventeenth-century Florida and its people. In Australia, in 1988, Captain Phillip did not repeat his voyage from England, but local communities were to be drawn into the celebrations through a traveling exhibition. As the show went from town to town, local groups were invited to present their own unique display in the exhibition in a special space set aside for them. In this way the exhibition was to "guarantee" that it was "not some controversial view imposed from Sydney." Here the spectacle provided for the "townsfolk" was not the Tall Ships or Phillip's landing; instead, the aim was to focus on "the familiar, [the] local, artifacts and images."[45] Through the selection of its own imagery the locality could presumably constitute its own history, but within the framework of the national past being produced in Sydney.

Organizers of these colonial observances invariably found that they not only had to contend with contests over the form and content of the festival and the manner in which local commemorations were or were not related to national images. There were also significant challenges to the fundamental meaning attributed to these events. At one level this related to how participants in some of the festivities perceived them. The very nature of a public festival left room for participants to ascribe different meanings to the exhibitions and events. This was no more evident than in the Australian bicentenary celebrations of 1988 when it was the spectacle of the occasion that triumphed over the "'celebration of a nation.'" The crowds lining Sydney Harbor on 26 January did not, by and large, carry Australian flags; the pleasure craft in the bay outnumbered and overshadowed Phillip's First Fleet; and Australia Day 1988 turned into a "glorified celebration of Sydney Harbour," probably the "greatest one-day spectacle . . . in one city" in Australia.[46]

Perhaps even more significant, movements in Australia and the United States questioned whether there should be a celebration or commemoration at all around a moment selected to mark European founding or settlement. A great deal of opposition was directed at these commemorations, which acquired appellations such as "festival of hate" or "festival of conquest." In Australia, various Aboriginal organizations declared 26 January 1938 a Day of Mourning and Protest. At a conference of representatives of these organizations in Sydney, on the day of the "150th anniversary of the Whiteman's seizure" of the country, speakers asserted that the Aborigines had "no reason to rejoice on Australia's 150th birthday." One hundred and fifty years ago the land belonged to their forefathers, but now they were being "pushed further and further into the background." A resolution was passed unanimously protesting "against the callous treatment of our people by the whiteman during the past 150 years" and appealing to "the Australian nation of today to make new laws for the education and care of the Aborigines." Fifty years later the bicentenary provided the focal point for "Treaty 88," a campaign for, among other things, a treaty between the Aboriginals and the Australian government, protection of Aboriginal sacred sites, and the "international recognition of Aboriginals as a *people*." A key moment in the campaign was a direct inversion of the moment of colonial founding, when an Aboriginal person landed at Dover Beach in England on the very day that the flotilla of Tall Ships and the First Fleet sailed into Sydney Harbor.[47]

The Columbus quincentennial saw the amount of opposition to celebrating or commemorating the festival of founding reach unprecedented levels throughout the world. In the United States the National Council of Churches called for the quincentenary to be a time "for penitence rather than jubilation." The 1992 alliance, a coalition of Native American groups, coordinated by Suzan Harjo, saw no reason to celebrate "murder, pillage, rape, destruction of the major waterways, destruction of the land, the destruction and pollution of the air," all of which, these groups maintained, had been initiated by European westward expansion. They therefore organized their own events for the quincentennial. These included a campaign for land and treaty rights, an hour of silent mourning on 12 October 1992, spattering Columbus statues with blood, and putting Columbus on trial and hanging effigies of his likeness. In Guatemala, the Second Continental Gathering of the 500 Years Campaign of Indigenous and Popular Resistance announced that commemorating Columbus would be tantamount to a celebration of "ethnocide and genocide, which cost . . . ninety million victims alone during the conquest and the colonization." The Caribbean Organization of Indigenous People not only objected to the celebrations in very strong terms but claimed they were a celebration of victory, for, despite the arrival of Columbus, "the fact that indigenous people still survive today is a tribute to their resistance." In Britain the playwright Harold Pinter set up a "500 Years of Resistance" group to support those across America who were resisting Columbus. As part of an attempt to broaden the anti-Columbus campaign even further, Antonio Gomez, the information director of the Indian Treaty Council in San Francisco, attended the congress of the ANC in South Africa in July 1991, explaining to delegates how 1492 "really represents the start of the process which led to the slave trade" between Africa and America. His message was well received, and the president of the ANC, Nelson Mandela, promised to join in the protest as replicas of Columbus's ships sailed into San Francisco. As a result of these campaigns, when October 1992 came around the commemorations had fizzled out and low-profile activities were the order of the day.[48]

The counter-histories that emerge in the festival of founding tend to build their narratives around two components: pre-conquest societies and the impact of western (or eastern) expansion. The date of founding becomes the marking point of this narrative, re-cast as the onset of conquest. All that had happened before this founding/conquest in indigenous societies is then cast in an environment-friendly, mother earth, classless aura, whereas after conquest/ founding, the earth is destroyed, corruption occurs, and societies become ridden with structural inequalities and either collapse or are destroyed. "The Untold Story," which teachers were encouraged to recite to young children in schools in the United States in 1992, started off in pre-conquest times:

> Once upon a time a group of people lived on an island, Bohio (now called Hispaniola) in the Caribbean. These people, whom I consider my people, were proud of their island. They built beautiful farms and villages from dirt and rock. They respected the plants and animals. Many people lived on Bohio. They called themselves Tainos.[49]

Then three boats appeared "far off in the ocean" and life began to change. Massive amounts of gold and capital flowed from America to Europe, "plague and pestilence" began to pervade the American continent, poverty and tyranny became the order of the day, the environment, which the "native people" had so loved and protected, was destroyed, and slavery, with its legacy of racism which "still haunts America," was introduced. Yet this was not entirely a story of gloom and inevitable destruction. The light at the end of the tunnel in the anti-celebratory narrative was the resistance of "Native Americans," who were, in the face of Columbus, asserting "their culture and traditions," establishing a unified front, exposing "the hidden history of colonialism," and building a new world "based on justice."[50]

As the official festival programs have been seen as "renovating European celebratory narratives," so these anti-celebratory campaigns have been cast as being in stark contrast to the official versions, asserting "a counterhistory," revindicating "lifeways," and consolidating "struggles for territory and autonomy." But to read these anti-celebratory narratives as direct descendants of struggles against European domination is merely to invert the process of reading the official version by easily slipping the production of the past into a framework of repression and resistance. Once again, the ways that apparently conflicting pasts engage and interact with one another are ignored. The date of founding/conquest in America, for instance, is ironically the beginning of history for both pasts. For those in favor of celebrating Columbus, it is the beginning of history in terms of the start of the written record as opposed to the archaeological, whereas for the opposition it is the date when almost ahistorical indigenous lifeways change as historic events start to occur. Moreover, it is the narrative of the founder figure that remains the pivot of the story. The counter-histories may "distort, twist, or invert" his image, but, like a mirror, they still "reflect the original image" and "the original text." The essentials of the story thus remain very similar, and, more often than not, they affirm the existence of a national past around the moment of founding and conquest.[51]

What is notable is that the "European narrative" was implicitly produced in conversation with manifestly antagonistic versions of history. This is perhaps more obvious in the more recent festivals of founding where the criticism of the Eurocentric nature of the proceedings has led to alterations in conceptions of founding. In Australia, as noted earlier, it led to the creation of "multiple journeys," and in the United States the voyage of Christopher Columbus was not considered, in 1992, in the "multicultural, interdependent, ultrasensitive modern world" as the discovery of America but the collision of two worlds that transformed both the East and the West.[52]

Van Riebeeck's Journeys

In South Africa in 1952 it was the Dutch commander of a revictualing station at the Cape, Jan van Riebeeck, who upstaged both the Portuguese, who, from the voyage of Bartolomeu Dias in 1488, had come to regard "South Africa . . . as a province of the little kingdom of Portugal," and the British, whose moment of landing in Muizenberg in 1795 was long regarded by "educated men" as the beginning of "noteworthy" South African history.[53] Van Riebeeck's landing at Granger Bay in April 1952, like that of Columbus in the United States in 1992 and Phillip in Sydney in 1988, was made possible only by both the public and the historical pasts. This book is a journey into these pasts, relating how a story of progress came to be told about Jan van Riebeeck in 1952 and how that story was contested every step of the way.

The first part of the journey attempts to plot some of the histories of the framing moment, examining the representations of Van Riebeeck and the landing, and how they were located within different histories before 1952. This stage of the journey offers a package tour of the Van Riebeeck experience over three hundred years, from the moment of landing, through the unveiling of his statue on Adderley Street, Cape Town, in 1899, to the start of the celebrations of the hundredth anniversary of the Great Trek in 1938 at the base of his statue. The journey focuses on three selected histories: the April commemorations of founding, school history textbooks, and the diary of Jan van Riebeeck. From these pasts and their differing meanings, the organizers of the 1952 festival were able to select, highlight, and discard in order to ensure that Van Riebeeck and his crew landed safely at Granger Bay.

Once the organizers came around to giving content, meaning, and shape to a South African past Van Riebeeck had created, no single European narrative could easily be drawn on. There was the story of the struggle of the Afrikaner against the rule of the Dutch East India Company and British imperialism, highlighting the Great Trek, the Anglo-Boer War, and Paul Kruger, who stood up against the might of the British Empire. The narrative of gold and diamonds told of struggles against anti-capitalist forces to build an industrial South Africa, typified by the "achievements" of Cecil John Rhodes who wanted to build an imperial road from the Cape to Cairo. Often linked to this narrative was the "British achievement," the introduction of "civilized" values to Africa, which emerged triumphant particularly against what were called "the kaffir hordes" on the eastern frontier. At times all these different histories were complementary, but they stood equally in contradistinction to one another. Was Rhodes, for instance, the villain of the Jameson Raid, which tried to topple the government of the Boer Republic headed by Paul Kruger, or was he the builder of the South African economy? Were missionaries the bearers of civilization or obstacles to the expansion of effective settlement? These were the sort of conflicts the organizers had to battle as they sought to reduce South Africa's space to a stage, where time unfolded in a logic of its own and where history was re-cast as History, an impersonal force which was "the playwright, co-ordinating facts into a coherent sequence."[54]

When Van Riebeeck discovered South Africa in 1952, the country and its public past he was presented with had been established through an elaborate series of negotiations. There had been bargaining and arbitration over the differing European narratives, between oppositional and European narratives, between order and spontaneity, and between authenticity and spectacle. The second round of the journey in this work takes readers through these multiple transactions, starting at the pageant which was meant to begin the past but which was almost the end point of the festival, namely, the re-creation of Van Riebeeck's landing on Saturday, 5 April 1952. This work then moves backward (or forward) to examine how differing pasts were accommodated, selected, and accorded place, form, and meaning in a continually re-constituted national past. These historical compositions took on a variety of forms: movies, theater, dance, radio broadcasts, published illustrated histories, and street pageants. As in the earlier part of the journey, it is not possible to take in all these momentous pasts and the processes of their production. The focus is on the pageantry in the streets of Cape Town and the festival stadium on the foreshore between 2 and 4 April 1952: the historical procession, the Malay and Griqua pageants, and the *volkspele* [national folk dances/games]. Although in some instances these moving processions of the past were not entirely representative of the broad range of official historical productions, for the sake of spectacle they stripped history down to its bare essentials and mapped out the broad outlines of how the distinctive episodes were to be cobbled together into national past(s). In this sense, the vehicles carrying participants aboard the floats into the past also transported the building blocks of a negotiated historical edifice for Jan van Riebeeck to receive on the sands of Granger Bay.

The third element of the journey takes us to the counter-histories produced around the Van Riebeeck festival. These included groups boycotting the celebrations and producing counter-histories, students refusing to participate because the planned festivities "showed a strong racial bias" and "a perversion of the true historical facts," and individuals appearing before the historical committees of the festival on behalf of "black history."[55] Unlike the public pageantry and visual tone characterizing the official festival, the opposition to the festival was dominated by the written and spoken word. It was through newspapers, variously titled as part of the "resistance" or the "alternative" press, that these campaigns were explained and propagated. In public meetings attempts were made to draw on a broader, more visible support base, which in turn could provide news for the press. Finally, books based on extensive research presented different versions of the past, and the opposition attempted to gain its historical authenticity from these writings.

This volume examines these three forms of counter-histories—the press, public meetings, and histories—in terms of their organization, structure, and dissemination. My concern is not to locate these forms within the discourse of repression and resistance but to explore the processes of their production in their interaction with the negotiated narrative of the nation that emerges from the organizers of the festival, almost simultaneously invoking and obliterating its "totalising boundaries."[56]

In spite of the sustained opposition to the celebration, the Van Riebeeck festival in 1952 attracted a large audience, some experiencing the events, pageants, and exhibitions firsthand by becoming part of "the crowd," others engaging in the festival vicariously by listening to their radios or watching *African Mirror* or *Ons Nuus* newsreels in the local movie theater as part of the entertainment package. Now, some fifty years after the festival, it is difficult to assess the audience response to what was seen and heard. The most obvious way to accomplish this is by using a procedure that has almost become a standing instruction to South African historians in the past twenty years: Simply go out with your tape recorder and interview those who were there! What needs to be considered in using this methodology are recent critiques of oral history: the way it sometimes acts to put words in the interviewee's mouth, the way testimonies are transformed into written texts with little consideration of the oral genres, and the way these testimonies, once written down, become sources to be mined for primary evidence. Taking full cognizance of these critiques, on the fourth stage of the journey I explicitly mine the oral testimonies that I and others have collected, along with school yearbooks, newspapers, and magazines of the time, to look at viewer responses to the Van Riebeeck festival fair, which had approximately eight hundred thousand visitors and was probably the most popular attraction of the entire festival. But in using the oral narrative, I make no claims to its ability to recover authentic consciousness or to offer a representative sample of a cross-section of visitors to the Jan van Riebeeck festival fair. Instead I use it, in chapter 4, to take the reader, along with the festival goers, on a guided tour of the fair, having explicitly constructed its itinerary and content from the historical record. Together we visit the English and Dutch villages built on Cape Town's foreshore, venture underground into a gold mine at the seaside, and gaze on the people referred to as "natives," living in their reconstructed homesteads. These exhibits at the fair, like the festival as a whole, did not "simply express a central, coherent communal meaning" but also evoked individual subjective responses. The guided tour is intended to draw out the different ways the exhibits on the foreshore were constructed and the visitors' various responses to the representations on display.[57]

By negotiating a delicate line between differing and contesting versions of the past and perceptions of its visual tableaux, the national histories of the Van Riebeeck festival were primarily concerned with re-mapping the bold outlines of the country. But in 1952, through the festival, an effort was also made to re-draw the map of local history, to name, frame, locate, and historicize the "internal 'contents'" of the land. A series of mail coaches traversed the country starting in January 1952, gathering local histories and providing the occasion for local festivals on their journeys to Cape Town to greet Van Riebeeck when he landed in April on the shores of "Darkest Africa."[58] This re-making of local history as the mail coaches returned to the "mother city" in 1952 is the subject of chapter 5.

These journeys in 1952 were in marked contrast to the celebrations undertaken in 1938 to commemorate the centenary of the Great Trek. The route taken in that year had been one of conquest: ox-wagons moving to the interior from Van Riebeeck's statue in Cape Town and enveloping local communities in celebration of a national Afrikaner trek. As the nine ox-wagons traveled through five hundred towns, covering the entire route of South Africa, streets were renamed after Voortrekker [pioneer] leaders, newly born children acquired names commemorating the trek, and speech after speech extolled the "virtues of the Voortrekkers" and their establishment of an "impregnable frontier for western civilization."[59] Fourteen years later the route was reversed, and Van Riebeeck's mail coaches provided a way to reclaim the discovery of the country and the land by incorporation rather than conquest, reconstituting the local through its reserved space in a national past.

Chapter 5, in its discussion of the mail coach "Settlers" journey through the Eastern Cape, takes an important premise as its starting point: What constitutes national and local history is not pre-determined, with local history merely inserted into the context of national history. Instead, the chapter attempts to examine the production and re-production of the boundaries of local and national pasts in the contests and negotiations over their contents and space. These contests were never more evident than in the eastern Cape region of South Africa, which Van Riebeeck's mail coach, "Settlers," traversed between February and March of 1952. Here, on the "eastern limits of the Cape Colony," the "frontier between white and black" dominated local pasts. Local public narratives recounted stories of a country where the "blood-curdling war cries of the Amaxhosa" were tamed by "intrepid fighters" and settlers in a "desolate" land "infested with wild animals and hostile Natives." Problems began to emerge when this local narrative encountered a national past surfacing on the streets of Cape Town, where claims were being made that "Van Riebeeck Never Saw the Bantu" and that "Xhosa and other tribes were then still unknown."[60] Clearly there was no easy fit between this national past, where people classified as "Bantu" were being excluded, and the national past being told in the eastern Cape, where the central narrative was on the encounters between black and white. As the mail coach "Settlers" traveled from Umtata through East London, King William's Town, Grahamstown, and Port Elizabeth to Cape Town, collecting local histories on its way, it had to mediate a path between these different pasts. Chapter 5 is the story of that journey through the towns of the eastern Cape, through local and national pasts, and the various attempts to define and fit the narratives together.

When Mayor Mieke Bloemendaal was greeted by Jan van Riebeeck on 28 October 1992, at an airport soon to be renamed Cape Town International, she was therefore not merely reasserting a Dutch/South African connection, stretching back to 1652, but her baggage contained more recent pasts which her hosts had helped re-create. These pasts had been constituted through a series of encounters in the early months of 1952, when the Van Riebeeck festival set in motion a process of mediation between differing European narratives, anti-celebratory campaigns, local and national history, and the spectators who "saw it all." This book explores how South African national pasts were produced for and through this commemorative event and the multiple confrontations over its contents. In these productions Jan van Riebeeck and his wife, Maria de la Quellerie, discovered that their ten-year sojourn at the Cape had been transformed into three hundred years of settlement, and it was their founding on the beach at Granger Bay in 1952 for which Mayor Bloemendaal was paying penance in Villiersdorp some forty years later.

1   Van Riebeeck's Pasts

When stories are recounted about the past of Jan van Riebeeck, the Dutch commander at the Cape of Good Hope between 1652 and 1662, they tell of his birth in Culemborg, his family background, his early days under the tutelage of his grandfather, the mayor of Culemborg, his apprenticeship as a surgeon, his joining the Dutch East India Company and being posted to Batavia, his becoming a merchant and administrator in the East Indies and then being sent home by the Company for misconduct, his marriage to Maria de la Quellerie, and his assignment to set up a refreshment station at the Cape. Over the next ten years there are accounts of his administrative duties, his encounters with the local populations, and his dealings with various Company officials, all of which terminate in 1662 when he departs for Malacca and his past at the Cape comes to an end.[1]

So much has been said and written of this past—some would say far too much—that it has become more than merely a set of stories about an individual's past. It has been accorded the status of being significant, of providing a context for a moment that is marked in different ways as the beginning of South African history: the beginning of apartheid, the beginning of colonialism, and the beginning of "western civilization" in southern Africa. The life stories that lead to this starting point, and the narratives of initial encounters set around the instance of proclaimed import, have been made so meaningful that the Professor of history at the University of Stellenbosch, H. B. Thom, could confidently assert, in introducing the 1952 edition of Van Riebeeck's diary, "Of the latter part of his life, little need here be said."[2]

To make this past into history, though, meant more than merely according it significance. A narrative had to be built up and gaps filled in, especially when these gaps were glaringly apparent. On one level this involved the historian in the metaphorical guise of detective, ferreting through archives, sifting through clues, and discovering missing links. One of Van Riebeeck's biographers, C. Louis Leipoldt, for instance, claimed that he had read all the relevant papers "printed and written" that were located at the archives in Cape Town, the Hague, and Batavia. But history did not merely fall into place through the process of discovery. The historian as storyteller had to take over, weaving the found and selected information into a good tale that reads well, giving the world "a formal coherence past 'reality' never had." In this process of reconstruction conjecture took over, and assumptions were derived from a sketched-out context, couched in a language of probabilities and possibilities. School "undoubtedly played an important part in his [Van Riebeeck's] training," wrote Leipoldt; one "may assume that [he] was taught Latin and perhaps a little Greek"; "probably . . . [his] grandfather . . . took care that the youngster should be properly grounded"; and "probably his own temperament" led him to choose the profession of surgeon. Leipoldt was so convinced that the context into which he had selected to write Van Riebeeck was crucial that he had "no shadow of a doubt that the liberal atmosphere in which he was privileged to pass his childhood left an enduring mark upon him, and that he reacted favourably to the cultural stimuli, whatever these might have been."[3]

Associated with this according of significance to Van Riebeeck's past and the construction of meaningful narratives of his life was the emergence of a series of historical debates. Was he born in 1618 or 1619? Was he nobly born, as Leipoldt claimed, or a lowly Company bureaucrat, as the Cape Colony's official historian, George Theal, suggested? Was he dismissed from the service of the Company for large-scale corruption or for merely augmenting his small salary? Was he really so interested in the Cape, or was it a stepping-stone to further his career? Was he indeed the author of his diary, or had administrative officers at the Cape written it? Was Van Riebeeck an "advocate of extreme and iniquitous measures" against the local Khoi population, or was his harshness infrequent and "made under extreme pressures and exceptional circumstances"? These debates, more than asserting difference, reflect an agreement over the "constitute requisites for debate": "knowledge, language, relevance, polarity, closure." There is a consensus that Van Riebeeck's past is important, that it is an issue of contestation, and that some form of truth about this past can ultimately be discovered in an undetermined future which will set the debate to rest. Its location as debate elevates it into the realm of critical discourse, seen as an integral element of the historical craft where the evidence can make one view "more veridical than the other."[4]

Van Riebeeck's past was therefore made into history by its being marked off as significant, through the construction of historical narratives around his life, and by the forging of related debates. This corresponds with the distinction between the past as "all that happened" and history as the according of significance to certain events in that past. The use of the passive voice would indicate that this signification occurred almost naturally, by a process of elimination and osmosis. In the academic world it is largely the historian or the professional chronicler who determines what should be the facts of history, facts which "other historians" then either accept or reject on the basis of the interpretation offered. What this formulation overlooks is that history is also very often made in the public domain, both in being authored by those who do not form part of the guild and by its authority being affirmed through public evaluation. There is more of a "shared author-ity" between the public domain and the academy in the constitution of historical "authorship and inter-pretive authority."[5]

In the making of Van Riebeeck it was this "shared author-ity" which changed his past into history. A central argument in this book is that a key moment around which this transformation occurred was the festival organized in 1952 to commemorate the three hundredth anniversary of Van Riebeeck's landing at the Cape of Good Hope. A range of academics, artists, dramatists, curators, dancers, athletes, and musicians meshed together in producing history which relied for its authority on public approval and intellectual scrutiny. Yet this moment was not one of beginning, where history was virtually created from the "sands of time." As "the world/the past comes to us always already as stories," so Van Riebeeck had acquired a series of histories before 1952. This chapter looks at those past histories, their constructions and meanings. It examines how Van Riebeeck and his past started to become history through commemorative events, school textbooks, and the publication of the daily journal of the Dutch East India Company at the Cape (Van Riebeeck's diary). The implication of treating each of these as discrete historical productions is that it does not pit one form of history against another in terms of its success or failure as a mobilizing agent but rather looks at how different forms of history perform different functions and interact with one another.[6] With other moments of Van Riebeeck's past appearance, these histories—in commemorations, schoolbooks, and the diary—offered, respectively, a tradition of ritual, an abbreviated past, and a historical authenticity. Those who organized his past in 1952 were able to draw on all these histories and their different offerings, incorporating, rearranging, and discarding elements from these various forms to fit in with the plans for the festival.

Commemorating the Past

The ritual acts associated with ceremonies of commemoration are generally seen as moments in which a shared or common identity is asserted. This identity is based on attempts to establish, through the ceremony, a collective memory where an "original narrative," usually built on the themes of "struggle, sacrifice, and victory," becomes the cohesive mechanism for community formation. This implies a notion of "spatial continuity," where the "commemorative ceremony" bounds a community into memory, in the dual sense of setting its limits and forging a singular identity. A sense of "remembering together" can become so powerful that what is shared is no longer the event itself but the memory of the commemorations.[7]

More than establishing spatial boundaries, these ceremonies also position individuals into communities as temporal entities. Time becomes part of a wider framework, where individual change, in its uniqueness and constant transformability, is "transcended . . . by ensuring the preservation of collective memory." People are brought into the community through historic time with its markers that signify before and after. This is not to argue that in commemorative ceremonies identities become fixed in the same time and with the same characteristics. Instead, they continually change and mutate "through the transformation of collective memory." It is precisely because of this transformability that commemorations, which evoke the past and construct and resurrect it for collective memory, are such a powerful force in constituting historical knowledge.[8]

Deriving information from the daily register of the Dutch East India Company at the Cape, it would appear that, on the whole, the commander had very little time for commemorative ceremonies in his period of residence from 1652 to 1662, even at the time of his arrival and landing. As with most "founders" and "discoverers" it was the first sight of land to possess/settle/inhabit which was regarded as the moment of significance and which did involve some sort of ceremonial activity. When the chief mate sighted Table Mountain on 5 April 1652, Van Riebeeck praised God, hoisted the flags of the *Dromedaris,* fired a gun, and rewarded the sailor with "four Spanish reals in specie." It was the "active gaze" on the land that was crucial, because it sought to turn claims into rights. Once the eye had been cast on the land as a supposedly rightful possession, then what was to follow in a seemingly seamless progression would be the naming and appropriation.[9]

The landing the following day, which later would become the central focus of the origin narratives, was barely remarked on in the journal and was accorded no significance as a first primarily because it was not one, either of European founding or settlement. The Cape, over the previous century, had become a frequent stopover route for ships traveling to the east, and indeed Van Riebeeck had spent eighteen days there when returning to the Netherlands from Batavia in 1648. Moreover, the English had established a settlement at Table Bay in the 1620s, although the crown never formally recognized it. It is little wonder then that, shortly after sighting Table Mountain on 5 April, Van Riebeeck sent two scouts ahead to "find out what ships—and how many—might be lying at anchor in the roadstead at Table Bay." Clearly there was an expectation that other ships from Europe, particularly the Portuguese and perhaps the English, would be at anchor. When the scouts reported, however, that there were no other ships, the *Goede Hoop* and the *Dromedaris* entered the bay and the captain was sent ashore to pick up post from previous Dutch ships that had stopped over and to acquire "some greens" for nourishment. It was only in the evening of the following day (7 April 1652) that Van Riebeeck finally went ashore, with no ceremony, "to consider more or less where the fort should be built," and then returned to the *Dromedaris*, which was to be both home and operational base for the next few weeks. Not until 24 April did he finally set up camp on the shore, without any fuss or bother. "We went ashore with all our baggage and family to stay there in a make-shift wooden hut—rather roughly constructed for the time being—in order that the work may proceed more satisfactorily." [10]

What was important for Van Riebeeck was to carry out his duties as a "servant of higher masters," God and the Dutch East India Company. The instructions to Van Riebeeck, whom the Company in no way regarded as either a discoverer or founder, had been to establish a fort so as to secure the revictualing station, and it was the ceremonies and identities established around the construction and occupation of this fort which were of prime importance in the first two years of settlement. Positioned between the sea in the northeast and the Fresh River in the west, this fortification signified possession against potential enemies—other European traders and the local Khoi inhabitants—who could threaten the Company's ability to secure a permanent refreshment station along a profitable trading route. In this vision Van Riebeeck defined the various identities along an insider/outsider frontier, with the fort and its inhabitants—the servants of the Company and of God—setting the bounds of inclusion/exclusion. The first ceremonies that took place more than a month after landing were therefore associated with establishing the identity of the fort and its inhabitants. On Sunday, 12 May, in a square in the incomplete fort, "the first sermon, and the Lord's Supper was celebrated," and three days later the fort was named Goede Hoop "in accordance of our instruction of our Lords and Masters [of the Dutch East India Company]." [11]

Only two years later, on 6 April 1654, once the fort had been completed and the initial settlement was able to secure itself against outsiders, did Van Riebeeck commemorate the landing. This ceremony is crucial as it sets up the genealogy for future celebrations of the landing, giving them a tradition to resurrect rather than a past to invent. The journal recorded the following:

> We have . . . resolved, and also for the first time begun to celebrate this 6th day of April in the name of the Almighty, and henceforth to set it aside for all time as a day of thanksgiving and prayer, so that our descendants may never forget the mercies we have received at the Lord's hands, but may always remember them to the Glory of God. [12]

Leipoldt refers to this moment as "the first public holiday" in South Africa; Thom noted, in a footnote to the diary, that "also the following two years Van Riebeeck celebrated the day of landing"; and when Van Riebeeck's day was commemorated in the twentieth century, reading this extract from the journal became a central feature of the proceedings. Yet it would seem that the landing was commemorated in 1654 because of the problems the settlement was experiencing at the time, particularly the scarcity of food and the concern over when the return fleet would arrive with relief. Indeed, before commenting on the day of prayer, the diary entry for 6 April 1654 is concerned that there is a lack of food "to fill the hungry bellies of the men." At this moment of intense stress, it seemed necessary to hold a small-scale ceremony, involving a prayer meeting, to give thanks, at least, to their "safe arrival." Also notable about this initial ceremony in 1654 is that, in as much as it commemorates the "safe arrival," it also locates the happenings in terms of the identity being established around the fortification, linking the landing with the construction of the fort "through the Holy guidance of God," the former facilitating the latter and the spatial ordering of the settlement in physical and cognitive terms.[13]

After this initial ceremony the diary records four further occurrences of this day of prayer—in 1655, 1656, 1659, and 1660—during Van Riebeeck's time as commander at the Cape. They all seem to have been low-key affairs, usually involving a prayer meeting led by a minister whose ship happened to be in the bay at the time. One must assume that in other years the ceremonies did not take place or that no minister was available at the time or that they were not recorded in the Company journal. In any case it would seem to indicate that, far from being important annual gatherings at which an identity based on landing or founding was inscribed into shared memory as a moment of "joy and gratitude" which the commander had "so piously instituted," they were insignificant when compared to attempts to secure the viability of the refreshment station for their Lords. A far greater moment of "joy and gratitude" was when the return fleet visited the shores of the Cape, bringing with it supplies for the station. Once the cargo had been unloaded and the ships had departed the Cape, the commander would issue orders for the Company servants to take a holiday and be treated with wine, food, and tobacco. This holiday is recorded in the diary as an "annual custom," indicating that rather than founding a settlement on 6 April it was maintaining a sometimes very precarious revictualing station that was more important for the Company's officials at the Cape.[14]

One hundred years later, according to *Drie Eeue: Die Verhaal Van Ons Vaderland* [Three centuries: The story of our fatherland]—a five-volume history of South Africa written specially for the Van Riebeeck tercentenary—there was much more enthusiasm for commemorating the landing than there had been in the early days of the settlement. Attempting to secure a direct lineage for a shared memory among a community identified as the "white race," the author of volume 1, Anna Boeseken, uses the *Journal of Cape Governors* (the *Dag Register*) as her primary source to relate how the first centenary of the landing was remembered with a series of prayer meetings throughout the Cape Colony, which by this time had extended some three hundred kilometers from the

Castle (which had replaced the original fort) on the shores of Table Bay. In churches from Stellenbosch to the Swartland, this history tells us, services were held on Saturday, 8 April 1752, to thank God for the landing, for peace, and for the produce of the land, and that there were now "enough whites" in the colony. Cast as a moment of divine intervention to parallel the events some hundred years previously, the weather conditions described in the *Dag Register* with almost monotonous regularity are transformed into a metaphor for the commemoration. The black storm clouds that had gathered earlier in the day gave way to bright sunlight [the landing of whites?] as shots were fired from the Castle and from ships in Table Bay. The brief description of the festivities ends with the Dutch governor, Ryk Tulbagh, who had just assumed his duty at the Cape, hosting a dinner for the "most distinguished officials, citizens and visiting foreigners" at the Cape.[15]

This description of the commemoration on 8 April 1752 is similar to Theal's in the second volume of his *History of South Africa,* first published in 1888. Relying mainly on a directive from the Political Council, which governed the Cape, he notes that the day was observed in churches "by the Europeans in South Africa as a day of thanksgiving to Almighty God for the undisturbed possession of the colony by the Company for one hundred years."[16] Although Boeseken and Theal differ in their narrative approach—for the former the climatic changes provide the metaphor for the nature of the celebrations, whereas for the latter the events are located within the administrative ambit of the Company—both emphasize the religious element of the centennial and the racial identification of the participants as whites or Europeans. In this way the line of descent to the present of 1888 and 1952 is established through giving history ("tradition") to a "race" which is defined almost as an immutable concept in a spatial location forever termed South Africa.

It is highly improbable that such a clearly defined sense of racial identity that Theal and Boeseken read back from the late nineteenth and mid-twentieth centuries existed in the Cape in the 1750s. Racial identities probably did exist in the eighteenth century, but people might not have described themselves specifically as white or black. This is not to deny that the social and cultural worlds of the eighteenth-century Cape were ascribed with racial meaning. Indeed, although the gatherings in 1752 possibly may not have been moments of explicitly asserting a white identity with a common racial heritage, they did set the [white] Christian world off from the [black] heathen one, the implication being that there was a natural hierarchy of domination. The sermon preached by Rev. Petrus van der Spuy in Cape Town on the centenary of Van Riebeeck's landing identified the settlers as the chosen people who had returned to Zion, located at the Cape. He used as his text Psalms 147:12–14 in which God is praised for strengthening the gates of Jerusalem, making peace in the realm, and filling its fields "with the finest of wheat." In these terms the Cape was the New Jerusalem, with a clearly inscribed border, keeping those who were not chosen (i.e., not born Christian) at a distance, and being rewarded for doing this by God with prosperity. This evocation of the Cape as a New Jerusalem and the return to Zion was a common theme among Dutch Reformed Church preachers at the Cape in the mid-eighteenth century. It enabled the settlers, by a strange reversal, to identify themselves not as intruders but as the true inhabitants of the land, and the slaves and local Khoi population as aliens.[17]

The positioning of this structure in 1752 was attributed not to Van Riebeeck or any other individual—his name is not mentioned in the *Governor's Journal* or the *Resolution of the Political Council*—but to the possession and occupation of the Cape, by the Company through the "will of God." Rev. Van der Spuy, who relied to a large extent on the Dutch East India Company for the position he held, did devote a small part of his sermon to Van Riebeeck, but mostly as a servant of the Company on which he showered accolades for its trading enterprise. To put it another way, in 1752 the commemorations were organized by the governor at the time, Ryk Tulbagh, in honor of the Dutch East India Company as the bearer of Christianity to the sub-continent. Tulbagh, who had just assumed the governorship, in turn, was able, through the ceremony, to establish his dual identity as both servant of the Company and of the settlers, an image he pursued relentlessly for much of his governorship; indeed, later he was written into settler history as a man whose "major achievement" was to codify the slave laws and restrict slaves' mobility, ostensibly making Cape Town a "safer place" for its white inhabitants.[18]

Only during the nineteenth century, when the Company station was transformed into a territorial possession, did Van Riebeeck begin to assume a major role on the historical stage. His initial appearance was during the brief interregnum at the beginning of the century when the Cape was handed back to the Dutch after a period of British occupation stretching from 1795 to 1803. In attempting to establish a sense of legitimate authority in the following three years when the Cape was part of the Batavian Republic—the Dutch East India Company had come to an end in 1798—the figure of Van Riebeeck became a symbol of continuity in a program identified by Commissioner De Mist as "re-establishment" after a "sad" interlude. This was no more evident than on 2 July 1804 when, in an elaborate ceremony, De Mist presented Cape Town with its own coat of arms—*Het Wapen Van Riebeeck* [The Van Riebeeck Crest]. The ceremonial activities started in the morning with a meeting at the Castle of the *Raad van Gemeente* [Political Council] which governed the colony. Thereafter the official delegation proceeded to the town hall, where, to the sounds of trumpets playing in the background, the new coat of arms, consisting of three gold rings on a red backdrop with an anchor, was displayed to all in attendance.

A twenty-one-gun salute was fired, and the members of the *Raad* hosted a special dinner for the local dignitaries. In speech after speech Van Riebeeck was toasted, and all generations were called upon to honor and remember his name as the "father," the "founder" of the "settlement," and the first "governor" of the colony. To crown the activities, the town hall was specially illuminated in the evening, providing a spectacle for the crowd of onlookers gathered to witness the day's proceedings, and Cape Town was designated by De Mist as Riebeeck's city.[19]

The ceremonial activities of 2 July 1804 mark a significant turn in the history of Van Riebeeck and his landing. No longer is the Dutch East India Company the focus of the commemorations. Instead, an individual is being associated with a beginning that is starting to place itself much more in the context of colonial settlement and its identity, with Van Riebeeck, the commander of a Company outpost, being transformed into a governor and founder. Clearly for the Dutch rulers the promotion of such feelings was a way to establish a sense of affiliation, particularly when their hold at the Cape was tenuous. Providing a local hero, who was also Dutch, could assist tremendously in this process of defending and maintaining their territorial acquisition. De Mist might well have been making a plea for affording the Batavian Republic a sense of longevity at the Cape when he urged the crowd to protect "his name (Van Riebeeck)" and "coat of arms" against "all foreign and domestic violence."[20]

This association with a local colonial identity, established during the Batavian Republic period, was the image that Van Riebeeck carried throughout much of the nineteenth century when the Cape was under British rule. Generally this took two forms, one related to a Cape Dutch identity and the other to a British settler identity. The assumption of an identity as ancestor of the Cape Dutch community was developed in the course of the nineteenth century by a Cape intelligentsia, most of whom were ministers in Dutch Reformed Churches in the colony. The settler community which had arrived in the Cape during Company rule was increasingly placed under pressure during the initial periods of British colonial rule as a result of periodic shortages of land and labor, accompanied by missionary accusations of inhumane treatment to the local population. Some of these settlers had moved northward in search of new sources of land and labor, outside the ambit of British control. Their journey of occupation, cast into History as an odyssey of pre-ordained founding, labeled the "Great Trek," amounted to turning their backs on the "colonial pioneer" Jan van Riebeeck and establishing independent Boer republics in the north. Alternatively, those settlers of Dutch, French, and German descent who remained in the colony, and had opposed the move to the north, became increasingly vocal about their land claims. Setting themselves up as occupying the moral high ground, they countered missionary assertions of unjust treatment by projecting themselves as the bearers of Christianity to a heathen continent. Van Riebeeck, instead of being rejected, was embraced as the initiator of the historical moment which established the "most successful of Christian settlements in Africa" and turned into, what one critic ironically termed, the "Saint of the Cape."[21]

This articulation tended to find expression in the more natural domain of intellectuals, newspapers, and journals, rather than in public ceremony. The one moment, though, when it did become part of ceremonial activity was in 1852, when the two hundredth anniversary of Van Riebeeck's landing was commemorated. Organized by the Dutch Reformed Churches in the Cape Colony, the ceremonies, held on Saturday, 6 April, took the form of "religious observance." By solemnizing the moment "when first European colonists took possession" of southern Africa and introduced the Christian religion, the arrival in 1852 was turned into His landing. The synod of the Dutch Reformed Church saw the day as one of "remembrance of the blessings Almighty God has been pleased to pour down upon the inhabitants" of "this part of Africa." In a notice in the *South African Commercial Advertiser* of the planned activities for the anniversary, the emphasis was on how the Dutch Reformed Church, for two centuries, had held up "the torch of truth to so many souls lying in the darkness of nature."[22] And when the "Divine Service" took place in Cape Town on 6 April, Rev. A. Faure, who had been the editor of the Dutch journal *Het Nederduitsch Zuid-Afrikaansche Tydschrift*, gave a sermon at the Groote Kerk in Cape Town that dealt with the history of the church in the colony:

> its early difficulties, its progress from small beginnings, and its present flourishing, and hopeful condition from which he deduced its duties, and pointed out the means by which it should devote itself to their fulfilment.[23]

This measured oration about church history contained little of a sense of mobilizing around the notion of shared "Dutchness." In rural centers of the Cape, however, a far more elaborate sense of ethnic identity formation was prevalent. When Minister Rev. G. W. A. Van der Lingen delivered his sermon in Paarl in April 1852, for instance, he augmented it with a great deal of polemic and likened Van Riebeeck to the biblical figure of Joseph in Egypt sent to deliver his people from religious decay. Van der Lingen regarded it as insulting and impolite that the "new colonists" were not paying sufficient attention to commemorating the landing—the British governor, Harry Smith, had decided not to declare the day a public holiday—and further berated Dutch speakers in the colony for forgetting their language and traditions. Yet these attempts at a specifically ethnic mobilization seem to have been exceptional at the time. The figure and moment of Van Riebeeck tended to acquire much more of a religious significance as the beginning in the progression which started when the "Christian community [was] established on the skirts of a Heathen continent" and ended in a past future over the next two hundred years with "the history of conversion and civilization penetrating from South to North, every corner of this hitherto dark and melancholy quarter of the globe."[24]

This self-representation by the Cape Dutch community as the leading Christian light in the colony, with Van Riebeeck the torchbearer, did not go unchallenged. Since the 1820s, missionaries, particularly those associated with the London Missionary Society, had been vocal in their criticism of the "un-Christian" behavior of the settlers toward the local Khoi community, their "violent dispossession," "hopeless bondage," and "wrongs and outrages inflicted on the innocent and defenceless." It was not so much that the missionaries did not want to bring what they defined as "light" and "civilization" to the "heathen"— indeed, they conceived of this as their major task—but that "oppression hindered the conversion and salvation of the Khoisan. . . . Without some degree of material prosperity . . . the labors of the missionaries to win souls for Christ would be in vain." Blame for starting the process of dispossession was laid squarely at the doors of settler society and the greed of Jan van Riebeeck, who, not satisfied with the directive of the Dutch East India Company to limit his activities to bartering with the Khoi for livestock, seriously considered becoming engaged in deceitful trading practices and perhaps even theft. Van Riebeeck, who had spent merely ten years at the Cape before moving on to what he saw as a more prestigious posting in the East Indies, thus became, in the missionaries' eyes, the personification of oppression against the Khoi and was thereby identified as the first settler.[25]

By coincidence, one of the most prominent of these missionaries, David Livingstone, was in Cape Town at the time of the 1852 commemoration and was scathing in his condemnation of the nature of the activities around the two hundredth anniversary of the landing. He saw the divine services as totally hypocritical, for, in his eyes, the Dutch Reformed Church had, for two centuries, remained silent and condoned "robbery and murder, provided the victims had black skins." Far from being the initiators of Christian principles, the Dutch Reformed Church was "the great bulwark of evil." It was Van Riebeeck, wrote Livingstone, the person being "associated [with] the introduction of Christianity" by the celebrators, who began this evil when he gazed with envy on the cattle of the Khoi.[26]

> We see the apostle of peace on earth and good-will to man utterly unable to restrain his greedy soul when viewing the herds of Hottentot cattle quietly feeding adjacent to the fort. He wonders at the mysterious dispensation of Providence, by which such fine animals have been given to the heathen. . . . This ancient Chartist coolly records his calculations as to how many of the

Hottentot *"cattle might be stolen with the loss of but a very few of his own party."*[27]

According to Livingstone, Van Riebeeck, rather than being venerated, should have been excommunicated from the church for asserting this claim to the possession of others as if it were a right. Livingstone even made this into a beginning in the "bitter" history of colonial settlement in southern Africa. It was, he declared, the first enunciation of the "Van Riebeeck principle" whereby the colonialists regarded the "heathen [as] given *to them* for an inheritance."[28]

The British settler image of Van Riebeeck seems to have emerged in the eastern Cape, where, in the 1820s, a subsidized group of immigrants had been brought in to form an agricultural barrier between the extended Cape Colony and Xhosaland. Although most of these immigrants had visions of becoming wealthy farmers, the more well off saw themselves in even more grandiose terms as changing into a rural gentry in an idealized little England on the eastern frontier, with the poorer immigrants working for them. The contradiction contained in these images led to the virtual collapse of the scheme, as many settlers migrated to towns to take up commercial and craft activities. Those who remained on the land increasingly came to rely on African labor, which was in very short supply. Around struggles to acquire land and labor from the African population, a British colonial identity was shaped based on a clear division between "civilization" and "barbarism." The settlers, both in the towns and the countryside, increasingly forgot their failures and portrayed themselves as the "pioneers of the Settlement who cleared the way for British commerce," the bearers of progress who felled *"the first tree . . .* commence[d] *. . . the first wattle and daub house*—and *. . .* [made] *the first furrow . . .* by a plough in the virgin soil." The Africans, who refused to acquiesce in the settler demands, were in turn depicted as "libidinous, uncontrolled, lazy," treacherous, "savages." At the forefront in promoting a British settler identity were the editor of *The Graham's Town Journal,* Robert Godlonton, and a local landowner, J. C. Chase, who together furthered an image of the settlers almost assuming a divinely ordained role as the bearers of civilization to Africa. Projected onto this racially constructed landscape, Van Riebeeck came to represent, for the British settlers, "one of us." Like them, he was now seen as an adventurer, founder, pioneer, who had planted the first vines and fig trees and had established the lineage of British "civilization" and European settlement in South Africa. At a dinner to commemorate the twenty-fourth anniversary of the arrival of the 1820 settlers, held in Port Elizabeth in 1844, a toast was drunk to Van Riebeeck and his "gallant band"; also a proposal was made that, as the day of Van Riebeeck's arrival (6 April) almost coincided with the day, 168 years later, when the first boatload of British immigrants arrived in the eastern Cape (10 April), that a date between the two "should be fixed . . . on which to keep in future one general holiday for both commemorations."[29]

The outcome of this identification of Van Riebeeck as part of the British colonial identity was that he became what the wealthy settlers imagined themselves to be: almost timeless English country squires. It was largely this image that was encapsulated in the mid-nineteenth-century painting of Van Riebeeck's landing by Charles Davidson Bell. Bell was a draftsman who had come to the Cape from Britain in about 1830, and later, after spending time on expeditions into the interior and taking up a series of clerical posts in the Cape government, he became Surveyor General. His strong identification with local Cape political circles and his training as a draftsman strongly influenced the subject matter he chose to portray: "native subjects." Yet this did not mean he was oblivious to the major trends emerging in English painting, particularly the concern with capturing broad landscapes, a trend associated in the Cape with the work of Thomas Bowler. Far from being a direct contrast to the work of Bowler, Bell's painting, particularly of the landing, blends his background of draftsmanship—the attention to ethnographic detail and the need to pinpoint people into carefully defined locations—with the English picturesque tradition and the Dutch historical movement of the nineteenth century. In the English tradition, broad landscapes were observed from a distance, with the emphasis on re-creating images on the "middle plane," situated between a shadowy foreground and a background receding in the distance. It is in this middle plane that the historical event is located and Van Riebeeck appears, attired in a long flowing English-style jacket, carrying a walking stick with a large silver top, accompanied by Cromwellian-type soldiers with guns and an enlarged version of the Company flag. Set slightly farther back, and blending into the background of trees and mountains, are a group of local Khoi inhabitants dressed in what appears to be tattered rags, all but one of them seated as they greet Van Riebeeck and his colleagues. The stark contrast in apparel, the spatial location of the two parties, and the portly pose of Van Riebeeck as opposed to the almost humble greeting from the Khoi group turn the landing into an archetypal first colonial encounter between the forces of "civilization" and those of "barbarism." Van Riebeeck, in his English guise of a rural landlord, is reinforced as the initiator of the civilizing mission in southern Africa, and his landing is being painted onto the canvas of the past as the starting point of history that Bell had helped to make.[30]

Yet, for all this association between an identity as an English settler and one as the bearer of "civilization," the response from the British colonial administration toward commemorating Van Riebeeck was lukewarm. The increasing appropriation of his figure by the Dutch-speaking intelligentsia tended to overshadow his English identity, and the administration considered that giving Van

Riebeeck undue prominence might serve to mobilize opposition to the colonial authorities. Thus only toward the end of the century, as British colonial ambitions in southern Africa extended their horizons, did the self-same Van Riebeeck, who had appeared in the painting by Bell, find himself perched on a pedestal at the end of Cape Town's main thoroughfare, Adderley Street. Dressed in the same clothes as in the painting, carrying the same walking stick, and assuming an almost identical posture, the statue, which was commissioned by Cecil John Rhodes in 1896 as a gift to the city of Cape Town, carries with it the colonial identity Bell had envisaged for Van Riebeeck. With his back to the shoreline, left fist clenched in determination, he stands gazing on Table Mountain as if asserting his claim to the land. The identity of the claimant, in this instance, was clear: it was Cecil John Rhodes, the major proponent of British imperial ambitions in southern Africa in the late nineteenth century. Rhodes was insistent that it be his name, and not the Scottish sculptor's, John Tweed, which would appear on the final product. Tweed was very much under Rhodes's patronage. He had been a relatively unknown sculptor brought from Paris to sculpt the gable above Rhodes's residence, Groote Schuur, as a scene depicting the landing of Van Riebeeck, an event that, for Rhodes, evidently marked the advent of his imperial aspirations. When the mayor of Cape Town unveiled the Van Riebeeck statue in May 1899, Rhodes was in London at the time, yet his presence seemed to dominate the proceedings, which took place under gloriously blue skies which seemingly miraculously had cleared (as in 1752), after days of incessant rain. The mayor of Cape Town was at pains to link the two "pioneers" of the colony, Rhodes and Van Riebeeck, who had "established effective government and introduced practical civilisation and the blessings of Christianity into this portion of the vast continent of Africa." Van Riebeeck even became the "Dutch Governor . . . who came and laid the foundations of the [British] colony," and the crowd who came to pay homage to him in 1899 were doing so "as citizens and also members of that great body, the English nation; they were there as free bodies of that great Empire to which they were all proud to belong."[31]

By the end of the nineteenth century Van Riebeeck had emerged and grown as a public historical figure, taking his place in a variety of ceremonial activities. This was clearly associated with the positioning and extension of colonial settlement in southern Africa. Although previous versions of his past were incorporated into this newly found historicity, he was now appropriated as the first settler of the colony, the first Christian, and the first colonial oppressor. In the early part of the twentieth century these identities were to be accentuated and incorporated into different forms as, in a series of commemorative performances, Van Riebeeck assumed an even higher profile in History.

His first major appearance in the twentieth century was during the pageant organized to commemorate the opening of the first parliament of the Union of South Africa in October 1910. The pageant was designed to establish South Africa as "A New Country," with a history that set up the colonial enterprise as the central motor and binding force of the past. Performed at Green Point, Cape Town, in almost perfect weather (the southeast wind, which had been howling for almost all of October, had suddenly dropped—another moment of divine intervention, following on 1752 and 1899?), the pageant, presented in tableau form over two days, told a story which moved from the days of "Primordial Savagery" in the mid-fifteenth century to its "defeat" in the "Grand Finale" in 1910. In between came selected moments in which the notion of a common progression toward this development obliterated all divisions and struggles within the settler communities over the nature and form of their colonial (and anti-colonial) identities. All were now conceptualized as fellow colonialists who had a "people's patriotism" and who had fought together for the "love of country." In their "life-blood," as if history had some inherited immutable genetic component, was the "Pacification of the Natives," the "Great Trek" which showed "the efforts of the Transvaal, Orange Free State and Natal to develop the country" with "the Bible in one hand, the rifle in the other" and the 1848 "opposition of the colonists to the establishment of a penal settlement in South Africa." Between 1854 and 1910, when the conflicts within the settler communities were at their sharpest and most brutal, there was no history, and a single tableau represented the period as "the vanquishing of savagery in South Africa by civilization and the evolution and development of the Nation's social and commercial conditions."[32]

Van Riebeeck's fit into this colonial unity was simultaneously difficult and yet easy. On the one hand, his association with a Dutch identity, defined largely through invoking the claim that he was the bearer of Christianity to South Africa, was problematic. This was an identity difficult to sustain in a commemoration seeking to establish a common sense of colonial identity, especially since, just less than a decade earlier, during the South African War of 1899–1902, British forces had been pit against an army, most of whom, although they may not have identified themselves as Dutch, largely spoke some form of Dutch. Hence, in the pageant, it was the more "neutral" Portuguese explorers, Bartolomeu Dias and Vasco da Gama, who began the process of marking and naming that ultimately led to colonization and who, "with flashing spears and flashing armour," planted "the first emblem of Christianity . . . on South African soil." But Van Riebeeck's past also fitted into this new South Africa. His role in the pageant was twofold. First, being the ancestor of Dutch-speaking South Africans, he was identified as being a component of South Africa's colonial population. It was this "new race" that the pageant classified as having arrived in South Africa with the landing of Van Riebeeck and "the Dutch pioneers." At the same time, Van Riebeeck was also able to assert an identity more in line with his image in the Bell painting and in the statue on Adderley Street. "The coming of Van Riebeeck," together with his "bearded mariners," was portrayed as "the first colonisation of the Cape." Although he did not literally take to the sea again, he did arrive onboard a reconstructed Italian ship dressed up, for the pageant, as the *Dromedaris*. In such a guise Van Riebeeck was not accorded the pole position in South African history but was seen, instead, as representative of specific processes attuned to the broad framework of a new history situated in time between "the days of the Portuguese" and "the British period" and spatially located at the Cape rather than South Africa. Still, Van Riebeeck's landing was marked as a crucial moment in this past, and, astonishingly, this led to his regeneration: He shed some 260 years to become an emblem of a new beginning in a country that now called itself South Africa. He started prancing about on his pedestal, wielding his walking stick like a baton, and exclaiming to surprised onlookers, " '*Allemagtig!* [Good God!] I feel quite young again!' " (Figure 2).[33]

Yet, when it came to establishing a list of public holidays for "The New South Africa," Van Riebeeck was not even considered. The basic principle underlying the listing of holidays were that they be appropriately arranged in both contemporary and commemorative time. Fitting them into contemporary time meant assigning them to days that would space the working year into manageable units and involved a discourse around concepts such as productivity, prolonged versus intermittent holidays, and "the wealth of the country." For example, in one such discussion, the King's Birthday was moved to August since too many holidays were already interrupting production in April and May. Fitting holidays into commemorative time, as with specific celebrations, involved placing them within a framework set by societal moments of historical import. Affirming South Africa as a union with a colonial heritage was the guiding principle for setting commemorative time in November 1910. The day union was declared, 31 May, became Union Day; 24 May was Victoria Day, bearing the "name of the Sovereign who reigned over the Empire when it went through its greatest crisis"; and 16 December was commemorated as a day of "national significance" to recall the victory of a group of trekkers who had left the Cape over a section of the Zulu army at the Battle of Blood River in 1838. The name accorded this day was not associated with trekker identity but with the Zulu king at the time of the battle, Dingane. This was not because the day eulogized Dingane in any way, but because the defeat of the Zulu army was conceptualized as a victory of the forces of colonialism and "civilisation over barbarism and heathenism," a motif that had been central to the pageant which had taken place a few days before the Public Holidays Act was passed in November 1910. For Van Riebeeck, though, who occupied a somewhat uneasy position within

2. Van Riebeeck is re-born for the establishment of the Union of South Africa. "*Allemagtig!* I Feel Quite Young Again," *Cape Argus,* Weekly Edition, 10 October 1910. Courtesy of *Cape Argus* and National Library of South Africa, Cape Town.

commemorative time and whose landing in April would have made the early part of the year even more unproductive, there was no space on the calendar.[34]

In fact, during the next decade, Van Riebeeck hardly featured in South Africa's commemorative past. His statue on Adderley Street was so neglected that it took on a "green and grimy" appearance.[35] It seems the only attempt to pattern a semblance of a memorial out of Van Riebeeck's landing came from the Algemeen Nederlands Verbond (ANV). Initially established in 1895 in Brussels, the ANV sought to establish a cultural heritage that linked together those people in a greater Dutch world who were identified (or identified themselves) as having "Dutch blood." To promote the "Dutch language, Dutch song, Dutch costumes and music," the ANV arranged concerts, held lectures, and distributed reading material at its various branches. Although founded in Belgium, its biggest branches were in southern Africa, where the organization had flourished on the Witwatersrand on the eve of the South African War. After the war it was resuscitated, particularly in the Cape, where its largest and main branch was set up in 1908. A central moving force behind the revival of the ANV and its shifting focus to the Cape was the rector of Stellenbosch University and Van Riebeeck's biographer, Prof. E. C. Godee Molsbergen. Molsbergen was a strong proponent of the concept of a greater Netherlands that would embrace Africa, Holland, and Flanders. He lauded the pioneers of Dutch colonization—Peter Stuyvesant in North America, Jan Pieterzoon Coen in the East Indies, and Van Riebeeck in Africa. With his guidance, the ANV played a major role in promoting Van Riebeeck as a key initiator of this greater Dutch identity and, in April 1918, held a lecture and musical program to honor "the arrival of Jan van Riebeeck at the Cape" and thereby form a "link between the ANV and Van Riebeeck."[36]

But this link went further, for, in the ceremony in 1918, a connection was starting to emerge, albeit tentatively, between those who identified themselves as part of a nation built out of a language constructed as Afrikaans and those claiming a Dutch heritage. In its past this Afrikaner nationalism had relied on a sense of independence, of breaking away to lay the foundations of a new nation. Taken as key moments in this History were the series of events turned into a journey of predestination and labeled the Great Trek and the struggles of the settlers against the officials of the Dutch East India Company in the eighteenth century. Establishing a European, and specifically Dutch, ancestry had little to do with a sense of nation. In the twentieth century this sense of national identity, based on a localized concept of independence, began to shift and to incorporate a sense of heritage. To broaden its appeal, the notion of being an Afrikaner became simultaneously more inclusive and more exclusive, incorporating a racial element of European ancestry and barring those who were "non-European." This had not yet taken the form of Holland becoming the "land of origin" of an Afrikaner nation, but it was F. W. Reitz, the former president of the Boer Republic of the Orange Free State—"a Republican at heart"—who was the keynote speaker on the occasion commemorating Van Riebeeck's landing in 1918. In previous ANV meetings he had insisted on telling his audiences about the way the Dutch had assisted Boer armies during the South African War of 1899–1902, clearly demarcating the Boers as Afrikaners and the Dutch as fraternal allies, and heaping inordinate praise on the Dutch royal house. This time, to coincide with the commemorative event, he delivered an oration in honor of Van Riebeeck, which the ANV yearly report described as "instructive and interesting." Once again Van Riebeeck was reiterating his claim as a Dutch ancestor, although this time he was finding a new group of descendants.[37]

This association between Van Riebeeck and elements within Afrikaner nationalist thought became even more prominent as the commemoration of the landing became an annual public ceremony in the 1920s. In 1921 the ANV applied successfully to the Cape Town City Council to hold a wreath-laying ceremony at the statue on Adderley Street on 7 April. Among the large crowd in attendance were the mayor of Cape Town, several government ministers, representatives of the Cape Provincial administration, and K. M. Jeffreys of the Van Riebeeck Society, an organization formed in 1918 to publish "rare and valuable" documents "relating to the history of South Africa." Using the entry in Van Riebeeck's diary on 6 April 1654 to give the ceremony a historical basis and a tradition—fulfilling "his" supposed wish that "the day of his landing . . . be *for ever* held in grateful remembrance"—homage was paid to the various forms of Van Riebeeck. He was embraced as the "First settler, though of Dutch race," "the Almighty Dutchman," "one of the most remarkable pioneers of civilisation in history," and as "founder of the great South African nation." The last acquisition was a very recent one, and, significantly, it was this aspect of the ceremonial orations that the Afrikaans press emphasized as it sought to indigenize the colonial settlement.[38]

This new indigenous form of Van Riebeeck increasingly came to the fore at the wreath-laying ceremonies the ANV organized over the next few years. He was given the title "*volksplanter*" [literally, nation planter] and hailed as the one who began the process of colonial expansion to the interior, thereby asserting his position in Cape Town as the start of, rather than the force against, the "Great Trek." In his newly found attire Van Riebeeck was domesticated into an example of a "*getroude man*" [married/honorable man] whose "married life was happy and blessed." This shift of focus from the event of the landing to the human characteristics of "the founder" was significant, as it now inscribed upon his way of life values associated with South Africa as home. Home had a dual meaning: It signified both a location of colonial settlement and, within that, a domesticity that gendered the colonial settler Jan van Riebeeck as a married man and Maria as his wife, the two creating an "exemplary marriage."[39]

As Van Riebeeck started coming home, calls were increasingly made to locate the landing within national commemorative time and to turn its annual anniversary into a public holiday. In 1925 the ANV submitted a proposal to the parliamentary select committee that was considering amendments to the Public Holidays Act to institute a Founders Day so as to recall "the day on which the first pioneer of European civilisation set foot on South African soil and established the permanent European settlement here." It was on his foundations, the ANV claimed, that South Africa "was building." Teachers would be called on to instruct their students of the significance of this aspect of the founding in the period leading up to the public holiday. The campaign also had the support of Prof. S. F. N. Gie, the first Professor of South African history at Stellenbosch University and a leading proponent of Afrikaner nationalist history. His European training led him not only to adopt an almost obsessive Rankean approach to the study of history but also to draw a distinction between anthropology, which he saw as dealing scientifically with the "illiterate and barbarian masses," and history, which he viewed as dealing with "the civilised nations." Locating the Afrikaner within history meant, for him, that the Afrikaners were inevitably part of the world that was "civilised" and "European" and that *volksgeskiedenis* [*volk*'s history] was really the "History of European Civilisation in South Africa." In this racially constructed notion of history Van Riebeeck and his crew were the European "founders of our South Africa, the South Africa of the white man," and the "birthday" of South Africa was part of the "Historical development of the Dutch Nation." Gie was concerned to mark the day of landing not merely as a commemoration of an event or an individual but the start of history itself. In the light of the meaning he thus accorded the event, he called for Van Riebeeck's landing to be placed on the calendar as a "national festival."[40]

With concern over contemporary time paramount—"I know of no other country in the world that is so 'holiday ridden' as South Africa," asserted the chair of the select committee investigating amendments to the public holidays act—and in spite of support from some members of parliament, attempts to place Van Riebeeck in commemorative time fell on deaf ears. What did occur, nonetheless, is that the distance between Van Riebeeck and the Afrikaner nationalist past tended to lessen. The outcome of this ever-diminishing distance was that in 1938, when the centenary celebrations of the "Great Trek" were arranged by the Afrikaner nationalist cultural organization, the Afrikaans Taal en Kultuur Vereniging [Afrikaans Language and Cultural Association]

(ATKV), Van Riebeeck featured prominently. The plan for the *Eeufees* [centenary festival] was for a series of ox-wagons from different parts of the country to travel the "Road of South Africa" to Pretoria where the foundation stone of a Voortrekker monument was to be laid. Traveling through different towns, the *fees* drew together the white Afrikaans-speaking population "stretching from the Cape to Pretoria" in "a massive cultural orgy." Local festivals were held as the ox-wagons passed through the towns, men grew beards, women donned *kappies* [bonnets], and streets were named after Voortrekker leaders. The selected starting point of this trek to the north was not the eastern Cape, where most of the trek leaders had begun their journeys in the 1830s, but the base of the Van Riebeeck statue on Adderley Street, Cape Town. Whereas one hundred years earlier the move northward had spurned Van Riebeeck and his various forms, he was now incorporated into the trek as the starting point of a history predetermined by God. The two ox-wagons were beginning their journey, claimed the Afrikaans newspaper, *Die Burger,* at the spot where "nearly 300 years ago, Van Riebeeck responded to God's calling and began the process of *volksplanting.*" All South African history was now cast as one long continuous Afrikaner trek from one "*volksdaad*" [*volk*'s deed] to another. It started when Van Riebeeck landed and established "the cradle of our South African civilization" at the foot of Table Mountain, and it reached its turning point when Sarel Cilliers made a prayer to God before the battle against a section of the Zulu army at Blood River in 1838. The next *volksdaad,* the trek of 1938, was to bring the history to its destination in a future, Afrikaner-led "white South Africa." As wreaths were laid at the base of Van Riebeeck's statue, speeches were made, Bibles presented, and the ox-wagon—named after the trek leader Piet Retief—departed on the first stage of its journey to the Castle, built between 1666 and 1705 to replace the original fort constructed by the first commander of the Dutch East India Company at the Cape. Van Riebeeck surveyed the scene in a "calm and sedate" manner, and gazed bemused over the thousands that had gathered to pay homage to him as he, somewhat surprisingly, re-emerged as the "*Volksplanter.*"[41]

A direct outcome of this association between Van Riebeeck and an Afrikaner nationalist past was that Afrikaans cultural organizations started to participate far more actively in the April commemorations, instructing groups of schoolchildren to learn and recite the Van Riebeeck prayer and compiling material so that a "historically correct" portrayal of Van Riebeeck could emerge. H. B. Thom, Professor of history at the University of Stellenbosch, wrote a pamphlet, which was published by the Federasie van Afrikaanse Kultuurbewegings [Federation of Afrikaans Cultural Associations] (FAK) and the Cape Town City Council, calling for Van Riebeeck day to become one of "national commemoration." Evoking the words of his predecessor in the history department, S. F. N. Gie, he called on the government to "create the opportunity for the holding of worthy and fitting commemorative functions, and at the same time perform a resounding cultural act." Although Thom's plea was not heeded, the enthusiasm within Afrikaner nationalist circles was so overwhelming that, with much assistance from the FAK, in 1940 the celebrations of the landing took place on a "grander scale," not only in Cape Town but also in other towns and cities in South Africa. The FAK, established in 1929 by the Afrikaner Broederbond, presented itself as the umbrella and central decision-making body for more than three hundred Afrikaner cultural organizations. It decided on what constituted Afrikaner identity and sought to promote it through various media. By 1941, along with the ANV, the FAK had assumed almost total control of the arrangements for the celebrations. Although representatives from the Cape Town City Council, the Dutch government, the Boy Scouts, and the Caledonian Society were invited guests, Afrikaans cultural bodies, which turned up in full force, dominated the proceedings. The ceremony itself, though, was not reduced to outpourings of Afrikaner nationalist rhetoric. Indeed, no speeches were made and the focus was on asserting a European heritage. Thus, after Van Riebeeck's pledge had been recited and all the invited organizations had laid the wreaths, it was the National Anthem of the Netherlands that was sung.[42]

This increasing involvement of the FAK in the proceedings and the more popular appeal of the ceremony led to a great deal of friction over who the appropriate organizers for the commemorations should be. Although the conflict that emerged mainly consisted of debate regarding organizational expertise and access to appropriate resources, it reflected contestation over the symbolic appropriations of Van Riebeeck's past. Some pressure came from within Afrikaner nationalist ranks for the ANV to step down completely from its role in the organization of the commemoration, because it was "an association whose membership was largely composed of foreigners."[43] This was probably the clearest expression of Van Riebeeck assuming a local nationalist identity and attempting to cast off his colonial imagery. The ANV was taken aback by this outburst in the pages of the Afrikaans magazine, Die Huisgenoot, and in its reply to the editor took pains not to place Van Riebeeck in a Dutch past but to assert the South African Afrikaner connections of the ANV:

> More than a third of our members are sons and daughters of South Africa with typically Afrikaner surnames. Of the other two thirds, more than a half are old Dutch people who have been naturalised citizens of the Union for years. Some of them obtained their citizenship in the days of Kruger and Steyn. In the past, people like President Reitz and Senator François Malan were honorary presidents of our branch.[44]

In addition to the problems raised over the ANV's organizational role, the FAK was also concerned about the way the Cape Town City Council was assuming more direction in terms of the proceedings at the statue on Adderley Street. The ceremony had taken on a very somber character, the City Council was making its presence felt by ensuring that the organizers had to obtain permission to use the statue site, and it was even rumored that "God Save the King" might be included in the proceedings. The FAK, feeling it was being maneuvered into an inferior position with regard to Van Riebeeck, withdrew from organizing the wreath-laying ceremony, labeling it "merely a formality." Now asserting that the form of the ceremony did not matter—in any case, it took place at the base of the statue of that arch-imperialist, Cecil John Rhodes—they arranged an evening ceremony in the Hofmeyr Hall. The Cape Town City Council, realizing that the ceremony at the statue was acquiring a broader public appeal among the white population of the city, stepped into the breach and, from 1945, Van Riebeeck Day was "officially commemorated by the Council." As the Batavian governor De Mist had done almost 150 years earlier, Cape Town was redesignated *Riebeecks stad* [Riebeeck's city], with its origins and character symbolically represented as European.[45]

By the mid-1940s, through these various acts of commemoration, the meaning and identity of Van Riebeeck and the landing had shifted dramatically from the days of European trade and settlement. From the seventeenth and eighteenth centuries, when the central theme had been the landing as a religious signifier of possession by the Dutch East India Company, to the latter part of the nineteenth century, when the focus on Van Riebeeck as an individual was as a forebear of colonialism, he changed, in the twentieth century, into a European founder of an indigent nationalism. This is not to argue that these images and identities merely replaced the former ones. Indeed, not only did the past images remain but aspects of these were retained and incorporated as new identities emerged. As the three hundredth anniversary of 1652 approached, the historic times of Van Riebeeck, constructed and resurrected for collective memory through the commemorations, varied from the Christian lineage, the pre-destination of an Afrikaner *volk,* the ancestry of Dutch-speaking South Africans, to a legacy, or a somewhat tarnished reputation, derived from colonization. The tercentenary festival of 1952 drew on these pasts to construct Van Riebeeck in its own image, an image that often had to negotiate a tricky path between these historic times.

Schooling the Past

Shifting identities associated with Van Riebeeck and his landing that are similar to those established through commemorative time can be tracked through an examination of school textbooks used in South Africa from the early nineteenth century to the 1940s. The Dutch ancestor, the colonial settler, the Christian bearer, and the *volksplanter* are all in evidence and follow a temporal routing that seems to follow the commemorations. This is not altogether surprising given that school texts over this period became major instruments of socialization through attempting to establish a formal coherence, often related to a national past, and, by stripping history to essences, protecting the self-identified group from "'cognitive chaos.'"[46]

Yet textbooks do not merely reflect social and political circumstances nor do they reproduce exactly the same historical meanings as the commemorations. Textbooks in themselves produce specific forms of historical knowledge that can be located within a unique register where there is a specific context, a distinguishable prosaic pattern, and a social relationship in which structures of authority are mutually reinforcing. The context is nearly always the school or college classroom where, since the development of mass printing in the nineteenth century, textbooks have become the primary medium for education. It is a truism that "students' school work often begins (and in some schools ends) with the textbook." If one accepts this assertion, then by analyzing textbooks one can ascertain the nature and content of the knowledge "that is supposed to be transmitted in the classroom." The language of textbooks is built on the premise that the questioner already knows the answer to questions she or he asks. To perform this function more effectively, textbooks are designed to clearly demarcate the "correct answers." The emphasis is on providing definitions, "declarative sentences," and listing, labeling, and numbering points. In a very real sense, textbooks are the ultimate expression of a writerly text, where the reader is allowed little space for his or her own reading of the text. Textbooks "*say* what they *mean* and mean precisely, neither more nor less than, what they *say*." Finally, textbooks maintain social relations of authority in that their assertions are "transcendental," seemingly originating from outside the direct realm of the speaker. The teacher and the student combine in a process that repeats and reproduces the structure and content of the textbook, with the teacher quizzing the student's grasp of the assigned knowledge. This invests the words in the text with an appearance that they are beyond criticism in that they are not seen and heard as "the personal whim and limited experience of the speaker."[47]

Although this conceptualization of the language and authority of textbooks is a general one, it does seem to be applicable to history texts used in schools. Causal factors and outcomes are often neatly packaged into listings, giving reasons for and results of, which the student is obliged to provide in terms of answers. The central story of the past is clearly demarcated, and anything that might be considered extraneous, complicating, or additional is either discarded or reduced to a block alongside the main text. In this form, the nature of history is ultimately one of deriving essentialisms that have to be transmitted in the classroom context. The constituent parts of that essential knowledge are often at the heart of struggles over what should be taught as history in schools: Should it be Eurocentric or Afrocentric, should it emphasize content or skills, should it tell about individuals or larger contexts, should it narrate a story or provide a package of sources? Although these seem to be issues of contestation, what is clear from all these sites of struggle is that a consensus exists that there is a basic or core knowledge of history that must be authorized in the classroom.

One of the first history textbooks to be used in classrooms at the Cape was for schoolchildren who were schooled in Dutch. *Geschiedenis van de Kaap de Goede Hoop* [History of the Cape of Good Hope] was published in 1825 and written by Joseph Suasso de Lima, a schoolmaster at the Evangelical Lutheran High School in Cape Town. De Lima, who was of Jewish descent, had arrived in the Cape from Amsterdam, had engaged in various unsuccessful business ventures, and took to teaching, translating, and writing plays for the Cape Town stage. In these undertakings, particularly for his satirical writings and what were considered irreligious ideas—he once suggested that dancing be associated with prayers—he often acquired many enemies, especially from sections of the Dutch-speaking community.[48]

From the moment of its publication, De Lima's book was severely criticized. It has been called "elementary," "disjointed," "full of errors," "one-sided," "lamely written," "beneath all criticism," and, rather patronizingly, "quaint." These critiques, although containing a large measure of validity, do not examine how De Lima's textbook embraces a certain type of knowledge of the past and turns it into history. Underlying the text is a sense of creating a local identity based on colonial settlement embracing settlers from disparate areas of Europe. The subject characterized as the means to achieve this is history, "an authentic account of prominent events." Cast as role players, inventors, and discoverers in a world of progress, individuals, through their actions, were seen as influencing the course of events. This represented a significant shift away from the educational system in the Cape in the eighteenth century, where religious instruction dominated and history hardly featured in the curriculum. In De Lima's world of the early-nineteenth-century Cape, recently colonized by Britain, establishing and specifying individuals into discernible locations was becoming more important than imparting religious guidelines. To accomplish this transformation from sacred to secular history, it became crucial to import what today is specified as the subject of geography into history and for students to be able to spatially locate their individuality on a map of manageable, discrete entities. De Lima's book begins with a series of questions to students requiring that they pinpoint themselves on a world map. Once the text has been geographically demarcated and mapped out, individuals appear to take their role in the temporal routing of history to discover, arrive, possess, and settle. After settlement, it is the governors of the Cape who provide the markers of change in an extended chapter 9, covering almost three-quarters of the book, entitled "Continuation."[49]

De Lima places Van Riebeeck's departure from Holland to the Cape to take possession of the land in the name of the Dutch East India Company together with the landing on 6 April 1652 as the starting point of the history of the *Vaderland*. Although he does list other European traders who called at the Cape before 1652, he claims that they did not attempt "to retain this outpost." Clearly, for De Lima, Van Riebeeck's establishment of a revictualing station signified possession in colonial terms by the "father" of the land. "From that moment, in my opinion, history begins," asserted De Lima. In the three pages of the history that follow (chapters 7, 8, and the beginning of the lengthy chapter 9) the emphasis is on Van Riebeeck's trade relations with the local inhabitants, the "resistance" to the settlement from the "*Hottentoten*," who are portrayed as being thieves and robbers, and the characterization of Van Riebeeck as an "honourable and brave" man. Framing these events and individual actions is, once again, De Lima's concern with establishing how the Cape is spatially constructed. He tells how Van Riebeeck commissioned the first map of the Cape in 1657 and continually desired to extend the boundaries of the "colony." For De Lima, the Cape had always been a bounded colony, from the time of the establishment of the revictualing station, marked off by the first governor at Riebeeks Kasteel, "the area where his first border was."[50]

The accuracy of this statement and of De Lima's many others might be debatable; what is clear, however, is that his concern was to specify local space and to turn the Cape into a European place. This was a crucial component of the knowledge of history that *Geschiedenis van de Kaap* sought to impart. It was reinforced by incorporating lessons in geography and civics into history. The authority was conveyed by the listings and by the question-and-answer format, defining historical knowledge as supplying the correct answers to the questions as specified in the text. The extent to which De Lima's textbook was used and its knowledge of the past transmitted in the colony beyond the classes at the Lutheran school is not known, and indeed it might only have been regarded as being of curiosity value at the time. There are indications that its use was limited, as it could not be used in English medium schools, and there was a great deal of disaffection with De Lima in Dutch intellectual circles. It must also be remembered that not until the late nineteenth century was history taught as a specific subject at schools in the Cape Colony, which was also the case in Britain. If, however, having access to the vast array of textbooks produced subsequently, one wanted to "see progressions that didn't exist at the time," *Geschiedenis van de Kaap de Goede Hoop*, instead of being dismissed as having "no influence on the course of South African historiography," can be viewed as the first of a kind, containing many of the features that were to characterize South African history textbooks for the next century and a half: its transformation of geography and civics into history, its emphasis on designating the local, and the learning of predetermined answers. Moreover, Van Riebeeck appears in the past at the beginning of history, reinforcing both the temporal identity he was starting to establish in commemorative time as a figure of colonial settlement and his spatial identity at the Cape of Good Hope with its ever-expanding borders.[51]

In the fifty years following the publication of De Lima's *Geschiedenis*, history remained a peripheral subject in most schools in the Cape Colony, constituting only a small part of the English-language syllabus. English history from the Battle of Hastings in 1066 to the Battle of Waterloo in 1815 formed the basis of what was taught in this section of the curriculum, with the emphasis placed on nurturing a sense of colonial loyalty. It was only in the 1870s, with increasing competition for colonial possessions among European countries and the extension of British imperial ambitions in southern Africa and the antagonisms this aroused, that schools came to place greater emphasis on history as a subject. On the one hand, this history highlighted a colonial identity, extending the previous stress on English history to incorporate loyalty and devotion into the expanding empire. On the other hand, and in seeming contrast to imperial history, texts were also written in a language that was starting to identify itself, though somewhat hesitantly, as Afrikaans—indeed, the authors of one of these texts apologized for incorrect spelling because no dictionary in this language was yet available—accentuating struggles for independence against colonial authorities. Yet, as is shown below, both these histories relied on a framework of colonial identities and had much in common, especially when it came to dealing with Van Riebeeck and the landing.[52]

The most widely used textbook in the Cape Colony in the 1870s and 1880s was Alexander Wilmot's *History of the Cape Colony for Use in Schools*, published in 1871. This was a condensed version of the *History of the Colony of the Cape of Good Hope*, written by John Chase, which had appeared two years before. As with De Lima, it is the concern to establish spatial locations that frames this school text. In this case, though, the concern is not only to situate the colony at the Cape of Good Hope; two-thirds of the book is devoted to the interior space of European expansion, labeled "the frontier." These boundaries of the frontier, established in time and space as the key signifiers, enabled Wilmot to set up racial dichotomies of "civilization/savagery," with colonization as the bearer of the former and the "Natives," initially called "Hottentots" and later "Kafirs," as the bearer of the latter.

The stress on the (British) colonial encounter casts Van Riebeeck not at the beginning of history but as a colonial official who was merely carrying out his job effectively. The crucial date for Wilmot, therefore, is the one that denotes the beginning of governance and administration. The concept of the Cape being always/already a colony is utilized to assert that "Commander Van Riebeeck assumed the government of the embryo Colony upon the 9th of April, 1652, when he issued a proclamation as "Senior Merchant," taking formal possession of the country, and enacting various regulations.[53] This is followed by an account of some of the "difficulties" Van Riebeeck encountered at the Cape in effectively carrying out his administrative duties: "He had not only to provide against attacks from the natives, but to keep the servants of the Company in order." All in all, the period when Van Riebeeck was governor at the Cape is portrayed as a deeply unhappy time in his life as he desperately sought to be posted elsewhere. Yet Wilmot does maintain that in spite of the "troubles" he faced Van Riebeeck stoically carried out his orders to the letter, attending "assiduously to the interests of his employers." By obeying, ordering, building, arranging, systematizing, and proclaiming, Wilmot turned Van Riebeeck into the almost ideal (British) colonial official.[54]

Die Geskiedenis van Ons Land in die Taal van Ons Volk [The history of our country in the language of our *volk*] by S. J. du Toit and C. P. Hoogenhout, published in 1877, was explicitly written against Wilmot's imperial past as "corrective to the 'official' history books that are used in schools." There are clear indications, though, that it was not only a school text. It was produced by the Genootskap van Regte Afrikaners [Fellowship of True Afrikaners] (GRA), a group of teachers and priests in the western Cape who, in the face of apparent discrimination against them by British imperial interests, were attempting to promote a language they were codifying as Afrikaans as a means to engender a popular indigenous nationalism in a territory encompassing the British colonies and Boer republics, defined as "South Africa." In their manifesto, they distinguished themselves from other sorts of Afrikaners as the only "True Afrikaners," claiming neither English nor Dutch legacy but a separate and distinct Afrikaner lineage. History was seen as crucial in furthering this sense of "True Afrikaners," giving them an identity with a characteristic, relatable past. In *Die Patriot,* the newspaper of the GRA, it was claimed that this history was a most effective way of developing nationalism, as it would tighten the familial bonds of love among the *volk.* Imparting this past was seen as a cross-generational task but one that would begin with children, who needed to be acquainted "from their childhood of the trials and sufferings of their fathers in this land where foreigners now seek to tread us under foot."[55]

To provide these "True Afrikaners" with a history, a new space, situated beyond the frontier, was mapped on the southern African landscape. The emphasis on difference and independence moved *Die Geskiedenis* outside the boundaries of the Cape Colony and its imperial surroundings to encompass a territory called "South Africa." After 145 pages dealing with the periods of the Dutch East India Company and English rule at the Cape, the next 90-odd pages takes the reader, with the trekkers, across the borders, on "one of the most important events in the history of the colony under the English." It follows the "Refugee Farmers" as they struggled, and not always successfully, to establish independent republics north of the Cape Colony in Natal, the Orange Free State, and the Transvaal. By according a special location in the text to the latter events, it meant they were also given their own time, which did not flow directly from the chronological sequencing of events in the Cape Colony.[56]

The historical ancestors of those who occupied this independent space and time are established early on in *Die Geschiedenis* where the writer distinguishes between three classes of people at the Cape in the initial phases of settlement: the officials of the Dutch East India Company, the indigenous "natives," and the group of "Free Burgers" who had either purchased or rented plots on which to farm. The latter are identified as the forefathers and are attributed with building the colony in the face of opposition from the other two classes. Du Toit's venom is particularly directed toward the employees of the Dutch East India Company, whom he maintains had the means to colonize but refused to do so. Instead, he claims that they were only interested in making profits for themselves and the Company and that they not only hindered but directly opposed colonization, oppressing *"die arme Boere"* [the poor farmers] in the process (18).

Van Riebeeck, far from being taught in schools as a founder figure in the early Afrikaner nationalist past, is a much more ambiguous figure and the role he played far more uncertain. He was, on the one hand, the "Founder of the Cape Colony" (17), which enabled the *boere* to establish their farms, but he was also an employee of the Company, which seemed intent on victimizing the *boere*. For all its avowed anti-imperial intentions, *Die Geskiedenis* thus relies heavily on Wilmot's *History of the Cape Colony* when dealing with Van Riebeeck. As for Wilmot, the signifying date is 9 April 1652: "The administration of Van Riebeeck at the Cape really begins on the 9th April 1652. Because on that day he issued a proclamation taking possession of the land in the name of the company and enacted various laws" (5). The resemblance to Wilmot's text is so apparent that one wonders whether the authors merely copied the extract, modified it slightly, and then translated it. Similarly, Du Toit repeats Wilmot's assertion that Van Riebeeck did not have a happy time at the Cape and that he was desperate to be sent elsewhere: "He had troubles from all sides. On one side he had to be wary of the wild natives and on the other side his own people." The final verdict on Van Riebeeck in *Die Geskiedenis* is also lukewarm. It outlines his accomplishments in the planning and construction of the settlement, and is largely derived from Wilmot: "He was here for ten years, from 1652 to 1662. When he arrived here there was nothing. Now there is a Castle, houses, gardens and farms." Even these achievements are stated blandly and are not directly tied in to the person of Van Riebeeck. Clearly *Die Geskiedenis* did not want to diminish the accomplishments of the Boers by heaping accolades on Van Riebeeck, the Company official (7, 17).

The essential pasts of both Wilmot's and Du Toit's textbooks were thus firmly located within an imperial framework, where Van Riebeeck appeared as little more than a competent colonial official on the landscape. This spatial mapping of his past seemed at variance with the ways he was being commemorated, at almost the same time, as the first settler, the first Christian, and the first colonial oppressor. Yet in all these commemorative forms Van Riebeeck, the colonial official, was omnipresent, albeit playing different roles. What the school texts of Wilmot and Du Toit did was to give the official a basic narrative, situated in a more specific space, which was to be transmitted, memorized, and tested in the classroom rather than remembered in the commemoration of people and events.

From the 1890s a new set of textbooks were superseding those of Wilmot and Du Toit. These textbooks, either derived from the work of the colonial historiographer of the Cape government, George Theal, or written directly by him, underwent many reprints and revised editions and became the basis for most South African school histories in the twentieth century. Theal also maintained that many other writers of school history texts in the 1890s and 1900s were making considerable use of his material without his permission.[57]

Theal's textbooks were "most-eagerly awaited" at the time, since he was regarded as the preeminent historian of southern African, with a reputation for intensive archival research and extensive detailed historical narratives, often extending into numerous volumes. The style of his histories was also conducive to the textbook format. His explicit aim was merely to "state nothing but the facts" in "plain language," and often his histories were lengthy listings of events, names, and places, the very stuff of which school history textbooks, in their search for essentialisms, are made.[58]

This concern with listing items of significance was paralleled in Theal's school texts by the specifying, naming, and placing of individuals. This had been a characteristic of the previous texts cited, but Theal took this a step further by providing maps, pictures, and replicas of documents. All these illustrations were offered as a means toward greater precision, toward ensuring that the student saw the past instead of having to rely on imagination from the printed word, which both the author and teacher could regulate only to a limited extent. With pictures, this control could be increased. The dates told students which were the most important events to recall in Theal's South African past, whereas maps and pictures showed how they were to be coded, placed, and stored in the visual imagination.[59]

A central image Theal wished to convey was of clearly demarcated racial identities that could be distinguished by physical and what he called "cultural" characteristics. In his school history, *Primer of South African History*, he placed the inhabitants of South Africa on an evolutionary scale. At the bottom of the rung he placed the "race" that he said "lived by hunting alone," "the Bushmen." He cast them physically as being "of small size, of a yellowish brown colour, very fleet of foot, and very sharp-sighted." Above them came the "Hottentots," "who had tame animals, but did not till the ground" and were, in Theal's image, "larger in size, and much less wild" than the "Bushmen." On the next rung of Theal's racial evolutionary ladder came "The Bantu," who, like the "Hottentots," "had tame animals," but, in addition, "tilled the ground." Members of this race, according to Theal, "were larger in body than either of the others, and their colour varied from deep brown to black." Yet, despite their agricultural pursuits, "the Bantu" were not viewed by Theal as a fully cultured race, as "they had no other clothing than skins of animals. . . . They kept no sacred days and had no churches. . . . They could not understand each other's languages." By implication, it was the "white race" (Theal does not define them physically) that had all these attributes (presumably all "whites" dressed in "proper" clothes, went to church, and could understand one another perfectly well), that was "fully accultured," and that stood at the apex of Theal's racial hierarchy.[60]

Once these races had been firmly established in the introductory pages of Theal's text, they were then mapped onto South Africa and its past events. The "Bushmen" and the "Hottentots" were drawn as "Ancient inhabitants" of a land that existed before history, before the naming and locating of places, with maps showing "how little was known of South Africa when the Dutch first settled here" and the land was "as good as unknown." The "Bantu," however, were not situated on this pre-historic map but, instead, were shown to be migrating southward from Asia in a similar fashion to the Portuguese who were exploring the Atlantic coastline of Africa from the mid-fifteenth century. Theal's history textbooks are unclear as to when and where this "Bantu migration" began and how it proceeded, but he is definite that "the Bantu" had not reached South Africa by the time of European exploration. Thus Theal not only "did more than anyone else to establish a pseudo-scientific basis for the myth of the empty land," but he detailed and inscribed it in the texts and consciousness of South African schoolchildren for decades to come.[61]

It was Theal's land, virtually devoid of historical markers, the site of "ancient inhabitants" and "migrating Bantu," that the Portuguese first "discovered" in the late fifteenth century, setting up crosses and naming places to signify their visits. But it was not until the mid-seventeenth century that the passing visits to Theal's "empty land" were turned into European "foundations" when the Dutch East India Company sent its representative, Jan van Riebeeck, to establish a refreshment station "on the fertile ground at the foot of Table Mountain." For Theal, the arrival of Van Riebeeck in 1652 is clearly a turning point for South Africa in terms of its encounters with his racial hierarchy of history, as it signified, for him, "the date from which the history of white people in South Africa commences." He even introduces into the South African past a priest who accompanied Van Riebeeck on his journey to the Cape, William Wylant. Theal, wanting to establish an ancestry for the "white race," urges his readers to remember this name "because a son of his was *the first European child born in South Africa.*"[62]

As the "European founder," Van Riebeeck himself is not given the adulations one might have expected from Theal. He is described as "a little, active, quick-tempered man" who "remained ten years at the fort as commander" and was then transferred, after numerous requests for promotion, to India, leaving the settlement at the Cape "in a fairly prosperous condition." Between his arrival and departure, a rather bland chronological narrative is offered, which follows Van Riebeeck's journal and extracts elements that highlight building, planting, trade, and conflict with the "Hottentots." This all leads to the scenario Theal sketches of the eve Van Riebeeck takes leave of the settlement in 1662, with "the Hottentots" no longer being any "trouble" and each ["white"] farmer having "his little farm marked out." Theal's lukewarm description of Van Riebeeck and of the events during his tenure as governor at the Cape can probably be explained by Theal's attempts to write "white" history, which undoubtedly made him sensitive to emergent Afrikaner nationalist versions of the past, where the role of Company officials was often harshly criticized and the exploits of the independent groups of "European" farmers was highlighted. In this respect, it is interesting that Theal follows Du Toit's *Geskiedenis* and refers to the farmers who established plots along the Liesbeek River in 1657 as "*the first real South African colonists.*"[63] These seemingly contradictory forces were then situated within Theal's particular brand of the past, where recounting facts was central—a trend the form of school textbooks accentuated—to produce a negotiated Van Riebeeck whom schoolchildren could view as the bearer of whiteness, a builder of the colony, but no more than an adequate official.

Although Theal dominated the South African textbook market, his work and its pre-eminence was challenged by Dorothea Fairbridge's *History of South Africa*, published in 1917 by Oxford University Press. Like Theal's schoolbooks, Fairbridge's *History* was extremely popular and enjoyed numerous reprints. Fairbridge was a prolific writer whose field extended beyond the narrow realm Theal would have defined as history, that is, the collection and narration of "facts." In addition to the *History*, she wrote five novels, nonfiction books dealing with "old Cape culture," travelogues, and edited diaries and letters. She was also a regular contributor to *The State*, a magazine that promoted the Union of South Africa, debated its symbolic forms and appropriations, and "was devoted to the overnight construction of a new ameliorative South African identity that would permit reconciliation between the English and the Afrikaners."[64]

It was Fairbridge's interest in establishing colonial unity as part of the British Empire that was the thread running through nearly all her writings, her *History* in particular. The constituent parts of Fairbridge's South Africa seem quite similar to those Theal advocated, with phenomenological descriptions attributed to her racial categories of "Bushmen," "Hottentots," and "Bantu." Although she accords the "Bantu" more land than Theal does, the idea of a vast uninhabited interior before the advent of the Europeans is still pivotal. And it is these Europeans who are depicted as the bearers of "civilization." Although there were "inevitable" clashes "when the forces of civilization c[a]me into contact with those of the primitive races," it is these "civilized" forces who ultimately (and also inevitably?) triumph in Fairbridge's pre-determined past and who are carried through the narrative "to see the work of Union carried to its completion."[65]

Yet, for all its apparent similarities with Theal's school textbooks, Fairbridge's *History* is also markedly different from Theal's *Primer* and *Short History*. This was a result, in part, of a personal animosity between the two—Fairbridge was assisted in her historical endeavors by Hendrik Carel Vos Leibrandt, who had been appointed, above Theal and much to his chagrin, as Keeper of the Archives in 1880—as well as her approach to the writing of history.[66] Theal, as noted above, wrote history in a chronological sequence, providing facts along a linear, systematically arranged, horizontal axis. Fairbridge, on the other hand, was much more interested in the symbolism of events, persons, and images of the past. In her model of history, time was not conceived purely in the progression Theal advanced but as selected moments that emphasized significance and subjective experience. Thus, instead of recounting the past by simply listing facts, an approach that dominates most school texts, Fairbridge's *History* was related as a story. Historical personages along the progression of time were given character and personality, gardens and buildings were imbued with meaning, and events were described in graphic detail. Symbolism, rather than facts, comprised the essential details of Fairbridge's past for schoolchildren.

Fairbridge's symbolic past was organized in the Union of South Africa, which, in turn, was located in the British imperial world. Individuals were agents of the past and were measured in terms of their effectiveness in carrying out a pre-determined imperial mission. The person at the apex of Fairbridge's imperial hierarchy was Cecil John Rhodes, who, from the age of eighteen, "dedicated his life" to the "service" of "Empire and of united South Africa." The story of his life was compared to the mythical tale of Dick Whittington, a poor boy pre-destined to become Lord Mayor of London, and that of the biblical character Moses, who saw the Promised Land—"a fusion of the great white races of South Africa"—in a distant vision but never entered it.[67]

If, for Fairbridge, it was Rhodes whose "vision" and "greatness of soul" had brought South Africa to the verge of Union under the British flag, it was Jan van Riebeeck who started the process of imperial unity in her *History of South Africa*. This was similar to the way Rhodes himself had conceptualized Van Riebeeck when he commissioned the statue on Adderley Street, Cape Town, in 1896. Fairbridge heaps inordinate amounts of praise on Van Riebeeck, certainly far in excess of any of the textbooks previously mentioned. He is described as "a man of indomitable courage and great resource and perseverance" who, with his "great qualities," "set a fine example." The focus of the section dealing with Van Riebeeck is on the development of the Company gardens to supply the passing ships and on the construction of a Great Barn (Groote Schuur) as a granary. Both these activities are used as emblems to link Van Riebeeck with the coming of Union, where the germination and growth from seeds planted in the soil serves as a metaphor for the coming of Union: "The Union of South Africa has grown from the little vegetable garden of Jan van Riebeeck." A short while later in the narrative, the Great Barn is used to symbolize solid beginnings and, disregarding chronological forms, symbolically links Van Riebeeck, Rhodes, and the Union. "On foundations of van Riebeeck's barn two centuries and a half later another great South African [Rhodes] built the house which he left as the residence of the Premier of United South Africa."[68]

Importantly, it is Van Riebeeck as an individual that is emphasized here as the builder of foundations and the first colonizer. The chapter dealing with Van Riebeeck makes no mention at all of the members of the independent farming community that developed after 1657, which both Du Toit and Theal had labeled as the first colonizers. When the chapter concludes with Van Riebeeck's departure, no reference is made of his eagerness to take up another posting, and he is eulogized for his "infinite courage, self-sacrifice and determination." It is the imperial agent, in this case dressed as the highly effective Company servant, who is decisive in Fairbridge's world, where loyalty to the "Motherland in the North Sea" matters most of all.[69]

Fairbridge's textbook is also notable for the much more substantial appearance of Maria de la Quellerie, sometimes called "Van Riebeeck's wife." In both De Lima and Wilmot she is not even mentioned, not in name or even as a "wife." Du Toit makes a fleeting reference to her as "his wife" in connection with outbreaks of disease at the settlement, and Theal, in his *Primer*, remarks that Van Riebeeck "had his family with him." In *Our History in Picture*, there is an illustration of Maria with the caption, "Portrait of the wife of Jan van Riebeeck," but whereas Theal provides historical notes with the other pictures, no text appears with this one.[70] Fairbridge's entry on Maria, although quite brief, says far more than any of these other textbooks. Like most of the characters that appear in Fairbridge's past, Maria has been given iconic qualities.

> His wife, Maria de Quellerie, was a daughter of Minister Gaasbeeck of Rotterdam, and she displayed a serene endurance of peril and discomfort which must have been of infinite assistance to her husband.[71]

This short portrait is placed toward the end of a lengthy paragraph that praises the "qualities" of Jan as a "good all-round man" and is located chronologically between the departure from Holland at the end of 1651 and the arrival at the Cape in April 1652. In a text littered with descriptions and illustrations of imperious men, from Van Riebeeck to Harry Smith to Cecil John Rhodes, who are conquering and "civilizing" on the road to Union, this entry seems a bit out of place. The only other woman of whom there is a lengthy account is Lady Anne Barnard, who accompanied the Colonial Secretary, Andrew Barnard, to the Cape in the late 1790s. In editing a selected collection of Lady Anne Barnard's correspondence in 1924, Fairbridge praised these letters as being the result of endeavors of someone who employed a "brilliant pen." In the *History*, published seven years earlier, Lady Anne Barnard is described as "a woman of great charm," and Fairbridge situates her within the symbolic narrative of progression toward Union by remarking on the parties she gave in the Castle "in the hope of drawing the two [white] races together." In comparing these entries and looking at their textual location, it is difficult to draw any substantial conclusions about the symbolic representation of women in Fairbridge's past. Clearly, there are women in this past and in the future of the Union who have played important roles and will continue to do so. It is the specific nature of that participation that is difficult to define, and I would suggest that perhaps Fairbridge is struggling to define it herself. On one level, it seems that the two women she chooses to highlight are similar in as much as they portray the function of white women as one of assistance, in any way possible, with what is a perceived as a "manly task" of bringing about Union. Maria does this by "enduring" and Lady Anne Barnard by hosting parties. Yet, Lady Anne Barnard is also portrayed as being someone who was "brilliant," who wrote with "infinite candour" and "had keen powers of observation." In this light Maria de la Quellerie pales by comparison, and it would seem that the role model of the "white women" that Fairbridge prefers is located in her representation of Lady Anne Barnard. Maria de la Quellerie, therefore, seems to enter the textbook past as a reminder to readers that there were women in South Africa's past, that they played an important part in "man's progress," but that this role should be carried further to enable women to become critical observers of "man's world"—to give "an honest picture of the Cape at that time"—rather than to be "enduring" appendages.[72]

Over the following three decades, as the subject of history in South African government schools came to be shaped around notions of citizenship and the constituent and conflicting components of "the nation," it was taught on a large scale in primary and secondary schools. There was a veritable explosion in the textbook market as schoolteachers began writing texts themselves, superseding in output the professional historians and the novelists who had dominated thus far. This proliferation of school history tended to take place in the context of a highly regulated system as book committees were set up in the provinces to approve or recommend certain texts and a centralized matriculation system left little room to deviate from the given syllabus. The textbooks that appeared were issued with a stamp of government approval and bore titles such as *Juta's History for Matriculation Students* and *New History for Senior Certificate and Matriculation*.[73]

The overwhelming trend in history textbooks was that they became even more essentialist, sometimes with brutal elimination of any content considered extraneous to the central narrative of the past. This was partly a result of texts now being written for schoolchildren in the junior standards, where legislation prescribed history as a compulsory subject. In addition, the textbooks were addressed to teachers, a large proportion of whom had little prior training and lacked basic historical knowledge. They were intended "to give [teachers] assistance by steering them in the right direction." Even if teachers had some historical knowledge and training, the textbooks were also necessary to ensure that teachers taught the correct history for the matriculation examination. Textbooks were thus intended to provide both "Teachers and Students with what was prescribed in the new history syllabus," and authors were often apologetic in case their readers thought they had not achieved this. One author expressed the wish that, although his text was lacking in parts, that it would be of help to more than one teacher; another, although admitting to large gaps, urged teachers to treat his book more as offering a type of "first aid."[74]

As more and more material was excised from school textbooks to equip teachers and students with an examinable past, history became a series of listings, points, and abbreviated summaries. Books were published that contained "a brief resume of the principal facts of the history of our South Africa" compiled "for examination purposes." Learning about the past became the ability to memorize an inventory of causes, effects, advantages, disadvantages, men, and events. In the first ten pages of *Juta's History and Civics for Junior Certificate (Departmental Examination)* by Cecil Lewis, readers were provided with definitions of six terms used by the Dutch East India Company, three advantages of the Company, and nine rules the Company drew up for the independent burgher farmers. *The New Matriculation History,* written by Eric Stockenstrom, catalogued eight reasons why the Company did not want to expand the settlement at the Cape of Good Hope. These lists of facts and reasons were complemented by names and terms, highlighted in bold print, giving students and teachers key words to recollect in an already abbreviated past.[75]

The historical basis for these inventories was derived, more often than not, from the authority in South African facts, namely, George Theal. Textbook histories freely admitted that they borrowed liberally from Theal, to the extent that he became the "mainstay" for many of them.[76] As was seen earlier, these facts were built around the concept of a white settler history as the bearer of civilization. This provided a foundation from which history syllabi were constructed on notions of civilization, with a white South African past located in a broader framework of Western progress. The division of school history into two sections, South African and General (or European) History, reflected this tendency to establish an overall historical context of a "civilized past" that bounded the "white race" of South Africa. In the South African section, syllabi emphasized the "advance" of "Western civilization" over the "native races," whereas General History was about how "civilization" had emerged triumphant over "barbarism" in Europe, with the latter providing the role model for the former. Although any explicit reference to racial categorizations was being omitted in many textbooks and replaced with terms denoting a more neutral-sounding "civilized" history, the story of South Africa's past, in schools, became one which was aptly titled "The White Man and the Sea."[77]

This theme of the development of "Western civilization" became apparent particularly, but not exclusively, in textbooks written in Afrikaans. As was seen in the commemorations of the 1920s and 1930s, the political movement associated with Afrikaner nationalism was attempting to claim a European heritage in order to attract a broader constituency in a limited racial framework. In the context of the school textbook market, where certain books such as Fairbridge's were asserting an allegiance to Union as part of the British Empire, the challenge for writers of Afrikaner nationalist history was to claim an independent past in South Africa while at the same time developing a generic racial origin that was not tied to a specific imperial loyalty. S. F. N. Gie's *Geskiedenis van Suid-Afrika* [History of South Africa], which appeared in the *Voortrekkereeks Skool-handboeke* [Voortrekker series of school handbooks] in 1940, was the clearest expression of this independent Afrikaner past being meshed with a European ancestry. Gie acknowledged that he largely left the "native" out of his textbook because he wanted to emphasize that it was impossible to tell the "Civilized History of South Africa in South Africa" without taking into account the contact "that has always existed between the white man and the old cultural circles over the sea." A reader published some twenty years earlier was even more emphatic about what it considered *Vaderlandse Geskiedenis* [History of the fatherland]. It would not dwell on the successive "Kaffir Wars," where imperious characters like the British governor Harry Smith strode heroically on the battlefields of the "civilizing" frontier, but on "Cultural History or The History of Civilisation, on the evolution of our *Volk*." [78]

The shift toward an ever-diminishing past, combined with the increasing emphasis on the development of "Western civilization," almost obliterated "the natives" from South African history being taught in schools. Whereas, previously, textbooks such as Theal's and Fairbridge's had introductory chapters entitled "The Ancient Inhabitants" or "The Early Inhabitants," the textbooks of the twenties, thirties, and forties had opening chapters that bore titles such as "The European Settlement—Result of Trade Enterprise" or "The Discovery of the Sea Route to the East." [79] It was now the Portuguese seafarers—Bartolomeu Dias, Vasco da Gama, and Antonio d' Saldanha—whose tales were recounted in the beginning of history at the end of the fifteenth century. They became the discoverers who placed the Cape and South Africa in a European world and its somewhat abbreviated "civilized" past.

The implications of this condensed past for Van Riebeeck were astonishing as he moved from an episode that appeared after a few chapters in school history to a site that was very near its source. Soon after the Portuguese merchants, he emerged, usually at the start of chapter 2, in an image that projected him as the man who found the land "wild and empty." The reason the land was in this barren state, according to this textbook, was not because no one was around but because "no white men [were] to be seen." Clearly, without the "white race," there was only "barbarism" to be found in the pages of the *Leesboek oor Ons Geskiedenis* before 1652, with the local inhabitants not even accorded the status of being humans. Van Riebeeck as "white" thus became "the first human" to settle in South Africa, a "Founder and Builder" of "European civilization." Schoolchildren were told he was "a great man" because he did more than he was "obliged to do" and thought of things that would "make life and the world better." A similar process was related in Afrikaans and Dutch textbooks. Whereas in 1916 he was not one of the "Great Men of South Africa," by 1924 the date of Sunday, 7 April 1652, was being invoked as the beginning of the past, proclaimed as the day that "THE FOUNDER OF SOUTH AFRICA!" landed.[80]

As in Fairbridge's text, in the textbooks of the 1920s and 1930s it is Van Riebeeck as an individual who comes to the fore as the man who shaped the transformation that led to an extension of the settlement. Roles of the independent burgher farmers and Van Riebeeck, instead of being distinct and oppositional processes, were rolled into one, with both placed very near to the beginning of the past. This increased prominence of the individual as founder was reflected in the proliferation, in school textbooks, of images of Van Riebeeck and the landing. His statue on Adderley Street, Cape Town, commissioned by Rhodes, became the icon that adorned the front cover of textbooks and readers published by Juta, photographs of his portrait were more widely used, and Bell's painting of the landing was either reproduced or depicted in an illustrative format.

Yet some textbooks were still slightly hesitant in delivering a historical judgment on Van Riebeeck, expressing certain reservations. As a representative of the Dutch East India Company, he was labeled a tricky manipulator, a "*slim*" Jan, and a "Little Thornback," implying that he was both clever and wily but somewhat unrefined. Although he "tried to deal wisely with the free burghers," he was castigated for not encouraging colonization, "for the country needed white colonists more than anything else." It is this sense of Van Riebeeck not going far enough that seems to permeate these judgments. He is praised for accomplishing a great deal but then criticized for not having had knowledge of the future, "a vision of what the Cape is like in our days." This is a vision of South Africa as being the land of the "white man," with claims of legitimacy being based on initiating and sustaining "civilization." Gie congratulates Van Riebeeck for not allowing the "Hottentots" access to certain portions of land, because, Gie says, they indulged in "the politics of robbery."[81] This example Van Riebeeck gives is not good enough for Gie. To promote the cause of "white" possession, Gie wants to extend Van Riebeeck's claim to a legal principle that "no individual or nation has absolute rights to the land. If someone wants to remain in possession he must display his right through his use of the land. A nation is obliged to make as much use of his land as is possible for the service of humanity.[82] Here "whites" become legitimate possessors, as they are portrayed as the colonizers and, by extension, the "workers of the land." Van Riebeeck, to the extent that he did not promote the colonizing enterprise, is therefore not given an entirely unblemished record. At the same time, however, he is "forgiven" because "he did his very best."[83]

And what about Maria? In pasts littered with genealogical tables, lists of summarized points, and maps and charts, Maria was almost nowhere to be found. She appears in only two of the ten selected textbooks from this period.

She may surface in other history textbooks, but this selection of texts does seem to indicate that Maria was not considered a significant component of the chosen, condensed past, extending a trend that was evident since De Lima's book in the 1820s. The two books that do mention her are both written in Afrikaans and in an atypical narrative style in that it is extensive and makes use of an illustrative technique using numerous examples. In Gie's *Geskiedenis,* she is mentioned only with regard to her marriage to Jan van Riebeeck in 1649, where she is described as coming from a "good civic family," just like Jan. *Kykies Vir Kinders* by Nico Hofmeyr recounts Jan's first night after landing at the Cape. In this imaginary tale, Jan is feeling lonely and far away from home on a deserted west coast of Africa. Transferred for the purposes of dramatic effect from the *Dromedaris* to a tent on the beach, the only comfort is from "his good wife" and her child. He asks her, "Wife, how are we going to endure it here?" There is no reply, but Jan is able to pass the night sleeping peacefully and, in the morning, is invigorated and ready to start working. "Oh, this man set us an example! He could work, this Jan van Riebeeck, the doctor-soldier," exclaims the storyteller. In these brief encounters with Maria (in the previous example her name is not even mentioned), it is Jan who is still the central figure in the past. For Gie, Maria provides Jan, and the "white race," with "good breeding," and, for Hofmeyr, she is Jan's only comfort, a reminder both of his former home far away and of the prospect of constructing a new home. Maria, in both these senses, becomes an integral component, if not a central one, of the development of a "white nation," her role as a woman being seen as provider of pure blood and a good home.[84]

Thus, on the eve of the tercentenary festival that was to celebrate his landing, Jan van Riebeeck was approaching the beginning of school history texts, and the "natives" were slowly being edged out. His spatial location in the text was paralleled by his placement on a geographical mapping of the past. Initially a colonizer at the Cape, by the mid-twentieth century he had started to become a figure of "the west" in a country called South Africa. Maria was largely left out of this past, but, when she did appear, it was as reproducer and housekeeper of this "nation." This positioning of Jan and Maria in school textbooks is commonly represented as being a result of the rise of Afrikaner nationalism in the late nineteenth and the first half of the twentieth centuries. As Afrikaans historiography sought to gain political power through presenting its own versions of the past, it was that history, with Van Riebeeck at the fore, that fed "into the school books that the great majority of literate South Africans experience."[85] Certainly this contributed to the emergence of Jan van Riebeeck at the beginning of the past in school textbooks. But the process was extremely complex as he did not always fit into an Afrikaner nationalist past, and at times a more positive image of him was projected by those texts which promoted a British imperial past and future, and were in direct opposition to the Afrikaner nationalist project. In a very important sense, it was the very nature of the form school history took, its commitment to specifying spatial positions and presenting essential ingredients, stripped of complexity for both teachers and students, that paved the way for Jan Van Riebeeck's emergence on the introductory pages and the front covers of the textbook past and the almost total neglect of Maria.

Diarizing the Past

In 1921 Nico Hofmeyr, a former school inspector and popular writer of historical tales in Dutch and later Afrikaans—more than one hundred thousand copies of his *Kijkes in onze Geschiedenis* [Glimpses in our history] were published in Holland in the 1890s—decided to target his stories to a younger audience, a market that had recently widened considerably with the emergence of history as a primary school subject. His *Kykies vir Kinders* [Glimpses for children] was an attempt to move away from the conventions of school textbooks where history was constituted by lists of facts and logical conclusions, all carefully demarcated. To make history more attractive for his younger readers, he decided to give life to the past by incorporating a personal touch into the telling of the story, embellishing historical personages with specific characteristics and adding lengthy poetic descriptions of the surroundings. In relating the landing of Van Riebeeck, he transfers the biblical allusion from the first chapter of the book of Genesis—"The land was desolate and empty"— onto the shores of Table Bay to depict an image of white arrival as the very start of time itself. But it is not only the created event of white founding, set amid the rolling breakers and majestic beauty of Table Mountain that makes it historic for Hofmeyr. What makes it historic for Hofmeyr is also the start of the written record of the past, signifying real historical evidence. The very first point he tells his readers about the arrival in this "desolate and empty" land is that Jan van Riebeeck kept a diary.[86]

> He wrote about one thing and another every day in his diary. We can still read this book today. Wasn't this a good idea of his? For sure: now we can see everything through his eyes and feel everything with his heart.[87]

For all his literary allusions, Hofmeyr clearly wants to affirm a notion of history based on the written archive, where all the stories he recounts are supposedly verifiable by referring to the document of origin. Van Riebeeck's diary both begins his tale of the past and provides it with a written source that inscribes veracity and authenticity.

Not many historians today would follow Nico Hofmeyr's approach to written documents in general and to Van Riebeeck's diary in particular. They would point to other evidence, such as oral traditions and archaeological remains, as equally valuable sources of the past. Moreover, all this evidence would not be accepted at face value but would be cross-referenced for accuracy and placed in context to determine the recorder's subjective position. Yet, in spite of this circumspection, experiences recorded in a diary still retain a predominant sense of conveying historical authenticity, transmitting an authoritative voice of the past and credible substantiating evidence for any historical narrative. If diaries are considered contemporaneous to the events being related and analyzed, their reality effect is greatly enhanced, providing historians with a veritable mine of information to unearth, located at the core of the events from which the history emerges. Once discovered, substantiated, and contextualized, diaries often become the very basis of history, giving it origins and a validated past, enabling historians to do what they like to do best, "begin at the beginning."[88]

If, as has been suggested, celebrations established different forms of Van Riebeeck in commemorative time before 1952, and school texts situated him in a named, abbreviated space, then the publication of the journal which describes, in diary form, some of the daily occurrences when he was commander at the Cape of Good Hope gave him substantial authentic evidence to become part of history. Before 1952 the journal—sometimes incomplete, sometimes featuring only selected portions—was published four times. It first appeared in the 1820s, in serialized form, in the Dutch periodical *Het Nederduitsch Zuid-Afrikaansch Tydschrift*. Toward the end of the following decade, the colonial official Donald Moodie translated and included large portions of the journal in his collection, *Official Papers Relative to the Condition and Treatment of the Native Tribes of South Africa*, which had been commissioned by the governor, Benjamin D'Urban. Between 1884 and 1893, mainly using the written copy of the diary located in the archives at the Hague in Holland, W. J. Brill edited three volumes of the journal for the Historische Genootskap van Utrecht [Historical Society of Utrecht]. Finally, in 1897, the keeper of the Cape archives, H. C. V. Leibrandt, published a summarized version of the journal in his *Precis of the Archives of the Cape of Good Hope*. These publications set the stage for a major debate in the 1940s, initiated by H. B. Thom, the History Professor at Stellenbosch University, over whether Van Riebeeck was the author of the journal as all these editions had implied. As the landing was becoming commemorated and written into the past as the beginning and a first, so, through all these versions and the emergence of a historical debate around its authorship, the journal was being transformed from a Company record to a bimonthly serial and then into "the first major historical source published in the Cape Colony."[89]

This assertion that the journal was not always already a historical source implies that a document used later as historical evidence neither starts off nor automatically proceeds through life in this form. This may seem to be stating the obvious, yet historians, in using documents in a very narrow way as primary sources, often neglect the fact that these actually change form, as does the text at times, in the very context of their production and re-production.[90] Van Riebeeck's journal, which appeared in *Het Nederduits Zuid-Afrikaansch Tydschrift* in 1824, was a different document from that which appeared as an archival piece in the 1890s and later as the setting for historical debate over its authorship in the 1940s. By tracking the document that is sometimes entitled "Van Riebeeck's journal" on its pathways into history and the realms of scholarly debate, one can begin to unravel the various ways that its meaning and its being altered, through the processes of its production, so that by the late 1940s it was well on the way to providing historical authenticity to the beginning of a South African past that starts with Van Riebeeck.

At all trading posts of the Dutch East India Company in the seventeenth and eighteenth centuries the commander was obliged to ensure that a record was kept of activities at the station and to pass this on to the Company offices in Amsterdam and Batavia. At the Cape three original copies were made of the daily record of events during Van Riebeeck's tenure as commander, which were later labeled as his diary. Two of these, per instruction, were sent abroad, and one remained at the Cape where it was later deposited in the archives. In the course of time (it is unclear exactly when) seventy pages of the original document housed in Cape Town, dealing with the period from December 1651 to November 1652, were lost, other pages started to crumble away, and the ink began to fade. The copy that was sent to Batavia was not recovered and the one in Holland, discovered in 1853, was kept in the Dutch archives, in reasonably good condition, scattered among the collection of papers from the Cape. It was by turning these fragmented, at times barely legible, Company records into a coherent, partial whole that, at various times, Van Riebeeck's diary was constituted.[91]

When the Dutch periodical *Het Nederduitsch Zuid-Afrikaansch Tydschrift* decided to present a serialized version of the diary to its readers in 1824, it did not have much to go on. Probably not knowing about the documents in Holland and Batavia, in all likelihood those involved used the manuscript in Cape Town as the basis of their work. Presumably they found the daily register among the official documents at the government offices in the old slave lodge at the top of Adderley Street, where they were under the jurisdiction of the Colonial Secretary, who bore the official title of "Secretary and Registrar of Records." All government records had been transferred to this building between 1810 and 1814 after the Castle, where they had been housed previously, had become the sole preserve of the military establishment when the British assumed control of the Cape. As Thom points out, there is little indication of how the editor of the *Tydschrift* actually went about the process of selection, transcription, and presentation of the diary. The fact that, when it was published, it failed to include Van Riebeeck's journey to the Cape indicates for Thom that, by this time, a substantial portion of the first part of the diary had already been lost. Documents were not well protected in the slave lodge–cum–government offices and it was not unusual for them to be removed, damaged, or sold to private individuals.[92]

Yet the decision to begin the version in the *Tydschrift* with a reference to the entry on 5 April 1652, when the land was sighted and the associated monetary reward paid out, may also reflect a conscious choice to highlight the moment of sighting and landing as the start of the narrative of the past. The *Tydschrift* was founded by a group within the Cape Dutch intelligentsia in 1824 and edited by Rev. Abraham Faure, who, as was seen earlier, played a major role in organizing the two hundredth anniversary activities to commemorate Van Riebeeck's landing in 1852. For most of the contributors to the *Tydschrift*, who were teachers in Cape Town and more at home in print than in public displays of commemoration, the periodical became the major vehicle to promote a Cape Dutch identity with a historical and particularly spiritual basis. Articles were written which dealt with religious topics, such as ways to serve God and Christian principles, as well as with individuals and events from the Cape Dutch past from which they claimed descent. Van Riebeeck came to embody both these aspects. He became the progenitor of a constructed, unbroken lineage, whose birth was determined by an event, namely, the moment of arrival at the Cape. In addition, he was labeled "father RIEBEECK" and imbued with a "holy spirit" which made him behave in a most "pious and Christian way." The Cape Dutch designated and identified themselves as his descendants, the bearers of Christianity to southern Africa, and turned his landing into a moment of great religious significance.[93]

The Van Riebeeck diary, as it appears in the *Tydschrift*, is treated as the founding document of this Christian world that the Cape Dutch intelligentsia sought to construct at what they called "this outpost." Faure saw it as his duty to clutch the diary from the abyss of amnesia before the "nibbling mouse" destroyed the basis of this past on paper. The memory he wanted to produce by publishing the diary was a sense of "knowledge of the Fatherland," defined neither in Holland nor in England but at "this southern point" where Van Riebeeck faced and dealt with "many problems" in establishing the "Christian settlement." Events not directly related to this central theme, such as the voyage to the Cape, were at times left out of the *Tydschrift*'s diary, and those regarded as central were highlighted. The clearest example of the latter is the decision in 1654 to commemorate the landing. The entry for 6 April appears in the same typeface as the rest of the periodical, but the proclamation by Van Riebeeck that this date should be permanently instituted as a day of prayer so that their descendants do not forget "the mercies we have received at the Lord's hands," appears in italics. By alerting readers to this entry, Faure was attaching to a Christian identity a principle of beginning with a legitimacy of historical-religious ancestry in the pages of their founding text.[94]

To assert that the diary assumed biblical proportions in the pages of the *Tydschrift*, though, would be taking this linkage with a Christian identity a little too far. There was a recognition in the first issue of the periodical that to carry too much religious material might alienate readers and that it was neces-sary to mix it with more enjoyable matter. When excerpts from the diary first appeared, in the following edition, the editor expressed the hope that it would provide every South African with pleasant reading. Every second month, start-ing in 1824, readers of the *Tydschrift* could follow, in serialized form, the diary of Van Riebeeck, with the editor at times filling in gaps when he felt there were problems of continuity. He also contributed speculative material when he thought it necessary to provide historical background that readers might not have at their fingertips. What readers were thus encountering when they read the daily journal of the commander of the Dutch East India Company at the Cape of Good Hope between 1652 and 1662 was, more than anything, a serial-ized story of the past. It was a story with strong religious overtones, to be taken immensely seriously, and at same time a story to enjoy and follow, with eager anticipation, every second month. This diary, unfortunately for its readers, had to come to an abrupt end four years before Van Riebeeck left the Cape, when the magazine closed down in 1840.[95]

As the serialized diary in the *Tydschrift* was drawing to a premature end, extracts from the "Journal of Commander Jan van Riebeeck," translated into English, appeared in *The Record or A Series of Official Papers Relative to the Condition and Treatment of the Native Tribes of South Africa*, compiled by Donald Moodie. Officially commissioned in 1836 by the governor of the Cape, Benjamin D'Urban, *The Record* was compiled in response to a dispatch from the Secretary of State for Colonies, Lord Glenelg. In this missive, forwarded to Cape Town from London at the end of 1835, Glenelg severely castigated the colonial government at the Cape for its "native policy" which had "pro-voked" the Xhosa into invading the colony. Based on the evidence before him, which largely emanated from the missionary John Philip, he proclaimed that, in the light of the way the colonial administration was dealing with the Xhosa, the Xhosa had "ample justification" for their invasion of the colony. It was to counter these accusations from London, based on Philip's evidence, that Donald Moodie, an ex-magistrate and Protector of Slaves in the Eastern Divi-sion of the Cape Colony, was appointed, on a salary of £400 a year, to unearth as much documentation as possible on "relations between the colonists and the tribes." He devoted his time to "beavering away among the records of the central government" and writing letters to magistrates in each district, attempting to locate documents which would refute Philip and hence Glenelg. In this pursuit he collected piles and piles of manuscripts, a small proportion of which was published in three volumes of *The Record* between 1838 and 1841. Van Riebeeck's diary, which Moodie placed as the starting point of "native policy" of (British?) colonial administration at the Cape, found itself at the beginning of these *Official Papers Relative to the Condition and Treatment of the Native Tribes of South Africa.*[96]

Whereas the *Tydschrift* sought to establish a Van Riebeeck ancestry for a Dutch Christian identity at the Cape through the publication of the diary, *The Record* made the diary into a document that reflected colonial policy. It was not so much that Moodie, "like all historians . . . wanted to begin at the beginning . . . of the Cape colony." When the Cape Colony began was not a cut-and-dried issue. Clearly the selection of Van Riebeeck as the starting point of the Cape Colony was partly in response to Philip's accusation that Van Riebeeck had treated the local population inhumanely. But Moodie went further and wanted to establish a genealogy that gave colonial policy, in respect to the local population at the Cape, a legitimate and long-standing inheritance. Many of the extracts he selected from the diary for publication dealt with "native affairs," and he interspersed these with proclamations and Resolutions of Council to show "how well" Van Riebeeck had treated the Khoi. To enhance the dramatic effect, apparently he even shifted dates in the diary. For instance, to establish a sequence of events leading to the implementation of policy, he moves a meeting with "a party of about 9 or 10 savages of Saldahna" to 8 April. In this meeting the diarist records how Company soldiers interposed themselves between the "Saldania" and the "*strandlopers*" [frequenters of the sea shore] to avoid conflict. Moodie follows this up with an extract from a proclamation by Van Riebeeck on 9 April that "all kindness and friendship" be shown to "the wild people." In all other versions of the diary, the events Moodie ascribes to 8 April took place on 10 April. The imperative to explicitly demonstrate "native policy" as a logical evolution to correspond to supposed knowledge of local conditions seems to have been the basis for Moodie's selections and ordering of the diary in his *Record.*[97]

Moodie also takes advantage of the Dutch translation to establish a sequence of good relations that Van Riebeeck supposedly initiated. In the events cited on 8 (or 10) April, the diarist relates that "David Konink, with two assistants and two soldiers . . . were met by the said 9 savages of Saldania, and treated by them in a very amiable and handsome manner, so as to excite wonder." It is not exactly clear who initially treated whom amicably. In a later translation the diary reflects no such ambiguity: "Skipper David Coninck . . . encountered the

9 Saldania savages who adopted such an amicable and pleasant attitude that it was almost a wonder." Moodie's version might be ascribed to his particular translation, still the version of events he offers readers is vague and could be read as an example of how well Company officials were approaching the local population.[98]

To label the document included in Moodie's *Record* as "Van Riebeeck's diary" is therefore probably a misnomer. Moodie's explicit intention was not to include the entire diary. He was only interested in events relating to "the Native Tribes," and he selected extracts accordingly. The daily weather reports were excised, and other events, such as the day of prayer on 6 April 1654, are mentioned but given much less prominence than in the *Tydschrift* version; indeed, in the example cited, no description of the day's proceedings is given. Translated, edited, and rearranged to fit into Moodie's ordering of the evolution of colonial policy on the spot, Van Riebeeck's diary became the founding document for an image that British officials at the Cape were attempting to depict in the mid-nineteenth century. Like the Van Riebeeck in Moodie's *Record,* these officials portrayed themselves as carrying on a well-established tradition of showing utmost care and benevolence toward the "wild savages" of southern Africa, whether they are "Saldania" or Xhosa.

In the late nineteenth and first half of the twentieth centuries, Van Riebeeck's diary began to shift from its position as a delineator of inheritance and identity to a document that became authenticated as a source of history. There were three stages in its transformation into the realms of verifiable past. The first involved the collection of various fragments into volumes that were devoted entirely to publishing the diary as a whole. This was in marked contrast to the serialized and fragmentary nature of its appearance in the *Tydschrift* and *The Record*, respectively. Second, the diary was accorded a designation as a historical document of import by being among those selected and placed among a collection of papers officially labeled as a colonial archive, constituted at the Cape in the 1870s. Finally, it was the explosion of historical debate in the public domain over its authorship that paved the way for its entry into history as a corroborative past.

The idea of publishing Van Riebeeck's diary in book format was initially mooted, in Holland, in 1848, by the Historical Society of Utrecht. The idea was given further impetus when, in 1853, a member of the society, P. A. Leupe, discovered among the Dutch government papers an extant copy of the diary, including the section on the outward-bound voyage omitted by the *Tydschrift*, which had been "received from the Cape by the East India Company (Chamber of Amsterdam)." This early section was subsequently published, along with extracts from the *Tydschrift*, in a booklet that ended with events from October 1652. It was not until 1884 that the society began publishing the diary in book volumes, completing the work in 1893, with Van Riebeeck's departure to Malacca.[99]

The stated aim of the editor, W. G. Brill, was to arouse interest in South Africa among people in Holland, perhaps to establish affinity with the group of Dutch speakers who, at various times, held the reins of power in the northern part of South Africa. To help establish this connection he assigned himself the task of reproducing the diary "in its original form," leaving out no detail, in case "some reader or other might consider that in an omitted passage there might have been some information meriting his interest." In spite of criticisms that Brill did not accomplish his aim of publishing the diary in its entirety—he left out the weather bulletins (in favor of what he called more "important issues"), the voyage to the Cape (since he relied, for the first seventy-two pages, on directly copying the version from the *Tydschrift*), and some letters and parts of official proclamations—he did set the diary on the course of becoming allotted to verifiable history. Its derivation from a society solely committed, through its *Kronijk* [Chronicle] and other publications, to establishing and disseminating facts about the past contributed to its assignation as a historical source. But it was the very fact that the diary was published as an (in)complete historical document that gave it its status. In later years, when a new edition of the diary was being published, the Utrecht version was called "the main source of information for anyone studying Van Riebeeck and his time at the Cape." Another editor, who expressed misgivings about the shortcomings of the Utrecht volumes, still acknowledged that they were of immense value, because it was "the only published source from which we can draw complete and reliable information about the founding years." Van Riebeeck's diary was being established on the route into history by becoming a published source of the past.[100]

Publication was one way of establishing a document as an authentic historical source. Another was to locate it among other selected documents in a depository that provided restricted access, namely, an archive. The influence of Rankean ideas on history in the nineteenth century, with their focus on scientifically establishing empirically verifiable sets of facts, had attributed almost fetishistic powers to the concept of an archive and gave manuscripts a seemingly magical aura that only those who knew and learned the secrets of discovery could unearth. In 1876 the government of the Cape set up a commission "to collect, examine, classify and index the archives of the colony." The outcome of this commission was that a special fireproof room in the Surveyor-General's office was set aside to store the records of the various administrations of the Cape from 1652 to 1806 (which included the manuscript of Van Riebeeck's diary). In 1879 George Theal was appointed, in a temporary, part-time capacity, as "Officer in Charge of Colonial Archives." Theal was immediately overwhelmed by the abundance of materials available in the Cape archives, and saw his future career mapped out before his eyes. But Theal's assumption that he would become the official magician who would discover and order the secrets of the South African past did not materialize. When the government, in 1881, converted the post into a full-time "Librarian of the House of Assembly and Keeper of the Colonial Archives," Theal, much to his fury and dismay, was overlooked, and H. C. V. Leibrandt, a liberal church minister who had limited experience in sorting out the records of the landdrost at Graaff-Reinet, was appointed. Theal was later chosen as Colonial Historiographer. The result was a bitter rivalry between Leibrandt and Theal, alluded to earlier, which came to the fore, in part, in their respective interpretations of historical events and persons. Leibrandt, for instance, tried to show that Governor William Adrian Van Der Stel was not the tyrannous despot he was depicted as, initially by the burghers, through their complaints at the time, and then by Theal, as a historian. Yet this conflict went deeper and centered around Leibrandt's official designation as Keeper of the Archives. Theal, deliberately flouting Leibrandt's position, sometimes withheld from Leibrandt documents that were in Theal's personal possession and then published his own collections, one time apparently using material Leibrandt had acquired on a trip to Holland, without acknowledgment. At stake here was access to and control of the archives and the secrets of history, Theal assuming, as a preeminent historian, that his rights had precedence, and Leibrandt, in his official position as the keeper, believing likewise.[101]

One issue on which Theal and Leibrandt confronted each other in their dispute about archival material was Leibrandt's penchant to publish and translate documents in précis form. One of the documents Leibrandt summarized and translated was Van Riebeeck's journal for the years 1651–53. His rationale in compiling these translated summaries was to widen public access to archival material, particularly for English readers unable to understand the Dutch documents. The précis project was part of the much broader political initiative that he, along with people like Dorothea Fairbridge, was involved in, that of establishing a white unity in the context of the British Empire. Theal could not accept summaries of documents. He had published abstracts himself but found them unsatisfactory and, after returning from Europe in 1894, condemned the practice as worthless and lacking historical accuracy. In spite of this criticism from Theal, the historian, Leibrandt, the custodian, continued to publish summaries and translations of materials in the archives, and this included Van Riebeeck's diary, which appeared in 1897. Leibrandt's selection of the diary for publication in summary form made it more than an official document of the past located in a designated archive. It singled it out for wider accessibility as one of the most "valuable sources of information."[102]

Leibrandt's translated summary of the diary resembled textbook productions of the past. By reducing the diary to its abbreviated essence, he transformed it into a historical document whose facts could easily be read and understood in English, without readers having to plow through and translate endless pages of Dutch text. Readers interested in additional information were presumably being encouraged to explore the archives themselves, whereas others could continue reading without the interference of particulars Leibrandt had decided were irrelevant and inhibited the flow of facts. The summary also lightened the process of dipping into the text to find specifics, although, with much of the text excised, precise details could only be found in the Utrecht text or by examining the archives directly. For the latter reason, H. B. Thom labeled Leibrandt's diary of Jan van Riebeeck "defect[ive]" and "not very reliable." But what Leibrandt had accomplished was to distinguish Van Riebeeck's diary as a superior historical source. Through his custodianship of the diary in the depths of the parliament, where the archives were located after 1884, with his publication of a précis of all three volumes, signifying it as a document of import, and by making "the essence of an important archival document available to the English-speaking world," Leibrandt had firmly established the diary as an archival document imbibed with the magic of historical discovery. The implication, in Leibrandt's terms, was that Van Riebeeck's diary was no longer being produced as a document of identity and curiosity with archaic value but as a document of history for a "white" South Africa that formed part of the British Empire.[103]

The publication and location of the diary in the latter part of the nineteenth century had clearly set it apart as a source of history. When consideration was given to re-publishing the diary in the 1940s, the debate that took place among professors over its authorship secured its status as a historical document. This scholarly debate to make the diary into history-as-discipline derived its authority by not merely revolving around the production of material but concurrently addressing how the past was read and interpreted in a space—the terrain, issues, and form of debate—common to the participants. Establishing positions in the debate was as much about negotiating this space as it was about the intellectual content of the presentation.[104]

The debate over the authorship of Van Riebeeck's diary in 1944 was demarcated in a dual setting. On the one hand, the dispute evolved in an academic setting as it concerned the intellectual expertise of its two chief protagonists, H. B. Thom and D. B. Bosman, Professor of Dutch-Afrikaans Linguistics at the University of Cape Town, each presenting his authoritative position based on his academic discipline. The debate itself, however, was not conducted within the realm of the academic world but in the pages of *Die Huisgenoot* [The family companion], the popular Afrikaans magazine that had been established in 1916.

Die Huisgenoot was directed toward a market of readers whom it believed typified the Afrikaans household, with the emphasis on women and family as the bearer of an Afrikaner identity. Its contents ranged from short stories, items of cultural interest, and articles on aspects of an identified Afrikaner history to a special section for "the wife," which dealt with home maintenance and domestic responsibilities. Because of its emphasis on educational material, the magazine was popularly labeled " 'the poor man's university.' "[105] In its pages the two academicians, Thom and Bosman, had to present their arguments to a much wider public, one not always attuned to the niceties of the debaters' academic positions. Thus the manner in which Thom and Bosman presented their academic credentials to readers often assumed primary importance in the debate. It was their presentation, and the imaging of their expertise to the readers of *Die Huisgenoot* over who really wrote the diary, that made the diary into a document of the scientifically verifiable past.

But before the debate entered the pages of *Die Huisgenoot,* the first salvos were fired at a meeting of the Van Riebeeck Society. This organization, officially established in 1918, had about one thousand members in the 1940s. It was primarily involved in publishing documents on South African history that its nine-member council, drawn mainly from academics at the Universities of Cape Town and Stellenbosch, determined to be of value. What constituted value was open to interpretation, but, from the organization's list of publications, construed as worthwhile were accounts of missionaries, travelers, and settlers. At a council meeting in 1940, Prof. D. B. Bosman's proposal that the society "arrange for the editing of the Journal of Jan van Riebeeck" in view of the approaching "300th anniversary (in 1952) of the landing . . . at the Cape" was accepted. Thus the diary was accorded the status of being one of the most important sources of a South African past, so determined by the Van Riebeeck Society, which now undertook the task of broadening the diary's accessibility by publishing it. Between 1940 and 1946, however, apart from some preliminary transcribing of the manuscript in the Cape archives, little was done to carry this project to fruition. What did occur, though, was that one of the prime movers behind the project, H. B. Thom, began to raise serious doubts about the authorship of the diary. To the astonishment of some members at the society's annual general meeting in 1943, Thom produced evidence to show that "although Van Riebeeck's name is usually associated with the Diary he did not write it."[106]

Early the following year Thom reproduced his evidence in the pages of *Die Huisgenoot.* He pointed out that, given Van Riebeeck's duties as commander, he would have had little time to make entries in a journal, that much of the diary is written in the third person, that different handwritings are apparent in the script, none matching Van Riebeeck's, and that even after Van Riebeeck's departure from the Cape in 1662 the same handwriting that appeared in the diary immediately before he left is still evident. Thom also dismissed the option that Van Riebeeck might have dictated the diary as it was not the commander's duty to engage in the keeping of records. This task fell to his secretarial and accounting staff, and this was apparent from diary entries that referred to events around the fort even when Van Riebeeck was not present. Based on this evidence, Thom concluded that Van Riebeeck did not write the diary, that it was nothing more than an official document of these first ten years at the Cape recorded in an ordinary daily journal that the Dutch East India Company insisted should be maintained at all its posts. He therefore suggested that the journal be more appropriately titled "*Die Kaapse Dagregister tydens Van Riebeeck, 1652–1662*" [The daily register at the Cape during the time of Van Riebeeck, 1652–1662].[107]

The rejoinder came a few weeks later from Professor Bosman. Asserting his position as a linguist rather than a historian, he claimed that writing two thousand pages over a ten-year period would not have taken up a lot of Van Riebeeck's time. The linguistic style of the diary was also similar to that of other documents attributed to Van Riebeeck; further, writing in the third person was the convention of the day and considered more courteous and appropriate than writing in the first person. He did not regard the handwriting evidence as conclusive, claiming that all extant copies of the diary, including the one in the archives in Cape Town, were copies. Finally, he pointed out that only Van Riebeeck could have written certain moments in the diary, as they express his innermost thoughts and feelings. All this "internal evidence," Bosman's term, was enough to convince him that Van Riebeeck indeed wrote the journal and that it should be called the *Dagverhaal van Jan van Riebeeck* [Diary of Jan van Riebeeck].[108]

Thom's reply was to assert historical methodology as scientific and to claim that Bosman had overlooked important issues relating to the use of evidence. Thom maintained that he could point to many documents written in the same linguistic style as Van Riebeeck's but that had in fact been written by a variety of Company officials. Moreover, he declared that it was misleading to cite an average length of diary entries, as some were quite lengthy and must have taken a long time to write. Further, to his mind, the personal entries in no way offered conclusive proof that Van Riebeeck was the author. Insisting on the validity of his argument that the diary was written in the third person—for whatever reason—he also maintained that Bosman did not address Thom's most convincing pieces of evidence, that the diary was written while Van Riebeeck was absent from the fort at Saldanha Bay and that it continued in the same script even after Van Riebeeck left the Cape in 1662. For Thom, this was indisputable proof that Van Riebeeck did not write the diary and that Bosman was "not sufficiently trained in the methods of historical inquiry."[109]

Although no definitive conclusion had been reached, the debate between Thom and Bosman in the pages of *Die Huisgenoot* came to an end. Yet by engaging in this debate over the authorship of the Van Riebeeck diary/journal/daily register in the pages of this popular magazine, they had established the diary as an authentic source of momentous historical import. Their styles had at times resorted to the polemic, with rhetorical questions replacing sustained argument and issues often left hanging with "I would rather leave it there." Couched in these popular techniques, they proclaimed their academic credentials and expertise in dealing with the issue under debate. Bosman claimed that although he was not acquainted with the sources and historical research of any other period, as a "language historian" he had been interested in Van Riebeeck's diary since 1922 and had written a book, *The State of the Afrikaans Language in the time of Jan Van Riebeeck.* Thom, in questioning the authorship of the diary, portrayed himself as one on a quest for historical truth, fighting against uncritical acceptance, "the number one enemy of real historical writing." To reach conclusions without historical proof, as he claimed Bosman had done, was sacrilegious and not part of the discipline of history. In both these instances, though, through the assumptions of expertise, Van Riebeeck's diary had become a subject of historical debate that could be treated seriously, analyzed for veracity, and effectively used as historical evidence by those trained in the respective disciplinary methodologies. On the public terrain, where the debate was conducted, the diary was being established as a document of interest and importance that people in the know could argue about. When the most public event associated with Van Riebeeck took place eight years later, the tercentenary festival associated with his landing, it was not altogether surprising that these two, self-styled protagonists were to be most immediately responsible for the diary's re-publication by the Van Riebeeck Society. Bosman was to be the editor of the Dutch edition, writing the introduction and the notes on language usage, and Thom was to prepare the English edition and provide the "necessary historical annotations" for both versions.[110]

By the mid-1940s Van Riebeeck's diary was a different document from the one that had started off its life in the offices of the colonial secretary and every second month in the *Tydschrift*. Its status as a source of history as a verifiable past had been established through its publication, its archival location, and its being debated in a magazine that focused on items of interest for the home. With the three hundredth anniversary of "the landing" approaching, Van Riebeeck was clearly being established as a figure with a historically written past. Although it was not clear that his diary enabled readers to "see everything through his spectacles and feel everything with his heart,"[111] it authenticated a past that began to clear the way for his landing in 1952.

Moments in Van Riebeeck's Past

If one tracks Van Riebeeck's past through a variety of public forms into the 1940s, a picture emerges of Jan van Riebeeck drawing ever closer to the beginning of a South African past. The wreath-laying ceremonies at the base of his statue on Adderley Street were becoming increasingly popular and the site of intense controversy over who should be the appropriate organizers, Van Riebeeck and Maria were acquiring a more prominent position in school textbooks, and his diary was being validated as a historical source.

This marking of Van Riebeeck and the landing as a character and a date of significance, respectively, had as much to do with the interventions of designated historians as with those associated with the production of history in the public domain. In the profession that emerged in the nineteenth century in South Africa, historians, like Theal and Thom, undoubtedly contributed a great deal to this signification through their various publications and by participating in historical debates. Often it was their interventions which established the authentic aura for events and figures of the past, setting them in the realm of critical discourse. At the same time, a range of organizations and individuals were producing their own Van Riebeecks, sometimes using the work of professional historians, but also drawing on one another in establishing their veracity. Missionaries, teachers, artists, politicians, colonial officials, theologians, governors, commissioners, novelists, and cultural organizations all shaped their own and other images of Van Riebeeck and his past. Their Van Riebeecks were shaped as much by their political contexts as by the formats in which they produced their pasts.

The result of these complementary and often contradictory productions of Van Riebeeck's past was that, by the 1940s, he had not merely become the figure of the Afrikaner nationalist past.[112] In one sense he was becoming a *volksplanter,* but at the same time his imperial imagery remained very strong. Seen as a religious founder by some, others associated him with oppression and destruction. At times he was the Dutch ancestor; at other times he even became English. In some instances he combined elements derived from these various versions of his past. There was not a singular Jan van Riebeeck in South Africa's past. With the three hundredth anniversary of 1652 on the horizon, a way had to be negotiated between these multiple pasts by those who were involved in organizing the tercentenary celebrations. This was necessary to ensure that Van Riebeeck landed safely on the shores of Granger Bay in April 1952.

2 "We Build a Nation"
The Festival of Unity and Exclusion

Granger Bay is a small, protected inlet immediately to the west of Table Bay. It is adjacent to the Victoria and Alfred Waterfront, a resurrected part of Cape Town Harbor with a complex of shops, restaurants, bars, museums, hotels, and movie houses, all set in an imagined world of a re-constructed British maritime past (see Figure 3). For Granger Bay, being sited in this locale has meant that it has become the scene of a flurry of construction activity to service visitors to the consumer emporium on the Waterfront. Roads around the bay have been widened and re-directed to lead to the Waterfront, with parking lots and garages built for the increased volume of motor car traffic and hotels erected for tourists in this "place of pleasure and entertainment within a pretty 'historic' setting." Granger Bay is not unaccustomed to providing the facilities for the re-presentation of history in the public vista. In April 1952 it was the stage for a pageant of the past in which Jan van Riebeeck, accompanied by his family and a group of soldiers, re-created their landing at the Cape three hundred years earlier. This scene was the culminating drama in a government-sponsored festival, conceived as being integral to the construction of a past and future South Africa based on a form of racial exclusivity, which simultaneously proclaimed itself to be nationally inclusive. With Van Riebeeck as its central icon, the festival was designed to "commemorate the establishment of the White settlement at the Cape of Good Hope by Jan van Riebeeck three hundred years ago," utilizing as its central theme "We Build a Nation."[1]

At the time of the Van Riebeeck festival of 1952, Granger Bay contained none of the amenities that would be built some forty-odd years later to accommodate visitors to the Waterfront. The beach was mainly "just a bunch of rocks," and, although there was a narrow strip of land, it was littered with stones; indeed, the entire area around the bay was generally considered "dirty and unromantic." The organizers of the pageant had searched for a site for Van Riebeeck to come ashore but could find nothing suitable. They considered Woodstock Beach but found it too flat and aesthetically unpleasing. The other alternative, the harbor, did not fit into the historic motif, as its facilities were considered too modern to provide an appropriate backdrop. In spite of all the difficulties associated with Granger Bay, one could still land there, as evidenced by fishing boats docked on the beach. Anna Neethling-Pohl, the pageant mistress, and V. J. Penso, the chair of the *Dromedaris* sub-committee of the festival, therefore chose Granger Bay as the site where Van Riebeeck would set foot on

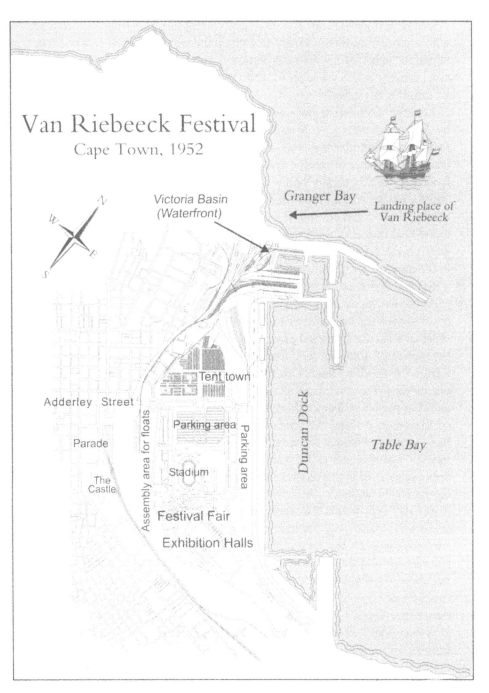

3. Map: VAN RIEBEECK FESTIVAL, CAPE TOWN, 1952. James Whitelaw, Design Matters, based on maps of Van Riebeeck Festival Terrain (Transport, Traffic Routes, Car Parks), drawn by the Cape Town City Engineers Department, Bax Collection, Manuscripts and Archives Division, University of Cape Town Libraries.

5 April 1952. In mediating between reconstructing an appropriate historical site with an aura of authenticity and tidying up the area for participants and spectators, an "ugly" fishing shed was destroyed, another building was camouflaged as a bush, the beach was cleaned, and the sand was leveled without "touching its unspoilt character."[2]

Just after 10:00 on the morning of Saturday, 5 April, Jan van Riebeeck (played by André Huguenet), with his wife Maria (Frances Holland) and their son Lambertus, disembarked from a replica of their ship, the *Dromedaris*, and, with the assistance of marine cadets from the South African Nautical College, landed at the tidy theater on the beach at Granger Bay. As they came ashore, Van Riebeeck, with a broad smile, motioned to his family, soldiers, and crew to step forward and advance toward a small hillock. There, in full view of the crowd that had assembled, twenty thousand–strong, he planted the flag and, gazing upon Table Mountain, took possession of the "large and beautiful land" in the name of the Dutch East India Company (see Figure 1).[3]

But the drama on the beach at Granger Bay could not end there. More of a spectacle was necessary to satisfy the audience, which had waited patiently for hours to view the proceedings. In the planning stages, Anna Neethling-Pohl, in order to make the historical drama as realistic as possible, had wanted to base the morning's activities on the beach on entries in Van Riebeeck's diary. Unfortunately the diary made little mention of the landing. So the script that was ultimately written and approved by members of the *Dromedaris* sub-committee, and that players rehearsed three or four times before the actual performance on the beach, divided the ceremony into two parts. The first began after the flag-planting ceremony, when a group of Griquas—handpicked by the government's Commissioner of Coloured Affairs after other "non-whites" who had been approached by the festival organizers had refused to participate—playing the part of *strandlopers* [literally, beach strollers], emerged from their hiding places and approached Van Riebeeck. On orders from their commander, the soldiers accompanying Van Riebeeck brought forth a chest containing various trinkets, pieces of copper and mirrors, which were then handed over to the *strandlopers* as gifts. Van Riebeeck made a speech proclaiming that they had not come to make a profit at the expense of the people but to bring order and the light of civilization. The Griquas acting as *strandlopers*, per instruction from Anna Neethling-Pohl, displayed appreciation for these words and for their gifts from Van Riebeeck and the "civilized world," bowing before him and retreating with expressions of pleasure and gratitude. The radio commentators, broadcasting the ceremony to listeners around South Africa on that Saturday morning, marveled at how the organizers had stopped at nothing to make the production so historically authentic in this well-rehearsed, scripted past, largely derived not from Van Riebeeck's diary, as the commentators assumed,

4. Jan van Riebeeck (André Huguenet) and Maria de la Quellerie (Frances Holland) on the Kat balcony at the Castle of Good Hope, April 1952. Manuscripts and Archives Division, University of Cape Town Libraries. Photo: *Cape Times.*

but from the painting by Charles Davidson Bell, with Maria and Lambertus now joining the soldiers and sailors on the canvas of the past.[4]

The release of pigeons, accompanied by another shot from the *Dromedaris,* signaled the second, more symbolic phase of the ceremony, marking it off from the "real history" which had just been enacted. Maria handed Jan a box containing eight scrolls signifying "The Treasury of the Nation": religion, Roman-Dutch law, freedom, language, agriculture, industry and commerce, defense, and the arts. Each scroll was then presented to prominent individuals who were designated by the festival organizers as "representatives of the people."[5] A musical flourish from the South African Police Band completed the ceremony on the beach, after which Jan, accompanied by Maria, were conveyed to the Castle, where they posed for photographs before taking up residence in the nation that had been built exclusively for them (Figure 4).

This re-creation of the event of landing as colonial settlement, at the end of a week of drama, speeches, pageantry, and displays in Cape Town, was the fount for the beginning of the past that the Van Riebeeck festival of 1952 sought to portray. Like the landing itself, this national past was not an easy one to produce for the festival. It did not flow spontaneously from the moment specified as origin to the sands of Granger Bay some three hundred years later. The path to an "existence as separate people" was littered with events and personalities that inhabited a past ridden with conflicts. In a festival "primarily concerned with the constructive growth of [an exclusive] South Africa," the past had to be tidied up, certain incidents deleted, others camouflaged, and the ground leveled to produce "the story of White Civilisation in South Africa." Once the past had been cleaned up, it had to be planned and rehearsed to provide a continuous visual spectacle for the crowds who gathered on the streets of Cape Town, at the specially constructed festival stadium on the foreshore and on the beach at Granger Bay.[6]

How these events were tidied up and negotiated into and out of the past in arranging for the arrival of Van Riebeeck and associated festivities that first week of April 1952 is the focus of this chapter. Examined first are some of the initial planning stages of the festival in the late 1940s, and the multiple and changing character of its objectives. Attention then shifts to various individuals and committees, and shows how the past was organized and authorized in different ways to constitute the festival. Finally, two selected events in the festival week of 30 March to 6 April—the People's Pageant and the Pageant of the Griqua and Cape Malay—are examined in detail to demonstrate how they contributed to the construction of various elements of Van Riebeeck's past.

Planning for Van Riebeeck

As emphasized in chapter 1, the landing of Van Riebeeck in 1652 was not a naturally occurring event automatically marked as a beginning. Only through commemorative ceremonies, appearances in textbooks, and the publication and accessibility of Van Riebeeck's diary did he begin to approach a starting point of the South African past. Similarly, the three hundredth year since the landing was not automatically associated with the notion of anniversary. Therefore, in tracing the origins for the planning of events to commemorate the landing in 1952, one does not look for linear connections that would lead to the point of anniversary and festival. Instead, one follows a multiplicity of beginnings, at different times and locations, some linked to one another, others falling by the wayside, some ultimately incorporated in what became the government-funded Van Riebeeck tercentenary festival.

Chapter 1 has alluded to several of these beginnings. In 1940 the Van Riebeeck Society had already resolved that 1952 was a date of significance and had decided to issue a commemorative edition of the diary. Subsequently it was resolved that, in addition to a Dutch version, an English translation would be produced so as to broaden demand for and accessibility of the proposed publication. By 1947 translators had been approached, the archives had requested a copy of the diary kept in the Hague, and H. B. Thom had applied for special leave from his teaching post at the University of Stellenbosch to "undertake the editing and general supervision of the *Dagboek* [Diary]." School texts were also bringing Van Riebeeck to the fore and starting to emphasize the landing in 1652 as the beginning of South African history. Annual ceremonies on 5–8 April at the base of the Van Riebeeck statue on Adderley Street and in Hofmeyr Hall had become commonplace. The Cape Town City Council, the Algemeen Nederlands Verbond (ANV), and the Federasie van Afrikaanse Kultuurverenigings (FAK) were all co-operating and competing to organize the wreath-laying activities.[7]

In addition to these moments, in 1946 a lecturer in the Department of History at the University of the Witwatersrand, Arthur Keppel-Jones, had written a future history of South Africa entitled *When Smuts Goes*. According to Keppel-Jones, who has subsequently been labeled the "historian who had turned to prophecy," the purpose of the book was twofold. First, the book predicted that the National Party, led by D. F. Malan, then the opposition party in the South African parliament, held more popular appeal among the white electorate than seemed apparent through its somewhat poor performance in the 1938 and 1943 general elections. Second, the book warned that these Nationalists were dangerous, as they operated and asserted a policy of racial supremacy distinctly similar to that of the Nazis in Germany. If such a party came to power in South Africa, he maintained, the country would quickly slip into a morass and be faced with international condemnation, sanctions, and possible invasion.[8]

The book begins in 1952, with a tercentenary festival to commemorate Van Riebeeck's landing, presaging an election victory for the National Party over the governing United Party, led by Jan Smuts, in the same year. The central event of Keppel-Jones's imagined celebration was the landing of Van Riebeeck, who arrived on board the *Dromedaris* at Woodstock Beach on Sunday, 6 April 1952, after which a series of speeches were made by National Party politicians.[9] Keppel-Jones undoubtedly saw this future festival as a blatant attempt to evoke an Afrikaner past so as to further the agenda of the National Party.

> Throughout the length and breadth of the country, on hilltops and battlefields, at monuments and at the graves of martyrs, there were gatherings, speeches, and processions. In vine-clad Western Province valleys, in the dorps of the Highveld and Karoo, bearded youths and *kappie'd* [capped/bonneted] maidens dedicated themselves in an ecstasy of emotion to the *Volk*. Special numbers of newspapers retold the old story of the trials and tribulations of the *Volk*, its desperate rescue from the jaws of imperialism,

its great leaders, its true course on the *Pad van Suid Afrika* [Road of South Africa].[10]

Afrikaners who did not conform to the political ideology of the National Party were excluded by Keppel-Jones from participation in the festival. Keppel-Jones's use of predictive powers as a historian of the future to create a Van Riebeeck festival is a further indication that the idea that 1952 would be an anniversary of sorts was prevalent in the 1940s, although the form it would take was not automatically assumed to be an Afrikaner nationalist aura but was very much open to contestation. Those who could not envisage the future Keppel-Jones predicted were shocked by his book, and those in Afrikaner nationalist circles were angered because of the suggestion that National Party rule would bring the country to near ruin. Ironically, it was the description of the festival in Keppel-Jones's book and the attempt, consciously or otherwise, to subvert his claims (which were seen as an effort to poison a possible commemorative event) that helped shape the form of the tercentenary celebrations and Van Riebeeck's landing at Granger Bay on 5 April 1952, some four years after the National Party had already come to power.[11]

Certainly, some of the initiatives to hold a commemorative event to coincide with the three hundredth year since Van Riebeeck's landing did come from within Afrikaner nationalist circles, as Keppel-Jones predicted. The Afrikaans Taal-en Kultuur Vereniging [ATKV; Afrikaans Language and Cultural Association], which had organized the 1938 Voortrekker Centenary festival, had, by 1947, established Van Riebeeck committees at several of its branches throughout the country. The strongest drive from within Afrikaans nationalist circles to promote Van Riebeeck, though, came from the FAK, which had actively participated in the annual wreath-laying ceremony at the base of the Van Riebeeck statue on Adderley street on 5–8 April to promote the idea of Van Riebeeck as the *volksplanter*, only to withdraw when it felt that the Cape Town City Council was dominating the ceremony. At its Congress in July 1945, the FAK appointed a commission, which included among its ranks Prof. H. B. Thom, charged with the task of establishing a committee that would take the necessary steps toward ensuring that the landing of Van Riebeeck would be celebrated in April 1952 in a dignified and proper way. The committee, which included representatives from the Dutch Reformed churches, the ATKV, and various women's organizations, held its first meeting in April 1946. It decided to proceed with the organization of a commemorative festival on 6 April 1952 which would have a specifically Christian and Afrikaans character. Other groups, such as the Cape Town City Council and the United Party government, were warned that, if they intended to hold a commemoration, they could not do so without the approval and cooperation of this FAK sub-committee.[12]

The tentative ideas that were advanced by the FAK sub-committee coincide with the way that the 1938 Great Trek centenary celebrations were held, with the emphasis on the establishment and furthering of a unified Afrikaner identity. *Die Burger,* the Cape-based Afrikaans-language newspaper, which had called for the United Party government, led by Jan Smuts, to take the lead in organizing the 1952 celebrations was told, in no uncertain terms, that it was through "our (the FAK) committee that Afrikanerdom could be represented in this issue." In calling for *Die Burger* to come into line with the position from the north (the center of the FAK's power base was in the Transvaal), the FAK *Van Riebeeck-Feeskomitee* asserted that it did not want the Afrikaans press issuing contradictory statements as it would weaken the FAK's self-proclaimed position to represent the "organised Afrikanerdom in the cultural sphere" and its right to "take the lead as far as possible." The committee also informed Jan Smuts, the prime minister, of its existence and of the planning that had already taken place for a festival in 1952. He was told that a festival so envisaged would take on a "genuine Afrikaner character," with Van Riebeeck being celebrated as the founder of the "Afrikaner nation, with its own language, culture and national nature."[13]

Despite the claims by the *Jan van Riebeeck Feeskomitee* in 1946 that it had already made considerable progress in planning for a festival, over the next two years very little was done to further the aim of establishing Van Riebeeck with an Afrikaner character for 1952. The response from the prime minister's office to correspondence from the FAK was unfavorable; the government refused to lend support to a festival that it said promoted sectional interests. Any historical occasion had to be organized on a broad national basis by the government and not by a limited body like the FAK, claimed Smuts. An executive committee of the larger *Van Riebeeck Feeskomitee* was established to respond more immediately to this issue and to other matters demanding urgent attention. Much of its time was spent in attempts to set up a meeting with Smuts in order to clarify its position, a meeting which had still not taken place by January 1948, the prime minister purportedly being otherwise engaged with overseas trips and the British royal family's visit to South Africa. The executive committee also sent letters to editors of Afrikaans newspapers asking them to encourage annual celebrations of Van Riebeeck Day by the *volk,* urged affiliates to devise programs for 6 April 1952, and laid down guidelines for participation. The most crucial instruction was that the festival had to be primarily for the "white population" and that "racial apartheid" had to be strictly adhered to. People designated to be of mixed race, and labeled coloureds, would be allowed to participate, as long as they used Afrikaans as their "home language" and the FAK could "negotiate safely" with them. Indeed, representatives of the Dutch Reformed Mission Church saw a huge potential in facilitating this participa-

tion as it could lead to the development of cultural organizations among coloureds who speak "our language," especially in the western Cape where coloured Afrikaans-speaking schoolchildren outnumbered white schoolchildren
by about ten thousand. This involvement in the festival, however, was specifically to be in separate organizations and events. Determining the nature of this
involvement in the festival, and facilitating it, would be the Dutch Reformed
Mission Churches and the FAK, working within a framework expressed metaphorically as that of child/parent and master/servant.[14]

While the FAK was planning its Van Riebeeck festival, the Cape Town City
Council was setting up its own special committee to deal with Van Riebeeck
and 1952. At the beginning of 1946, one of the local English-language newspapers in Cape Town, the *Cape Times*, had started promoting calls for a tercentenary festival. It reported how Cape Town City councilors were discussing the
idea; it published letters from readers asserting that such a festival should sur-
pass the Empire exhibition held in Johannesburg in 1936; and, in an editorial,
it called for planning to start immediately. In March 1946 the mayor of Cape
Town, acting on an instruction from the City Council, announced that he was
going to chair a committee which would approach the government "to formulate plans for a festival along national lines," an initiative which received the
wholehearted support of the editor of the *Cape Times*.[15]

It would appear that much of the correspondence and many of the claims
by the FAK to serve as the primary organizers of a festival in 1952 were directed against this special committee, particularly since it was the City Council
that had usurped the ceremony at the statue and was giving it a flavor that did
not fully accord with Afrikaner nationalist sentiment. The notion of the 1952
festival that was being discussed in the pages of the *Cape Times* and in the
Council chambers was also at odds with the idea the FAK was proposing. One
reader of the *Cape Times* suggested that instead of having "a definite Afrikaans
colour," a Van Riebeeck festival should have "a South African colour" which
would include "all sections of the population," a sentiment that was echoed by
the editor and the Council's special committee. The latter insisted that the festival be "non-political, non-sectarian and non-sectional." It is not entirely clear
who comprised, in these terms, "all sections of the population," but the way in
which the ideas were being couched, in terms of "British tradition" and "Afrikaans colour," would seem to indicate that the "South African colour" being
referred to was white.[16]

This notion of a Van Riebeeck festival embracing "all [white] sections" had
a much closer affinity with the ideas of the United Party government of Jan
Smuts. Apart from assuring the Van Riebeeck Society that it would provide
£1,000 toward the cost of producing the diary, however, the government did
not seem to be devoting much attention to the prospect of a festival in 1952. It

could not find time to meet with the City Council's special committee and, by February 1948, had not responded to the committee's request for the government to express its views on the tercentenary. The *Cape Times* attributed this largely to the time taken up arranging for the British royal family's visit to South Africa in February and March of 1947. By prioritizing the royal visit, the government was not only making history in terms of re-creating past events, as the trek celebrations did and as a planned Van Riebeeck festival envisaged, but also in the sense of creating first and significant occasions. From the time the royal family landed, they were making history "before our eyes": King George VI was "the first reigning monarch of England ever to set foot on South African soil"; the royal cavalcade in the streets of Cape Town was the highlight of "a momentous day"; the opening of parliament by the king was a "Historic event in the mother city"; the commando which escorted the royal family into the Transvaal town of Ermelo was "a reminder of past history as new history is made"; and "a new chapter was enacted" in the history of Pretoria, as "their majesties and the two princesses paid the city the honor of a personal visit." On this journey the royal family enveloped a range of symbols of the past into their epoch-making historical tour, so much so that South African history was brought into their all-embracing gaze and under their supervision. They were entertained with folk dances "by young men and women descended from the Voortrekkers"; they were greeted by a group of Boer veterans from the South African War (1899–1902) "beneath the statue of Louis Botha"; they were welcomed by "witchdoctors in ancient dress and grotesquely painted faces"; they listened to "native children" at Lovedale mission singing about Ntsikana, "one of the earliest Bantu converts to Christianity"; they were presented with a miniature ox-wagon in the "old Transvaal capital," Pretoria; and in Eshowe a "Zulu warrior," who had fought against British armies, "proudly showed [the king] a wound that he had received in the battle of Isandhlwana in 1879." The bringing together of history in these ways through the pageantry of the royal tour was a way for the government to mobilize popular support around a series of symbols which were not derived from the Afrikaner nationalist past, as had been the case with the 1938 trek, but from a setting in which the image of the British royal family was the cementing force. Very importantly, this was not cast as an imperial visit, but one of making and participating in history itself. This was no more evident than when, on an "epoch-making day in South African history," the King visited the military base at Voortrekkerhoogte, wearing for the "first time . . . the uniform of a Field Marshall in this country." Alongside him was Jan Smuts, and "it was the first time that two field marshals have appeared together in this country." Through the royal family, South Africans were being invited by the Smuts government to become part of, and indeed to make, world history with an associated set of symbols that claimed universality. The almost natural symbolism of all-embracing history supposedly gave it power to counterpose, and indeed submerge, local images, which would then be cast as parochial and largely insignificant on the stage of world history. The government could find little time for Van Riebeeck, as the royal family "passed ... [his] statue" and proceeded "on into Adderley Street" at the start of their tour.[17]

The historic symbolism which Smuts and the United Party government used during the visit seemed to have mobilized popular support, as the streets thronged with thousands upon thousands of cheering spectators greeting the royal family. As part of the tour itinerary, Smuts had taken his guests to Standerton, the constituency he represented in parliament. The commentator on an *African Mirror* newsreel called this a proud moment for both Smuts and his constituents, for seldom had "a politician in any country been able to bring such honour to those who have supported him so staunchly." On 24 April, when the royal family departed, it was Van Riebeeck who, lifting his hat as he gazed out to sea, bade them farewell, with the words: "Not Good-bye but '*Tot siens*'"[*au revoir*]. On his statue the dates 1652 and 1947 were now imaginatively inscribed, as if the royal visit symbolized the culmination of a past which he had begun (Figure 5).[18]

This support for the government among those who were allowed to vote proved to be more apparent than real. Just over a year later, the United Party was voted out of office by many of the same people who had come out to wave the British flag and extend "their own warm welcome" to the royals. The "staunch supporters" in Standerton voted for the National Party candidate in their constituency, Wentzel du Plessis, who defeated Smuts by 224 votes. The drawing power of the universal historic imagery that Smuts and the royal family had brought with them was tenuous. It was not easy to dissociate the royal family from a British imperial imagery, especially when the essential core of the Afrikaner nationalist past, which had been constructed over the past fifty years, had been based on the fight against imperial control. Even though former enemies of British imperial forces had greeted the king, the leaders of the National Party were not on hand to welcome the royal family when they arrived in Cape Town. Moreover, there was no resonance with a local identity and past that the universal historic symbolism could draw on. The royal visit had not been able to sustain a national past that enveloped all within a (British) commonwealth, and it was the anti-imperial history of "The Great Trek" and a still somewhat ill-defined racial policy termed apartheid—which vacillated between the total removal of African labor from white areas and a more limited notion of the government introducing stricter measures to control the "necessary" African labor—that emerged triumphant among the largely white electorate.[19]

5. Jan van Riebeeck bids the British royal family farewell after their visit to South Africa in 1947. "Not Good-bye, but '*Tot siens*'" [*Au revoir*], *Cape Times*, 24 April 1947. Courtesy of *Cape Times* and the National Library of South Africa, Cape Town.

The National Party victory did not immediately provide a boost for the public past of Jan van Riebeeck. It was the cross-class alliance among whites with an identity determined as Afrikaans, and a past written as a struggle for freedom, that had provided the basis for the success of the National Party and that needed to be continually reinforced in the initial phases of its rule. The opening of the Voortrekker Monument near Pretoria in 1949 provided the ideal platform to re-enact the pageantry of 1938 and to strengthen the associated symbols of what was proclaimed to be the "Biggest Festival in History." In much the same vein as the ox-wagons had trekked from various parts of the country to Pretoria in 1938, a group of *rapportryers* [dispatch riders], based on the commando system used by Boer armies, brought messages from the *volk* in "distant places" to the monument, stirring up "enthusiasm and national feeling" in the process. Between 14 and 16 December, at the monument itself, a series of historical tableaux were performed as part of a "mighty festive symphony with vast movements," with the emphasis on a *volk*'s history that moved from "Struggle to Victory." They took the audience on a journey with the trekkers from the time that the trek leader, Piet Retief, had met and been killed by the Zulu king, Dingane, to the "Freedom Flags" of the independent Boer republics and the "scenes of mourning" after the defeat of the Boer armies by the British in the South African War of 1899–1902, and ended with victory in "The Present" with the opening of the monument in 1949.[20]

The highlight of the proceedings in 1949 came when, at midday, the rays of the sun bore down through an opening in the roof of the monument onto a cenotaph bearing the inscription *"Ons vir jou Suid-Afrika"* [We for thee, South Africa]. D. F. Malan, the prime minister, asserting that these words should now become "engraved deeply and indelibly on the heart of every Afrikaner," gave the signal for six boys and six girls dressed in Victorian garb representing trek outfits to open the doors of the huge granite monument designed to eulogize the Voortrekker past. Inside the monument was a historical frieze sculpted out of marble, representing twenty-seven selected episodes in a history of the trek from the time of departure from the Cape to the establishment of independent Boer republics in 1852. In these scenes of "trials and tribulations," "sacrifice and suffering," all culminating in a pre-determined "logical conclusion" of an independent South African Republic, the frieze was intended to document and set forever in marble "the Afrikaner's proprietary right to South Africa."[21]

Yet, for all its associations with sustaining an Afrikaner past and identity, there were indications at the proceedings of the inauguration and the symbols contained within the monument that the Voortrekkers were now being used to construct more than just an Afrikaner nationhood. At this particular point in its history, it was becoming increasingly important not just to "reinforce the superiority of white Afrikanerdom" but also to promote the cause of a broader exclusive white South African nationalism. The hold the National Party had on state power, just over a year after the election, was extremely fragile. This was not only because of the narrowness of its election victory; it was also a result of the pressure it was under to come up with a policy that would deal with the growth in African urbanization and the accompanying upsurge in political militancy in the 1940s, perceived by most whites as an imminent threat to the supremacy they had taken for granted. In this tenuous position, the "quest for legitimacy across [white] class lines" became a crucial component of Nationalist political strategy, playing a major role in formulating Apartheid policy, and a history and identity for whites as whites that reinforced and authenticated their notions of supremacy. The Voortrekker past that had been produced since the 1870s was not ideal for these purposes, as it set itself against other white identities, but at the same time it was the most imminent History that Nationalists could draw on, as was evident at the opening of the monument. A keynote speaker, Justice J. C. Newton Thompson, was specially selected by the festival organizers to represent what was designated as the English-speaking component of the South African white population at the inauguration. Speaking just before D. F. Malan's main address, he called on "both sections [which] are originally descendant from . . . European civilization" to come together so that it would be possible to speak of the "white community" as "the South African nation." The crowd of some 250,000 responded to his speech with rapturous applause. D. F. Malan spoke of the Voortrekkers as having blazed the trail of an independent South African nationhood based on the maintenance of white paramountcy and white race purity. Inside the monument itself, one of the twenty-seven friezes displayed on the interior walls depicted a little-known historical scene in which a representative of the English-speaking settler community at Grahamstown handed over a Bible to the trek leader, Jacobus Uys. Although he did not hand over the Bible personally, William Rowland Thompson, the frontier merchant who was an ancestor of Justice Newton Thompson, was present at the scene. And thus a past was linked together in the trek to both a present and a future of whites bound together by the monument. In this respect, the monument became a symbol of the whiteness borne by the Voortrekkers, who repeated endless colonial progressions into the "darkness" of the African interior through their journey of conquest. Through this journey, the Voortrekkers, in 1949, became the true founders of white South Africa, outstripping potential all-comers, including Van Riebeeck.[22] It is not an individual but the generic "Voortrekker, wife and family" who, as an entity, were presented as enabling the process of pure breeding to continue across the frontier of race. Van Riebeeck, the lone man on the coastal plains, could not be the founder of white South Africa in the past of the Voortrekker Monument without his family to accompany him.

In as much as the royal family was not quite able to dissociate itself from its imperial past, it was not easy for the Voortrekker past to cement a white nationalist identity and an anti-imperial history. Many of those whom the Nationalists sought to incorporate within the monument could not associate themselves with a history that was, at its core, based on a struggle against people they related to as ancestors. Although a great deal of enthusiasm was expressed in sections of the English-language press for the way that the proceedings were a display of "goodwill" and "unity"—*The Star* newspaper in Johannesburg published a special booklet comprising a series of articles on the "Great Trek" and photographs from the inauguration that told a "heroic story . . . which . . . stirs the English-speaking South African also, because these Voortrekkers are our people"—there was some unease about the "high pitch of Afrikaner fervour" evident in the celebrations, the way that the Voortrekker past was being portrayed as the main event in South African history, and how this was being linked to the struggle against the "mighty enemy from Europe" in the South African War. The historical tableau which depicted the plundering of Boer farms by British forces and the grief of Boer women in the war was criticized for opening up old wounds and being at odds with the theme of the monument, *"Ons vir jou Suid-Afrika"* [We for thee South Africa]. In addition, the view of the Voortrekkers as conveyors of civilization and progress was not one that historians, who had written in English, had placed at the forefront of depictions of the trek. Indeed, they had portrayed the trekkers as "rude frontiersmen" who had "fled to the wilderness" once they had been confronted with the "light" of "civilization" which the British had ignited from the "torch of enlightenment carried ashore by Van Riebeeck." *The Star's* special inauguration booklet also referred to the Voortrekkers as having developed "prejudices" and "limitations" as a result of their "long isolation on the old Cape frontier." The ambivalence toward the proceedings and the monument itself was expressed in a cartoon that appeared in the *Cape Times* on 17 December 1949: On a scroll, a map of South Africa appeared, its top part containing a likeness of the monument with the year 1949 A.D. inscribed on it. On the bottom portion of the map was a large question mark with the years 2000–3000 A.D. written next to it (Figure 6). The future of the Voortrekker past was clearly not one in which the cartoonist of the *Cape Times* felt secure. To establish a white past required a much more ambiguous ancestry than the Voortrekker Monument could provide, but one that still maintained, at the same time, a substantial historical record. In a sense, Van Riebeeck and his many histories were eminently suitable for this role, and even though he did not yet have a prominent family to land with at Granger Bay, the coincidence of the three hundredth year since his landing provided the ideal moment to claim another set of historical events as the basis of a white identity.[23]

Even while the inauguration of the Voortrekker Monument was being planned, the FAK's *Van Riebeeck-Feeskomitee* was starting to change its direction, in the wake of the 1948 election victory of the National Party. Chaired by the Minister of Native Affairs, E. G. Jansen, the committee suggested to the new government that a proposed Van Riebeeck festival assume a national character

6. The inauguration of the Voortrekker Monument in 1949, soon after the National Party had come to power promising to implement a policy of apartheid, raised questions about the future of the country. "Whither, South Africa?" *Cape Times,* 17 December 1949. Courtesy of *Cape Times* and the National Library of South Africa, Cape Town.

by drawing the races together to organize and participate in the anticipated events. Races, in these terms, bore no reference to a biological essence but to what was deemed to be an ancestry based on language and culture, one related to an Afrikaans-speaking world, the other to an English-speaking one. Assuming the mantle of representative of the race of Afrikaans-speaking whites, the FAK recommended that the government appoint a central committee to organize a "national festival" in 1952, incorporating the executive of the FAK's own committee, the administrators of the provinces, G. Siemelink (from the ANV),

T. B. Davie (the vice-chancellor of the University of Cape Town), and four English speakers. This committee, it was envisaged, would organize the festivities on a "nation wide" basis and also seek out the co-operation of groups in Holland. A Cape Town committee, with representatives from "interested population groups in Cape Town" would be responsible for arranging a series of events in the city, which would provide the main stage for Van Riebeeck, his landing and his past.[24] Through these committees the festival would celebrate a commonality of all whites as a distinct nation with their joint past derived out of Europe and Van Riebeeck, which would set them apart from and above the "uncivilized" natives of Africa.

In order not to distract from the inauguration of the Voortrekker Monument, these plans were deliberately kept under wraps until 1950. To keep the recommendations alive, though, representatives from the FAK's committee met and corresponded regularly with government ministers. There was some concern that if the government did not proceed to appoint a festival committee, it would lose the initiative to do so as there was already some talk of the Cape Town Chamber of Industries deciding to stage a large exhibition on its own. To facilitate the planning process, the FAK extended invitations to a broader range of participants to constitute a *Breë Komitee van die Van Riebeeck Feeskomitee* [Extended Committee of the Van Riebeeck Festival Committee] to meet with the Minister of the Interior, T. E. Dönges, on 10 March 1950. At this gathering Dönges said that the government was totally supportive of the plans that were emerging from the FAK for a Van Riebeeck festival. Not only would it appoint the central and Cape Town committees on the basis recommended by the FAK—in the latter it was also deemed necessary to include a "few ladies" as well—but it went further and pledged government financial backing for the organization of the celebrations by these committees. Clearly the government perceived that by according significance to Van Riebeeck, and by assuming a leading role in enabling his landing and his past to take place, it might strengthen its claims to legitimacy.[25]

Almost a month later, to coincide with the annual commemoration of the landing, Dönges issued a press release announcing that the government would lend its support to a Van Riebeeck tercentenary festival to be held in 1952. The central arena for such a festival, Donges declared, would be Cape Town, a move the local English daily, the *Cape Times*, enthusiastically approved, proclaiming the city to be "the very place where those early settlers established and consolidated a beach-head for Western civilization in a continent that was undoubtedly a dark one." A sixteen-person Cape Town committee, which the minister nominated and the mayor immediately convened, with representation from the English-, Afrikaans-, and Dutch-speaking communities, was to set plans in motion for the festival.[26] This committee, to a large degree, was an attempt to amalgamate the two groups that had been at loggerheads over proposals for a Van Riebeeck festival in the late 1940s, the Cape Town City Council and the FAK, with the government, which, for all its Afrikaner nationalist associations, represented as the neutral arbiter and the cementing force.

Further than announcing that a central committee would be appointed later to coordinate the festivities throughout the country, Dönges gave little indication at this stage of the proposed content that a Van Riebeeck festival would take. In spite of Van Riebeeck's emergence in commemorations, textbooks, and the diary, he was not a character that automatically evoked a set of associated historic events, and it was to be left in the hands of the committees to plan his past. Sections of the English and Afrikaans press immediately began to speculate over the nature of the proposed events for Van Riebeeck. Suggestions were made that a monument be built on Signal Hill, that Dutch warships call in on Table Bay, and that a group of Van Riebeeck's direct descendants visit the Cape. One of the most talked about and extravagant ideas was that Van Riebeeck should set sail again from the Netherlands, re-creating his voyage three hundred years previously, emulating Henry Hudson who had sailed to New York in 1909 to participate in the three hundredth anniversary celebration of that city, organized by the American Scenic and Historic Preservation Society.[27] In all these suggestions the central focus was on establishing a European and specifically Dutch ancestry with little direct association with the local national past that followed.

This shifting of the direction the Van Riebeeck festival was to take was not received with unanimity within Afrikaner nationalist circles. M. C. Botha, who was the organizer of the 1949 inauguration of the Voortrekker Monument, and who was touted as the organizer of the Van Riebeeck festival, expressed the fear that by attempting to be an inclusive white occasion, it would water down the emerging trend toward establishing an Afrikaner ancestry through Van Riebeeck and the Dutch, which historians like S. F. N. Gie had promoted. Disregarding any conflict that occurred between settlers and the Dutch East India Company, as well as the changing nature of the Dutch inheritance, it was claimed that the Dutch culture borne by Van Riebeeck was so strong that it was able to maintain itself through the period of British colonial rule in the nineteenth century, to emerge triumphant, in the form of the Afrikaner nation in the twentieth century. In terms of this logic, a Van Riebeeck festival should be a celebration of this supposed Dutch/Afrikaner linkage, where the English would be represented but would play a "subordinate role."[28]

Botha must have felt that his worst fears of the festival losing an Afrikaner nationalist flavor with a Dutch heritage were being realized when the Cape

Town committee began to meet and consider ideas for the central theme. There were some thirty-nine proposals, and although many of them referred to specific events rather than an overarching thematic conceptualization, there was little to suggest that an Afrikaner/Dutch lineage was being considered seriously. Proposals ranged from the establishment of a Tercentenary Tuberculosis Trust to staging a motor car Grand Prix, restoring and preserving buildings, exhibiting books, paintings, and photographs, holding a wine festival, re-enacting Van Riebeeck's landing, and constructing a Dutch village to declaring South Africa a republic. Probably closest to Botha's conceptualization of the festival were the recommendations for a pageant of the past re-enacting events from Van Riebeeck to the present and the idea that a genealogical record of old Cape families be compiled as a national monument. While the executive of the Cape Town committee—which labeled itself the Tercentenary Action Committee— did not rule out any of these proposals, it initially favored as the central theme the establishment of a Health Fund and the construction of a concert hall on Cape Town's foreshore. The latter was regarded as eminently advantageous to some members of the committee, as it would not only have symbolic significance in making Van Riebeeck into a Christopher Columbus "marking the transfer of the culture of the Old World into the new," but it could be used, could raise money, and, unlike the Voortrekker celebrations, would present a "living" monument.[29]

Setting up Van Riebeeck against the Voortrekker Monument in such a way was undoubtedly to raise the ire of the promoters of Afrikaner nationalism. Even before the Cape Town committee had met to consider the various proposals, M. C. Botha from the FAK had called on the government to relegate this committee to the status of local organizers. Dönges, to avert any clash which might occur over the theme and to ensure that the Cape Town committee would not undermine any plans the government might have, moved hastily and appointed the central committee, to be chaired by E. J. Jansen, the Minister of Native Affairs, which would "coordinate all [Van Riebeeck] festivals in the Union and abroad." Although the relationship between this committee and the Cape Town committee was never spelled out, it became apparent that the central committee would make decisions on what it considered to be national matters, such as the theme, and the Cape Town group would concern itself with submitting proposals and making arrangements for events in the city. The *Cape Times* expressed slight misgivings over this move, hoping that the central committee would not become the "plaything of small-minded sectionalism" as it claimed had occurred during the Voortrekker celebrations. *The Argus* was also hesitant about these sections emerging on the committee but expressed its reservations more in terms of how it conceptualized the festival than by raising possible doubts. It presented the Van Riebeeck festival as a moment of reconciliation in which differences would be forgotten to recall and relive "the long gone days which were the beginnings of White civilization in South Africa," casting the intervening period into the abyss of collective amnesia for the history of the white nation to emerge.[30]

A notable shift in discussions over the envisaged composition of Van Riebeeck in 1952 took place immediately after the appointment of the central committee. It was not so much that the conceptualization of the festival took on an Afrikaner nationalist aura, as the *Cape Times* feared it might, but the idea that Van Riebeeck had to be constituted in some way as a figure with a national past became the focus of deliberations around a "basic principle." Echoing the shift in direction of the FAK, C. F. Albertyn, from the Afrikaans publishing house Nasionale Pers and editor of the magazine for the Voortrekker youth movement, *Die Jongspan*, who was on both committees, suggested that the "spiritual" theme be "We Build a Nation." In this schema South Africa consisted of two nations, English and Afrikaans-speaking whites, who would be united through Van Riebeeck, with settlers and settlement forming the basis of an "indigenous" festival. To realize this theme in practical terms, Albertyn suggested that each visitor carry to Cape Town a stone of a specified size that would then be used to build a monument. By the time the central committee had its first meeting at the beginning of September, though, no final decision had been reached about Albertyn's proposed theme, or any other for the festival, and it was concluded that Van Riebeeck would have to wait for written proposals to be submitted before his future and his past could be resolved for 1952.[31]

The Cape Town committee, now under pressure to present a national theme, relegated the idea of a concert hall to a local issue and, in its place, presented a revised proposal with Table Mountain as the focus of the festival. Fitting in with the concept of founding, it presented Table Mountain to the central committee as the "monument" with an ancestry based on a European gaze, "seen by Sir Francis Drake and by the early seafarers" and where "Van Riebeeck laid the foundations of a new nation under its protective walls." It was not only these European antecedents that appealed to the Cape Town committee but also the way that Table Mountain was able to couple this ancestry with a sense of being indigenous. The mountain was conceptualized as "our incomparable heritage," a "national temple" that should be protected and preserved. As part of the conservation of the past and celebration of Van Riebeeck's landing, the committee suggested that the "noxious weed Haxea" should be removed from the mountain and that there be a planting ceremony of indigenous trees on its slopes. Albertyn's scheme of everyone bringing a stone to Cape Town to build a monument could also be incorporated into this format, as the stones could become part of the walls of a summerhouse to be erected on the mountain. In an almost contradictory sense, to commemorate Van Riebeeck was seen as a way to return to and replant the seeds of a native history with a European past.[32]

Although this theme was more appealing to the central committee than the envisaged concert hall, it was still seen to be expressive of local rather than national ideas. This committee did not view this theme as capable of defining and sustaining a national past, as the Cape Town committee suggested it would. The mountain could be imaged "as sacrosanct in the hearts of the people," but its associations were overwhelmingly related to a specific city and the way that city constituted its inhabitants in terms antagonistic at times to an Afrikaner nationalist identity. Table Mountain could thus be considered, along with various other themes, as forming part of the Van Riebeeck festival, but the central committee would not entertain the idea of it forming the central theme.[33]

The rejection of Table Mountain did not mean that the government was intent on sponsoring a festival for Van Riebeeck where "the historic emotions of 1938 were . . . due to be repeated in a slightly different medium" and where Afrikaners were called on to display solidarity with the National Party. There were three crucial problems associated with developing a tercentenary festival with an exclusive "Afrikaans outreach." First, that approach might not be able to sustain the response of 1949, given its closeness in time to the previous commemoration. Second, the figure of Van Riebeeck, the company servant, was not immensely popular within Afrikaner nationalist circles where the Dutch East India Company had been portrayed in its past as the enemy of the burgher farmers. Finally, the power base afforded by a white Afrikaner nationalism would always be severely limited. Maintaining power in a context of racial exclusivity meant that it was necessary to draw other pasts and identities into constituting a white nation. The coincidence of 1952 provided the ideal stage to promote a racially based nationalism in which the anti-imperial symbolic baggage associated with the "Great Trek" could be incorporated and attuned to a broader exclusive racial past. Albertyn's proposal of a festival that commemorated European settlement and its past, delineated between 1652 and 1952, was very much in line with this thinking. In October 1950 the central committee decided that "South Africa After 300 Years: We Build a Nation" was to be the theme of a tercentenary festival in 1952, where a past of "ancestral immigrants" emanating from Van Riebeeck would be created as a "symbol of national unity," asserting simultaneously both racial power and exclusivity.[34]

Negotiating and Authorizing Van Riebeeck's Past

The key modernizing alibi the central committee presented for Van Riebeeck to declare this racial power for a nation designated as his descendants was that the festival was "to show 300 years of civilisation in South Africa." A white South African nation, defined in and through the festival, would become the bearer of the "torch of Western Civilisation to this southern corner of Africa," following which it had "matured over 300 years." In this conceptualization it was progress, derived from Europe, which started the past and then went through a process of maturation to move inexorably toward its "own way of life and its own mission." Depicting this process of beginning, progression, and achievement of a self-proclaimed separate nationhood for Van Riebeeck became the organizing principle for the events of 1952.[35]

The central committee planning the festival incorporated into the schematic conceptualization of the specific events some of the suggestions that had already been made before the decision to have an all-embracing theme. With the need to show beginning and progress, a major focus, the committee decided, would be on the past, with a series of historical exhibitions. Among other items, these involved a reconstruction of the *Dromedaris* and the landing of Van Riebeeck, a show depicting highlights of South African history over three hundred years, and, in order to make the festival into a spatially national event, the journeys of progression that had occurred during the Voortrekker celebrations were to be re-created by having mail coaches travel to Cape Town from different areas of the country. To present the achievement that had derived from this past, a large exhibition or festival fair was visualized which would display the economic structure of the nation as being based on agriculture, industry, and mining. Complementing the more "material" "picture of how far we have progressed as a nation," there would be depictions of cultural advancement. Art exhibitions, musical concerts, dramatic performances, youth displays, and sporting competitions would take place in Cape Town throughout February and March 1952, much of it centering on the Castle, which was proclaimed to be "South Africa's oldest and most memorable building." The proposal that Table Mountain become the central theme of the festival was also merged into this jam-packed program. The organizers signaled their intention to have Table Mountain declared a national monument, linking the nation not merely with a European past but rooting it in a "symbol . . . of conservation" in a ceremony of "Dedication to the Soil."[36]

Presenting a past for Van Riebeeck was no easy matter. The initial problem was deciding on the form a public performance of the past should take. In 1910 a historical pageant had been held at a designated venue, and, in debates over the program for the 1952 festival, that earlier pageant was recalled as a "magnificent show," one that could be emulated as an appropriate model because of how it linked the performers with their direct ancestors. Similarly, at both the laying of the foundation stone and the inauguration of the Voortrekker Monument, a series of historical tableaux had been performed. Many of the initial suggestions made to the Cape Town committee in 1950 had favored the revival of this format, the general idea being to present selected moments in a history, thereby establishing in the public vista a sense of identity that was defined both in a particular space, namely, South Africa, and a linear sequence of a determined historical time that led from Van Riebeeck's landing to the present of 1952. The pageant thus extended the notion of locating individuals in commemorative time specified by a singular ceremony or designated holiday to one where an extended past became the focus of establishing a public identity in a history where parts were carefully chosen, scripted, and rehearsed. Moreover, the pageant also involved notions of much more public participation, where the crowds of onlookers could respond almost immediately to an array of visual images. One proponent of this scheme, A. J. Bosman, was so enthusiastic about it that she sent the committee a list containing "pageant procedure" derived from the experience of pageants that had been held in the United States. Yet the problem with pageant format, as was the U.S. experience in the early parts of the twentieth century when pageants were a popular form of commemorative celebrations, was that the carnival atmosphere might prove to be so overwhelming that the occasion would lose its aura of the genuine historic. The outside stage also made it difficult to create a serious ambience that would enable the performers to focus the audience's attention on the historic scenes. Although dramas had been re-enacted at the Voortrekker celebrations, the emphasis had been on public talks, with speeches drawing on historical episodes to establish and sustain an image of a united *volk* to which every Afrikaner owed his or her undivided loyalty. In considering the appropriate forms for staging the past in 1952, members of the government insisted that it maintain a sense of solemnity as "an historical occasion." The festival was to be a "devotion to the past" and should not be turned into a carnival or a "national fair." For the organizers of the Van Riebeeck festival this meant that, much like their American counterparts some fifty years previously, they had to decide "how . . . they [could] elicit the enthusiasm and cheers . . . without sacrificing the marrow of patriotic and moral exhortation customarily put forth in the historical oration." The Afrikaans dramatist Anna Neethling-Pohl, who had organized historical tableaux for the 1938 Voortrekker festival, was adamant that, given these sorts of problems and the difficulties in achieving an adequate response, she would never again become involved in a similar sort of production.[37]

Yet, in spite of all her protestations, Anna Neethling-Pohl was cajoled into becoming the organizer of the historical pageant for the 1952 Van Riebeeck festival and was seconded from the South African Broadcasting Corporation for a year to carry out this function. Her previous experience in 1938, her association with Afrikaans drama, and her study of pageantry abroad—in 1949 she had toured Europe, observing many pageants and speaking to their organizers

—seemed to make her the most eminently suitable choice of the Van Riebeeck festival pageant sub-committee. But Neethling-Pohl was insistent that, based on her experience and her study of pageants, the various historical tableaux could not be presented on stage in the form of singular episodes. When she appeared in May 1951 before the pageant committee, which had been assigned the task of ensuring that a national past would be displayed in April 1952, she outlined instead plans for a procession of history through the streets of Cape Town. The advantage of such a schema, she maintained, was that it was able to display singular episodes within a holistic past, in which history became a flowing river that united its tributaries into a nation that grew and developed as the procession wound its way through the streets in a sequence that, like the textbook past, was one of "causes and results." The seamless, developmental nature of the moving pageant would also lend a sense of inevitable progression to a history that was selected, presented, and carefully laid out so as to become "unchangeable." This clearly fitted in with Calvinist notions of predestination that, in many ways, informed Afrikaner nationalist political ideologies. But Neethling-Pohl did not envision the format of history in the moving pageant in such limited terms. By gazing on this episodic, sequential, preordained, moving past, she envisaged that members of the crowd who gathered in the streets would be able to recognize, with a feeling of "joy," their specific place in a collective history that had become visually knowable and forever fixed as "*our* history." Through the procession of the past, the onlookers could come to identify themselves as "citizens of South Africa."[38]

The major problem with this type of moving history in the gaze of the general public was that, in spite of Neethling-Pohl's determination to have it tightly secured, there was little control over the way the crowd constituted itself and how it identified with the events in the procession. She was not unaware of this problem. Soon after she arrived in Cape Town to organize the pageant for the Van Riebeeck festival, she witnessed a demonstration by the Torch Commando, an organization originally constituted by former servicemen in the Second World War, who were protesting plans by the National Party government to eliminate people from the voters roll who were racially classified as coloureds and still had the franchise in the Cape. Totally unsympathetic to the cause of the protest, she expressed shock and outrage at the makeup of the crowd that filled Cape Town's streets from the Parade to St. George's Street, which she referred to as a "hysterical mass." What particularly upset her was that she saw little sense of discernible racial identities displayed by the protesters. "It was a real mix-up," she declared. "White, coloured and black sang Tipperay together and carried smouldering stinking torches."[39]

A few months later, members of Cape Town City Council were expressing similar fears, although their major concern was that the gaiety and frivolity associated with street processions might excite itself into a semblance of disorder which they did not want for a serious historic occasion. This was expressed in the concern that the pageant may turn into a "hospital rag," referring to the annual float parade by students from the University of Cape Town to raise money for medical institutions in the Cape Peninsula. While recognizing these problems, the pageant committee was impressed with Neethling-Pohl's suggestion for a moving pageant. Staging the past on the streets in the form of a procession would enable more people to view the past; it would also overcome the complication of how to deal with details of language usage that might occur if items were staged in a theatrical arena. It was also maintained that street processions did not necessarily have to take on the appearance of a "hospital rag" and that similar events in Cape Town, Coventry in England, and Otago in New Zealand had been "solemn and impressive." Problems of racial delineation, which were essential if white nationhood was to be the central focus of the festival, could be effectively dealt with by arranging separate pageants. But most of all, the pageant committee was confident that in Neethling-Pohl they had found a person who could assert the necessary control over the past, ensuring that it was presented in an attractive manner while preserving the historic nature of the occasion. "Miss Anna Neethling-Pohl . . . besides being a student of history, has carved for herself a niche in the theatrical world not only as an actress but also as a producer . . . who has recently attended similar pageants in Europe." Given all Neethling-Pohl's experience, the pageant committee was confident that there would not be a "properse mix-up."[40]

Charged with controlling the presentation of the past for the [white] nation, Neethling-Pohl set about drawing up draft scripts for a pageant of the past that was to take place a few days before Van Riebeeck was due to land at Granger Bay. Some six months before Neethling-Pohl's appointment, discussion around the historical presentations for the festival had already begun in a sub-committee chaired by C. F. Albertyn. The framework decided on was to present about twenty events starting with pre-discovery—"what the first whites encountered here"—followed by selected highlights to be chosen by professors from university history departments in South Africa. Most of the events selected, in fact, arose from discussions between J. C. Pauw, the organizing secretary of the festival, and H. B. Thom soon after the sub-committee had met in November 1950. In Afrikaner nationalist historical circles Thom was regarded as an expert in his field. He had gained a reputation among his students for his knowledge of the birth of "White South Africa," his obsession with establishing factual veracity, information that was "precise, systematic, objective," and his ability to link together in a "symbiotic relationship . . . the demands of academe and the demands of the 'volk.'" Given these qualifications, he was in many ways the ideal historian to give the past of the Van Riebeeck festival its authority. Neethling-Pohl used the material that Pauw had received from Thom for the scripts she drew up. Intensely aware that the form of the past for which she had strongly motivated necessitated perhaps more than a brief notion of the real historic to give it validity, she submitted drafts for the moving pageant to Thom for approval. Although there is no indication of what his comments were, they were taken extremely seriously and immediately implemented in the revised text. Thom thus bestowed the blessing of his empirically based white history on this play of the past.[41]

Thom's role in authenticating the presentation of the past went much further than making recommendations for the pageant. At the time when Neethling-Pohl was involved in making arrangements for the procession, Thom had been granted special paid leave by the University of Stellenbosch to edit Van Riebeeck's diary for the Van Riebeeck Society. Although this aspect of his work was less highly visible than the pageantry with which Anna Neethling-Pohl was involved, and festival organizers had not set up a special committee to deal with the diary's publication, it was the diary that gave the festival as a whole the effective means to realize its historical authority. Thom himself recognized the importance of the diary in giving authenticity to Van Riebeeck's past and, although his wish was rejected that the diary be given what he called its "correct title," *Die Kaapse Dagverhaal tydens Van Riebeeck* [The daily record at the Cape during the time of Van Riebeeck], to indicate that Van Riebeeck was not really the author, he devoted his time to editing the diary methodically using copies obtained from the Hague. The government, recognizing the importance of producing the diary in time to coincide with the festival, gave Stellenbosch University a grant of £3,976 so that it could find a temporary replacement for Thom while he edited the diary. The Van Riebeeck Society, aware that the diary was not part of its usual publication program, convened a special editorial committee. With that committee's assistance, by March 1952, Thom, together with D. B. Bosman, who worked on the Dutch edition, had completed the task of editing volume 1 of the diary at a cost of some £10,000. A total of 4,500 copies of the diary were printed, 3,000 in English and 1,500 in Dutch, in time for the pageantry in Cape Town's streets and for Van Riebeeck's landing at Granger Bay.[42]

Initial sales in March 1952 seemed to indicate that the diary was very popular. Within two weeks of its publication, it was reported to the Van Riebeeck Society that half the print run had been sold. However, apparently these figures were highly exaggerated, since, by September 1952, only 2,203 copies had been sold, and Van Riebeeck Society members had purchased just over half of these. To recover costs, sales urgently needed to be increased, but attempts to market the diary proved fruitless. Even some twelve years after the Van Riebeeck festival, although the Dutch version had been sold out, 1,757 copies of the English edition remained unsold. This would seem to indicate that the diary in itself held little popular appeal, although the *Argus* did publish it in the form of a daily cartoon strip and *Die Burger* carried brief excerpts on a daily basis. But, in spite of its unpopularity in the form in which the Van Riebeeck Society produced it, the diary was crucial to validating the past of the festival. As had been the case at the beginning of the twentieth century, when the editing and publication of Voortrekker's diaries by Afrikaner nationalist historians had helped transform the concept of the movement of farmers into the interior of the country into the reality of a "Great Trek" that became "beyond dispute," so the publication of Van Riebeeck's diary made his past into empirically verifiable fact. It also gave a beginning and an associated scientific historicity to the notion of three hundred years of settlement that would encompass all that was made and selected to follow in the play of the past into the factual real.[43]

In a sense, Thom's role in authenticating the past for the Van Riebeeck festival through selecting the key events for the pageant of the past, refining the script, and editing the company record was an expected one. He had, after all, played a major role in contributing to public historical debates about the diary in the pages of *Die Huisgenoot,* was the prime mover behind the call to make Van Riebeeck Day a public holiday, and appeared on various committees associated with planning the festival from the mid-1940s. Probably even more significant in giving the past of the festival its authority, though, was that it became associated with the category of history rather than politics, the former identified with objectivity and neutrality, the latter tainted with partisan affiliations.

A clear indication that the festival was being distinguished as a historical moment came when the Council of the University of the Witwatersrand decided to commemorate the tercentenary by conferring eight honorary degrees on South Africans "who had distinguished themselves in connection with either the cultural and economic development of the Union, or the elucidation of its past, or the interpretation of its present problems to the world." Two features characterized the list of people the Witwatersrand University Council selected to receive these degrees. First, in a delicate balancing act, and in keeping with the festival's notion of a white nation drawing the English and Afrikaans races together, both Afrikaans- and English-speaking figures were awarded degrees. Sarah Gertrude Millin, the writer whom the University Council proclaimed as "uncontestably the most prominent South African writer of our generation in the English-speaking world"—many years later, the novelist James Coetzee described her as "a woman imbued with the racial prejudices of white South African society" who used "her novels as a means of propagating and justifying these principles"—was awarded a degree alongside the Afrikaans literary figures J. D. du Toit (Totius) and D. F. Malherbe. The

Afrikaans newspaper, *Die Vaderland*, praised the university for the latter two awards, maintaining it showed that the Afrikaans language belonged to all South Africans and was also the "heritage of the English speaking South African." Second, recognition was given to individuals who were involved in the production of history. The historian Eric Walker, whose work was cited as defining "the main outlines of the story of South Africa," Helen Mckay, the unofficial curator of the Africana collection at the university's library, and C. Graham Botha, South Africa's chief archivist between 1919 and 1944 were all awarded honorary degrees. It is difficult to establish direct connections between the work of these producers of history and the history being produced for Van Riebeeck in 1952. The closest link, perhaps, may be seen in the illustrations from Botha's *Our South Africa* (1938), used, with acknowledgment, for *Our Three Centuries*, which Victor de Kock compiled for the festival committee in 1952. Nonetheless, the recovery, systematizing, and writing of the past by these producers of history whom Wits University honored was being recognized as constituting part of a corpus of South African history that the festival could and did draw on. The honorary degrees bestowed on these historians gave the festival the aura of being about history as a scholarly pursuit and not a political or playful drama that the pageantry might invoke. The festival organizers viewed this as particularly important in order to counter the prediction made by a history lecturer at the University of the Witwatersrand, Arthur Keppel-Jones, that Afrikaner nationalists would use the pageantry associated with the festival to further their political aspirations.[44]

The organizing committee for Van Riebeeck seized on the opportunity to promote the festival as history of the white nation by arranging for the graduation ceremony to be broadcast nationally on radio by the South African Broadcasting Corporation. Yet, for all the publicity given to the honorary graduates and their achievements, the occasion did not entirely conform to the festival organizers' expectations. In his speech at the graduation ceremony, University Chancellor Richard Feetham used the concept of race to designate categories of white, non-European, and African instead of English and Afrikaans, the designations to be used in the festival. Arguing that the Van Riebeeck festival was an opportunity to "review the past and assess the future" along these much broader racial lines, he called on whites to use the knowledge derived from history and science about "the unity of the human race" to rid themselves of "the idea of innate racial superiority." More effort, he maintained, should be placed on developing an African intelligentsia which would serve its own people and the country as a whole so as to ensure that the South African nation would be built "together with them." This was certainly not the story of separate pasts and the growth of a white nation that the Van Riebeeck festival committee sought to portray and wanted to hear. Nevertheless, the activities surrounding the awarding of the honorary degrees to the English, the Afrikaners, and the producers of history still enabled the graduation ceremony to give a semblance of authenticity to Van Riebeeck's past, but perhaps not quite as much as he would have expected.[45]

Richard Feetham's slight subversion of the past of the festival was an indication that its reality effect was neither easy to control nor constitute merely by relying on the words of the Stellenbosch professor, the primary sources, and the notion that what was being dealt with was history. There were marked divisions over the makeup of a South African nation and its history. Once the draft scripts for the pageant of the past began to circulate in the public domain, sometimes inadvertently, these divisions began to manifest themselves. In building a nation on its own terms, the festival organizers often had to negotiate and accommodate these different histories into its History in order to legitimize its activities as broadly historical, rather than political.

Responsibility for the initial script for the historical procession lay with Anna Neethling-Pohl and members of the pageant committee, whom the festival organizers defined as people "well versed in history." Although they were averse to committing acts of "violence" against "the facts of history," this committee, which contained English and Afrikaans speakers in equal proportion, worked within a paradigm of presenting a past to and for Van Riebeeck that would entail "give and take" to make it into a broadly acceptable settler history. The result was that the first script that they approved for the historical procession in the streets of Cape Town (there had been six previous drafts for a stage show, based on discussions with Thom) was approved only after lengthy negotiations over the past in order to arrive at unanimity. This consensual past that was eventually scripted commenced in "Africa: Dark and Unknown" and ended with a float entitled "Africa Liberated." The intervening seventy-odd floats would emphasize European settlement, focusing on specific events that were determined as signifying aspects of English and Afrikaner pasts, including some of the tension between these two, and ending with a coming together in a white settler nation with an indigenous history constituted as South African. Among the people and events depicted as leading to settlement were to be the Portuguese seafarers, Vasco da Gama and Bartolomeu Dias, reaching the Cape and planting crosses; Sir Francis Drake reporting to Queen Elizabeth that he had just rounded the "fairest Cape"; and the "Flight of the Huguenots" from religious persecution in France in 1685 (eventually) to take up residence at the Cape. All this flurry of pre-(and post?) settlement activity lead to the scenes of the "*Nederlanders Se Volksplanting*" [Dutch *Volks* Planting] in 1652 with floats depicting the three ships in Van Riebeeck's fleet: the *Dromedaris, Reiger,* and *Goede Hoop.* After the moment of settlement, the Afrikaans and English races were to be forged separately in the pageant. Events that emphasized the past as a struggle for freedom, "The First Free Burghers," "The Revolt against William Adriaan van der Stel," and "The Great Trek," were presented as crucial in the making of the history of the Afrikaners. In the English history, in contrast, it was the contributions of individual personalities, "Lady Anne Barnard receives guests at a ball," "Lord Charles Somerset Goes a Hunting," and "Pringle and Fairbairn Fight for the freedom of the press," that were selected as significant moments for the pageant. Some of the conflicts between these two pasts were to be displayed: members of the London Missionary Society were presented in 1811 as falsely accusing the settlers of mistreating the local Khoisan inhabitants; in 1902, after scenes depicting the "*Tweede Vryheidsoorlog*" [Second War of Liberation] between the British and Boer forces, a group of sixty women and children, dressed in black mourning apparel, would march to signify the way the British had treated Boer women in concentration camps during the war. These conflicts would be remembered, but at the same time would make way for a process of unity of settlement and nationhood in a special "South African float" which would provide the finale. As "South Africa" would make its spectacular entrance into the specially constructed fifty thousand--seat stadium at the foreshore, it would be encircled by all the other floats of events and personalities of the past, bringing them together in an Africa that had just been seen to be liberated by a history presented as "white civilisation."[46]

Armed with this script, Anna Neethling-Pohl approached various commercial concerns based in Johannesburg, including the massive Anglo-American Corporation, to sponsor individual floats. Much to her alarm, they almost immediately raised objections about the omission of certain events from the pageant, such as the Act of Union in 1910, and the way that many of the depictions were offensive to whites who claimed to have an English ancestry. What this precisely alluded to became evident when the script was passed on to the press —by whom is not entirely clear—and one of Johannesburg's English language newspapers, the *Rand Daily Mail*, ran excerpts from the program with an accompanying editorial which maintained that the overwhelming impression being created in the pageant was one of an Afrikaner people struggling against their antagonists in the form of British domination. The two floats singled out were the ones dealing with the Boer War and the Philanthropists. The latter, the editorial asserted, was a gross distortion of the missionaries' efforts to bring "some kindly Christianity into the brutal frontier life," and the former, with its "legions of mourning women," was a "dainty dish for the racialists." To place the "race which produced Drake, Raleigh and Cook" into a South African past that was based on "partnership" rather than "bitterness," the *Mail* suggested there should be floats of the British defeating the Zulu, protecting Table Bay, mining gold, and fighting communist forces in Korea. This was clearly not the reaction Neethling-Pohl was hoping would emanate from her visit. Arthur

Wilson, the head of the Anglo-American Corporation's public relations division, expressed the sentiment that Neethling-Pohl had shown political naïveté in distributing the document in Johannesburg, rushing in like a fool "where angels fear to tread."[47]

Indeed, Neethling-Pohl's actions appeared to have had almost dire consequences for the organization of the festival as Transvaal industrialists threatened to withdraw en masse. Jacques Pauw, the organizing secretary for the festival, who had acquired a masters degree in history at Stellenbosch University in 1929—first studying under S. F. N. Gie and then Gie's successor, J. A. Wiid—and who had subsequently become a schoolteacher before taking up a post as the public relations officer of the Bloemfontein City Council, arrived in Johannesburg shortly after Neethling-Pohl's departure in order to encourage participation in the envisaged festival fair and met with a stony response. It seemed wherever he went the festival was being referred to as "a second Voortrekker Monument," a reference to some of the events at the inauguration in 1949, and a political maneuver for the Nationalists to win the 1953 election. This scenario for the Van Riebeeck festival, which had echoes of Keppel-Jones's book, was what the organizers had been desperately seeking to avoid through their insistence on the historic nature of the proceedings. It would seem that once the past the festival sought to portray was seen by Transvaal industry and the *Rand Daily Mail* to be hostile toward whites—who claimed an English heritage—it had crossed the border from history into politics. The Johannesburg National Party newspaper, *Die Transvaler,* on the other hand, hoped that the festival committee would not heed these criticisms, maintaining that to do so would be "a violation of the truth." The true history of South Africa, as *Die Transvaler* asserted it, was that "respectable Afrikaners" had been falsely accused by missionaries, that many of the self-same Afrikaners had moved northward because of British "misrule," and that the "imperialists and capitalists" had used the imprisonment of children and women in concentration camps to break Boer resistance. If this history were not to be part of Van Riebeeck's past, then, threatened *Die Transvaler,* Afrikaners would stay away from the festival.[48]

But Pauw was confident that the National Party, with the weight of its party organization, its affiliation with a myriad of cultural organizations, and its newly acquired state power would be able to sustain white Afrikaans-speaking support for the festival. His major concern was the grave implications that a withdrawal from the largest representatives of capitalist interests in the country —the Anglo-American Corporation and the Chamber of Mines—held for the Van Riebeeck festival. Not only might it indicate that the fair which he was directly involved in planning could flop, as other industrial concerns followed their example and withdrew, but that Van Riebeeck's claims to be asserting white "racial unity" in 1952 could be undermined. This closely echoed the sentiments of the editor of the *Benoni City Times* who argued that instead of "putting white against white" by consistently dredging up "the tragedies of the Anglo-Boer War," the festival should promote a "united race." This was largely a response to increasing African urbanization on the East Rand (where Benoni was located), which had taken place in the 1930s and 1940s as large numbers of secondary industries established their operations there. Conditions in many of the African townships in the area were particularly poor, and in the late 1940s and early 1950s more radical African political activity had emerged with the Communist Party mobilizing popular support around local grievances. The editor of the *Benoni City Times* articulated this as a "black peril," and he advocated that it was necessary to counter it with a racially exclusive white unity. The historical representations being proposed for 1952 would, according to him, merely serve to divide the white race and lead to a time in the near future when the country would be "overwhelmed by the Bantu." To defy this perceived threat, he suggested that the Van Riebeeck of the 1650s and the president of the Transvaal Republic during the Boer War in the 1890s, Paul Kruger, be brought together in a display of white "*EENDRAG*" [UNITY] in 1952.[49]

Pauw sought to cement this racially exclusive unity after cracks had begun to emerge when the pageant program had been inadvertently released to the press at the beginning of July 1951. He recommended that a massive publicity campaign be launched, which would draw in both the National and United Parties and thereby pronounce the festival as "non-political." Furthermore, he suggested to the festival fair committee that an investigation be instituted into how the script had been leaked and that public procedures be implemented to discipline whoever was responsible for releasing what was now conceptualized as an unauthorized past. Finally, he advised the committee to move quickly and publish a revised history without the "objectionable floats."[50]

Pauw moved swiftly to ensure that his proposals for damage control were implemented. Although there appears not to have been an internal inquiry into the release of the pageant script, he issued a statement saying that Van Riebeeck's past for 1952 had not yet been finally approved and that suggestions on historical items were still most welcome. The chairs of both the central and Cape Town committees issued statements that the festival would be "non-political" and, on 18 July 1951, released a final script that had been sanctioned by their respective committees and hastily approved by Thom. In this revised past a much more delicate balancing act was employed to produce a history that would find broader acceptability in what was envisaged as a white nation, especially from those interests who had financial muscle. The missionaries were no longer presented as false accusers but as "clashing" with "European settlers" over "treatment" of "the Hottentots." Instead of being enemies, the British and Boer generals were now to ride side by side as "great" leaders, "cou-

7. Certain incidents that showed conflict between what was perceived to be Afrikaner and British pasts had to be toned down for the Van Riebeeck festival. The float in the pageant of the past on the South African (Anglo-Boer) War was altered from a procession of Boer women, dressed in black, mourning the deaths in British camps, to one symbolizing "the end of republics and the courage and endurance of the Boer people." National Library of South Africa, Cape Town. Photo: *Cape Times.*

rageous" and "famous" strategists. After the Anglo-Boer War, the presentation would no longer be "The flags of the Republics at half-mast accompanied by women forming a guard of honour" but would simply be entitled "The End of the War." The women would no longer wear mourning apparel but would be dressed in white and escort a float that symbolized the demise of the Boer republics (Figure 7). Six drummers would herald the final chapter of the pageant entitled "THE ROADS CONVERGE" with floats depicting the Act of Union in 1910 (representatives of the colonies meeting "on equal footing"), portraying the recognition of Afrikaans and South African involvement in both world wars, with no mention of the intense and bloody conflicts that had taken place over the decision to participate. The final float would be a horse-drawn chariot, ridden by a young boy and girl bearing the South African flag and adorned with emblems of the provinces.[51]

This revised past was greeted with far more enthusiasm from the English-language dailies and the major industrial and commercial concerns in the country. In general they agreed that the committee, in presenting its program for the past, had been able to stabilize history, seen as a body of factual knowledge, with politics, seen as the arena of conflict between whites claiming different beliefs, thereby enabling the former to dissociate itself from the latter. Van Riebeeck's past, which now bore the official stamp of approval from the festival committee, was congratulated for eliminating events from the past which "could offend," producing a "picturesque," "dignified (if not comprehensive) survey of white South Africa's progress since 1952," and being "a faithful reflection of the cavalcade of South African history." The Cape Town Chamber of Commerce proclaimed the new past with its excisions and amendments to be "well conceived," and the Transvaal Chamber of Mines was now ready to embrace the festival with unbridled enthusiasm, promising to build the biggest mining exhibit ever seen in South Africa at the festival fair on a plot adjacent to a reconstruction of Van Riebeeck's birthplace, Culemborg. The only hesitation concerned how the scripted pageant would actually be translated into visual representations on the day of the pageant. Although the editor of the *Rand Daily Mail* was still wary, the editors of both *The Star* and the *Cape Times* were confident that, given the pronouncements from the festival committee and the way that conflicts over the historical episodes had been handled, this was an "exaggerated suspicion."[52]

Within Afrikaner nationalist circles, there was a less enthusiastic response to the depictions of the past that would now parade down Cape Town's main thoroughfare, Adderley Street. Their reactions were mostly, though not entirely, representative of the provincial divisions and different ambits of Afrikaner nationalist power. In the Cape, the Afrikaner nationalist movement had grown in the 1910s and 1920s in large measure on a well-established base of agricultural capital. From the security of this position, which had developed gradually over the past few decades, and a close affiliation with Van Riebeeck stretching back to the 1920s, *Die Burger*—which had started in 1915 with funding from Stellenbosch wine farmers—came out strongly in support of the revised festival program. The editor maintained that the script for the pageant had not distorted, sentimentalized, or erased episodes from the past for the sake of the festivities. Nonetheless, he added, in its work the committee had not highlighted the scenes of conflict and thus managed to present an impressive past "without fear or prejudice." In the northern provinces of the country, Afrikaner nationalists were far less pleased with the revised script. Being economically and politically less secure, much of their recent success had been based on the mobilization of an exclusive Afrikaner identity by a group of teachers, church ministers, and civil servants, which coalesced around the Afrikaner Broederbond and its affiliated cultural organizations, the ATKV and the FAK, as witnessed in the trek commemorations of 1938 and 1949. These groups had already been uneasy even in the early planning stages that the Van Riebeeck festival would at least neglect, and at most undermine, this sentiment, which had relied heavily on mobilizing an Afrikaner nationalist past. When the script of the past was published in July 1951, this cautionary approach again manifested itself, although the level of critique within different Afrikaner nationalist circles in the north varied. *Die Vaderland,* a newspaper associated with an older, and less virulent form of Afrikaner nationalism that identified itself with the former prime minister, Hertzog, for instance, lauded the festival committee for being able to produce what it called an objective past out of the profusion of conflicts between settlers. It did feel, nonetheless, that a large part in the pageant was being given to the "Small Englishmen in our midst," disproportionate to their role in South African history. It also wanted the Second World War taken out of the script, as it was too contemporary and too similar to the issues of current political conflicts, and indeed had led to a rift in the government over its participation in the war. *Die Transvaler,* which was linked more closely to the Afrikaner Broederbond and was deeply distrustful of the Cape branch of the party and its mouthpiece, *Die Burger,* was much more disparaging of the history being proposed for the pageant. Speaking on behalf of the "great majority of Afrikaners," it pointed to defects in the program that did not accord with "the Afrikaner who knew his national past and felt with it." This national past, according to *Die Transvaler,* was being undermined in various ways: the role of women in Afrikaner history had been neglected, and prominence had been accorded instead to the wife of a British official at the Cape, "the frivolous Lady Anne Barnard"; the constitutional development of the Union of South Africa was distorted, with all the accolades being heaped on the previous constitutions of the Cape and Natal and no recognition given to the achievements of the Boer republics in this regard; the Second World War had been incorrectly represented by overlooking the opposition to the war from many Afrikaners; and, in what it called the most serious omission, the women and children who died in concentration camps during the South African war were to have no "place in such an historical pageant." These excisions and distortions of what had previously been constituted as key and essential ingredients of an Afrikaner past led the editor of *Die Transvaler* to conclude that the Van Riebeeck festival was becoming "Not a True Reflection" of South African history and could lead to massive protests from Afrikaners. A letter to the newspaper the following week echoed these sentiments and reminded readers how a watered-down version of Afrikaner "tradition" had threatened to dominate the proceedings at the inauguration of the Voortrekker Monument in 1949.[53]

These objections were taken a step further at the beginning of August when members of an ATKV delegation presented a list of observations on the pageant to a Mr. Reeler of the festival's central committee. Their remarks closely resembled the objections raised in *Die Transvaler* but went further to outline general principles the delegates felt had not been properly considered. They wanted answers to certain questions: How had it been decided to incorporate some historical events and exclude others? Was spectacle or historical value the criterion? How were organizations allocated to their respective presentations (with English organizations being given more prominence than their Afrikaans cultural counterparts)? And how was the actual historical content of the floats being determined (for example, by what procedure was it decided that certain events, like the Great Trek—"on itself enough for an entire programme"—were to be reduced to singular episodes in South African history)? Regarding specific examples, members of the ATKV delegation pointed to the inclusion of what they saw as unimportant and meaningless events in the pageant—for example, a hunting party given by the British governor, Lord Charles Somerset; a dance hosted by Lady Anne Barnard; and the Dutch governor, Simon Van der Stel, riding in his coach—at the expense of what they viewed as "influential and far reaching" historical processes, such as the role played by Afrikaner women in South African history. The delegation called on the festival committee to clarify these and other issues and to publicize more broadly the names of those taking part in the proceedings.[54]

Although the outcome of the above meeting was never reported, the protest actions *Die Transvaler* had predicted did not materialize. One change which was made in the pageant was to label the Republic of the Orange Free State a "'Model' State" so as to counter the Cape colony as the bearer of constitutional development. Despite this modification, the ATKV was not satisfied with the outcome of the negotiations. So, much to the ire of Anna Neethling-Pohl, the ATKV, and the FAK increasingly withdrew from participating in the Cape Town events so as to organize local Van Riebeeck festivals in the Transvaal where they could have greater say over the content. The ATKV invested far more time and energy in organizing the mail coach processions throughout the country. In addition to rambling off to their own terrains, the Afrikaner nationalist organizations in the north went to great lengths to devise schemes which would highlight the role of Afrikaner women in the portrayals of South African history. The *Vrou en Moeder Beweging* (Wife and Mother Movement), the women's equivalent of the ATKV, offered its expertise to towns and cities in the Pretoria-Witwatersrand region to assist in arranging historical depictions of Afrikaner women. Floats such as "South African Womanhood" and "Wife and Mother" began to appear in local Van Riebeeck festivals. For the national commemoration in Cape Town, the pageant sub-committee provisionally approved the design of a float originally entitled "Womanhood" for the "Pageant of the Present"—which was to take place directly after the "Historical Pageant"—but suggested that its appellation be altered to "Woman and Motherhood" to reflect "all aspects of the activities of women." These aspects, as they appeared "enthroned" on the float, asserted a seemingly natural progression in the lives of all women, moving in four phases from infancy to youth, marriage, and, ultimately, the "perfection" of motherhood. This was clearly in accord with the *Vrou en Moeder Beweging*, whose president had claimed, in 1948, that, despite women having moved into occupations previously occupied by men during the Second World War, their primary "purpose in life was to marry and rear children."[55]

Other than portraying woman as wife and mother in the float processions, this image was promoted by popularizing the icon of Maria van Riebeeck as the housewife who devoted her life to Jan and other "womanly" tasks. The government's Department of Agriculture, which, since 1949, had published the "first Official Journal for the Housewife," *The Woman and her Home*, produced a special edition for the Van Riebeeck festival with a front cover showing "The Wife of Kommandeur Jan van Riebeeck." Among its contents for discussion were "The Cape in 1655–1656," "The Costumes in the Time of Jan van Riebeeck," How to "Plan Housework"—which included caring for children, preparing meals, cleaning, gardening, shopping, care of domestic animals, relaxation, and entertaining guests—and "Typical Dutch Recipes." The issuing of one-penny stamps depicting a portrait of Maria by Dick Craey, which formed part of a commemorative set for the tercentenary, also brought Maria's image into the household. To memorialize the "kindly, devoted and tolerant," "Mrs. Van Riebeeck," the Cape Town City Council named a street after her, and the Dutch royal family signaled its intention, on behalf of the people of Holland, to present Jan and the city with a statue of "his spouse," Maria. This Maria was given a history of her own, through the publication, in Holland—under the auspices of *Zuid-Afrikaansche Stichting Moederland* [South African Foundation Motherland]—of the biography of the "Housewife of Jan van Riebeeck," who accompanied her husband to the furthest reaches and enabled him to accomplish his tasks in the world. The Afrikaans woman's magazine, *Sarie Marais*, began a "Search for Jan van Riebeeck's Wife" to play that role in the pageant of the landing of the *Dromedaris* at Granger Bay. The essential criteria for the part required that she be small in stature, about twenty-three years of age, and have dark eyes and light brown hair so as to match the Craey portrait. No acting ability was necessary; selection would be based on the contestant's resemblance to Craey's painting based on a photograph displaying a head and shoulders portrait, which contestants were asked to submit—"snapshots" were inadmissible. The winner would receive £75, a trip to Cape Town, an appropriate costume to wear, and the honor of standing silently alongside the eminent South African actor, André Huguenet, who had been specially chosen to play the part of Jan van Riebeeck, first onboard the *Dromedaris,* then on the beach of Granger Bay, and later on the balcony at the Castle. Her only duty was to serve wine to her husband and the accompanying soldiers and then to present Jan with the cask containing the "Treasury of the Nation."[56]

Maria's emergence from virtual obscurity in South African history to become Jan's silent partner on the beach at Granger Bay was partly related to the centrality of the discourse of *volksmoeder* to Afrikaner nationalism since the latter years of the first decade of the twentieth century. The maternal duty of Afrikaner women in the service of the *volk* was built around images of the suffering mother and child during the South African War, promoted by the Afrikaans poet Totius, in magazines and newspapers like *De Zuid-Afrikaan* and *Die Brandwag* and through organizations like the *Afrikaanse Christelike Vroue Vereniging* [Afrikaner Christian Women's Organization] (ACVV). This allusion of maternal duty to the *volk* was later encapsulated in the *Vrouemonument* [Women's Monument], which was unveiled in Bloemfontein in 1913; its central image was that of a statue of a seated, forlorn-looking woman with a dying child in her arms. Standing behind her is another woman, in Voortrekker garb and bonnet, who gazes toward the horizon. A plaque, inscribed on the monument, indicates that it was erected "to remember the 26,370 women and children who died in concentration camps and other women and children who died in the war 1899–1902." Although the proceedings around the unveiling of the monument did not emphasize motherhood, the visual imagery was of a "weeping victim," a suffering, stoical mother of children whose image was expanded to become the mother of the *volk,* defined through the monument as the "Fatherland." The appearance of this *volksmoeder* discourse in the first decade of the twentieth century largely arose from the concern, particularly among Dutch-Afrikaans–speaking men, about women's changing role in society, the heated discussions around the extension of the franchise to women, and the increasing numbers of women entering both the educational sphere and the workplace. Women's organizations like the ACVV were also extending and defending their operations beyond the realm of the home. In this context it was not sufficient to regard Afrikaner women as merely part of the domestic sphere but to incorporate the private domain of mothering into the service of the *volk.* In the 1920s, with white Afrikaans-speaking women moving into urban areas in ever larger numbers and taking up employment in factories, and with the enfranchisement of white women becoming imminent, patriarchal relations of domination in "white" households came under increasing threat. Within Afrikaner nationalist circles it became increasingly necessary politically to actively encourage women to enter the public sphere, but still to define this participation through the home and the mother. A consistent attempt was made to promote a link between motherhood and serving the needs of the Afrikaner nation through magazines like *Die Huisgenoot* and *Die Boerevrou*. Coupling ethnic and gender identities through the idealized "mother in the house" as a universal category provided the bonding to shore up the imagined community of white Afrikaners. *Die Boerevrou* linked motherhood with the promotion of the "Afrikaner nation." Afrikaner women were assigned the task of bearing, rearing, and educating Afrikaner children for the *volk*, both in the private sphere of the home and in the public arena of welfare organizations. To be an effective *volksmoeder* meant to reproduce not only in physiological terms but also to advance the *volk* through "support [of], interest [in] and dedication" to an Afrikaner history, language and culture.[57]

The construction of the *volksmoeder* not only relied on establishing a sense of internal coherence but also on situating the discourse in opposition to an external identity posed as a threat, in this case black men and women. This "peril" was located within both the domestic and public spheres, where job protection and maintaining the "purity" of Afrikaners in the household were articulated, in magazines like *Die Boerevrou*, by asserting racial exclusivity and superiority. In the 1930s the much more virulent form of Afrikaner nationalism which emerged under the auspices of the *Gesuiwerede Nasionale Party* (Purified National Party) and the Afrikaner Broederbond took this racial enmity even further, railing against trade unions like the Garment Workers' Union for not providing adequate job security for its members, who were largely white Afrikaner women, protesting against black workers in the clothing industry, and conducting election campaigns around the issue of racially mixed marriages. In the 1938 general election campaign, Afrikaner men were cast as the saviors of white women from the "grasp" of black men. This campaign was used to reassert the control which Afrikaner men had gradually lost, as women were becoming both sexually and economically independent in urban environments. The idea of *volksmoeder* encompassed and indeed depended on this sense of a racial othering to demarcate its boundaries and constitute its communal membership. Visually this was embodied in the statue of a Voortrekker woman that stood thirteen feet high at the entrance to the Voortrekker Monument, providing protection to two children. The statue, in the words of the monument's designer and architect, Gerard Moerdyk, was to mark the pivotal role that Voortrekker women had played in bringing whiteness to the southern African interior by accompanying their husbands. In its position of prominence it was symbolic of "White South Africa" warding off the forces of darkness and "barbarity" as represented in the sculptures of black *wildebeeste* [gnus] embedded in the rock alongside it. The zigzag design at the top of the actual monument was intended to symbolize fertility and the *volksmoeder* in her reproductive role in "making and keeping South Africa a white man's country."[58]

When members of the FAK went to Reeler to express their misgivings about the proposed pageant, it was precisely on these grounds of asserting and maintaining racial purity that they articulated their disappointment over the exclusion of women from Van Riebeeck's history for 1952. It was the women, they asserted, who had provided the men with white companions and who had held the family together, and thereby women were "absolutely essential" in ensuring "the whiteness of the developing *volk*." An article, "Pioneer Life of the First Farmers," that appeared in the special Van Riebeeck festival edition of *The Woman and Her Home* similarly placed great emphasis on the role of the woman as homemaker in the sense of maintaining both domesticity and racial purity in the "unsettled" world of the frontier. Women were commended for turning the wagon into a home where they could make clothes, soap, biltong (jerked meat), and bread. It was also through marriage that the women enabled the men to preserve "their race," the "bond" preventing those "who for two centuries had so little contact with the civilised world, from falling into miscegenation."[59]

Much as the Van Riebeeck festival was not a direct outcome of the political machinations of Afrikaner nationalism, this emphasis on white women in 1952, symbolized in the iconization of Maria, was not solely an extension of *volksmoeder* discourse. Her image was also being popularized as the Cape's first lady, in the sense of being the wife of a colonial governor of the Cape—although Van Riebeeck was not a governor but a commander—and someone who combined tolerance with an appropriate application of knowledge. In this appellation as a "lady" she acquired a series of physical and moral virtues: "fair skin and intelligent eyes" with a look that spoke of "decisiveness" and "virtuous yet distinguished womanhood," "dark hair and a generous mouth," "practical common sense," "courage and determination," and "patience and understanding." This "charming woman," with a much less ambiguously noble ancestry than Jan's, bore a very close resemblance to the colonial images of Lady Anne Barnard that Dorothy Fairbridge had fostered in the 1910s and 1920s which were now being advertised in the program for the pageant of the past as those of "culture and refinement." As with Lady Anne, it was this gentility that enabled Maria to "bring the races together" by hosting parties of both English and Dutch men at the fort in an imaginary "little Colony." Maria de la Quellerie became a "woman of breeding," who, after being welcomed by "a group of savages" at the Cape, lived a "lonely, isolated life" because she had no one from "her own social sphere" with whom to communicate, and she feared the "little, brown Hottentot men." Yet it was this isolation that made Maria, more than Jan (who sometimes dirtied his hands in the employ of the Company) the bearer of a European racial essence that was constituted in social terms as innately aristocratic, her blue blood bestowing on the Company fort the title of "THE FIRST HOME" at the Cape "colony."[60]

Maria's colonial imagery coalesced with a shift that was starting to occur in Afrikaner nationalist discourses of women in the 1950s. The narrative of Afrikaner women as housewives and mothers of the community of the *volk* began to incorporate a much greater sense of modernity rather than relying on a traditional past. This was no more evident than in the magazine, *Sarie Marais*, that had launched the search for Maria de la Quellerie. Published in the Cape by Nasionale Pers, which also published *Die Burger*, it marketed itself primarily to young Afrikaans-speaking women. Although it included items of historical interest, its areas of concentration were stories of romance and how Afrikaner women had achieved success. An example of the latter was a feature by André Huguenet, where he looked at the role of five women who were involved in staging, and acting in, dramatic productions. Included in Huguenet's article was a brief account dealing with the founder of the *Volksteater* [National Theater] in Pretoria, Anna Neethling-Pohl. In 1951–52 *Sarie Marais* also ran a controversial column entitled "Tell Me Doctor," in which a doctor gave advice to "mothers, young women, daughters" on "specific ailments and dangers to which they are exposed as women." The magazine received a flood of letters, some offering support for the informative function the column was supposed to be performing, but others condemning it for showing no respect for the privacy of the body. The editor defended the column on the basis that medical knowledge was an absolute necessity for the modern woman. This modern woman, as characterized on the front cover of *Sarie Marais*, wore the latest fashions, smoked cigarettes—which were manufactured by the Rembrandt Tobacco Corporation in factories where the employment of "white girls" was preferred—and drank tea. The latter image represented a marked shift away from *Die Boerevrou* where the drinking of coffee had been the metaphorical device used to draw the women into a bounded community around the imaginative ceremony of imbibing the *volksdrank* [*volk*'s drink]. Drinking tea was regarded as the preserve of those who were "uppity" and would not associate with the "real" *boerevrou* around the coffee table. By 1952 tea drinking had become associated with a knowledge of the modern world, and the "Women of South Africa" became "ladies" who were now to be found sitting "Round the Tea Table" discussing matters of topicality rather than communality.[61]

Although white women were still identified with the home and Maria was given the appellation of "THE FIRST HOME MAKER," the person who won the competition to "Act Van Riebeeck's Wife at [the] Festival" was more than merely a face to match the Craey portrait. Frances Holland from Durban was an actress who had appeared on stage, in movies, and on radio. Apparently quite fortuitously she was, as well, a descendant of both the 1820 settlers from England and the Voortrekker leader Andries Pretorius, thus embodying (and reproducing) the drawing together of the European "races" which Lady Anne Barnard and Maria de la Quellerie had previously worked toward and which Jan van Riebeeck was ritualizing in 1952. Her husband, Douglas Fuchs, was the regional director of the South African Broadcasting Corporation in Natal, a good friend of André Huguenet, and the chair of the Durban Van Riebeeck festival committee. Yet it was as Frances Holland and not as Mrs. Douglas Fuchs that Maria took her place on the beach alongside André Huguenet in 1952. In a ceremony from which she had previously been excluded by both the Company diarist and the artistic imagination of Charles Davidson Bell, she now "stood at Jan's side in the presence of the men who formed his small band of pioneers and . . . listened to the simple service when he planted the flag."[62]

The "Hunt for the 'Ideal South African Woman' " did not manage entirely to clear the way for the landing of the Van Riebeecks on 5 April 1952 and the production of their past in the streets of Cape Town on the preceding two days. Indeed, it was the overseers of Van Riebeeck's city, Cape Town, where Van Riebeeck had landed and where the mayor presided over Council meetings in a seat named Van Riebeeck's chair, that were proving to be a major obstacle to staging the past. The central committee had estimated that the cost of the festival would be in the region of £350,000. With the government willing to provide a £125,000 sponsorship and the Cape Provincial Administration £50,000, the Cape Town City Council was asked to contribute £75,000 to make up some of the leeway. Taking into account the income that would be derived from visitors to the city during the period of the festivities and the possibility that any surplus funds could be used to develop a cultural center in Cape Town, the festival committee did not view such a proposal as unreasonable. But with the city facing a deficit of almost 1 million pounds and accusations in the local press that spending the money on one festival would be extravagant, the City Council vacillated for more than six months before deciding the amount it would contribute toward the festival.[63]

Given the Cape Town City Council's interest in the mid-1940s in organizing the annual wreath-laying ceremony at the base of the statue on Adderley Street, its initial enthusiasm for organizing its own Van Riebeeck festival, and the mayor's participation on both the central and Cape Town committees which the government had appointed for the festival, such a lukewarm response may seem surprising. Clearly pecuniary issues were at stake, as the City Council had not envisaged spending large sums of money when it had initially embraced the idea of a Van Riebeeck festival. The Town Clerk, in 1948, had drawn on the examples of the "simple thanksgiving service[s]" in 1752 and 1852 to advocate a similar type of commemoration in 1952.[64] But the major problem lay with the manner in which the various festival committees were constituting Van Riebeeck for 1952, with the city having hardly any say in the portrayals of the past, despite it constituting the central stage. When the opposing factions lined up against each other in the City Council, it was the historical depictions that had already been decided on for Van Riebeeck and "his city" that were the battleground of the heated exchanges over monetary allocations.

One group led by Joyce Newton Thompson—the wife of Justice Newton Thompson, who had delivered the speech prior to D. F. Malan at the inauguration ceremony of the Voortrekker Monument—attempted to persuade the Council to approve the £75,000 allocation. Newton Thompson, like her husband, was concerned with establishing a national identity based on a sense of Europeanness. She was responsible for bringing to life, for the 1952 pageant, the Thompson-Uys meeting on the eastern Cape frontier, which had been inscribed on the frieze of the Voortrekker Monument. Her successful idea for the float was that Martin Thompson, the great-great-grandson of William Rowland Thompson, the frontier merchant, would take the part of his great-great-grandfather and hand over a Bible to Jacobus Uys, the Voortrekker leader, who would be portrayed by Jacobus Uys "of this generation complete with whiskers and beard grown for the occasion." By reviving this minor incident, linking the past and present through the "blood of the fathers," writing the magistrate, who had actually handed over the Bible in 1838, out of history (William Rowland Thompson had made the address prior to the presentation), and defining the partnership down the generations through a mutual symbol representing a founding document of civilization, the float was intended to impress upon viewers "the harmonious working together of the two principal European races in this country." In this framework of European nationing, the City Council was being "tarred with the brush" and accused of being miserly through its reluctance to contribute a substantial amount to the "national event," to play its "civic" role as "the oldest city in South Africa," where "white men first settled" and to demonstrate how it had guarded "the hedge he [Van Riebeeck] planted to show the Hottentot marauders how far they should go."[65]

Those opposing the Cape Town City Council grant to the festival came from a variety of positions. Mention has already being made of problems with the form of the past and fears that the moving pageant could possibly turn history into a farce. There were also objections similar to those of the *Rand Daily Mail*, with specific reference being made to the float depicting the "Downfall of Republics" as stirring up animosity between the "European races." Further disapproval revolved around how the settler nations of "civilized" South Africa were being selected, including German immigrants but excluding Scandinavians, Jews, and people of Eastern Europe. The most substantial objection with the history that had been selected for the pageant of the past was that it had, by and large, omitted "non-Europeans" from the nation and that, when they had been incorporated, it was in negative terms of darkness and barbarity shown to contrast with the light of "European civilisation."[66]

A Cape Town City Council group, led by Sam Kahn, had voiced this last objection. Later, Kahn argued at Council meetings in 1951 that although historical depictions considered offensive to sections of the white population claiming an English heritage had been removed from the past, no such sensitivities were being displayed with "scenes depicting the Native people." He specifically referred to the floats "Africa Dark and Unknown" and "The Pioneers on the Border Face Disaster" as spectacles where the blacks were shown "solely in a primitive and barbarous state." Kahn went further to present suggestions for the inclusion and alteration of some of the scenes. Depicting the emancipation of slaves was, in his terms, an absolute priority for a national history, and this should be linked to the movement of farmers northward in the "Great Trek." Furthermore, the context in which certain historical depictions were being framed, he argued, should be changed so as to incorporate generalized notions of, and struggles for, liberty and freedom. For instance, the float that had been re-named "The Clash with the Philanthropists" after industrial concerns in the Transvaal had voiced objections, he suggested, was a "falsification of history"; it should show, instead, how missionaries had enabled the process of slave emancipation to take place and how they had consistently pointed to the inhumane treatment of black laborers. The "Freedom of the Press" float, which emphasized the "independent" development of the settler population, he asserted, should become more all-embracing and encapsulate the "Struggle for Personal Liberty." Kahn viewed the scripted pageant of Van Riebeeck's past, as it stood, merely to reflect a limited notion of South African nationhood, encompassing only whites, and he therefore believed that the City Council should not contribute a single penny toward the festival.[67]

Although Kahn did not have whole-hearted support in the Council for his recommendation, the Council had sufficient reservations not to approve the £75,000 until a specially designated deputation had met with the Cape Town committee of the Van Riebeeck festival to discuss the Council's concerns about the program. The meeting with the delegation, led by Kahn, which took place on 24 August 1951, was quite unremarkable; the Cape Town committee studiously noted down every point made, promised to pass the queries on to the pageant committee, and then said it would forward a reply as hastily as possible to the Council's finance committee so that it could make a recommendation on sponsoring the festival. Five days later the pageant committee met and sat for four hours drafting a response to the City Council, hoping that in so doing they would show that they had "honestly endeavoured to portray Western Civilization in South Africa" and would thereby "satisfy critics."[68]

The pageant committee, forced to articulate a link between specific historical episodes it intended to portray and the thematic conceptualization of the
festival, forwarded a document to the finance committee of the Cape Town
City Council in September 1951 that attempted to clarify and justify its nationing claims. This was expounded in two ways. The first reasserted the festival as
a display of a nation with a past that was historically authentic. Many of Kahn's
suggestions and amendments were carefully and meticulously attacked, on
"historical grounds," as inaccurate and false. Conversely, items included in the
pageant program were defended as "objective portrayals of historical facts."
The prime example of this resort to historicity was when the document dealt
with Kahn's proposal that the emancipation of slaves be linked to the "Great
Trek." Using Theal's *History of South Africa* and Agar Hamilton's *Native Policy
of the Voortrekkers,* the committee provided evidence that the trekkers had not
opposed the "gradual manu-mission" of slaves and that, when they had established independent Republics in the north, slavery had been outlawed. In these
terms, Kahn's suggestion was not only inappropriate but was totally out of
order as it was a "falsification of history." When it came to giving the pageant
as a whole a historical stamp of approval, the authority on which the document drew was the Superintendent General of Education, Dr. W. de Vos Malan,
who had praised the scripted past for its "accuracy, completeness and imparti-
ality." [69] Even though the decision not to evoke the word of Prof. H. B. Thom
in this specific context might have been because of his close association with
Afrikaner nationalist politics, the choice of de Vos Malan seemed to infer that
history, as it was transmitted in the classroom, was the generally approved and
acceptable past.

Second, the document explicitly provided a racial classification for the nationing that the festival and pageant were attempting to display. The nation
and its past with which the festival was concerned, the document claimed, were
those of the "European race groups" from England, Holland, France, and Germany who, in the committee's terms, were responsible for the "growth and
development of Western Civilization in South Africa." Those who were considered not to have this line of descent, "the Coloured and African," were assigned to different racial categories of "non-European" and "native" and would
be incorporated into exclusive pasts and allocated a "Special Pageant." This
was more than merely a reiteration of some of the suggestions that had been
made during the early planning stages of the festival, when the idea of possible
separate displays for coloureds had been mooted by the FAK. Faced with the
need to specify the nation racially, the organizers were now defining the "non-
European" as a counter to "us," the "pure" and, at the same time, indigenous
South African "European" nation. The latter would provide assistance to the
former to "find his place [and his past] in the pattern of this new unity-in-

diversity of the South African state." This "place" would be "his own legitimate sphere" in separate nations defined by racial essence.[70]

Of course, problems arose when this racial separation being proposed for the festival was countered by the "facts," as suggested in a letter written to the *Cape Argus*. The writer claimed that, as the Dutch governor Simon van der Stel's mother was an Indian woman from Mauritius, a coloured man should play that role in the pageant. Such supposed "facts," which could prove to be uncomfortable, were not even considered by the pageant committee. Instead, it stuck rigidly to the general guidelines to be followed for "non-European" participation in the Van Riebeeck festival that insisted on "special" events for those who were not part of the "new nation." On the one hand, these events were to display an essential "non-European" lifestyle: "tribal" structures, "natural" musical rhythms, craftwork, and home industries. On the other hand, there were clear guidelines to exhibit "the influence of Western civilization on the Non-whites." This involved replacing the superstitious with the rational—the "disappearance of witchcraft"—the "old tribal laws" with "Western" forms of government, polygamy with "family life," and incessant "tribal wars" with "Personal Freedom." Ultimately, under "Western" tutelage, the outcome would be the development of separate, but as yet not clearly defined, "Non-White independent units."[71]

On the basis of these guidelines, the festival committee decided that for those they defined as the "native population," the festivities would consist of events depicting "the meaning of white civilization for the Natives." Primarily this would be visible through a display which would be constructed at the festival fair by the Native Affairs Department (NAD), depicting a "Bantu village" that would show the transformation of "native life" from a state of tribalism to one of modernity, under the guidance of Europeans. In the latter state the "Bantu" would be able to "serve his own people." There was to be no pageant in the streets of Cape Town in which Africans could participate, but the NAD planned to hold a "*Bantoe-fees* [festival for the Bantu]" in the township of Langa where there would be sporting activities, open-air film shows, and choir competitions and where "a number of cattle would be slaughtered for the people." These planned events, when linked through the festival with the symbols of white nationhood in the past and present, were a component of the government's attempts to portray the control and management of the growing urban African population by the Native Affairs Department "as part of the natural evolution and structuring of South African society." Africans were marked as essentially tribal, having no place in the city except as sojourners to perform laboring tasks, although the specific terms of their temporary location were contested and remained undefined until the late 1950s. Their natural place and history were therefore defined not in "the west," but in a "separate sphere" where the modernizing "tribe" would enable them to "cultivate their traditions." In the western Cape, this took on a very distinctive form: the implementation of a policy that gave preferential employment to laborers who were racially labeled as "coloured" rather than "native." Through the Coloured Labour Preference Policy (which was also administered through the NAD), the western Cape, and Cape Town in particular, was constructed as "unAfrican," a place of European founding and settlement with workers who were "coloured" and not essentially "tribal." One "ratepayer," who urged the Council to support the Van Riebeeck festival, described areas where Africans lived in the Cape Peninsula, like Windermere, as a "stain . . . at our main entrance." With Africans excised from "the west," from its cities, its histories, and its place of founding (the "mother city"), it is not altogether surprising that, when Van Riebeeck landed at Granger Bay in 1952, he found that "the Bantu" were "not indigenous to South Africa." In fact, he "never saw the Bantu" until the second half of the eighteenth century when "Governor Joachim van Plettenberg . . . established the Fish River as the boundary between the European and the non-European." As the *Rand Daily Mail* put it, rather facetiously, there was not even going to be a "very small float, somewhere at the back" which contained a hint of a suggestion that "the non-Europeans may have taken some little part in the development of the country."[72]

People who were defined not as "natives" or "Bantu" but still "non-European," were to "organize their own program" under the direction of the Commissioner for Coloured Affairs, I. D. du Plessis. A special day in the final week of the festival program, prior to the "People's Pageant" and the landing of Van Riebeeck, was to be set aside "for the Coloured and Malay communities." Anna Neethling-Pohl would assist in organizing events for the day which would take place in the main arena, the fifty-thousand–seater festival stadium, on Wednesday, 2 April. Clearly people designated coloured were being assigned a past in the "progress" of "western civilization" but still apart from Van Riebeeck and his history. This accorded with notions of coloureds as "good old types" who were "reliable" workers and docile subjects. Indeed, until the 1920s, Afrikaner nationalists considered some coloureds, who spoke Afrikaans and generally followed the Islamic religion, and were specified as Malay, to be part of South African history as the oldest element of the *volk* who had arrived at the same time as the whites and had always been civilized. Only when Afrikaner identity became associated much more closely with whiteness, particularly in the 1930s, did a Malay identity as separate and clearly distinguishable from an Afrikaner one become widely promoted. I. D. du Plessis, the poet and journalist who held a post as lecturer in the Department of Afrikaans and Nederlands at the University of Cape Town before devoting his full-time attention to the Coloured Affairs Department, spent a great deal of time constructing a Malay history and culture, so much so that D. F. Malan labeled him the "king of the Malays." In 1944 Du Plessis published a book entitled *The Cape Malays* in which he defined a "pure" Malay physical type—just over five foot tall, with "olive skin," a "flattish face, high cheekbones, black (slightly slanting) eyes, a small nose, wide nostrils, a large mouth, hands and feet small and delicately formed, thin legs, coarse, straight black hair and a sparse beard." He also assigned them specific customs and traditions, among these the "Malay sword dance known as the *Chalifah*" and the "magic" of "Malay tricks." And, finally, he selected a Malay history for them which revolved around a Van Riebeeck–type founder figure in the form of Sheik Yusuf, who was banished to the Cape from the Dutch East Indies in 1694, and which included their participation in battles alongside colonial troops, sometimes against the "natives" on the frontier. When Du Plessis was appointed chair of the "Malay and Coloured" sub-committee of the Van Riebeeck festival, he brought all this "knowledge of the Malay" with him. He concentrated on developing a program for Malay participation in the festival that virtually coincided with the various sections in his book. There were two elements to this. The first consisted of an exhibition of Malay arts and crafts that was to be displayed as part of the "Historical Exhibition of the Arts" in the Castle of Good Hope, but in a "coffee room specially set aside by the military authorities." The exhibition was to be one of colour, "customs, rituals and observances," where the work on display was not categorized as art (as was the rest of the exhibition in the Castle) but as a collection of domestic household items that revealed the "lure of the exotic" in Malay "civilisation and culture." Second, the script for the Malay pageant on Wednesday, 2 April, that Du Plessis presented to the festival committee was saturated with the religion, customs, traditions, and "tricks" of the Cape Malay that he had re-produced in his published text. At the beginning of the procession, of course, there was history, and Sheik Yusuf was to step ashore with two wives, fourteen friends, and some servants to be welcomed by the governor of the Cape. For coloureds who were not defined as Malay, no details had yet been worked out, but a space in the program was left open so as to allow "any organised coloured groupings" the opportunity to take part in Van Riebeeck's festival.[73]

The finance committee did not receive all the details on "non-white" participation outlined above but, on the basis of the explanation and information for "special events" that was conveyed to it, it decided to recommend to the City Council that it should contribute £50,000 toward the festival. Kahn considered the festival committee's reply to be lame and feeble; all it did was display how the events being conceptualized would be discriminatory, partisan, and laden with historical distortions. He argued that £50,000 was still excessive and reiterated that the Council should make no monetary grant to the festival. Other members of the Council, unwilling to antagonize the government and the festival committee, were more willing to compromise, and, after a three-and-half-hour debate behind closed doors on 27 September 1951, the Council decided, by a vote of 18 to 15, to contribute only £25,000. Joyce Newton Thompson was incensed, and on 12 October 1951 she submitted a motion for the decision to be rescinded and for the Council to grant at least £50,000 toward Van Riebeeck and his festival. Her call received the support of the editors of both *Die Burger* and the *Cape Times,* the former accusing the Council of merely penny-pinching and the latter claiming it was causing irreparable harm by playing the "dog in the manger role" and voting to contribute a totally insufficient amount. Other councilors also backed the resolution to rescind the £25,000 grant in order to "further race relations," where races were defined in terms of European derivatives.[74] Kahn rejected these pleas for reconsideration out of hand.

> If I thought this was being organized truly as representative of Western civilization I would have supported it. But what Western civilization has apartheid? This Festival is a tawdry, meretricious interpretation of our history. It entirely excludes non-Europeans. The challenge to us is whether we regard non-Europeans as part of our nation or not. If our slogan is "We Build a Nation" the non-Europeans must take part. But the Government is slashing and dividing the nation. Their motto should be "We Divide a Nation."[75]

Once again a lengthy debate ensued and when the time came to vote, the Council was split exactly down the middle (19 votes for and 19 against). After it had "wrangled for months for the few paltry pounds to be spent," the original motion to grant £25,000 to the festival stood, and the promoters of Van Riebeeck accused Cape Town of forgetting South Africa.[76]

Yet the Cape Town City Council had not abandoned Van Riebeeck entirely. As Fritz Sonnenberg, the mayor of Cape Town, pointed out, the City's Engineers' Department had spent huge amounts of time clearing up and transforming the "sandy waste" of the reclaimed foreshore into a suitable festival venue. At its own cost—£10,000—it had floodlit the approaches and a replica of the Van Riebeeck statue, provided a parking area, and erected temporary street lighting. With funding from the festival committee, it had constructed a temporary sub-station and installed the necessary cables to provide electricity to the site where the pavilions and the stadium were located. The festival committee was later billed £84,530 by the Council for these services, which included £7,924 for traffic control. When the latter amount was queried by the festival committee, which considered it part of the normal line of the traffic officers' duty, it was reduced by £5,000 in consideration for the "underlying purposes of the festival." The Town Planning Department supervised the layout of the fairgrounds and the tent camps where visitors could stay and arranged the location of parking areas and the stadium. The Council also provided £12,000 for building a Cape Town pavilion at the festival fair, allowed the festival free use of the City Hall and the City orchestra (salaries of members for the period, totaling £5,374, were met by the Council), and sent a bust of Van Riebeeck which cost £473 to the town of Culemborg. Finally, the Council paid for an advertisement for Cape Town inside the official festival program at a price of £150. Kahn consistently opposed many of these allocations but was unable to put a halt to the support for these various projects by the Council. The only other festival scheme the Council opposed was sponsoring a mail coach, claiming it was illogical to have a Cape Town coach approaching its own city. Given these contributions to his past, Van Riebeeck could not have been entirely unhappy with the Cape Town City Council. Also consistent with the emerging policies of racial separation and domination that the government was pursuing was the scheme to "eliminate . . . black spots" in the Cape Peninsula where Africans were squatting on the borders of "European" territory and to erode any voting power Africans might have had in municipal regions by zoning areas where they lived into single large wards, thus effectively reducing the number of councilors they could vote for. Indeed, in one instance the central committee used Cape Town as an example of how apartheid was going to be implemented at the festival. Drawing on the case of Newlands rugby grounds in the city, where there were separate stands for coloured and white spectators, it assured National Party members that, likewise, apartheid was going to be "properly applied" at the festival. There would be segregated seating arrangements at the festival stadium and separate entrances to the fair grounds, the refreshment facilities, the post office on the site, and the replica of Van Riebeeck's hometown, Culemborg. The contradiction between what the *Argus* romanticized as "the old, happy life of the Cape, with its tradition of fair play for all races," and apartheid was not as marked as to make Cape Town "un-national" and "merely an appendage" of Van Riebeeck's South Africa.[77]

By the end of 1951 many of the arrangements for the festival had been set in place and, although Granger Bay had not been cleared entirely of its rubble, the arrival of Jan and Maria van Riebeeck on its beach now seemed imminent. But in the early months of 1952 all the planning that had gone into the festival events in Cape Town was nearly destroyed but, at the same time, was reinforced. The crisis for Van Riebeeck revolved around the National Party's intentions to disenfranchise coloured voters. To effect this action it had passed through parliament, in the first half of 1951, the Separate Representation of Voters Act. The United Party challenged the constitutionality of this act, first in the Cape Supreme Court, where the application was dismissed, with the United Party having to pay all legal costs, by Justices J. E. de Villiers, G. Steyn, and C. Newton Thompson, who found that a court of law cannot question the validity of an act of parliament. It was then taken on appeal, to be heard before five judges of the Appellate division, headed by Justice A. Centlivres. The scheduling of the case for 20 February 1952 meant that judgment, in all probability, would be delivered just as the Van Riebeeck festival was about to begin. Sensing that the judgment might put the festival in jeopardy, the chair of the central committee, A. J. van der Merwe, wrote to Centlivres asking him to "ensure goodwill" by postponing the delivery of the court's ruling until after the festival. Van der Merwe was concerned that the judgment could cause a rift in the "whole white population" that was being so assiduously constructed through Van Riebeeck and the accompanying festivities. He felt so distressed at the possible repercussions that he persuaded the prime minister, D. F. Malan, to write a letter to Centlivres along similar lines. But their protestations were to no avail, and, after a dispute over who could make the decision to postpone the case, the judgment was delivered on 20 March 1952, just three weeks before Van Riebeeck was due to land and with the festival fair already in full swing. The court ruled against the government and declared the Separate Representation of Voters Act invalid. The decision angered Malan and the National Party, who claimed it had created a totally untenable constitutional position and that the United Party, in taking up the case, had acted as if it were an agent of imperialism. This response by the ruling party and the decision of the court led to massive protest marches throughout the country under the auspices of the ex-servicemen's organization, the Torch Commando, where demands were made for the government to resign and for "the restoration of democratic government." What was significant for Van Riebeeck and his festival was that both those favoring the judgment and those opposed to it understood the events surrounding the court's decision to be a "constitutional crisis." In these terms the judgment had nothing to do with coloured voters per se but was all about politics defined as an arena in which whites were the exclusive role players.[78] The editor of the *Cape Times* expressed this most explicitly: "The fight to preserve the democratic principles of our Constitution is one between Europeans, and the non-Europeans would be well advised to leave the struggle to the Europeans.[79] This notion of politics as the preserve of the whites enabled Van Riebeeck to augment his position as the bearer of "western civilization" and its past in South Africa. Parties in parliament and the Torch Commando declared what was termed a "Festival political truce" for a three-week period from 29 March to 16 April 1952 so as to allow the pageantry to proceed without the encumbrance of the "constitutional crisis."[80] With politics defined in these racially exclusive terms, and being officially declared off limits, the Van Riebeecks could now take the stage with more composure as, and in, history during the first week of April 1952.

Van Riebeeck's Week of History

Moviegoers attending their local cinemas in the week of 9 April could watch a newsreel devoted to the beginning of the Van Riebeeck festival in Cape Town. The newsreel started its package of events with the service of "Dedication to the Soil" on the slopes of Table Mountain, which included the proclamation of Van Riebeeck Park by the mayor of Cape Town and a symbolic tree planting ceremony, introduced by D. F. Malan, on the metaphoric site where the "first seeds of civilisation were planted." The scene then shifted from the newly proclaimed Van Riebeeck Park, where low-flying aircraft skimmed the treetops, to the festival stadium on the foreshore to welcome the mail coaches from the various parts of the country at the end of their journeys across the land. There the mail coaches did their last lap around the track, after which a series of dances was performed evoking "the first romantic days at the Cape of Good Hope, here where the source of civilisation shot out the tips of its spears far and wide."[81]

What the moviegoers did not see were the pageants (ignored by the newsreels) on the special "day for Malay and Coloured communities," Wednesday 2 April. These events very nearly had to be abandoned because of the massive boycott of the festival by the people the organizers had termed "non-European." The planned "*Bantoe-fees*" in Langa never took place, many of the participants of the Malay pageant withdrew, and the organizers had a great deal of difficulty finding a group of coloureds to render some scenes.[82] Ultimately, I. D. du Plessis managed to scrape together some people under the ethnic classifications of Malay and Griqua to perform in a pageant consisting of selected events and personalities in their alleged histories.

The Griqua pageant, which had been arranged rather hastily, was built around the Griqua as a distinct, separate racial entity, striving for its own national identity. Nine events, beginning with the first Outeniqua contact with Van Riebeeck, depicted the growth of the Griqua "*volkie*" [little *volk*] under the leadership of the Kok and Le Fleur families. This "growth" was mainly about movement of the Griqua to various parts of the country, culminating in "the founding of Kokstad" and the "the Griquas under their leaders, Andrew, Abraham and Stockenstroom le Fleur." Accompanying the pageant was a choir that rendered a regular "praise to the lord" in the Dutch Reformed Church and called it their "*volkslied*" [national anthem], "*God, Ewig Groot en Goed*" [God, Forever Great and Kind]. The Griqua who were interviewed on the radio after the pageant said that their participation in these events had already been prophesied in 1927, to show the world their *volk*, their origins, their racial phenotype, and their ambition for a homeland. Trying earnestly to show that the

8. A special day was set aside at the Van Riebeeck festival for people who were called "Malay" and "Griqua." One of the items performed was the Lingo dance, a dance that was supposed to be part of "Malay" tradition that was largely created by the academic I. D. du Plessis. Manuscripts and Archives Division, University of Cape Town Libraries. Photo: *Cape Times.*

Griqua were not insignificant, the interviewer remarked that, judging from the five hundred participants who had been gathered from all corners of South Africa, he had never imagined there were so many Griqua in the country. The interviewee could only agree. They were even "many more than I thought," he replied.[83]

The Malay pageant, as scripted and commentated by Du Plessis in the festival stadium, combined selected snapshots of history with caricatures of contemporary culture. The "great legend" of the "Malay nation," Sheik Yusuf ("Joseph"), stepped ashore, next arrived a group of political exiles to "form the nucleus of the Malay craftsmen of the Cape," and then the Malay Corps participated in the Battle of Blaauwberg in 1806 and later in a battle on the eastern frontier. Once the history of the Malay had been dealt with in two episodes, namely, founding and providing assistance to colonial forces, there were snippets of Malay "culture," ranging from the "Lingo dance," Malays in sport, and trade displays to a Malay fisherman and fish sellers (Figure 8). As in the exhibition at the Castle, the essence of the Malay, conveyed in the floats of Sheik Yusuf and his followers, was one of "colour and beauty and fine craftsmanship" derived from Du Plessis and his racial classification of a people with "slim, and delicate hands."[84]

It is apparent that these Malay and Griqua pasts and cultures were not given much prominence in the context of the festival, and little attention was devoted to staging these productions. Almost apologetically, I. D. du Plessis claimed that the intention was not to create a finely tuned, faultless presentation but rather to evoke the pleasurable warmth of "a really enjoyable school concert." The praise in the English and Afrikaans press for these simple, amateurish depictions were along the same lines. "The infectious gaiety of the Cape non-Europeans in a carnival mood swept through the audience," wrote the *Cape Times* reporter. An overseas visitor was quoted as saying, "This is the first time I have really felt the Festival atmosphere." *Die Burger's* daily reporter at the festival felt that a professional production could not hold up a light to this sort of concert, which even children enjoyed. All those who were not present (and there were many) had missed one of the most beautiful and major events at the festival, the reporter claimed. Yet, clearly they had not. What they had missed was an almost pathetic performance in the pouring rain for the sake of Van Riebeeck and his "white admirers" in order to show that there were some "non-Europeans" who were well disposed toward them and their apartheid policies. With the boycott of the festival so successful, the "perseverance" of the Malay and Griqua participants enabled the sparse, largely white crowd to reflect that they and Van Riebeeck had accomplished one of the "greatest and most worthwhile" moments in "coloured relations."[85]

These pageants of colour (but not race, in the festival's terms) primarily conveyed a message of separate groups, with their own traditions and proto-histories. Du Plessis reminded audiences that the Griqua and Malay had "specific needs" related to their ethnic identities. *Die Burger* remarked that the pageant showed how trekking and craftsmanship had become almost an innate part of the Griqua and Malay respectively. It suggested that each should acquire their own land to perpetuate their own genetic pool. The values of "commitment to tradition," "pure blood," and "ownness" would become anchors of a future "united" South Africa, advanced by a possible territorial division. By separating the country into separate racial pockets, Van Riebeeck, on the eve of his people's pageant the following day, could assert with some measure of confidence that his national festival was being organized "by whites for whites" in order to tell, first and foremost, a story of "white achievements."[86]

While the festival events were already under way in Cape Town, the final touches were given to the historical creations for the pageant of the past at Wingfield Airport, which became "a nation's historical workshop." After all the problems associated with devising the script, this part of the operations was proceeding smoothly. In the evening, as the Malay and Griqua pageant was winding down, and as the floats made their way from Wingfield to the stadium to prepare for the following day's procession in the streets of Cape Town, a major and unforeseen difficulty emerged. A huge storm broke out and rain came down in buckets; after it abated, a ferocious wind continued. Anna Neethling-Pohl was in a quandary: "I wondered what could be saved and how. . . . I had a strange feeling beforehand that we were going to have good weather on the days of the pageant, but that storm was a miserable disappointment for me." With leaders of the various floats and the press gathered around, she decided to take a chance and issued a statement that the procession would go ahead, "even if it pours with rain and there are no spectators in the stadium. We have come too far, worked too hard to not keep on going to the end." In the early hours of the morning floats were repaired, with each helping the other out. Later, Neethling-Pohl would report that, for her, this was the highlight of her experience as pageant mistress. "I have never before seen such co-operation and wonderful togetherness in our country," she wrote to the pageant committee. "I have never experienced such a spontaneous, determined action interspersed with humour."[87]

Much to Neethling-Pohl's relief, when dawn came the skies were clear—another moment of divine intervention following on 1752, 1899, and 1910?—and the streets were rinsed after almost twenty-four hours of intermittent rain. "The sun was at its best" to reveal to the public a monumental history pageant premised on white unity and supremacy: the "People's Pageant." The key reference points of the pageant were two floats constructed by the Speech and Drama Department at the University of Cape Town. As per the script, at the head of the procession was a float which served to justify processes of conquest and settlement in South Africa: "Africa Dark and Unknown." Masked figures, attired in black robes and shackled in chains, marched alongside the scene of a despotic figure who held them in "mental and spiritual darkness" (Figure 9). One and a half hours later, the same float reappeared but in a different guise. "Africa Awakes" contained a scene of figures dressed in white, symbolizing "youth, strength and purity, the foundation on which rests the freedom of the individual and of Africa as a whole."[88] In presenting a contrasting image to "Darkest Africa," it reinforced notions of European settlement as the motor force behind a "natural" phenomenon of historical evolution, from darkness to light, from slavery to freedom. The radio commentators enthused over the transformation:

> From a situation of fear, a period followed of struggle, change, tension, defeat and victory and slowly that character of darkest Africa changed and gave rise to a new nation with its own cultures, its own language, its own direction, its own idealism and its own art.[89]

9. The float "Darkest Africa," presented by the Speech Training and Drama Department, University of Cape Town, at the People's Pageant, presented Africa as dark and
barbaric prior to the arrival of European settlers. National Library of South Africa,
Cape Town. Photo: *Cape Times, The Festival in Pictures,* Cape Town (1952).

Thus, as "Africa Awoke," "We Build a Nation," presented by Mrs. D. F. Malan,
the wife of the prime minister, and sponsored by the Association of Chambers
of Commerce and *Die Afrikaanse Handelsinstituut* [Afrikaans Commercial In-
stitute], appeared to bring the procession to its predetermined finale. This float
was much more than a simple horse-drawn chariot, ridden by a young boy and
girl bearing the South African flag and adorned with emblems of the provinces,
as had originally been envisaged. It now depicted two huge models of white
horses of about three to four meters in height, "rearing their forelegs in the sky,
drawing a chariot, guided by a white clad youth [a Springbok rugby player]
with a young girl holding the Union flag beside him." This was intended to
symbolize the "courage, faith and strength" with which "the young South African nation enters the future" (Figure 10). South African history was thus cast

10. The float procession ended with "We Build a Nation," presented by Mrs. D. F. Malan. This float was supposed to symbolize the coming together of the South African settler nation in 1952. National Library of South Africa, Cape Town. Photo: *Cape Times.*

as a progression away from darkness and toward "European civilisation," the seeds of which had been "planted three hundred years ago" when Van Riebeeck landed at Table Bay.[90]

The intervening floats traced moments in this "history of enlightenment," as the nation came into being based on the co-operation of ruling classes, in a history that had been negotiated so as to be largely devoid of conflict. Although there were still some scenes depicting an Afrikaner past as a "struggle for personal liberty"—included in this section was the revolt of the burgher farmers against the Dutch East India Company—the Boer War had been sanitized, Thompson presented Uys with a Bible on the outskirts of Grahamstown, and the last Transvaal president, Paul Kruger, followed shortly thereafter on a float depicting the man who had been instrumental in a bid to overthrow his government in the 1890s, Cecil John Rhodes. But "the Legacy of Rhodes" made no mention of his "ridiculous . . . childish . . . farcical" attempted coup d'état. For the pageant committee, the legacy of Rhodes, who in his day had praised and monumentalized Van Riebeeck, consisted of his "influence on education, agriculture, transport and native welfare." Although Rhodes was not exalted and placed on the same level as Van Riebeeck, as the writer Sarah Gertrude Millin had hoped he would be (as she expressed in an article in the Anglo-American Corporation's journal, *Optima*), he became, alongside Kruger, part of three hundred years of a South African past, proudly proclaimed as an "apostle of Apartheid—the separation, the apartness, of black from white."[91]

The nation depicted in the pageant was founded by the efforts of all settler communities. The Dutch, the English, the French, and even the Scots and the Germans contributed to this nation, in processes ranging from *volksplanting* to the mineral revolution. The uitlanders who arrived in the 1880s and 1890s contributed most to the development of mining, transforming the Transvaal "into one of the richest territories in the world." Although this had brought with it "some difficult problems" (this was clearly a deliberately understated reference to the Anglo-Boer War), the central theme of the pageant asserted the development of settler co-operation in the founding of Van Riebeeck's South African nation.[92]

"I Land Together with Van Riebeeck"[93]

Jan and Maria van Riebeeck, of course, were given a separate ceremony in order to accord them a place of prominence in the founding of the white nation. Although there were five floats in the people's pageant depicting their arrival and early days of settlement, their landing was dramatized on its own on Saturday, 5 April. With the way safely negotiated over the past year and the beach cleared of all its rubble, few problems were encountered with the landing. Although there might have been some difficulties with the swell as they had to go in stern first for visibility's sake, instead of facing the sea and pulling in to the shore, the water was calm, making the maneuver relatively simple. The only problem was with Maria, for whom it was the first time at sea, and who was sick onboard the *Dromedaris*. Yet Frances Holland was determined to carry on and was brought ashore to accompany Jan on the sands of Granger Bay. As they stood on the beach together with their son, Lambertus, and a group of students from the University of Stellenbosch who acted as soldiers, they were no longer merely *volksplanters*, the originators of colonialism, or the bearers of Christianity. As a family they were set to take up residence in the Castle of

Good Hope as the founders of a European settler nation and, according to *Die Transvaler*, the initiators of the government's policy of apartheid.[94]

The apparent ease with which the landing took place, the huge crowds that gazed at the pageantry on this and the preceding days, and the way the events proceeded almost without a hitch formed the basis for an enthusiastic response. The English press and the Afrikaans press were both overflowing with effusiveness for the festival, in general, and the pageant of the past, in particular. Drawing on the conceptualization of the festival as the celebration of a national past, there was a great deal of agreement with the claim that Van Riebeeck had managed to overcome sectionalism among South Africans who could now identify themselves as Europeans. Anna Neethling-Pohl was even more ebullient, asserting that she knew, from her experience of working on the pageant, that the South African nation existed and that it was united. This unity, for her, was almost metaphysical: "There was a spirit of being together, of joy at being together, a pride in being a part." Even more significant, this identity, united as European, and derived from the Van Riebeecks, was cast as the South African nation. It was in these terms of racial exclusivity that the festival became "truly national," a "sweeping . . . example of national unity," and, according to J. G. N. Strauss, the leader of the United Party, an exhibition of how the "greater unity" of "Afrikaans and English-speaking South Africans" was able to transcend a "serious crisis in our national life." This almost divinely ordained "greater unity" that the Van Riebeecks had brought with them in 1952 had safeguarded racial purity, guaranteed that "the White groups" had "not been overwhelmed by the native and Coloured peoples" and would ensure that they [the "White groups"] would still be "as flourishing as ever in another 300 years."[95]

Yet the same tensions that had surfaced in the planning of the festivities had not disappeared. *Die Burger's* festival correspondent felt that the overall thematic symbolism of the festival had been lost because of the variety of events, that "national symbols," such as the anthem, "Die Stem" (the other South African anthem at the time was "God Save the Queen"), and the South African flag, were not evident enough, and that the float "We Build a Nation" was lost in its position at the end of the procession. Moreover, the correspondent claimed, the crowds, by and large, were Afrikaans-speaking. This was attributed to white English-speakers' attitudes toward the festival having being "poisoned" by Arthur Keppel-Jones's book *When Smuts Goes*, which presented the commemoration at the start of "his alarmist future history." There was also some feeling, in the more liberal sections of the press, that the festival had possibly widened the "gulf between the White and non-European communities" and, while they regarded it as unthinkable to "surrender . . . White leadership in South Africa," some "fair reform" did seem necessary. But the most substantial dissenting voice against the festival and its representations was swept under the carpet and labeled as largely insignificant. A massive 95 percent boycott of the festival by those who were termed non-European was conveniently ignored by a Van Riebeeck who said that from the beaches of Granger Bay he had managed to spread a message of "good will and understanding between white and non-white."[96]

3 Contesting Van Riebeeck's Nation

At the "zero hour of our national life," as Jan, Maria, and Lambertus van Riebeeck were making preparations for their landing at Granger Bay to commemorate "their three hundred years of rapine and bloodshed" and to prepare themselves for "another evil era of piracy and oppression," Silas Modiri Molema, historian and treasurer of the African National Congress (ANC), opened the twentieth annual conference of the South African Indian Congress (SAIC) by calling on the delegates to "gird [their] loins" and brace themselves to "reverse the dismal and tragic history of past years." In the months that followed, he said, Van Riebeeck and company would feast on "our defeat" and "our tears."[1] He urged the audience, though, not to be "carried away like chaff before the wind,"

> Nor hold a candle to our shame and sorrow,
> Nor flatter the rank breath of white South Africa,
> Nor bow our knee to their idolatries,
> Nor coin our cheek to their smiles,
> Nor shout in worship of their echo.[2]

Molema's speech was received with acclaim by the audience, and the SAIC passed a resolution to support a campaign of defiance against apartheid's unjust laws. It decided to work together with the ANC to call on "hundreds of thousands to [come] to the meetings and demonstrations on April 6" and participate in the "first stage in the struggle . . . for the ending of oppression."[3]

Just over two months later, on the eve of the beginning of the festival week in Cape Town, the day before D. F. Malan opened Van Riebeeck Park and the mail coaches ended their journeys at the stadium on the foreshore, about six thousand people gathered on Cape Town's Grand Parade to declare their intention of intensifying a boycott campaign against Van Riebeeck and his festival. Adjacent to the Castle where Van Riebeeck was about to take up residence, the speakers faced the crowd from a platform adorned with an image of "the founder" turned upside down and defaced with a large X (Figure 11). Held under the auspices of the Local Co-ordinating Committee of the Non-European Unity Movement, the meeting was addressed by many of its leading lights who spoke both of how the "*Herrenvolk*" had consistently attempted to "break the nation" and how the Unity Movement, through promoting a boycott of the festival, were, in reality, the true builders of the nation. Dealing with the former theme, speakers such as Hosea Jaffe, Dan Neethling, and Jane Gool drew on historical

11. Anti-Van Riebeeck Festival Protest Meeting, Grand Parade, 30 March 1952. On stage, from left to right, are Phyllis Ntantala Jordan, Willem van Schoor, S. A. Jayiya, Goolam Gool, Dan Neethling, and Jane Gool. Halima Gool, courtesy of Allison Drew. Photo: Ralph Taylor.

events—the alienation of land, the disenfranchisement of "Non-Whites" and the exploitation of workers—to show how a policy of "Divide and Rule" had been used to block the "unity of the oppressed." Other speakers, like Ben Kies, Willie van Schoor, and Isaac Tabata, used local and international examples— such as the way teachers were participating in the boycott of the festival and the liberation movements in other parts of Africa, China, and the Middle East —to illustrate how nations could be built through "great liberatory struggles." The crowd responded to their entreaties with enthusiasm and resolved to re-affirm the boycott of the festival, escalate its application over the next two weeks as the festival reached its climax, and support "the struggle to build a real nation of all South Africans, irrespective of race, colour, creed or sex."[4]

The seeming ease with which one can apparently move, in a narrative of national resistance, from the SAIC conference in Johannesburg at the end of January, which proposed to take action against Van Riebeeck, to a Unity Move-ment meeting at the end of March, which celebrated and further encouraged the boycott of his festival, belies much of the conflict that went into formulating responses by those individuals and organizations who were opposing the commemorative events in the streets of Cape Town and beyond in March and April of 1952. In as much as the festival, which presented itself as a seamless, unbroken exhibition of past and present settler unity, was the outcome of a range of conflicts over both the appropriate form and content of its varying displays, so the pasts which contested Van Riebeeck's nation were as heavily disputed in terms of their presentation and substance. Clearly, different political organizations were involved in opposing Van Riebeeck, and many of the disagreements over the appropriate responses to the tercentenary festival were related to their divergent objectives and strategies. Yet, while these political organizational imperatives were often crucial in demarcating the nature of the rejoinder to Van Riebeeck, the calls for a boycott of the tercentenary were, by and large, a direct response to the attempts by the organizers of the pageantry and exhibitions to incorporate specific groups into the structures and events of the festival, particularly the separate ones set aside for people categorized as "non-Europeans." The organizers encountered a great deal of resistance to their incorporative campaign from various sectors, structures, and individuals. This chapter examines these opponents of Van Riebeeck who surfaced during the preparation for and in course of the festival. It explores the different forms they assumed as they converged with, and diverged from, one another in their interaction with the negotiated narratives of the nation emerging from the planners of the tercentenary and the landing at Granger Bay.

Boycotting Van Riebeeck

In the latter part of 1951, as the final touches were being put into the Van Riebeeck festival programs, the organizers of the various sub-committees that dealt with specific aspects of the proceedings set about the task of locating the thousands of participants who were required to put the show on the road. They scoured schools, universities, and youth and cultural organizations in order to fill the places. Their recruiting efforts largely paid off as hordes of white schoolchildren were enlisted to scuffle "through the dust, bellowing a song of white ascendancy."[5] Although the primary purpose of the festival revolved around establishing a sense of this European-derived settler unity, and thus constructing a white racial national identity, the organizers were also concerned with promoting "non-European" identities in bounded ethnic (or proto-ethnic) categories that would be beholden to the "European race." This was a key feature of emerging apartheid policy in the early 1950s, where the task of extending and maintaining white rule was no longer merely conceived in terms of exercising racial control over the majority of the population but involved splitting "the majority into compartmentalized minorities." To make these "ethnic minorities" into "believable" and durable entities, they had to be constructed in terms of selected and featured aspects of "historical and cultural experience."[6] As was seen in chapter 2, these experiences were promoted in the festival through the planned separate events and displays that were arranged for those demarcated as not constituting part of Van Riebeeck's nation. There was to be a "day for the Malay and Coloured Communities," a village at the festival fair to be "inhabited by tribal natives," and a *"Bantoe-fees"* [festival for the Bantu] in Langa township involving sports, choral singing, and the slaughtering of animals, as well as special "cheap days" to enable coloured teachers and students to inflate the numbers at the festival fair. But, unlike the masses of white schoolchildren who participated in the mass displays, finding ready groups who could join in these separate activities proved far more difficult. Many of those whom the festival organizers specified as "non-European" decided that they would not partake of the segregated and rather measly offerings of Van Riebeeck's "Jong Suid-Afrika." Eighteen hours after the "Youth of South Africa" had delivered their message and rendered their oath to the crowds that had amassed, Adam Kok, Sheik Yusuf, Stockenstroom le Fleur, and the Moslem Lads' Brigade performed their "special pageant" on a rainy autumn day in Cape Town, in an almost deserted stadium, to a handful of spectators.[7]

This bizarre, farcical, and at the same time almost eerie event in the midst of all the revelry and drama that the festival was producing had been shaped the previous year when the organizers had approached coloured school principals in the Cape Peninsula to bring their pupils to the envisaged festival fair. This fair was a mammoth and enormously expensive undertaking, and, from the outset, the organizers realized that the only way to recoup some of the costs was if "non-Europeans" attended. Moreover, coloureds attending the fair would be confronted with displays that clearly showed whites as pre-ordained bearers of experience, civilization, and ability and would thereby re-establish an affiliation of "thankfulness" and congenial servitude toward whites, constructed as the good old times—before the days of "mischievous, ignorant and unthankful agitators"— that had existed in a mythical, rural "old Cape." "The relationship on the farm between ourselves and those who served us could not have been happier," wrote a visitor to the "Coloured section of the exhibition at the Castle." "They were hardworking and happy folk and served us willingly and cheerfully all their working lives." By going to the festival fair, coloureds could also see "the products which were processed by their labour" and thus could re-affirm maternal ties of servitude to the "white man" in terms of "their own" possession. This was expressed metaphorically through the festival message which the white Dutch Reformed Church (DRC) wanted "non-Europeans" to imbibe: Coloureds, who belonged to the mission church, needed to place them-selves so as to recognize their position as the "daughters" of the "*Moeder Kerk*" [Mother Church].[8]

If the principals of coloured schools could be persuaded or cajoled into bringing along groups of pupils to the fairgrounds, it would both solve the numbers problem and relay this festival message from "mother" to "child." The latter metaphor was appropriate for promoters of the festival as they regarded young people as malleable entities whose minds needed to be shaped. To facili-tate the participation of youth in both racial and generational terms, the festi-val was publicized by asking schools to sell, for nine pence, a medallion made of cupro-nickel, which depicted Van Riebeeck in an imperial pose, flanked by a boy who was about to place a wreath on his head and a girl holding a palm leaf. For the organizers, these attempts at popularizing an image of Van Rie-beeck, in anticipation of participation in the festival program, floundered, as not only were pupils unable to afford purchasing what was regarded as a non-essential item but also because the scheme encountered a group of teachers, organized in an articulate, vociferous constituency, who were vehemently op-posed to the festival and its racially exclusive nationing. The Athlone Princi-pals' Association, with representation from "23 non-European schools having a total of 10,500 pupils" in the Cape Peninsula, decided that it would not take the children whom they taught to the celebrations which were "glorify[ing] white domination," exhorted parents not to buy the "badges of shame," and announced to D. F. Malan that he could go about building his nation without them.[9]

These principals from Athlone were aligned with the Teachers League of South Africa (TLSA), an organization that in the early 1940s had become a po-litical battleground for groups that coalesced around the issue of participation in a government-established separate advisory board for coloureds, which car-ried the title the Coloured Advisory Council. In 1944 the Anti-CAD (Coloured Affairs Department) faction of the TLSA, which was dominated by a radical, largely university-trained, intelligentsia, defeated the more conservative fac-tion, led by G. Golding, who advocated taking part in government structures in order to preserve a racially designated coloured identity and sectional interests, and assumed control of the organization and its official mouthpiece, *The Edu-cational Journal*. Golding left the TLSA, formed the Teachers Educational and Professional Association (TEPA) and the Coloured People's National Union (CPNU), rejected black unity as he claimed that coloureds had a closer affinity with whites than with "natives," and called for segregated residential areas. The newly radicalized TLSA, on the other hand, became a key player in the Non-European Unity Movement, a broad front of organizations formed in late 1943 to fight racial domination and segregation, and to reject racial identities as imposed constructs. Along with the Anti-Coloured Affairs Department (Anti-CAD), the All-African Convention (AAC), the Cape African Teachers Association (CATA) and the African Political Organization (APO), the TLSA adhered both to the ten-point program of democratic rights that the Unity Movement advocated and to a policy of total non-collaboration with structures and institutions associated with racial segregation. Although issues of when, where, and how boycotting should be applied were hotly debated within the Unity Movement, boycotting tended to be advanced more in terms of a principle than a specific strategic tactic. Regarding boycotting government structures as "the primary weapon of struggle," it was necessary to do much more than merely support a boycott of the Van Riebeeck festival; rather, with "enthusiasm and self-sacrifice," it was necessary to "intervene and put these principles and strategies into practice."[10]

This enthusiasm to confront Van Riebeeck by the broad front of organizations associated with the Unity Movement was also directly related to its continual use of history-as-lesson to effect its ten-point program and the strategy of non-collaboration. "The liberatory movement," wrote a reviewer in the Unity Movement's newspaper, *The Torch*,

> must be built upon a scientific analysis and understanding, upon the hard-learnt lessons of the past, upon principles, and carried forward consciously by our practical work based on theories derived from that historical understanding. A proper history is a useful weapon in this whole process of emancipation.[11]

When W. P. van Schoor delivered the TLSA memorial lecture in 1950 entitled "The Origin and Development of Segregation in South Africa," his aim was to show that history was an absolutely necessary signpost toward achieving liberation. "A people desiring to emancipate itself," he asserted, "must understand the process of its enslavement." There were differences within the Unity Movement about what these historical processes entailed, but they tended to revolve around colonial dispossession, the almost inevitable bankruptcy of those who collaborated, heroes of resistance, and the artificial imposition of racial categories. Some of these aspects were evident in "A History of Despotism: The Why and Wherefore of South African History" by Nxele, which had been running in *The Torch* since 1949. Van Riebeeck was referred to as a "frustrated imperialist" who "fought the indigenous people for land and slave labour," the "Hottentots" were stubborn resisters "fighting against foreign conquest," and the racial category "white" was one by which "the slave-owner and governing group from Holland, from Europe, with the pink-yellow-blotchy colour" "miraculously" came to be known.[12]

So prepared was the TLSA for the coming of Van Riebeeck that, very soon after the government's announcement in April 1950 that it planned to stage a tercentenary festival, branches were canvassed on what action to take. According to *The Educational Journal,* the executive of the TLSA, as a result of the feedback received, passed a resolution in October 1950, well before any plans were in place to create separate events for coloureds, opposing the festival, dissociated itself from the proceedings of the festival, and urged branches to engage in history lessons, "enlightening members and the public on the historical facts concerning the arrival of Van Riebeeck and the reasons for the present celebrations." This might be a highly idealized depiction of how the TLSA arrived at the decision, but it does indicate that there was a keen interest in TLSA circles (particularly among the leadership) in mobilizing against a festival which promoted a racially exclusive nationalism, utilized history for that purpose, and was "trying to inflict" that history "on the oppressed."[13]

The Educational Journal, in line with the TLSA resolution taken in October 1950, ran a monthly "Van Riebeeck Series" in the first half of 1951, to provide the "full facts" on the events leading to the landing in 1652 and its immediate aftermath. These presented facts were explicitly directed against the festival and its central icon to enable teachers to engage in what was termed a "critical discussion and revaluation" of "the subject of the *Herrenvolk's* Tercentenary Celebration." What is eminently notable about these articles—"Forgotten Past" by David Stuurman, "Gold, Gospel and Glory" by John Parish, and "The Settlement: Reasons and Consequences" by Harold Kapman—is their presentation of the past in an almost academic discourse, providing references, a bibliography, and a contextualization of events in a framework of African history, political and economic transformation in Europe, and the expansion of trading operations in the East Indies. It was the authority and seriousness of these articles, together with their presentation of a selected, partial past as completely open to interpretation and critical discussion, that was to form the basis of persuading teachers that depictions of the arrival of Van Riebeeck as a "white man's duty" or a "civilising mission" were "rationalisations and untruths" to justify "the present state of affairs."[14]

When the twenty-five Athlone Principals announced that they would be discouraging their pupils from participating in the festival in any form, they received the full backing of the TLSA. At the Regional Conference of the South Western Districts Branch of the League, held in the small southern Cape town of Oudtshoorn, the executive of the TLSA issued a statement that teachers should not permit their pupils to buy the Van Riebeeck medallions and should work, instead, toward organizing a boycott of the celebrations. Significantly, at the same time, the TLSA resolved to oppose the opening of a college for the training of coloured teachers in Oudtshoorn. The lack of study facilities and boarding accommodations in the proposed college, the plan to lower entrance qualifications for women, the structural nature of the buildings—"prefabricated hutments"—and its location, far removed from major urban areas, were cited as reasons for the denunciation of the project. Such facilities and their condemnation paralleled the constant criticism by coloured teachers of a lack of wage parity between themselves and white teachers, the latter receiving far higher remuneration than their coloured counterparts. Coloured teachers, therefore, found they had little enthusiasm or material incentive for celebrating the Van Riebeeck festival. Indeed, some teachers decided to reject the festival not because of a politically principled stand but because they wanted to assert an elite status as a "better type or thinking person," unlike the "coons and tribal dancers" who were "celebrating slavery" by participating in the separate events and from which "one couldn't expect anything better." Even the more conservative TEPA announced that it would not attend the festival, but at the same time it would not promote a boycott because it regarded the arrival of Van Riebeeck as an event of historical import, seeing him as "a pioneer of Western Civilization." [15]

The ability to mobilize support against Van Riebeeck from teachers who were termed coloured was also related to the transformation of their position as a designated racial grouping in the early years of National Party rule. Starting in 1948, trains in the Cape Peninsula were racially segregated, the ability of coloureds to move between racial groups and "pass for white" was severely curtailed by the Population Registration Act of 1950 which legislated racial categories, and the Separate Representation of Voters Bill, introduced in February 1951, intended to remove coloured voters in the Cape from the common voters roll. The Franchise Action Council (FRAC), a broadly based alliance linked to the ANC but at the same time enveloping a spectrum from "left-wing trade unionists" to "accommodationist coloured politicians," was formed to lobby and co-ordinate action against the Separate Representation of Voters Bill. Included in the ranks of FRAC were representatives from the SAIC, the Communist Party, the ANC, and Golding's CPNU. The Unity Movement saw the alliance as a sectional body concerned only with defending the interests of a single racial entity, pointed to meetings where the coloured vote was defended by speakers who argued that they did not want "to be reduced to the level of the Natives," and refused to join an organization they claimed had not broken down the "mental barriers of segregation" by behaving, acting, and thinking in terms of group interests rather than as a nation. Despite the lack of support from the Unity Movement, FRAC went ahead with its planned program of protests against the bill and called for a work strike on 7 May 1951. The Unity Movement declared this planned action to be "adventurist and irresponsible" and wanted no part of it. The CPNU, on the other hand, which had initially welcomed the tenor of FRAC meetings where speakers had warned about the dangers of becoming "like the African people," was unwilling to confront the government head on and withdrew from FRAC. Faced with a compelling need to publicize the planned strike, FRAC arranged a Freedom Fair at Maynardville in Wynberg which included sideshows, a Malay restaurant, and a performance by the government-sponsored Eoan coloured cultural group. Many of the fairgoers came in fancy dress—there was a "politically conscious gingerbread man" and an "apartheid miss"—and an announcer roamed the grounds reminding people about 7 May. This pageantry, when combined with a threat to what were perceived as racially based privileges, may have contributed to the partial success of the strike, particularly in the western Cape, although the Unity Movement suspected that employers and employees had privately agreed that they would work on a public holiday.[16]

Buoyed up by the success of what its deputy chair, Johnny Gomas, referred to as bringing "the Coloured people into action as no other organisation had done in the past," FRAC decided to add its voice to the growing call to boycott the Van Riebeeck celebrations. Unlike the TLSA and the Unity Movement, which condemned the entire conceptualization of organizing a Van Riebeeck festival, FRAC was more concerned with the specific arrangements, how festival committees promoted racial exclusivity by having no "Non-European . . . representation," and how the pageantry misrepresented South Africa's past by depicting the country's history as "of [and] for the Europeans only." Arguing that the arrival of Van Riebeeck was "an event of great historical significance," the statement issued by Gomas and E. Andrews, the secretary of FRAC, declared that the opportunity should have been used "to commemorate the first beginnings of co-operation between white and black." As this clearly was not the way the festival had been conceptualized and planned—a "biased and one-sided political and racial spirit pervades every aspect of the tercentenary," declared FRAC—it had decided to boycott all the official commemorative events associated with the tercentenary.[17]

The Unity Movement, which had, since 1950, been at the forefront of promoting a boycott of the festival, felt that FRAC was obfuscating the issue by dealing with the specific contents of the festival and seemingly implying that if substantial alterations were made they would encourage participation. The editor of *The Torch* wrote:

> The main reasons for boycotting this orgy of *Herrenvolkism* are that the national oppression and exploitation of the Non-Whites are to be celebrated, that the triumph of the Master-Race over Kaffir, Hotnot and Coolies is to be celebrated, that another 300 years of domination are to be heralded. No matter what *form* these celebrations take, no matter how many Non-Whites are bullied or seduced or fooled into taking part, no matter how wonderful the

exhibits and processions and side-shows, nothing can disguise the fact that the *Herrenvolk* is dancing and revelling upon our own enslavement. And only the slaves among us could consciously and voluntarily join them.[18]

The approach of FRAC, which presented non-participation in terms of lack of "non-white" representation in the events and history of the festival, would only spread "confusion and weakness" about the boycott, claimed the Unity Movement. What particularly worried the Unity Movement was that in late 1951 the organizers of the tercentenary were setting in place concrete plans to incorporate specific, separate, racially determined groups in the festival, thereby enabling "non-Europeans to have a . . . share"—if not an equal one— "in the celebration of their own enslavement."[19]

I. D. du Plessis, the Commissioner for Coloured Affairs, was attempting to organize Malay and coloured participants for their day at the festival. In his sights were the Cape Malay Choir Board, an organization he had helped to establish in 1939, and the Eoan group, the state-aided drama association for coloureds. While he was having limited success with his own society, the latter was proving to be much more hesitant about partaking of Van Riebeeck's offerings. Some members of the Eoan group wanted to participate in the events Du Plessis was organizing. Reasons for this varied from a willingness to "show how good coloureds were" to a fear that, if they did not join in, the government would withdraw its annual £400 grant to the organization. Reasons for boycotting the festival also varied. Some saw the festival as representing three hundred years of discrimination and saw no reason to partake in such a celebration. But others, like some of the teachers, asserted an elite racial status as coloureds and found the idea that they would have "to dance like Zulus and 'Kaffirs'" "unthinkable." Which of these reasons dominated in discussions is unclear, but combined they were enough for the Eoan group to decide that it would boycott I. D. du Plessis's Van Riebeeck celebrations.[20]

The refusal by members of the Eoan group to dance like "Zulus and 'Kaffirs'" was a direct reference to the organizers' attempts to involve another racially designated "non-European" group in the festival: the "natives" from the African township of Langa, eleven kilometers from the Cape Town city center. Selected inhabitants of the township were required to go on display at the Native Affairs Department Exhibit at the festival fair being organized in Cape Town for three weeks beginning on 15 March 1952. Using performers from the almost twelve thousand inhabitants of Langa for the display was seen as a way to cut down on the costs that might accrue if people had to be transported from other areas of the country and accommodated in Cape Town. But, from the outset, the NAD was aware that problems might arise in acquiring the exhibitors they required from Langa, fearing that "coloured threats to ban the Festival" might have spread to the township set aside for African residents in the Cape Peninsula. Wyatt Sampson, the NAD's Publicity and Liaison Officer, who was responsible for the "Bantu exhibit," together with S. Parsons, the Native Commissioner for Salt River, and Mr. Rogers, the NAD's manager of Langa, convened a meeting of organizations in the department's board room in Langa on 10 September 1951 in an attempt to pre-empt a possible boycott. To the approximately fifty people in attendance, they outlined plans to have a "real live African display" at the festival fair which would depict Africans prior to the arrival of Europeans (this included a "kraal" and "Native dancers" and "the best type of hut building"), to their education under European tutelage, and ending with "educated Africans on show." Claiming that this would be an opportunity for Africans to show the world that they were intelligent, Sampson urged them to co-operate with the NAD and to take part in the display.[21]

The response to the NAD's solicitations was not exactly what the department had hoped for. Some members of the audience claimed that they had previously co-operated with the government on several projects but "had regretted it" thereafter. Others refused to commit themselves and decided to convene a meeting of those who had a stake in the issue before submitting a formal reply to the NAD. One of the issues that those in attendance wanted clarified was the history on which the festival was being based. They appointed a special research committee, consisting of three African lecturers and teachers, "messrs A C Jordan, Siwisa and Kwebulana" to report back at the proposed meeting approximately two weeks later.[22]

The less than lukewarm response the NAD officials encountered was indicative of the lack of enthusiasm among the inhabitants of Langa toward the festival. What was jarring were the plans to present Africans in a tribal environment that portrayed the pre-modern life of people prior to European "civilization" as natural. The notion of innate underdevelopment was particularly insulting to those living in Langa who felt that they had moved far beyond the "tribal state." Indeed, by the 1940s, many of the inhabitants of Langa saw themselves as permanent residents of the city, living in a European-style community. They were increasingly intolerant of those who lived in rural areas, refused to marry people from the countryside whom they regarded as primitive and unsophisticated, and had established their own commemorations which marked the conversion of Xhosa-speaking people to Christianity and the beginnings of formal structures of education as pivotal moments in their lives. It was particularly African teachers in Langa who could not brook the idea of going on display. When I. D. Mkhize, the principal of Langa High School, circularized members of the Western Province Bantu Teachers League (WPBTL) to indicate the ways they could contribute to the Van Riebeeck festival, he received an angry rebuttal. The members of the WPBTL replied that they would not wear "*amabeshu*" (loincloths) and "teach Mpondo-Tswana-Zulu dances in tribal schools" at the festival. As an educated elite, they felt particularly insulted to be regarded as an easily malleable, "unthinking crowd."[23]

The meeting to decide on a response to the NAD was held at the Market Hall, in Langa, on 27 September 1951. A range of groups attended, some often having been at loggerheads with one another in the past. Among the groups were representatives of the Rugby Football Union, the Traders' Association, the Society of Young Africa, the Cape African Teachers Association, the National Council of African Women, the Langa Vigilance Association, and the local ANC branch. The presence of the ANC branch alongside groups aligned with the Unity Movement was particularly notable, as they had fallen out in the past on the issue of how to engage with government structures. Unlike the Unity Movement, the ANC and its allies, at times, tended to encourage individuals to participate on certain racially based government bodies, such as the Native Representatives Council and the Locations Advisory Boards, and advocated using the boycott only as "a tactic in the struggle." Yet the Unity Movement was hoping that the ANC, which was starting to take a much more radical turn under pressure from its youth wing, would begin to eschew a policy of involvement in certain segregated institutions. Although these differences still existed at the time of the meeting in Langa, they were temporarily set aside in the face of Van Riebeeck, so as to ensure that no one from Langa would take up residence in the "tribal village" on the foreshore.[24]

Befitting a gathering of "thinking African[s]," the meeting opened with a report from the history research group. A. C. Jordan, novelist and lecturer in African studies at the University of Cape Town, first outlined a process of European conquest that Van Riebeeck had initiated. Jordan referred to "land grabbing," the imposition of taxes to acquire labor, the exploitation of workers, and the denial of education to "non-Europeans." The second part of his report drew on examples in South Africa's past where collaboration in the "oppressor's wars" had not only gone unrewarded but had also led to greater repression: the Act of Union, which denied political rights to blacks, had been the "reward" for participating in the Anglo-Boer War; the shooting of people at Bulhoek and Bondelswartz had followed on the First World War; after "active service" in the Second World War, the strike by miners in 1946 had been quelled by the use of brutal force. This was clearly a warning to those who were considering imbibing the offerings of Van Riebeeck that they would be more than disappointed and would find themselves in conditions of even worse oppression. With a rhetorical flourish, he ended his speech: "What have we to celebrate? Can we celebrate our own enslavement?"[25]

The discussion that ensued after Jordan's speech was almost unanimous in its sentiments. The only dissent came from Julius Malangabi, past president of the ANC in the western Cape, who said that he wanted to know more about Van Riebeeck, not about South African history over the past three hundred years. In these terms, Jordan had not provided the type of history that Malangabi, with his limited notion of the past that the festival was seeking to portray, had expected when the research group had been appointed. Malangabi, however, found he had little support for his view:

> Miss M. Nongauza replied that Van Riebeeck regarded Africans as stinking dogs.
> Mr. Tukwayo, also replying to Mr. Malangabi, said the invitation was an insult. It was like a guest taking his dogs with him to a wedding party.
> Mr. Molelekwa said old men like Mr. Malangabi are incurable and should be isolated so as not to infect the younger generation.[26]

Johnson Ngwevela of the ANC and a member of the Langa Advisory Board also came out strongly against Malangabi and gave his whole-hearted support for a boycott of the celebrations. Much to the disappointment of the NAD, a resolution was adopted, at what its officials reluctantly admitted was a "well-attended meeting," to have nothing at all to do with the Van Riebeeck festival. The NAD decided not to pursue the matter further but to formulate specific alternative suggestions and, somewhat desperately, to search for "a place in the sun for a Native choir."[27]

For all its involvement in the particular issue around Langa's participation in Van Riebeeck's "tribal courtyard," the ANC was not devoting much attention to Van Riebeeck. This was because the resistance to the festival was secondary to the campaign of mass mobilization that was being planned against apartheid legislation, the former being a "prelude" to help achieve the latter.[28] In July 1951, at a joint conference of the leaders of the ANC, the SAIC, and FRAC, it had been decided to establish a council with representatives from these various organizations which would submit recommendations on how to proceed with a mass campaign to demand the repeal of the "oppressive laws" of apartheid. The Joint Planning Council, reporting back in November 1951, suggested that an ultimatum be sent to the government demanding the repeal of the laws by 29 February 1952. If the government did not meet this demand, the Planning Council proposed that the organizations take recourse to mass action, specifically defying the "unjust laws" and, in some instances, resorting to industrial action. It recommended two possible dates when this mass action should begin. The first and favored option of the Joint Planning Council was 6 April 1952:

> We consider this day to be most appropriate for the commencement of the struggle as it marks one of the greatest turning points in South African his-

tory by the advent of European settlers in this country, followed by colonialism and imperialist exploitation which has degraded, humiliated and kept in bondage the vast masses of the non-White people.[29]

The other possibility was 26 June 1952, which would recall the National Day of Protest which had taken place two years earlier when there had been a massive work strike in response to the killing of eighteen people in May Day clashes with the police on the Witwatersrand and the impending Unlawful Organisations Bill. Apart from practical considerations—would 6 April leave sufficient time to make the necessary arrangements for the campaign?—this was clearly a choice about the assignation of historical meaning. The date of 6 April, coinciding with the tercentenary, would emphasize the direct challenge being posed to Van Riebeeck and racial oppression. Such an explicit gesture would also fit the militancy of the ANC Youth League, whose president, Nelson Mandela, had warned that "the struggle should avoid the danger of bargaining for concessions." The date of 26 June, before 1950, had held no particular significance, but its association with subsequent events could help define it as a marker of resistance, when "the first steps towards freedom" were taken.[30] Navigating between historical meanings and organizational constraints, the ANC decided at its annual congress in December 1951 that protest meetings on 6 April would be "preliminary to a campaign of passive resistance" and only after these gatherings would the date to launch the campaign be chosen. In addition, the proposed action was linked directly to the Van Riebeeck festival. James Moroka and Walter Sisulu, the president and secretary general of the ANC, wrote to the prime minister, D. F. Malan, that "unless" the six "unjust laws," which they had singled out, were repealed, "the African people" could not "participate in any shape or form in such celebrations."[31]

Not only were many of the African people and others whom the festival designated as "non-European" refusing to partake of Van Riebeeck's nations, but those who were being trained thoroughly in the ways and means of the higher realms of "western civilization," which Van Riebeeck had supposedly initiated in southern Africa, were also reluctant to join in the festivities. As the schoolchildren from white schools had been taken along en masse to the festival, so the organizers expected that students from the country's universities would assist in building floats and acting in the pageantry, especially given the experience many of them had gained from their annual rag processions to raise money for various charities. And some students from the universities of Stellenbosch, Cape Town, Natal, Potchefstroom, the Orange Free State, and Rhodes did participate. This extensive list, which would seem to indicate that the universities overwhelmingly supported the festival, does not reveal the conflicts that took place in student bodies regarding the festival or that, at times, it was only individual departments or associations at the various campuses that were parading down Adderley Street that first week of April.[32]

In some cases students, either in mass meetings or through representative councils, rejected the festival outright as a "racially biased" "historical farce" and called on others in the university community to refuse to take part in it. The major debate among students at many of the English-language universities in the country revolved around the issues of academic and social segregation. Although very few black students were visible on these campuses, most of the students favored a policy of academic non-segregation while calling for social segregation. This meant the "admission of non-Europeans to the University, but for higher education purposes only, and not as equals in the social sphere." Black students should be able to use the same lecture theaters and libraries and write the same exams as white students, but they would have to live in separate residences and should not make use of the sporting and recreational facilities the university had to offer. When individuals from the Van Riebeeck festival committee approached students from these English-language universities to participate in the festival, the students adopted a similar attitude. In the Student Representative Council's (SRC's) discussions, students constantly reiterated that black students were not being permitted to participate fully and imbibe the offerings of the festival and "western civilization." This countered the principle of academic non-segregation, of which most of them approved. Thus, at the university campuses of Witwatersrand, Rhodes, and Cape Town, students were reluctant to bear, at the festival, the "torch of knowledge" as "leaders" who had taken root from "the seeds of European civilisation which were planted 300 years ago."[33]

Of all South Africa's universities, the one the festival organizers probably expected would offer the largest degree of participation was the University of Cape Town (UCT). This was not merely because of its location in "Van Riebeeck's city" but also because it represented an important element that had contributed to the development of what the festival defined as the English-speaking race. From very early on, T. B. Davie, the principal of UCT, had been included on the festival committee to represent English speakers. His wife, together with the University of Cape Town, presented the Higher Education float in the People's Pageant, bearing the "torch of knowledge" and "European civilization," through the offerings of different academic disciplines and faculties, to the African continent (Figure 12). Professor Mandlebrote from the History Department of UCT was, alongside H. B. Thom, a historical adviser for the festival, contributing "invaluable aid and advice" to Victor de Kock in compiling the official pictorial history of the festival, *Our Three Centuries*. As noted above, student expertise with floats was also required, and clubs and departments provided this. In addition, the annual rag procession was given the offi-

12. The "Higher Education" float represented various universities in the country and their academic disciplines as contributing toward growing the "seeds of European civilisation" in South Africa. The float was presented by Mrs. T. B. Davie and the University of Cape Town. Manuscripts and Archives Division, University of Cape Town Libraries. Photo: State Information Office, VR 266.

cial sanction of the festival committee, who, through negotiation, moved it forward to 29 March so it would not coincide with the major events of the festival, incorporated it into the official festival program, and promised to allocate funds to the procession (a figure in the region of £20,000 was mentioned). UCT also was charged with the task of staging the Higher Education exhibit at the festival fair, and T. B. Davie asked deans of the various faculties to convene a committee to facilitate this. Under Davie's guidance, this committee spent a great deal of its time arranging the science displays for the fair. In this latter guise, UCT was more than just a representative of an English heritage or a provider of pageantry but was declared, by the festival chair, to be the "oldest institution in our land for higher education." For playing a fundamental role in the "preparation of our youth in the service of the land and nation," UCT was being proclaimed, in its own right, as a Jan van Riebeeck.[34]

This claim did not sit well with some of the students at the UCT campus on Groote Schuur estate, bequeathed by Cecil John Rhodes. The major issue of the day at UCT was that of academic and social segregation. One group, largely

Afrikaans speakers, favored the creation of separate academic institutions for white and black students. Another group, clustered around the immediate past-president of the SRC, Zac de Beer (and including in its ranks Martin Thompson, who was to assume the role of his great-great grandfather on Adderley Street), defended academic non-segregation and social segregation, maintaining that social equality could not "operate in this country." A third group was inclined to do away with social segregation as well but felt that strategically it was better to keep to the "existing practice in the social sphere." Any attempt to push for equality in this area at this stage was seen as possibly undermining the policy of academic non-segregation that the university upheld. It was this latter group which proposed that the student body in no way whatsoever take part in the tercentenary celebrations.[35]

The sometimes heated debate over participation in the festival at UCT first surfaced in an SRC meeting on 12 September when a motion was placed on the table that it was the "right and duty of the University of Cape Town to participate in these celebrations." At the forefront of opposing the motion was Ronald Segal, a student who had arrived at UCT in 1950 from Sea Point High School, had fraternized with students and lecturers involved with the Unity Movement, and had immersed himself in cultural societies, teaching at "non-European" night schools and university politics.[36] Segal argued that because the festival and the pageantry were educationally pernicious, historically inaccurate, and racially exclusionary (some UCT students could not take part in the festival even if they wished to), the SRC should not support the motion. Other SRC members, drawing on their own studies to show that the pageantry had little historical veracity and that what was being presented was an outmoded conceptualization of South African history, supported him.

> Mr. Katz said that most scientific historians agree that the old historical interpretation of Theal, on which the pageant was based, was incorrect. If we supported the Festival we would be agreeing with this interpretation. Such things as the abolition of slavery, which had been of major importance in the development of South Africa . . . had not been included in the pageant, while such subjects as Lord Charles Somerset on a hunting expedition had been included. He was not against a historical pageant, but this was not a pageant, but rather a propaganda campaign.[37]

Another student concurred, referring to the pageant as a "historical farce" which had neglected so "great an event as the Emancipation of Slaves." It is not clear where these students had acquired this historical knowledge, but it is possible that Leonard Thompson and Jean van der Poel, who filled, respectively, the senior lecturer and lecturer posts at the time in the History Department at UCT, were teaching them. Their interpretation of South African history, which centered on the condition of "oppressed racial groups," differed markedly from that of both Theal and their department head, Mandelbrote, whose major interest was in the workings of colonial society, particularly the constitutional development of the Cape colony before and after the introduction of Responsible Government. These student voices, however, were in the minority, and Segal could not muster enough support to defeat the original motion to participate, proposed by J. M. Didcott and M. L. Mitchell, which carried by a vote of 9 to 6. The motion did add a rider, however, that the executive of the student body draw up a list of objections to the pageant program and submit these to the SRC for consideration at a later stage.[38]

A few days after this decision, fifty-four students petitioned the SRC executive to hold a mass meeting to re-consider the issue of participating in the festival. The meeting, which the SRC was constitutionally required to call, took place on 17 September, in Jameson Hall. About five hundred students attended, and Segal, once again, was the keynote speaker advocating a boycott of the festival. As he stood to speak, he recalls, students who were National Party supporters, and in favor of the festival and its objectives, started "howling and singing." This reminded Segal of his school days at Sea Point High where he was the subject of much verbal and physical abuse because of his wealthy background ("I was picked up by a driver in a Chrysler"), and because of his elocution, academic performance, and loathing of rugby. "It was school all over again, I thought; the bullies were baying."[39] Once the crescendo had died down, he began to speak and a silence enveloped the hall. At that moment, a feeling of "exaltation" filled him:

> I was hitting back at . . . a small cluster of taunting boys in a corner of the school courtyard. I don't suppose that I shall ever speak like that again, in a surge that left me drained and desolate afterwards. It must have been, it seems to me now, a sort of seizure, a convulsion of will to batter that wild jeering into silence.[40]

According to Segal, the hall erupted into applause when he had finished, and even the bullies "in the bays" of Jameson Hall had been defeated by his "will to overcome." Yet, because the meeting had run overtime and there was not a quorum in the audience, no vote was taken. The SRC decided to stand by its original motion to participate and to forward suggestions to the organizing committee of the festival as to how it should alter the pageant. These recommendations revolved around how to include "Non-Europeans" in a South African past: as soldiers in the two world wars, as part of "Education today," and as converts on the Moravian mission station at Genadendal. Although the pageant committee paid little heed to these suggestions, these ruptures at UCT, which were widely reported, did indicate, even though those opposing participation were represented as a minority of the student population, that there was not the unanimity over Van Riebeeck on Rhodes's estate that the festival committee assumed it could automatically count on. The strongest advocates of academic non-segregation and those who had acquired alternative knowledges of South Africa's past were fully prepared to confront the tercentenary festival and all its (mis)representations.[41]

As plans for the festival were being finalized at the end of 1951, therefore, it was increasingly apparent that the organizers were encountering opposition to their plans and their versions of the past from a variety of sectors, particularly from those termed "non-Europeans" whom the planners wanted to incorporate into separate programs. The most vocal opposition was from the Unity Movement, which saw the attempts to involve separate coloured cultural groups in the festival as the ultimate insult. Not only was the festival "glorifying . . . 300 years of violence" by "turning Van Riebeeck into a divine ancestor, a superman" and ignoring "the existence of millions of Non-white people who originally lived in South Africa," the Unity Movement claimed, but the festival was also assuming a stance of "supreme, if not sadistic arrogance to try and force the victims to celebrate as well."[42] Similarly the ANC, although not a prime advocate of the boycott of the festival, was using the date of 6 April 1952 as a marker of historical significance to launch its campaign of defiance. Yet many other reasons abounded for why Van Riebeeck was either being actively contested or ignored. These involved asserting the status of a racial or educated or "westernized" or university elite, with these categories overlapping at times. More often than not, these responses were related to the invitations the festival organizers had sent out to specific, largely racially categorized, constituencies. It was already apparent by the end of 1951 that many of these invitations were being spurned and that Sheik Yusuf would encounter problems in getting his company together. There was an imminent danger that his period of exile at the Cape might be lonelier than even he or the Dutch East India Company had anticipated.

Promoting the Boycott on Stage

From the last quarter of 1951 until Sunday, 6 April 1952, when the ANC held a mass rally on Cape Town's Grand Parade, the opponents of Van Riebeeck, who had already identified themselves in the previous months, launched an all-out campaign to promote the boycott of his festival. On these oppositional stages, oratory was the primary vehicle used to promote the boycott as histories were produced, sometimes in a very abbreviated fashion, explicitly linked to political programs. The appeal, or otherwise, of moral and political argument transmitted by the various speakers bore knowledge of the past to audiences as "They Marched . . . and They Listened."[43]

Yet this notion of persuading audiences through words was continually at odds with the need to play on emotions, metaphors, and excitement as a way to convey and acquire messages. This paralleled the very dilemma that had faced the pageant organizers, who were attempting to evoke an emotional response while ensuring that a serious historical message was being conveyed. Although the opponents of the festival were sensitive to the need for the dramatic, where borders between fantasy and reality were blurred and the visual and emotional were privileged, there is little evidence that they ever considered going to the extreme of staging elaborate pageants as the organizers of the tercentenary had. Finding appropriate models, particularly in Cape Town, for staging a spectacle of resistance must in itself have presented immense difficulties. The Moshoeshoe, Ntsikana, and Mfengu festivals, which had been celebrated in Langa in the 1940s and 1950s, were not spectacular and their appeal was severely circumscribed. They mobilized participants around ethnic and religious identities in programs usually involving a series of speeches, songs, and prayers, followed by eating and drinking. The annual New Year "coon carnival" processions by troupes of minstrels through the streets of Cape Town was generally seen by anti-apartheid organizations as a form of debasement, a series of playful antics that merely served to amuse the white onlookers. *The Guardian* had suggested that the carnival take on themes reflecting opposition to government policies or else it would basically simply remain a vehicle "to keep the coloured man a happy servant." And the University of Cape Town's hospital rag procession, which raised money for medical institutions in the Cape Peninsula, was hardly appropriate given its self-proclaimed intention to be conducted in "the spirit of the non-political" and its continued association with the organizers of the Van Riebeeck festival. Moreover, the opponents of the festival conjured up images of rag similar to those the organizers projected, seeing it as a "circus" that, in this case, was far removed from the "reality" which the "self-respecting non-Europeans" sought to portray.[44]

Extending the pageantry of the festival to the oppositional stage was also problematic in that play and drama might become the central focus. Although this could be utilized to convey different messages and to mock the drama the festival organizers presented, the pervasiveness of the festival's projections in newspapers and on film and radio made this difficult to achieve. If the dramatic were promoted still further, it might reproduce rather than undermine the images of the festival. Such self-styled Van Riebeeck festivals were commonplace on school stages in the early months of 1952. One such drama was re-enacted at Durban Indian Girls High School.

There was a delicious aroma of coffee in the air. The strains of "Die Stem" and the "Marseillaise" could be heard. Dainty Dutch vrous [women] and English and French ladies in the pretty gowns of the period tripped over the playground with their partners. Malay and Indian ladies in their graceful dresses and a Zulu intombi [girl], blowing her mouth organ, mingled freely with them. The tens and nines competed against one another by making models illustrating certain events in Cape history. The tens, who modelled the arrival of the 1820 settlers, took the prize. But the other two models made by the nines, illustrating the arrival of Van Riebeeck and the Great Trek, were also well done and the girls took great pains over them. The whole scene was one of great festivity—we were having our Van Riebeeck celebrations—the first of the many memorable events of this year.[45]

This play, which celebrated the landing and the history being associated with it, almost mimicked the pageantry of the festival, although the "free mingling" was not what the organizers had in mind for the streets of Cape Town. Children acted the parts of individual characters that were in the forefront of the pageant, assuming "adult roles" and possibly, in the process, acquiring the historical knowledge the festival sought to portray. Obviously this type of drama was not one the opponents of the festival wanted to encourage on a large scale as they sought to counter what *The Guardian* derisively termed the "the amateurish realism of the proposed tableau" for the streets of Cape Town.[46]

But pageantry did not necessarily have to copy the content of the festival, and, even when it did, that content might be subverted. Indeed play, drama, and festivals have been used over the centuries as key media to express political opposition. The public participation as actors and audience enables a challenge to the ordering that the organized pageantry attempts to establish. FRAC made one explicit attempt to mount a festival to counter the intentions of the Van Riebeeck celebrations. FRAC's commemoration, like the festival, was to include a series of historical tableaux, but, in contrast to the official script being written for the streets of Cape Town, the history FRAC presented would be both objective and based on a nationalism that drew together "all the sections of our people." The content of such a history was never made explicit, but a writer for *The Guardian* had suggested earlier that this history could include a series of figures from the past who could contribute dramatic material as "the greatest individual nation-builders": Simon van der Stel, the "Coloured man" who was "the most far-seeing . . . of the Dutch governors"; Moshesh, who "welded" the "Basotho people" from "fragments"; Shaka, who raised the "most powerful warrior empire south of the equator"; Gandhi, who left "his footprints" in South Africa; and Makana, "the Xhosa hero" who "drowned in captivity off Robben Island." This nation and those representing its past were

exclusively male, but, in contrast to Van Riebeeck's history, many races constituted this nation. Instead of being built on colonialism and its alibi, "western civilization," resistance to racial oppression was the force moving this history forward and it was racial unity that was needed to carry it further. Silas
Molema expressed a similar sentiment at the SAIC conference in January 1952,
when he called for "men and women of colour," "the Indian, the African and
the Eur-African or Coloured people" to unite as oppressed people in order to
fight for "common rights." Sub-committees of historians, artists, and dramatists were set in place to develop this inclusive national past, the Cape Town
City Council was to be asked for a grant of £500, and the mayor and three other
councilors were to be invited to sit on the pageant committee. There is no evidence that the Council, which had already donated some £25,000 to the Van
Riebeeck festival, was approached by FRAC in this regard. With FRAC spending most of its time on launching the defiance campaign in the western Cape,
their anti-Van Riebeeck celebration never came to fruition.[47]

Instead of parading in the streets and performing in stadiums, the opponents of the Van Riebeeck festival staged their opposition in rhetorical displays
in churches, market halls, and municipal buildings, on hillsides and in town
squares. The ANC and organizations aligned with it, in particular, made use
of these stages to promote and draw attention to their campaign of defiance
after D. F. Malan had turned down their call for the repeal of apartheid's "unjust laws." Casting apartheid as a natural system based on biologically determined differences, Malan not only had claimed that the structures and laws of
racial separation were just but that "natives" were in no way to be seen as constituting part of the same South African nation as those who represented their
ancestry as being derived from Van Riebeeck. Thus he castigated the ANC for
approaching him directly instead of going through the Native Affairs Department and suggested that the Bantu Authorities Act was "designed to give the
Africans the opportunity of enlightened administration of their own affairs."
This outright rejection by Malan of the ANC's call for all races to be part of
the same nation "of the land of their birth" left the ANC with little choice but
to embark on its planned defiance campaign and to spurn the separate offerings of Van Riebeeck as no "substitute for direct representation in the Councils
of State."[48]

With Van Riebeeck providing more of a vehicle for the impending action,
rather than being the direct focus, it would appear that the meetings around
the defiance campaign did little more than offer brief historical excursions.
From media representations of the meetings, it seems the emphasis was on support, organization, recruitment, volunteers, discipline, lessons, and funding in
order to prepare for action some time later in the year. Only Silas Molema, the
ANC treasurer, seems to have made extensive use of history. At both the South

African Indian Congress in January 1952 and at his home base of Mafikeng, where the ANC branch organized meetings opposing the local Van Riebeeck festival and launched the defiance campaign, Molema drew extensively on the past and berated Van Riebeeck for inaugurating the process of land dispossession.[49]

What is notable about these histories in 1952 is that they indicate a notable shift in Molema's political thinking. His previous historical writings were *The Bantu Past and Present* (1920) and *Chief Moroka: His Life, His Times, His Country and His People* (1951). In *Chief Moroka*, in the chapter dealing with "The Renaissance" of the Barolong with the assistance of missionaries, he included enthusiastic accounts of the 1938 and 1949 Voortrekker commemorations. He recalled that when the wagons of the symbolic trek reached Thaba Nchu in 1938, there to welcome them was Chief John Moroka who, in "fitting words" recalled "poignant incidents of a century previously" and presented the trekkers with an ox "to recall and renew the co-operation and friendship which had subsisted a hundred years previously between Chief Moroka and the Voortrekkers." The actual Voortrekker Monument he described as majestic, grand in conception, displaying a "wealth of design, and beauty of workmanship."[50] In 1952 Molema was labeling such commemorations on stage as "European festivals" which celebrated the destruction, exploitation, and degradation of black communities. The "salient" and "dominant fact of South African history," he told SAIC members, was

> that all the monuments, all the celebrations and all the feasts of the white
> man have a diametrically opposite meaning to the black man, because every
> monument of the white man perpetuates the memory of the annihilation of
> some black community, every celebration of victory the remembrance of
> our defeat, his every feast means our famine and his laughter our tears.[51]

The impending Van Riebeeck festival was another of these occasions, and Molema referred to it as a "frenzy of self-adulation."[52]

In rendering "the shameful catalogue of Oppressive Laws" to the audience in Mafikeng, Molema presented Africans as free, happy, and independent prior to the arrival of the European "pirates" from "across the seas." It was the "white adventurer, merchant and administrators" who undermined the work of the missionaries and the nineteenth-century imperial government by stealing "the land, and the cattle and the labour" from the "Black Man," barring him from the franchise and turning him into a "devil . . . [b]orn to serve his white master then go down like a dog into the grave." Van Riebeeck was the first of these pirates setting an example when he "cheated the African and stole his land." To participate in the Van Riebeeck festival, then, would be like "glorifying in their own defeat."[53]

These histories Molema delivered were similar to the one A. C. Jordan presented at Langa in September 1951. The story of conquest, dispossession, and enslavement, and the warning against collaboration, were all there. What is much more evident, however, is that although this type of history of South Africa as a European nation was not the one D. F. Malan and Van Riebeeck sought to portray, there was a marked, albeit unintentional, resemblance to the festival's histories. At the very core of the festival was the embellishment of a distinction between settler and African in order to provide Jan van Riebeeck with the alibi of history to commemorate his landing in 1952. By using the selfsame distinction, Molema was able to turn whites into Europeans, who brought exploitation, and blacks into oppressed people, who were inherently Africans. It was the latter he called on to unite and develop "race pride" so as to achieve salvation and liberation.[54]

Molema's extensive use of history at meetings leading up to the defiance campaign seems to have been exceptional. When history was brought onstage, it tended to be with a dramatic flourish that set it off from the preceding speeches. As was planned, most of these meetings took place on the weekend of 5–6 April 1952 in order to coincide with the Van Riebeeck festival and directly challenge the proceedings taking place on the streets of Cape Town. On 6 April, in Fordsburg, Johannesburg, the meeting started off with prayers, messages of support, and instructions for action, after which James Moroka, the president of the ANC, addressed the crowd. An almost complete silence enveloped the gathering as Moroka, adorned in a black, green, and gold "Mantle of Freedom," told his listeners that the celebrations of Van Riebeeck's landing ignored the "role of the Non-Europeans in South Africa." Van Riebeeck, he said, had brought slavery to South Africa, and this still pervaded white attitudes toward "the black."[55] In this abbreviated history for the political stage, Moroka cast all that was the South African past into the image of Van Riebeeck to create a history which used slavery as the icon of racial oppression for more than three hundred years, a history that needed to be dismantled by embarking on mass action against apartheid's laws.

This historical vision was repeated at other meetings around the country on 6 April. J. B. Marks, the Transvaal president of the ANC, gave a speech in Port Elizabeth where he labeled Van Riebeeck's day as one of protest "against 300 years of oppression on the non-Europeans in South Africa." In Alice, on the Friday before the defiance campaign meeting, in a Van Riebeeck day parade, the professor of history from Fort Hare, H. J. Chapman, had narrated a history from "the landing" through "the Huguenots," "the settlers," "the Great Trek" to "Commerce" as "the life blood of the nation." Two days later, at a "protest meeting" in the Bantu Presbyterian Church in Alice, the professor of African studies at Fort Hare and Cape president of the ANC, Z. K. Matthews, was calling "the past three hundred years" a time of "humiliations and indignities," when "the gulf between the inhabitants of this sub-continent" had widened "as a result of the short-sighted policies of those who had controlled the various South African governments during that period."[56]

The defiance campaign meeting on Cape Town's Grand Parade on 6 April focused largely on the festival and its interpretation of history. The spatial proximity to the festival and the lavish, incessant daily publicity given to its events made it difficult to ignore. On the afternoon of 6 April, the festival was reaching its climax in a formal service that contained little of the razzmatazz that had characterized the events of the previous days. A wreath-laying ceremony was performed in the presence of "high dignitaries" at the base of a replica of Van Riebeeck's statue on the foreshore, a prayer was read by the ambassador of the Netherlands, a series of mainly religious songs was rendered by the Transvaal Festival Choir, and the service was concluded with the singing of the Wilhelmus, the Dutch national anthem. The sense of simplicity that was brought to bear on the ceremony was intended to ensure that the festival would be seen as a serious rendition of a history which solemnly bound the settler nation together.[57]

As the festival endeavored to reach for the culmination and consecration of its past on the foreshore, on the Grand Parade speakers were referring to the proceedings taking place a few hundred meters away as a celebration of "300 years of white baaskap." Cissie Gool said that the festival was mere "gilded hypocrisy and distorted history" and that one float was missing from the pageantry and that was the "Float of Truth." This truth, said Johnny Gomas of the Franchise Action Council, was that, in the past three hundred years, the "non-Europeans had lost their rights more and more . . . and were today hated by the whites." The only recourse left was to fight for these rights by joining in the defiance campaign.[58]

The continual allusion to three hundred years at these meetings to promote the defiance campaign compacted the time of Van Riebeeck as the fount of all that followed in South African history. But the difference between these three hundred years and the years the festival organizers sought to promote was significant. In the festival's version Van Riebeeck provided the basis of the future, something on which to build. Those gathered on 6 April in Fordsburg's "Freedom Square," on Cape Town's Grand Parade, and in the Presbyterian Church in Alice wanted to bring that history to an end, to give it an aura of pastness. These "days of Van Riebeeck," stretching from 1652 to the present (1952), Moroka declared to be over: now "African, Indian and Coloured people were demanding their rights and freedom." Dr. Bokwe, the national chair of the ANC, asserted that the theme of the Van Riebeeck festival should not have been "We Build a Nation" but rather "We Bury a Nation." Rev. J. Jolobe called on Africans to "answer the call of destiny and fly like eagles to the skies of fame." What this call of destiny entailed was still rather vague but it did include a growing popular movement, aspiring toward African salvation. In this context, history (deriving, although not solely, from Jan van Riebeeck) as the bearer of modernity, had failed the test of time, bringing about "death, destruction, calamity, frustration and chaos," and now needed to be ended as "the struggle . . . against the oppression of the last 300 years" began.[59]

Although the defiance campaign meetings made limited use of history and contested the representations of the past being projected in the festival, those associated with the Unity Movement directed their focus squarely on the tercentenary and actively promoted the boycott of its events in the months immediately leading up to the landing of Van Riebeeck. Both the All-African Convention and the African Political Organisation, which by then were affiliated with the Unity Movement and supported its policy of non-collaboration, discussed the festival at length and gave their full backing to promoting an active boycott of the festival. But it was in Cape Town, where the Unity Movement had a large support base among teachers designated coloured and where the festival was making its presence most visibly felt, that the boycott campaign was centered. Meetings involving the Welcome Estate-Rylands Civic Association, Gleemoor Civic Association, Wetton Ratepayers Association, and the Bloemhof Flats Housing Scheme had already indicated their support of the boycott, and once the Unity Movement officially opened its campaign against the festival on 18 January 1952, others followed. Regular meetings to advocate the boycott were held throughout Cape Town, in the city center, District Six, and Schotsche Kloof, through to Kensington, Vasco, Elsies River, Kewtown, Grassy Park, and Nyanga. To persuade the two hundred to three hundred people who attended each of these meetings to keep away from the activities planned for the foreshore, they were given information about the type of history the festival sought to portray, as well as critiques of that history, and were consistently warned about the dangers of collaboration.[60]

Although these meetings were effective in mobilizing support for the boycott, members of the Unity Movement were uneasy about slogans and speeches becoming the basis for organization. Brief, performative speeches might attract followers who had a facile understanding, but many would lack the ability to advance the policy of non-collaboration. Although the dramatic was used effectively at times—"Let the masters celebrate," Mr. Tabata said amid applause, "for they will never again be able to celebrate. This is their last supper"—it was the spoken word, albeit on stage, as the conveyer of a sometimes lengthy history, that tended to dominate Unity Movement meetings where calls were being made to boycott the "Festival of Hate." The "educational work" of conveying a knowledge of the past on the political stage was the basis for achieving an "intelligent" "understanding" and "practical application of those ideas."[61]

These history lessons were similar to the ones the ANC was delivering in that slavery was the central motif characterizing South African history. Wycliff Tsotsi, the president of the All-African Convention, summed up South African history in one phrase: "the story of the military conquest and dispossession, of social ostracism and the political and economic enslavement of the indigenous African inhabitants of this country by European invaders." Various pieces of legislation were given the appellation "slave" to denote their oppressive content. At the meeting organized by the Unity Movement on the Grand Parade on 30 March, for instance, Ben Kies referred to the Act of Union as a "slave act." In Unity Movement pasts, slavery was also used as a vehicle to discourage participation in the Van Riebeeck festival, that event being condemned as a celebration of the former age. I. B. Tabata, speaking in Landsowne, gave the slave metaphor an international context, by relating how, in Haiti, old slaves would celebrate the arrival of new slaves by slaughtering a beast. This, he maintained, was how slaves were made to celebrate their own enslavement.[62]

A primary concern of these speeches was to challenge the festival organizers' authority to present a racially exclusive past as constituting South African history. The speeches continually emphasized that the "facts" the festival presented held little validity and were merely pieces of information being twisted to suit a political program of racial domination. Or, as Tsotsi put it, these bits of information were used to claim "a knowledge of South African History" merely based on "the colour of their skins." Yet, when it came to presenting South African history for a "true South African nation," as constituted by facts rather than race, race was the defining characteristic. Tsotsi's lengthy speech to the All-African Convention in December 1951—the reporter for *The Guardian* berated it as "pedantic"—was almost entirely a history lesson which, like Molema's addresses in Johannesburg and Mafikeng, countered Van Riebeeck's past by setting up categories of "African inhabitants" and "European invaders." He related the "wars against the indigenous peoples" to the need to supply passing ships from Europe, to make "White farmers wealthy," and to provide cheap labor for the "Europeans." Missionaries were singled out for the role they played "in the conquest and subjugation of the Non-Whites." After these wars, the Act of Union gave the "Europeans" political power by excluding the "Non-Europeans" and subsequently passing laws "against the Non-Europeans."[63]

Although the festival's past would not talk of race in these terms—its concern was the coming together of the white race into a nation—there was more than just a brief correspondence between the history Tsotsi was delivering and that of Van Riebeeck. To proclaim whites as being of European extraction was as central to the Van Riebeeck festival as it was for Tsotsi. For the former it was the source of "western civilization"; for the latter it was the basis for assertions of indigeneity, which "western civilization" destroyed. Moreover, in both instances, it was the nation that was seen as bringing race to an end. Race was conceived of as pre-modern, to be eradicated by the coming together of the founder nations under the aegis of Van Riebeeck, or through the "reason and principle" of the struggle against Van Riebeeck.[64]

Whether reason and principle comprised the force behind the boycott of the festival, there is little doubt that, as these staged performances to counter Van Riebeeck increased in regularity, the boycott gathered momentum. I. D. du Plessis's plans for the coloured and Malay day encountered even greater resistance, as his own creation, the Malay Choir Board, contemplated withdrawing but feared, if they did so, that they would not be permitted to use the Cape Town City Hall for their competitions in the future. By February 1952 more than half the main Malay choirs, including the Celtics and the Boarding Boys, had spurned invitations to perform at the Van Riebeeck Stadium because of their "duty to the people," and by the end of March all the choirs had decided to withdraw. Two jazz bands from Johannesburg, the Manhattan Brothers and the Shantytown Sextet, turned down offers of £400 to perform. The NAD, which had decided to proceed with its plans for a "tribal village" at the festival fair, found that the costs had gone up considerably, as it had to bring in "Natives from distant parts" to perform the roles assigned to them. Details of the "*Bantoe-fees*" in Langa had also been fleshed out to arouse interest. It was to include a program of children's sporting activities in the morning, a free lunch for all, a soccer match in the afternoon, and, in the evening, a "Native musical" and movie shows. Based on its previous experience of promoting the festival in Langa, the NAD was hesitant about officially sanctioning this program but decided it would award prizes for sports if the "Natives accept the invitation." In spite of all the offerings and incentives from the NAD, very few did, and the proposed "celebration" on the playing fields of Langa did not transpire.[65]

The Printed History Lessons

For all the gathering momentum of the boycott and its promotion on the political stage, the opponents of the festival felt that, to contest Van Riebeeck effectively, they had to challenge the historical authority that derived from the printed word. In order to "totally reject the . . . distortions and falsifications of history," it was, in the words of Dora Taylor (author of *The Role of the Missionaries in Conquest*) essential to "undertake the task of re-writing history." The Unity Movement, in particular, which was uneasy about mass political gatherings, asserted that writing and publishing history was a much more productive way of learning "lessons of the past." In written histories the "logical interpretation" and "direct quotation from, and numerous references to, old documents and diaries" gave the "point of view of the oppressed" more "of the truth" and "an honest beginning" than "slogans and mere speeches."[66]

Thus opponents of the festival produced a series of anti-Van Riebeeck publications to coincide with and contest the tercentenary, with political activists associated with the Unity Movement being the most prolific. Apart from *Missionaries in Conquest* and the articles in *The Educational Journal*, mentioned above, these publications included *Three Hundred Years* by Hosea Jaffe, articles in *The Torch* by "Boycott," under the title "The True Story of Jan van Riebeeck," and a chronology of the "wars and laws against us" in the "Special Boycott Edition" of *The Torch*. Other individuals and organizations published articles that challenged Van Riebeeck's history. The Forum Club, an organization created in the 1940s in Cape Town to encourage open critiques of the democratic movement, published a lecture given by Kenny Jordaan entitled "Jan van Riebeeck: His Place in South African History." Between February and April 1952, *The Guardian* ran a historical series entitled "1652—and All That" by Eddie Roux, author of *Time Longer Than Rope* and former Communist Party member. Finally, Patrick Duncan, a member of the British colonial service in Basutholand, who resigned his position to join the defiance campaign, writing under the pseudonym "Melanchthon," specially compiled and published a pamphlet for the tercentenary, which sold for one penny, entitled "Three Centuries of Wrong."[67]

In broad general terms these printed histories were all attempting to counter the official history of the festival. An essential element of the histories published in *The Guardian* and *The Torch* was an almost direct inversion of the historical representations of the festival. Sheik Yusuf, for instance, whom the festival organizers presented as an icon of Malay ethnic history, was changed, in the pages of *The Torch*, into a resister who believed in non-collaboration. The bushmen who were depicted as wild and primitive in the festival fair became communal owners of land, artistic geniuses, and inventive craftsmen, and were re-named Batwa. Of course, the greatest inversion was reserved for Van Riebeeck, who was described as a "mediocre surgeon" and a petty criminal who had "left Batavia under a cloud."[68]

These reverse images from *The Torch* and *The Guardian* were replicating the poster from the 30 March meeting on the Grand Parade of an upside-down Van Riebeeck with a cross defacing its façade. The point of departure of these published histories around the boycott was the same as that of the festival histories.

> Van Riebeeck remained the shaper of the South African past, and conflicts were reduced to an assessment of his moral qualities and his legacy. The debate moved little beyond whether Van Riebeeck was saint or sinner, superhero or criminal.[69]

But not all oppositional histories were the same. Roux's "1652—and All That," for instance, although it does posit the arrival of Van Riebeeck as a turning point which established a social and economic system of slavery that "has coloured the minds of South African white men ever since," is careful to point out that Van Riebeeck's occupation of the Cape was incidental. Roux also claims that the initial form slavery took at the Cape was mild compared to plantation slavery in the West Indies, allowing for the emergence of craft industries among the enslaved. This leads to the central point of his series, that black South Africans have contributed in many ways to the development of the country and that these contributions must be allowed to flourish by doing away with structures of racial segregation. In presenting this thesis, "1652" is much the same as Roux's work, *Time Longer Than Rope*, which was published four years earlier. Although *Time Longer Than Rope* was the first major Africanist work in South Africa, in that it posited the centrality of the struggle of Africans for their rights, the narrative presented consistently speaks for the "black man" and "his advancement" against the irrationality of race. In "1652," as in *Time Longer Than Rope*, race was presented as pre-modern and pre-enlightenment, and its elimination as the pre-requisite for nation building, inadvertently coinciding with similar notions of race as pre-national that the festival publicized.[70]

The Torch's "Boycott" was more concerned than Roux in challenging the festival's images directly and replacing them with truths. The "True Story of Van Riebeeck" was one of a "demoted, disgraced, sacked thief, begging and whining for a job"; the "truth about Sheik Yusuf" was that the Dutch regarded him "as an evil man" whom they "banished . . . to the Cape"; the "Strandlopers" who encountered Van Riebeeck were "skilled fishermen, expert workers . . . [who] made huts [and] played music"; and "the Batwa . . . were not less primitive than the old inhabitants of England or Holland." In the new history that "Boycott" presented, Sheik Yusuf, the Strandlopers, and the Batwa became heroes of non-collaboration, who did not succumb to Van Riebeeck and his followers. Clearly, the demarcation between lies and truth lay along the same divide as that of participation and boycott. This was the mirror image of the festival's construction of the space of the authentic past as being located within the history of its pageantry and publications. Both "Boycott" and Van Riebeeck offered virtually no escape from this history-as-mirror, the former "only knowable through a necessarily false representation" of the latter, thus threatening "to reproduce the static, essentialist categories" it wished to contest.[71]

The two lengthiest accounts that countered Van Riebeeck's history, by Jaffe and Taylor, also made extensive use of this inverted imagery. Both books engaged directly with the historical depictions of the festival and represented "appropriately adversary ideological history." In the case of *Missionaries,* the book also challenged accounts by mission-educated Africans, particularly those who were leading members of the ANC, such as Silas Molema, who had heaped inordinate amounts of praise on their teachers for bringing to "the Bantu, perhaps more than any other people," "civilisation, Christianity, and education." Far from being the bearers of light, Taylor argued, the missionaries had subjugated "the minds of the people" in order to ensure white domination. This was continuing through the maintenance of "an intellectual stranglehold over the leadership of the non-Europeans." This, perhaps, was the meaning of Taylor's challenge, given that the Van Riebeeck festival, in its attempt to create a settler past, did not paint missionaries in an entirely glowing light and referred in the float procession to the "accusation" by members of the London Missionary Society that the European settlers at the beginning of the nineteenth century "were ill-treating the Hottentots" as "entirely fictitious."[72]

The other dominating feature of both these works is their almost obsessive tendency to cite from documentary sources and, particularly in the case of Jaffe, to ensure that these were referenced. Within Unity Movement circles, this was the cause of much debate over whether the authors had achieved the appropriate balance between facts and analysis. One reviewer complimented *Three Hundred Years* because it contained both a "wealth of interesting historical data," which indicated "fine historical draftsmanship," and an "understanding and analysis which reveal the underlying social forces in the evolution of South African society." This was far more complimentary than A. C. Jordan's comment in his comparison of the two books. The "author [of *Missionaries in Conquest*]," Jordan asserted, "puts forward a thesis and facts [as proof]. . . . Facts and dates are used to support a thesis; unlike Mnguni [Jaffe], to whom dates and facts are ends in themselves." Both critiques point to the way history and political action, derived from the analysis presented, are regarded as indivisible in these works. Providing historical facts in the authoritative published account was important in as much as these facts were the conveyers of political lessons. In Taylor's introduction, she saw the stripping away of racial myths as "the way to liberating ourselves," while Jaffe's exposition was written to create an understanding of "how to transform the status quo." More than the historical characters and events that were sometimes presented in a mirror-like fashion, it in this insistence on the indivisibility of history-as-facts and politics that challenged the Van Riebeeck festival, where the history (as objective fact) was supposedly removed from politics and where a political truce was declared among the parliamentary parties for the three weeks of the festival so as to allow history to proceed through the streets of Cape Town unhindered. The histories by Taylor and Jaffe transformed these processions into sites of political contestation. Subjecting this festival truce to fact and analysis disputed the notions that South African history was about settlement, that politics was "between Europeans," reserved for the descendants of the settlers, and that "the non-Europeans would be well advised to leave the struggle to the Europeans."[73]

It would be erroneous to place all the published challenges to Van Riebeeck in the category of mirroring and inverting the festival's imagery. Kenny Jordaan's published lecture, "Jan van Riebeeck: His Place," contested the historical paradigms of both the festival and its primary opponents by suggesting that Van Riebeeck had nothing to do with the structures of racial domination that existed in South Africa in the 1950s. Jordaan argued that it was the mining revolution of the 1870s that destroyed pre-capitalist societies and created a universal system of wage labor in the region that underpinned the "national enslavement of the non-Europeans." This approach to South African history, which relied on Marxist theory together with documentary sources (Jordaan makes wide use of Van Riebeeck's diary) and what Jordaan admitted was the work of "the conservative historian Theal," was an entirely novel one that went far beyond the inverted past. Perhaps it was precisely the form this publication took which enabled it to produce a past that did not fall easily into the mirror categories of the festival and its opponents. A lecture to a small discussion group, which would always be on the fringe of the public terrain and hidden from its vista, was a safe place to present ideas that in many senses were beyond the mainstream of even academic history in South Africa at that stage. Here Jordaan was able to present his position for criticism and discussion to a small select audience. Those who were directly engaging Van Riebeeck in the public sphere, where what mattered were "weighty political considerations" and convincing audiences to reject the festival, could not make such bold, new, historical assertions.[74]

In the context of the festival, all these challenges in print—even when they mirrored the past that the organizers were attempting to portray—fundamentally contested the authority of the official historical depictions. The 1952 Van Riebeeck festival, although it placed great emphasis on visualizing the past, always regarded the written word of history as providing the authentic basis of its historical productions. Apart from Van Riebeeck's diary (which Professor Thom from Stellenbosch University translated and edited to coincide with the tercentenary), a range of publications was produced. Many of these bore the official stamp of the central committee of the festival and found their way into school libraries. Herschel School, for instance, noted that among its library acquisitions for 1952 were *Our Three Centuries, Three Ships Came Sailing, The Old Company's Gardens,* and *The Dromedaris: 300 Years.* It could also have ordered *Drie Eeue* [Three centuries], a five-volume illustrated history, specially written for the "youth of South Africa" by D. W. Kruger, Anna Boeseken, and A. Kieser; *Geskiedenis van Suid-Afrika* by A. J. van der Watt, J. A. Widd, and A. L. Geyer; and Maskew Miller's special set of publications for the tercentenary: *Overberg Outspan* by Edmund Burrows, *The Cape Peninsula,* edited by J. A. Mabbutt, and *First Ladies of the Cape* by Gwen Mills. Indeed, it was by defining and printing the word, the map, and the picture that the festival gained its sense of being history. A special exhibition was held at the South African Library, between 1 March and 5 April 1952, of books, atlases, and maps in its holdings "in commemoration of the arrival of Jan van Riebeeck at the Cape." Although in no way measuring up to the printed word of the festival, the plethora of historical material in newspapers, journals, books, and pamphlets which spurned Van Riebeeck and his past was able, at least, to confront him and his family with the authority of the printed word in different histories when they landed at Granger Bay in 1952.[75]

Yet the networks of distribution, which were controlled by the major publishing houses—like Juta's, Maskew Miller Longman, and Nasionale Pers— often working in conjunction with the government's education department, meant that many of these oppositional histories had a limited circulation. Very few copies of *Three Hundred Years* and *The Role of Missionaries,* for instance, were printed, and they were unable to find their way into most school libraries. They seem to have been most widely circulated among teachers who had affiliations with the Unity Movement, and who used the books, sometimes surreptitiously, as the basis of their history lessons. Even then the books found a limited readership; teachers, to evade school inspectors and to avoid disciplinary action from government officials, rarely made the books accessible to the students themselves.[76] Thus, although the published oppositional histories could challenge the word of the festival's texts, the limited and highly regulated access to the channels of government and publishing power effectively curtailed the ability of those producing material to counter Van Riebeeck and to establish a sense of authority for the pasts they presented.

"What Do the Bantu Think of the Festival?"[77]

Unlike the organization of Van Riebeeck's festival which coalesced into a series of official committees, those who contested his past and representations of it came from a variety of individuals and organizations, took different forms, and decided not to participate for markedly diverse reasons. Yet, for all these differences, the boycott of the events of the Van Riebeeck festival by those who were racially termed "non-European" was overwhelming. The "day of the Malay and the coloured" was turned into a Malay and Griqua pageant as Du Plessis scrounged around looking for participants. Very few coloureds attended the festival fair—indeed there were no "non-Europeans" on its first two opening days—and only a few curious "natives from Langa" visited the festival.[78]

This widespread rejection of the festival by "the non-European" did not go unnoticed by the promoters of the tercentenary, who continually tried to convince "the Bantu" to pay "homage to Van Riebeeck." In the Afrikaans magazine, *Die Huisgenoot,* E. L. Ntloedibe published an article entitled "What Do the Bantu Think of the Festival?" The article, which the editor of *Die Huisgenoot* was keen to assure readers was completely unsolicited, argued that the arrival of Europeans at the Cape had put an end to barbarism in South Africa, that the Great Trek had eliminated "tribal fighting," and that whites had defeated "Bantu imperialism." All these events, the anonymous writer maintained, resulted from keeping the races separate, indicating that the "only solution to the native question" was a policy of "total segregation." On these grounds, and because Van Riebeeck brought "civilisation to darkest Africa," Ntloedibe concluded that "the Bantu" should reject the boycott of the festival.[79]

Despite the claim of representativity in the article, where one anonymous opinion becomes that of all "the Bantu," and despite the claim of the report's apparent authenticity based simply on its being reproduced "unchanged," Ntloedibe's call clearly went unheeded, given the small numbers in the segregated section of the festival stadium and the official statistics from the festival fair indicating a 90–95 percent boycott of the celebrations by "non-Europeans." Phyllis Ntantala, who spoke at the meeting of the Grand Parade on 30 April, was elated: "The people were not there. What a flop for the government that had put up this show! What a success for the people's boycott!"[80]

Still, whether the boycott of the festival by "Non-Europeans" was an indication that after three hundred years the conquered "had become metamorphosed into potential liberators,"[81] as Hosea Jaffe asserted, is debatable. I. B. Tabata made claims similar to Jaffe's:

> Here for the first time all the Non-European sections had the opportunity
> of applying the boycott simultaneously. It gave them a feeling of solidarity.
> Throughout this whole period each one was keenly concerned with what his
> neighbour was doing; each group was deeply interested in the actions of the
> other. They felt that they were acting with a common purpose. Here was
> unity in fact. There was a common joy in the feeling that for once they had
> asserted their independence as a people.[82]

13. Sheik Yusuf was presented as the founder of a separate "Malay" nation at the Van Riebeeck festival. He landed at a virtually deserted Festival Stadium on 2 April 1952. Manuscripts and Archives Division, University of Cape Town Libraries. Photo: *Cape Times.*

Yet the independence and the unity Jaffe and Tabata perceived in the boycott were partially illusory. Despite the apparent gulf between the pasts being projected by those advocating a boycott and the pasts being proclaimed by the festival, the distance between them was not so great in some respects. Mirroring and inverting the settler past, deriving authenticity from the printed word, using the categories of European and non-European, and conceptualizing race as pre-modern all indicate an unspoken meeting between these two sets of histories and a certain dependence on each other. Moreover, the unity Jaffe and Tabata proclaimed was quite shallow; for example, the political struggles and divisions involved in mounting the boycott campaign were still very much in evidence. The Unity Movement and the ANC were each scathing about the other's performance. The ANC-aligned *Guardian* questioned whether boycotting in itself was an effective means toward mobilizing "the masses." "Will we have to wait another 100 years before we have the opportunity to see Messrs. Kies, Gool and Co. in action again?" asked the editor. The "Kahn, Moroka, Dadoo comedy on 6 April," replied the editor of the Unity Movement organ, *The Torch,* was "much ado . . . about nothing." And, even more apparent, although Tabata claimed that Van Riebeeck ironically was the "lever to the consciousness of the people in their struggle for liberation," the boycott was not always tied to principled political action. Many of those objecting to the festival were plainly disinterested: "they did not care about such celebrations," some thought the event had nothing to do with them, and others asserted a status as a racial or educated elite, "enlightened people" who were not about to sing and dance for Van Riebeeck.[83]

But whatever the reason for staying away from the foreshore and the events of the tercentenary, there was little doubt that the festival had not managed to persuade the "non-Europeans" to receive and accept Van Riebeeck's racial alibi that he was bringing Western civilization to the shores of darkest Africa. This rejection was most aptly expressed in the pages of *Drum* magazine:

> The year 1952 has seen a change. When the ruling elements said that the cele-
> brations were essentially theirs, but that they would like the non-whites to
> take part, the reply was an emphatic "Voetsak!" which in the Afrikaner lan-
> guage is usually taken to mean "Go away you rascal dog, I don't like you."[84]

"The boomerang [had] struck back!" and although Van Riebeeck had success-fully managed to persuade and convey thousands of "Europeans" to witness his progression from Granger Bay through the streets of Cape Town and into the Castle, he was unable to entice the "non-Europeans" to partake of his seg-regated and separate offerings. There were "no coloured children to sing and dance, no coloured performances or choirs," bemoaned *Die Burger.* There were only the Griqua, I. D. du Plessis's Cape Malays, and a forlorn Sheik Yusuf who landed at the lonely, desolate Cape on 2 April 1952 (see Figure 13).[85]

4 "'n Fees vir die Oog"
[A Festival/Feast for the Eye]
Looking in on the 1952 Jan Van Riebeeck Tercentenary Festival Fair

The 1952 Jan van Riebeeck festival was planned as a visual extravaganza, a "spectacle" more than an "experience." There were few speeches, leaving as much time as possible for the crowds to take in the constant array of sights and be "dazzled" by the "huge canvas." The processions in the streets of Cape Town, the various displays in the festival stadium, the exhibitions in galleries and museums, and the plays at the drama festival, like all the scenes at the festival, were intended to be *"'n Fees vir die Oog"* [a festival/feast for the eye].[1]

For those who could not make the trip to Cape Town, this visual production could be followed in the local movie theater while waiting to see Alec Guinness in that "Grand Comedy," *Man in the White Suit*, or Ivor Novello's "Wonder Technicolour Musical," *The Dancing Years*. Almost weekly, through the documentary newsreels *African Mirror, Ons Nuus,* and *British Movietone News,* a "voice-of-God" commentator took moviegoers to the Van Riebeeck celebrations. With the help of sound and musical effects drawn from a limited repertoire in their respective audio libraries, the commentary "mov[ed] the text forward" from the initial "preparations" for the festival in the latter months of 1951 to the arrival of Henry Moore's sculptures for display at the South African National Gallery and onto the beach at Granger Bay on 5 April 1952, when a group of Griqua, acting as strandlopers armed with bows and arrows, submitted to Jan van Riebeeck.[2]

The intention of the festival organizers was to have Jan van Riebeeck be the central figure in this lavishly illustrated history. Although the content of his story was always negotiable, it was planned that he and his landing were to become the pivot on which the story of South Africa would turn. In *Our 300 Years,* the pictorial history of South Africa commissioned by the central committee of the Van Riebeeck festival and compiled by Victor de Kock of the Cape archives (with the assistance of history professors at the universities of Stellenbosch and Cape Town), the pictures told a story that began at the Cape of Good Hope which, in 1652, except for a few "impoverished, famine-stricken, half-naked . . . savages" had "no inhabitants." That all changed on 6 April when, "in calm weather, a sail hove into sight. This was the glimpse of a small ship called the *Dromedaris.*" The newsreels, too, afforded the landing pride of place. The *Movietone News* report on the festival started with the "realistic" landing of Van Riebeeck at Granger Bay and was "followed [by] a mile long procession of floats through the streets of the city." Even a wooden replica of Van Riebeeck's statue, sprayed with sand to "give it the appearance of stone," was made so it could be placed at the center of the festival proceedings on Cape Town's foreshore rather than on the periphery at the end of Adderley Street, where he had stood since 1899.[3]

For the approximately one million people who witnessed the spectacle in Cape Town, though, Van Riebeeck was not what caught their attention. They were more eager to visit the specially constructed festival fair on the foreshore where they could look at some of the seven hundred or so exhibits on display, take in the experience of an English and a Dutch village, stare at "tribal natives," and then take a moon rocket ride at the amusement park.

> I went to the Festival on Monday for the whole day. I saw the gold-mining industry, the S.A.R. [South African Railways], the diamonds and Culemborg. After that I had lunch, and then I saw the Bushmen, the Natives, the dogs, the U.D.F. [Union Defence Force], and a Native weaving. I went down the gold mine and it was wonderful. The dogs did clever tricks. I liked John Cobb's racing car. I enjoyed everything so much that I would have spent every day of my holidays at the Festival.[4]

These sights at the fair, which people patiently waited in queues to experience and traveled the dangerous national road from Bellville to see, very nearly overshadowed Van Riebeeck.[5]

Like the visitors to Cape Town in 1952, this chapter looks in at the Van Riebeeck festival fair and examines it in the context of the plans for the festival as a whole. It takes as its starting point the premise that the fair is a "producerly text." Drawing on the distinction between a "readerly text," where the reader is invited to accept the intended meaning, and a "writerly text," which is never fixed but is open to being rewritten by the reader, the "producerly text" is one which, while signifying meaning, does not dictate the rules of reading and writing.[6]

> Rather it offers itself up to popular production; it exposes, however reluctantly, the vulnerabilities, limitations, and weaknesses of its preferred meanings; it contains, while attempting to repress them, voices that contradict the one it prefers; it has loose ends that escape its control, its meanings exceed its own power to discipline them, its gaps are wide enough for whole new texts to be produced in them—it is, in a very real sense, beyond its control.[7]

In this sense, the visitors to the Van Riebeeck festival fair were producers of their own images, meanings, and texts, unlike in the pageantry where the audiences were largely—although not entirely—cast as receptors. An examination of the fair, therefore, needs to highlight its intentions, workings, and deeper structures, as well as the productivity of the participant viewers in their verbal enunciations and their textual productions. Using publicity material produced for the festival, minutes, letters, and planning committee memorandums, newspaper, radio, and film reports, writings in high school yearbooks, and interviews with visitors, this chapter attempts to take the reader to the fair, go behind the scenes to view its construction, and gaze at some of the exhibits and the productions of people who visited "the show of the year."[8]

The Plans and the Chaos

The Van Riebeeck festival fair, opened on 13 March 1952 by Governor General E. G. Jansen and Minister of Economic Affairs Eric Louw, was officially proclaimed as Africa's version of the Crystal Palace Empire Exhibition held in London in 1851. Heralded as the initiator of a new era in the world economy, which would be influenced by the "entrepreneurship and wealth of Africa," the fair was devised to display "a complete panorama of South Africa's economic development."[9]

The fair was carefully planned to launch the second phase of the festival and to provide the central link in a continuum of events in Cape Town. The festivities in Cape Town were designed to start on 1 February with a series of sporting and cultural events in the festival's two main arenas. In the specially constructed fifty-thousand-seater Van Riebeeck festival stadium on the foreshore, the highlight was to be South African Athletic Championships in which Dutch athletic aces, Fanny Blankers-Koen and Willie Slykhuis, would participate. At the Castle, Cape Town's "oldest and most memorable building," which linked "the present with the distant past when the foundations of the European civilization were laid in South Africa," seven Van Riebeeck family portraits sent by the Dutch government were to be displayed at the "centrepiece of the historic art exhibitions." A month and a half later the focus was to shift from sport and culture to "material development," as the halls of the festival fair were to open their doors to reveal "the entire range of [South Africa's] industry, agriculture and commerce." Finally, at the beginning of April, Van Riebeeck would land, bringing with him his family and "civilisation" to southern Africa.[10]

But while these arrangements were carefully mapped out, it was difficult for the festival organizers to establish a "watertight system of hegemonic control." Whereas some museums can and do attempt to constrict meaning in exhibitions through their "institutionalised setting" where objects are often untouchable, a "religious silence" is imposed, and conventional methods of labeling and classification are used, in a festival, where the aim is to encourage inclusive participation through "acting, tasting, or feeling, in addition to looking," such restrictions become increasingly difficult. The almost utopian notion of inclusiveness contained in the festival is more than likely to "engender pariahs" and raise the specter of its exclusive nature, leading to non-participation by those the festival is seen to marginalize. For those who do come to the festival, on the other hand, the setting is not a "restrained and sensually restricted experience," and the audience is actively encouraged to involve itself in the exhibits. Some of the first scenes of the festival in Cape Town, for instance, took place almost incidentally at an unplanned venue—the railway station. Throughout March and April of 1952, the platforms were congested with a deluge of people. All main-line trains arriving at the station were fully booked by visitors to the festival. An additional twenty-five trains had to be laid on to convey "10,000 students, teachers, choristers, folk dancers, Voortrekkers and first aid groups."[11] The following scenes, constructed from contemporary reports and featuring the crowds that had gathered there, portray the disarray on the station's platforms in March 1952.

> Cape Town railway station, 6 March 1952. Crowds have gathered on platform 14. They are there to greet 11 "burly" white men who are travelling back to the Transvaal, after spending six months in Britain and France. When their boat had docked in Cape Town earlier in the day, Jan van Riebeeck had alighted from his pedestal to greet the men, and offered them his place, for the day, at the foot of Adderley street. Now, as they arrive to board the train that will take them to their homes, they are mobbed by the crowd. This is "a Jan van Riebeeck welcome home" for members of the victorious South African touring rugby team.[12] (Figure 14)

> Cape Town station, 7 March 1952. A crowd of people is waiting in anticipation on the platform. A train draws in. In one carriage the blinds are drawn to shield the occupants "from the curious stares of onlookers." As the train draws to a halt the occupants of the carriage disembark and huddle together nervously on the platform. A man, who appears to be in charge of the group, organises an impromptu press conference. He informs journalists that there was an initial reluctance by the group to come to Cape Town, "but when we told them it would mean new blankets and plenty of food and tobacco we had plenty of volunteers." He then gathers the group for a photo session and they barely raise a smile. And they keep quiet. Those who were hoping to see and hear more are disappointed. They must wait in the queues at the Van

14. Jan van Riebeeck welcomes home the South African rugby team after its
tour to Britain. *Cape Times,* 6 March 1952. Courtesy of *Cape Times* and
the National Library of South Africa, Cape Town.

Riebeeck festival fair on the foreshore where the bushmen from South West
Africa will be on display for the next three weeks under the supervision of
a professor of anthropology and now game warden at Etosha Pan reserve,
P. J. Schoeman.[13]

Cape Town station at the end of March 1952. The platform is crowded with
exhausted and grumbling schoolchildren who have just arrived on a special
train. From Cape Town they catch another train to Rosebank. From there it
is a two-mile walk to their camp. When the children arrive at the tents, they

see that they are on a slope allowing the rain to seep in underneath. The mattresses, filled only with straw, are hard and rocky. This will be home for the next week for twenty schoolchildren from Selborne Primary in East London, as they spend their time looking at the various exhibitions at the Van Riebeeck festival fair.[14]

The chaos at Cape Town Station highlighted the tension between the management and control that the organizers attempted to impose and the participation it wanted to encourage. Space was almost continually breached, control over the presentation became increasingly limited, and displays at times took on different meanings. The festival could not be totally controlled within the parameters for participation its organizers had set down, had located at prescribed sites, and had defined as manageable activities.

The Van Riebeeck festival was marked both by a large boycott and a distinct lack of singular direction among its various participants. As chapter 3 described, there was a large "non-European" boycott of the festival, despite attempts by the president of the conservative Coloured People's National Union, G. Golding, to counter this campaign by organizing expeditions for groups of coloured schoolchildren to see the "educational exhibits at the fair." At the festival itself, the large number of seemingly disparate exhibitions in different forms and venues, and the organizers' insistence that displays not be "like a museum," led, at times, to "messy events and disorderly, disputatious performances" instead of focusing on Van Riebeeck as a national symbol of white settlement. Special botanical arrangements at the station were trampled underfoot and potted plants were stolen. Festival visitors joked about the column that supported a replica of the Van Riebeeck statue, making up their own names for the character that gazed over the proceedings below. The schoolboys from East London "were all glad when the time came to go home," after spending a week in a tent at the Rosebank show grounds, which Cape Town's Medical Officer of Health had come close to declaring unsuitable for human habitation as the unsanitary conditions, exacerbated by "the presence of flies and fly breeding" at the horse stables, could lead to outbreaks of "dysentery, typhoid and gastro-enteritis."[15]

This is not to deny that Jan van Riebeeck became the lead actor on South Africa's public history stage from 1952. The association of the rugby team with Van Riebeeck was a clear indication of this. But the story of Van Riebeeck, "an historical tale without much emotional content," was constantly in danger of being relegated to the wings. When the time came for the planned third phase of the festival to reach its crescendo, the laying of the foundation stone for a proposed gateway to Africa and the placing of wreaths at the base of the Van

Riebeeck column, most people had lost interest in the proceedings. Only a few thousand people braved the cold wind and intermittent rain to attend the ceremonies.[16]

Going to the Festival Fair

In contrast to the public ceremonies of the final days, the fair on the foreshore, which had begun during the planned second phase of Van Riebeeck's festival, attracted almost constant public attention. On its worst days, when the wind blew and rain was a constant threat, some 15,000 to 20,000 attended the fair. On weekends and public holidays, crowds reached around 80,000. The fair was so successful that it was extended for a week after the formal ceremonies and pageantry were over. Many actually thought that the fair *was* the Van Riebeeck festival. Even a government minister, lamented *Die Burger*'s festival correspondent, talked of the fair as "the most important part of the festival." By the time the fair closed its doors on 14 April, total attendance stood at 887,648. Before leaving for home, the schoolboys from East London spent three days looking at the exhibition, saw "some beautiful models," and admitted that it was overall, "very good."[17]

Although special excursions to the festival fair were organized for schools, and at times it seemed the grounds were overflowing with children, gate receipts indicate that 70 percent of those who attended the fair paid two shillings, the entrance fee for adults. Once inside the fairgrounds, a multitude of hidden charges emerged. An additional entrance fee was required to see the replicas of the English and Dutch villages, rickshaw rides cost two shillings and sixpence a ride, and some restaurants charged between eight and twelve shillings for lunch. One visitor to the fair was so horrified at the high food prices that he exclaimed, "Do you think I own the gold pavilion?" The fears of C. J. Smit of Goodwood, who wrote a letter to *Die Burger* at the beginning of March, that the festival would turn into an occasion "only for the wealthy of my old little nation," seem to have been partially justified. Although some visitors saw the fair as a form of cheap entertainment, if one wished to do more than take free samples and collect brochures, one needed "money, money, money."[18]

Of the 800,000-odd visitors who did manage to attend, most were white, this despite the organizers' effort to attract coloureds to the fair by offering special cheap days. On the first two days of the fair, no coloureds attended at all. Although the number rose to about 2,000 a day, this was far fewer than expected. The projected total attendance at the fair of one million, of which half were expected to be coloureds, was not achieved, and the fair ran at a financial loss.[19]

Situating the Fair

The site of the Van Riebeeck festival fair was in a part of Cape Town that, until the 1930s, had been under water: the foreshore (see Figure 3). This area had been reclaimed from the sea in 1938 as part of the construction of a new dockyard, and, over the next decade, many plans for its use were drawn up, rejected, revised, and re-submitted. Finally, in 1947, a joint report, with a frontispiece photograph of the "'father' of Cape Town"—Jan van Riebeeck on his pedestal on Adderley Street—was published by a committee consisting of representatives of the South African Railways and Harbours and the Cape Town City Council. The report saw the development of the foreshore as part of the construction of a "New City," which would be characterized by its "Monumental Approaches." The approach from the sea side would lead onto a tree-lined pedestrian mall with a clear vista of Table Mountain, while, from the land, road traffic would be diverted onto a Grand Boulevard which would "[sweep] down the mountain-side in a series of smooth curves before entering the City in a broad park-like belt in the reclaimed area." At the intersection of these routes into the city, the foreshore would, it was envisaged, become the "Gateway of South Africa."[20]

To accomplish this task, new roads and a railway station had to be built, and some of the "troublesome," unplanned, "heterogeneous mass" of buildings which accommodated the "overwhelming influx of population from the countryside" had to make way for wide streets, spacious gardens, and "fine, modern" commercial, government, and residential buildings. The planners noted that while this process of reconstruction had been accidentally facilitated in Europe during the Second World War "through the appalling device of aerial warfare," the foreshore gave them the opportunity to "re-create Cape Town for the needs of modern life." Although it was claimed that this would mean "construction" rather than "destruction," the plan to create a new road system—which had already been envisioned as early as 1940—and to modernize the city by eliminating "slum areas," meant that a number of properties in District Six, the area that housed a large proportion of the "waves of impoverished workers" who had moved into the city, would have to give way to the Grand Boulevard. At a series of protest meetings in the early 1940s, when the initial plans were made public, the scheme was described as "wholesale eviction" and a "trick" to "disperse 27 000 ratepayers" under "the guise of slum clearance." These protests, combined with debates over where to locate the new station so as not to hinder the vista of the Monumental Approaches—eventually it was decided to build it below ground level—effectively blocked attempts to begin work on the foreshore scheme. By 1950 none of the planned developments had taken place, the foreshore had no roads, water, or electricity available, and the south-easterly wind made the area, at times, a "veritable howling desert, actually drawing the blood through the human skin."[21]

Other sites, such as Green Point Common, the Western Province Agricultural Association's show grounds at Goodwood, an amphitheater at the base of Table Mountain, and Wingfield Airport were therefore being considered as venues for the Van Riebeeck festival fair. All except Green Point Common were rejected almost immediately as they could not be prepared in time, there was a danger of rock falls from Table Mountain if the building operations were undertaken, and it was necessary to keep the airfield open to air traffic "due to the instability in the international situation." In the end the choice was narrowed down to either the foreshore or Green Point Common, and the Cape Town City engineer, Solly Morris, was called on to personally evaluate their respective strengths and weaknesses. Even though Green Point had a stadium already well under construction and the common had been used for the massive Liberty Cavalcade Exhibition in the Second World War, not altogether surprisingly he favored the foreshore which, only a few days before Morris submitted his report, had been officially incorporated into the city of Cape Town. He argued that the foreshore would be considerably cheaper because it had railway sheds that could be converted into exhibition halls (he estimated that the net cost on the foreshore would be £99,000 compared to £218,000 at Green Point), it was near the center of the city, the gardens that would be developed could become part of the Monumental Approach on the foreshore, and, even though it had been under water in 1652, it "historically mark[ed] the spot where Cape Town, and so ultimately the Union of South Africa, commenced its history."[22]

This fitted in neatly with plans for the foreshore to signify the space of Cape Town, in general, and the "vast area of virginal land," in particular, as "the first foothold of European civilisation in the sub-continent." Green Point, in Morris's eyes, paled in comparison. He claimed that although it contained greenery, it was "not attractive" when compared to the sandy, windswept wastes of the foreshore set "against the magnificent backcloth of Table Mountain," and, more important, it did not have the same "historical associations." For the Van Riebeeck festival committee, the idea of locating the festival fair on the site where history began was most appealing, as it coincided with the promulgation of Van Riebeeck as the initiator of "civilization" and the South African past. Moreover, here was the opportunity to "level" the ground and, like Van Riebeeck, build "a shining new suburb in the shadow of Table Mountain." The foreshore, in spite of its lack of amenities, its seemingly inhospitable surroundings, and a series of railway tracks that made the ground even more uneven, became the "ideal and only terrain" for the festival fair.[23]

On Show at the Fair

The festival fair and stadium, which ultimately cost in the region of £500,000, covered a fifty-acre site on the foreshore. There were three types of displays. Enveloping the site were specially constructed pavilions, which ranged in cost from £10,000 to £120,000 (Figure 15). These were mainly devoted to the larger industries, such as sugar, gold, and diamonds; the various provinces—including South Africa's colony, Namibia, which was named South-West Africa; some towns and cities; and the workings of select government departments. A replica of the marketplace of Van Riebeeck's birthplace, Culemborg, and a fanciful reconstruction of an English village, Much-Binding-in-the Marsh, were two of the major pavilions constructed. In the central area, on the eastern side of the fair, behind the gold and diamond pavilions, were seven hundred stands, located in halls (the converted railway sheds), where a variety of manufacturers, retailers, municipalities, and specific organizations exhibited their achievements. Finally, on the southeastern perimeter was the large amusement park, where rides included "the latest Dodge-em Cars, a trip through a haunted castle, the Helter Skelter and the Octopus."[24]

The intention of all these exhibits, under the broad theme "South Africa During and After 300 Years," was to show the development of "agriculture, industry and mining" since 1652. Other than that, visitors to the festival were left to their own devices in deciding what exhibits to see, in what order, and how each exhibit fitted in to the larger theme. This was in marked contrast to an emerging trend in expositions after the Second World War of providing an explicit narrative that attempted to control the viewing of the exhibits. This trend first made its appearance at the Festival of Britain in 1951, which commemorated the hundredth anniversary of the Crystal Palace Exhibition. The design of the main exhibition, on the South Bank of the Thames, with its "carefully organized routes" and "surface treatments of water, cobbles, grass or concrete," was "to guide visitors unobtrusively in the correct direction." In contrast, the Van Riebeeck festival fair seemed, in the words of Douglas Brown, the *Daily Telegraph*'s resident reporter in South Africa, to be a bit "higgeldy-piggeldy."[25]

There were six entrances to the fair grounds, two on the northern perimeter, three to the south, and the main entrance, near the main parking lot and bus terminal, on the western side (Figure 15). Most people entered the grounds through the main entrance. Straight ahead was a corridor that led directly to the large, dominating pavilions of gold, sugar, diamonds, and South African Railways and Harbours (plots 98–101). Along this corridor were a series of smaller displays, mostly devoted to implements for agriculture, light industry, and construction, a scene some fairgoers, who had visited agricultural shows,

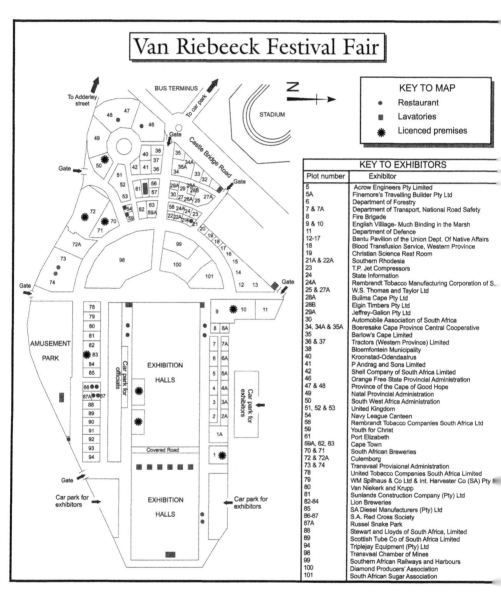

Van Riebeeck Festival Fair

KEY TO MAP

- Restaurant
- Lavatories
- Licenced premises

KEY TO EXHIBITORS

Plot number	Exhibitor
5	Acrow Engineers Pty Limited
5A	Finemore's Travelling Builder Pty Ltd
6	Department of Forestry
7 & 7A	Department of Transport, National Road Safety
8	Fire Brigade
9 & 10	English Villiage- Much Binding in the Marsh
11	Department of Defence
12-17	Bantu Pavilion of the Union Dept. Of Native Affairs
18	Blood Transfusion Service, Western Province
19	Christian Science Rest Room
21A & 22A	Southern Rhodesia
23	T.P. Jet Compressors
24	State Information
24A	Rembrandt Tobacco Manufacturing Corporation of S.
25 & 27A	W.S. Thomas and Taylor Ltd
28A	Builma Cape Pty Ltd
28B	Elgin Timbers Pty Ltd
29A	Jeffrey-Galion Pty Ltd
30	Automobile Association of South Africa
34, 34A & 35A	Boeresake Cape Province Central Cooperative
35	Barlow's Cape Limited
36 & 37	Tractors (Western Province) Limited
38	Bloemfontein Municipality
40	Kroonstad-Odendaalrus
41	P Andrag and Sons Limited
42	Shell Company of South Africa Limited
46	Orange Free State Provincial Administration
47 & 48	Province of the Cape of Good Hope
49	Natal Provincial Administration
50	South West Africa Administration
51, 52 & 53	United Kingdom
54	Navy League Canteen
58	Rembrandt Tobacco Companies South Africa Ltd
59	Youth for Christ
61	Port Elizabeth
59A, 62, 63	Cape Town
70 & 71	South African Breweries
72 & 72A	Culemborg
73 & 74	Transvaal Provisional Administration
78	United Tobacco Companies South Africa Limited
79	WM Spilhaus & Co Ltd & Int. Harvester Co (SA) Pty
80	Van Niekerk and Krupp
81	Sunlands Construction Company (Pty) Ltd
82-84	Lion Breweries
85	SA Diesel Manufacturers (Pty) Ltd
86-87	S.A. Red Cross Society
87A	Russel Snake Park
88	Stewart and Lloyds of South Africa, Limited
89	Scottish Tube Co of South Africa Limited
94	Triplejay Equipment (Pty) Ltd
98	Transvaal Chamber of Mines
99	Southern African Railways and Harbours
100	Diamond Producers' Association
101	South African Sugar Association

15. Map: Van Riebeeck Festival Fair. James Whitelaw, Design Matters, based on map in *Official Guide Book and Catalogue of the Van Riebeeck Festival Fair,* Cape Town (1952).

would have recognized. If visitors deviated to the right, in a southerly direction, they would enter the world of the provinces and the administration of South-West Africa (plots 46–50). This also led to the reconstruction of Van Riebeeck's birthplace, Culemborg. Heading north led to a maze of smaller agricultural and industrial exhibits, but, in all likelihood, would also take in the "Southern Rhodesia" pavilion (plots 21A and 22A), which included a reproduction of "the main wall and conical tower of the famous Zimbabwe Ruins," and the South African government's Native Affairs Department's "Bantu pavilion" (plots 12–17). Opposite the "Bantu pavilion" stood the English village "Much-Binding-in-the-Marsh" (plots 9 and 10). After the visit to the pavilions there remained endless rows of displays in the exhibition halls, stretching eastward beyond the city toward the suburb of Woodstock. Some had a specific theme: printing, wine, fashion, motorcars, education, and science. The organizing principle in these exhibits was usually a chronological narrative of progress from the times of Van Riebeeck toward a "promise for the future" of apartheid South Africa in an international world of development.[26]

While the Van Riebeeck festival fair might have seemed disjointed, two characteristics held it together: the assertion of national pride and the human showcases. This was reminiscent of the great world and empire expositions of the late nineteenth and early twentieth centuries. These "ephemeral vistas," starting with the "founding spectacle" of the Crystal Palace Exhibition of 1851, were media of nationing, rendering the world, the self, and the other knowable, and engendering self-regulation. These exhibitions sought "to place the people—conceived as a nationalized citizenry—on this side of power, both its subject and its beneficiary." Instead of self-discipline being engendered by a "state of conscious and permanent visibility" through the unseen, seeing supervisor, it was largely generated by casting the "eyes of the multitude" upon the "assemblage of glorious commodities," the "products of their labour," instilling a sense of national achievement.[27]

The power of this spectacle of industrial progress lay not merely in its own presentation but also in its juxtaposition with displays of primitiveness and backwardness. "Human showcases," often consisting of an array of "native villages," were a constant feature of the world fairs of the late nineteenth and early twentieth centuries, with the Paris Exposition of 1889 setting the trend. "Natives," who were "specially imported" to Paris from Senegal, Congo, New Caledonia, Gabon, Dahomey, China, and Java, spent their time in specially fenced enclosures, building their "huts," making items of clothing, and performing for the crowds of curious onlookers.[28]

These human showcases were presented in vivid contrast to the "triumphs" of "civilisation" and "industrial progress." The "constructed chaos" of the "jumble" of "native villages" on the Midway Plaisance in Chicago was displayed before the "colossal buildings," "massive machinery," and statuesque exhibits of the Colombian Exposition of 1893. Amid the "geometric" order and cleanliness of the Parisian exhibition of 1889 stood the "carefully chaotic" streets of Cairo. And, above all, stood the Eiffel Tower, "casting its shadow" over the "native villages" "like a giant Triumphal monument," in "[a] culture/nature juxtaposition of terrifying simplicity." As the world exhibitions placed the human race on an evolutionary scale, the national identity of "progress" and "achievement" became intertwined with a racial one. The boundaries of what was "self" and what was "other" were defined in terms of a racial type which was pronounced as being industrially advanced and having reached a higher stage of "civilization" than that achieved by the "savagery" of the "native condition." Through the exhibition, white citizens of the imperial powers became the "just beneficiaries" of this social evolution, bounded together and identified "in opposition to the primitive otherness of conquered peoples."[29]

The human showcases and "native villages" had gradually begun to disappear from the world's fairs by the 1930s after much protest and accusations of racism. In addition, ethnographic films and "pseudo-scientific anthropological treatises," richly illustrated with photographs, started to replace the human exhibits. Another reason might be that the supply of "native people" from some regions had begun to dry up, particularly from areas where the white settler populations exercised considerable local control over the "natives" through an assemblage of legislation, political structures, and notions of racial segregation. This was certainly the case in South Africa, which had supplied many of the human showcases for the world fairs. Colonial officials in Britain and South Africa at the end of the nineteenth century had reservations about these displays, fearing mainly that such displays might detract from the ability to supply and control labor for the mines in Kimberley and the Witwatersrand. In the 1930s, the South African government's Native Affairs Department was becoming increasingly concerned about the "detrimental" effect of these "excursions" and that it was losing its authority over the "natives" once they were in Europe or America. In spite of assurances from those organizing the expeditions that they would "keep Natives in compounds," applications to send "Zulu dancers" to New York, bushmen to London, and "Native singers" to Europe were all rejected by the department. The case of Captain van der Loo from Holland, who, in 1939, applied for permission to exhibit "25 kaffirs and some women and children" at the South Africa and Netherlands exhibition at the Hague, is a clear example of the implementation of this policy. He promised to cover travel and maintenance costs and to ensure that in Holland "the kaffirs would be strictly supervised." They would live in "an enclosed space in rondawels" in the zoo where they would be closely watched, never allowed to go out alone, and forbidden to drink alcohol. The department, however, was unconvinced and turned down his application. "Whatever measures of control may be exercised," maintained D. L. Smit, the Secretary for Native Affairs, these journeys made the "natives" "unfit . . . to resume their normal life in the reserves."[30]

Instead of sending "natives" abroad, they were displayed in larger numbers at South African exhibitions, where control could be maintained more effectively. In 1936, at the very first Empire Exhibition held outside Britain, Donald Bain, the big-game hunter, exhibited a group of bushmen at the Milner Park show grounds in Johannesburg. Beneath the huge central tower, with its radiating spotlight, and in the shadow of an enormous model airplane traveling along the world's "principal Imperial air routes," these proclaimed "living fossils" of the Kalahari were displayed for both locals and "travellers from the four corners of the world." A few years later, during the Second World War, "native performances" became a major attraction at a series of Liberty Cavalcades that were held throughout South Africa to raise money for the Governor General's War Fund and to tell "the story of a great war-time achievement by the home front." In the Cape Town cavalcade, held at Green Point Common in 1944, not only was there a "Native Village," situated adjacent to the "graceful" and "modern" building of the Soviet Pavilion with its dominating "high tower," but the "Native share" took on a much "more sophisticated character." At the "Dead Horse Gulch Dance Hall" a "troupe of native players" from Johannesburg sang, danced, and told stories through word and music about "their past and present existence in their native kraals."[31]

Like their counterparts in Europe and the United States, these human showcases asserted, through comparison with the industrial displays, the towering structures, and the pavilions devoted to demonstrating the progress of various nations, a human evolutionary scale with "western civilization" paramount. Moreover, they advanced a racial identity that associated whites in Africa as "European" rather than "native" and as the bearers of the first "lamp of civilisation" in southern Africa. It was from this initial spark at the "ancient Cape," asserted R. Stuttaford, chair of Western Province Liberty Cavalcade, that "lambent beams spread throughout the dark continent" of Africa. In these terms, the Second World War was being fought by "our lads" to defend Cape Town as the "cradle of civilisation." The native villages and performances thus served as a reminder to the largely white audiences in the southern-most part of Africa that, if they lost control, "the Darkest Africa of fiction . . . [was] not so far distant."[32]

The Van Riebeeck festival fair, with its multitude of human showcases, was, to a large extent, the culmination of all these displays, which were not solely of the "native" variety. Significantly, "European" life was also depicted in two village scenes, the market place of Van Riebeeck's birthplace, Culemborg (plots

72 and 72A), and, its English counterpart, Much-Binding-in-the-Marsh (plots 9 and 10). These were not displays of "backwardness" but evoked a discourse of "tradition" and "heritage" in a "quaint" "olde world." This enabled an alignment between nationhood, where citizenship and political allegiances were being demanded, and the evocation of cultural associations, where filial connections were presented as the collective tissue. The "tradition" and "heritage" mirrored the festival as a whole in that these two villages came to stand for different pasts being made into a shared national settler history. Their "quaintness" was more generic, suggesting a common ancestry in a rural past that followed a path to modernity through trade, transport, and local industries. Although there was little sense that the English village at the festival fair, Much-Binding-in-the-Marsh, was the hub of modern development, Culemborg, on the other hand, was presented not as a "dead village" but as a town "with over 10,000 inhabitants," "several local industries," "some famous Dutch cigar factories," and a center for the "production of furniture and glassware."[33]

Alongside, and set apart from these settlements which conveyed notions of a "European heritage" were a series of "native displays" where people classified as "black" were placed in a series of native villages. Like their counterparts in world fairs of the nineteenth century, these "native villages" presented an immediate comparison with the world of South Africa's heritage that was being portrayed as civilized and derived from the communities of Europe. The illuminated tower on the market square of Culemborg was intended to shine above the fair like "a beacon" of "civilisation," while, in its shadow, scattered around the show ground, a series of human showcases exhibited an essential "native condition," marked by "tribalism," "natural crafts," and "superstition." At the Bantu Pavilion (plots 12–17), the Native Affairs Department sought to interest the public in the "Primitive life of the Bantu," by having "real" "natives" "actually demonstrating their work and customs on the spot." "Native crafts" were performed "by skilled brown hands" and a "'witchdoctor' or tribal medicine man . . . display[ed] his herbs and paraphernalia."[34]

Although the juxtaposition of the modern and primitive was crucial to the way these "native villagers" were displayed to the visitors at the Van Riebeeck festival fair, merely depicting them as backward in contrast to the European settlers and their places of origin would have contradicted the Europeans' claim to be the bearer of civilization to Africa. Central to the colonial enterprise throughout Africa was the assertion of "progress for the colonial people . . . through the diffusion of 'modernization.'" This had been reinforced after the Second World War, as colonial powers, attempting to retain a degree of control in the face of emerging movements for independence, portrayed some type of "wise" and "benevolent" colonial rule—either politically, economically, or in both ways—as the means to sustain and promote development. In South Africa this diffusionist model of modernization was translated into "Betterment for the Bantu." On one level, this involved, at times, a series of haphazard government policies, which, from the late 1930s, sought to intervene in rural African communities that were becoming increasingly destitute largely as a result of land dispossession. The solution, put forward by the Department of Native Affairs, was not to consider the issue of land distribution but to institute "rational" and "scientific" farming methods which limited cattle holdings—"an essential part of any betterment scheme"—and fenced off areas to rigidly demarcate pastoral, residential, and arable land. At another level, betterment categorized race and gender as the determining features of advancement and development. The "Bantu men" were depicted as spending "much of their time in fighting and hunting," "forging assegais," ruthlessly killing off "all their male opponents," and seizing as many cattle as they could with complete disregard for "any tradition of husbandry," while the women tilled the soil with "primitive hoes," barely managing to "scratch the surface of the soil." The "White man," although he had inadvertently brought about an increase in stock and human population through "his knowledge of medicine and veterinary science," was characterized as bringing an end to "fighting and cattle seizing," providing education for "the rural Natives," and improving "their land" in the face of the "intensely suspicious" "Bantu." To leave the "natives" on display at the Van Riebeeck festival fair in a "primitive state" would have negated this supposed self-proclaimed concern of Jan van Riebeeck and the "White race" for "the dictates of Christianity and civilisation" and "the upliftment of the Bantu in all spheres—spiritual, physical and economic."[35]

With the South African government's apartheid policy starting to come under severe criticism, the Department of Native Affairs was concerned to portray this sense of "native progress" under white tutelage at the Van Riebeeck festival. Just less than £10,000 was spent by the department on its exhibit at the fair—exceeding the initial budget estimate by nearly £3,000—to create what the department considered to be the "correct impression" of "apartheid policy" for both local and international visitors. Instead of situating "native development" in the various provincial exhibits, which might have cost less but would have produced an "incorrect" image of an "integrationist policy," the department constructed a separate, "huge pavilion . . . for the display of non-European arts and crafts and all forms of development and achievement." Through this exhibit apartheid was to be deracinated, located within a "global view" of "civilizing influences," and turned into a "correct view" of what the "Government is doing for the Bantu" to "assist them to progress in their own sphere."[36]

To display this "raising [of] the native from his primitive state" under the aegis of "western civilization," apartheid, and the "white man," the Bantu Pavilion was arranged on an east-west axis in a series of courtyards through which the visitor would progress. The visit started alongside the northeast entrance to the festival fairgrounds, where a series of "cheap lorry sheds," adorned with gabled, cutout huts, invited the spectator to inspect the "Tribal Life courtyard." Here, adjacent to the "traditional . . . craftsmen and women of various tribes," performing their crafts for 7 shillings, 6 pence, per day, and the two "Zulu 'policemen'" from Pretoria who "acted their part" in "Zulu dress and character" "to good effect," sat Chief Moroka from Thaba Nchu in the Orange Free State, Chief Mohlaba from Letaba in the Northern Transvaal, and Chief Hlengwa from Umbumbulu in Natal. For 10 shillings a day these chiefs, on a rotational basis, deliberated "upon the affairs of their tribe" with the help of their counselors—who were paid 7 shillings, 6 pence, per day—and a teacher who assisted "the participants or 'actors' in producing life-like representations of the conduct of tribal business." After leaving the chief, his counselors, and their instructors to their deliberations, the visitor moved eastward to a "courtyard of a native school," where a group of pupils from Besonvale Institution in Herschel put up a "splendid performance" in a demonstration classroom under the supervision of their "native teacher," Mr. Diau. Finally, the visit ended in the "Progress Courtyard," where the Native Affairs Department declared itself to be the facilitator of "native advancement." The agricultural betterment schemes which made "the Bantu . . . adopt productive rather than destructive farming methods" were demonstrated, a government clinic displayed "its . . . activities on behalf of the Native population" and took "care of Native casualties at the Fair," and a "neat modern self-built Native home" was shown in the process of construction by Phineas Leballo and Alfred Mohale. Like all those on exhibition at the Native Affairs pavilion, these builders were presented as "Bantu pupils of state training institutes."[37]

However, these pupils sometimes got out of hand and did not co-operate with the Native Affairs Department. The first problem had been to find "natives" who were willing to go on display in Cape Town. Initially, the Native Affairs Department had hoped to draw on "local natives" resident in Langa, but the strength of the boycott in the township made this virtually impossible. Fears were raised that the display might have to be abandoned, and it was only after scouring the country, offering material incentives, and transporting people "at considerable expense" from as far afield as Sterkspruit—in the eastern Cape, more than a thousand kilometers from Cape Town—that exhibits were found for the "bantu pavilion." Then, when the exhibitors arrived in Cape Town, they were made to feel very unwelcome in Langa. They were thus forced to stay at a "vacant military camp" at Firgrove and were transported to Cape Town each day in a truck by Obed Ambrose Mashaba, a cinema announcer from the NAD head office, who drove recklessly, reaching speeds of fifty-five miles per hour. Even though the "native exhibits" were isolated at the camp, it still seemed as though they were being pressured to "desert the undertaking." Only after the Native Affairs Department officials in charge of the exhibit called on chiefs Moroka, Hlengwa, and Mohlaba to act as "stabilisers" was the withdrawal of the "100 Native" demonstrators averted. At the camp itself, complaints were emerging over the food and drink arrangements. Under pressure not to alienate the "natives" they had managed to entice to Cape Town, NAD officials gave special permission "for the 'home brewing' of ±15 gallons of K/beer [Kaffir beer] per day at the camp for consumption by the native inmates." Finally, rickshaw pullers from Durban, although not part of the NAD display, started taking the festival organizers "for a ride." Brought down from Durban at a cost of some £2,500 to take visitors around the grounds, they began to bypass the special ticket system, whereby they would receive 20 percent of daily receipts as their wages, and pocketed money for the rides directly from their passengers. Only after fair officials threatened that they would hire out the rickshaws to the "Zulu boys" at £2, 10 shillings, per day and that those from Durban would have to pay for food and board from their daily earnings did this practice come to a halt. Overall it seemed that the local officials had as much trouble controlling the "natives" at home as when the latter had traveled abroad to be exhibited.[38]

Across the path from the NAD pavilion, on the northern side of the festival grounds, was the English village Much-Binding-in-the-Marsh, devised by two "anonymous" "English-born South Africans" and supported by a consortium of business interests in Cape Town and Johannesburg. In its evocation of an almost timeless rural past "for old times' sake," Much-Binding had more to do with demonstrating a heritage of Englishness as a constituent part of the South African nation being proclaimed under the aegis of Van Riebeeck than displaying development and progress. The village was named after a British Broadcasting Corporation (BBC) radio sitcom that was set on a Royal Air Force base, turned country club. The program originally ran on the BBC between 1947 and 1953 and was broadcast in South Africa, initially on the English service and later on the newly established commercial station, Springbok Radio, in the early 1950s. A sense of English farce pervaded Much-Binding-in-the-Marsh when the air base, turned country club, found a new form as a "typical hamlet" of "the Southern Counties of England" at the Van Riebeeck festival fair in Cape Town. The village had its "Norman" church, "Tudor-style" buildings, a "typical ... English 'local'" called "The Lion," its "quaint" "Old Curiosity Shop" and a village Green. "Proper British people" with "British accents" directed visitors to various parts of the village. To expand even more on its being "pretty authentic," there was a replica of one of the "old English forms of punishment," a set of stocks, that proved to be the most popular section of the village. Much-Binding, which in England did not "exist at all," was brought to life at the Van Riebeeck festival as an old-fashioned, somewhat comic, and considerably sanitized version of an idyllic English rural past. In the words of one visitor, "It seemed as if a little bit of England had dropped right down into South Africa."[39]

Even though Much-Binding did not make apparent assertions to progress, comparisons were drawn between it and the pavilion of the Native Affairs Department (plots 12–17). Structures in the former, with its brick and stone buildings, were presented as much more stable and the result of carefully applied, learned skills. The latter were described as an outcome of natural abilities with not always the most desired results. In the "Tribal Life courtyard" visitors were able to see a group of "unhurried" Zulus, under the supervision of Wyatt Sampson—publicity officer of the NAD—living in "specially constructed kias," building "the best type" of rudimentary huts, while they eyed "the neat thatching of Much-Binding-in-the-Marsh village with a considerable amount of envy."[40]

A much starker juxtaposition took place in the southwestern corner of the fair grounds. Grouped together, near the Marine Drive entrance to the fair, were the United Kingdom pavilion (plots 51–53), the building that exhibited the South-West Africa administration (plot 50) and the town of Culemborg (plots 72 and 72A) In the United Kingdom pavilion, images of "the great British contributions" to Van Riebeeck's nation, which had not been very apparent at Much-Binding, especially those relating to the subject of advancement, found their place. Across the way the village of Culemborg, built by a special Netherlands Van Riebeeck Committee that was constituted in Cape Town in 1950 "on the initiative of the Consul-General of the Netherlands, Dr. H. J. Levelt," combined elements of a small-town Dutch heritage with a strong assertion of technological expertise, especially in maritime matters. Adjacent to Culemborg and the United Kingdom pavilions, was the "big draw" of the South-West Africa pavilion. Here a group of bushmen were displayed as primitive peoples, "essential Africans," who hunted, lived in a world of ecological symbiosis, and were represented as a people without history.[41]

The United Kingdom pavilion, which the British government presented, exhibited democracy and technology as being Britain's national achievements. One display consisted of a series of technical inventions, "from the latest farm machinery to the jet engine from the Comet aircraft" and its radar. The other, transported in full from the Festival of Britain, was an exhibition of a history of parliamentary democracy, from "its early days until modern times." Not only were these exhibits supposed to indicate an advanced society, but they were also a perfect fit with the "We Build a Nation" theme. They laid out paths to progress through technology and citizenship as having an "honoured place in the growth of present day South Africa." The festival fair organizers pushed

16. Van Riebeeck's birthplace, Culemborg, at the Van Riebeeck festival fair in Cape Town. Manuscripts and Archives Division, University of Cape Town Libraries. Photo: *Cape Times.*

this correspondence even further by asserting that South Africa's parliamentary system was based on the British model, completely ignoring the claims of most of South Africa's inhabitants to citizenship and the franchise.[42]

Diagonally opposite the United Kingdom pavilion, but described in the *Official Festival Programme* as being "near the native village," Culemborg deliberately set itself apart from other exhibits at the fair. It held a special ceremony at which the Dutch ambassador Jan van den Berg, the patron of the Netherlands Van Riebeeck Committee, Cape Town, laid its foundation stone; it was designed so as screen the town off from the goings on at the rest of the fair; and it charged an entrance fee to indicate that it was not "an ordinary exhibit but an experience." Paralleling the English experience at Much-Binding, the Culemborg pavilion proclaimed a European heritage of Dutch descent to visitors to the festival fair. The market square, the town hall, the barrel organ, the hand pump, and the "fantastic puppet plays" offered by the "'old Culemborg comity'" were all intended to create an "atmosphere of Holland" (Figure 16). But this was not altogether a timeless past of tradition. Culemborg sustained a history through its claim to significance as the place where Jan van Riebeeck and hence the settler nation were born. In a special "Jan van Riebeeck-Room" in the town, models of Jan, Maria, and their son, Lambertus, were exhibited in "a wonderful, soft light" surrounded by "heavy . . . straight lined oak furniture," old maps, and paintings by the "Dutch masters." Culemborg became the link between the festival fair and the history depicted at the festival. Like its historical ancestor, Culemborg in Cape Town stood out "as a separate entity" amid "the bustle of the foreshore," affirming Holland and Van Riebeeck, respectively, as the "land of descent" and the founder of a "new nation."[43]

In contrast to Much-Binding, but along similar lines as the United Kingdom pavilion, Culemborg presented itself, and Holland more generally, as arenas of progress and advancement in specific spheres. The festival fair guidebook emphasized that behind the facade of the gabled houses at Culemborg "the very latest of Holland's modern achievements" were on show. These included a "Magic Garden" built by Philips Electrical Company, a model of the Amsterdam's harbor works, exhibits showing the activities of Dutch shipping and airlines, and the workings of a glass factory. In the Culemborg Town Hall, the major exhibition depicted the technology being utilized in "Holland's fight against the sea." An explicit connection was made with the festival in that one of the major firms involved in the hydraulic operations in Holland, the Hollandsche Aanneming Maatschappy, was presented to the public as the same company "which carried out the reclamation in the Cape Town foreshore, where the Van Riebeeck festival is now being held." The ancestors of these Dutch people were being celebrated in 1952 as the bearers of the torch of "Western Christian Civilisation" to "the dark continent of Africa."[44]

That "darkness" was on show at the South-West Africa pavilion where the group of bushmen, under the supervision of the anthropologist-cum-game warden, P. J. Schoeman, performed daily. In the gaze of curious onlookers, armed with their cameras, who might have just paid a visit to Van Riebeeck's birthplace, they sat, talked, posed, and crafted bows and arrows. Represented as the "earliest Natives," the bushmen were placed by the festival organizers on the bottom rung of a human evolutionary scale, at the first stage of human development. Unlike the NAD pavilion, where the emphasis was on progress under the auspices and control of people who claimed a European descent, in South-West Africa's "modernistic" building, with "displays of the social and economic development of the territory," the bushmen were displayed as an example of a primitive racial type with little or no prospect for advancement, other than to be placed in a bushman reserve. In contrast, the "European races," on show alongside the bushmen, were asserting their heritage and development as components of a future, racially exclusive, modern South African nation.[45]

As indicated in chapter 2, this development of a white settler nationalism, which would cut across class and ethnic divisions, was central to the conception of the Van Riebeeck festival as a whole. In the festival fair specifically it was intended to feature prominently through highlighting local manufacturing industry. Unlike the agricultural sector, which was largely seen to be the preserve of Afrikaner farmers, and the mining sector, which English capitalists were perceived to dominate, secondary industry was represented as a [white] South African achievement. Local manufacturers, with the assistance of sympathetic governments that had imposed tariff barriers, had increased the value of produced goods from £84 million in 1925 to an estimated £1 billion in 1951. The exhibition halls at the fair, located behind the large pavilions devoted to transport and the mining and sugar industries, were designed not only to display this "astonishing development" but also to portray it as the height of national achievement. Numerous displays of industrial development were presented in a relatively ordered fashion. Bearing some resemblance to the construction of the Festival of Britain, but on a much more limited scale, the viewer was supposed to start "at one end of the halls with the products of the primary industries (mining, agriculture, forestry, and fisheries)" and then trace "the story of each product as systematically as possible." Under the watchful gaze of the "patron saint of South African business," Jan van Riebeeck, the festival fair was to reveal "the richness and vigour of the young industries of South Africa."[46]

Central to this image of national development was one of progress through science. Science was depicted as the thread that "wove" the country together, from the days of subsistence agriculture through the growth of markets to the stage of "industrial development" and the emergence of large towns and cities. In the Hall of Science at the Van Riebeeck festival fair, visitors were invited to view this "great scientific progress." They could see how geologists had mapped the minerals of "the country's industrial centres," how the government-funded Council for Scientific and Industrial Research, with its "extensive laboratories" and "large staff," set industrial standards and solved "scientific problems in industry," and how, like Van Riebeeck, veterinary scientists were fighting and conquering "parasites and disease." The only aspect of science not allowed to be displayed at the Van Riebeeck festival was the theory of evolution. Whereas the "native" showcases constructed an imagined racial evolutionary scale within the "human race," in the "Hall of Science" evolution, with the consent of the South African Archaeological Society, was banned "as it might offend [the] sensitivities" of those who "truly believe that fossil material represents dead species in a prolific creation but proves nothing more." This enabled "European" religion to sit, somewhat uneasily, within a rational mode of scientific enquiry and progress, whereas "native" belief was cast as superstitious and hence backward.[47]

These interconnected conceptions of "national development" and "western progress" were central to the Van Riebeeck festival fair. With such a variety of exhibits on display, however, they were difficult images to sustain. Even Van

Riebeeck's guiding finger could not direct visitors to what they should see and experience. Unfortunately, for those who wanted the festival fair to focus on secondary industry and scientific progress, these halls attracted little attention. Of the £416.19.10 spent on producing five thousand booklets for the Hall of Science, for instance, only £36 was recovered from sales. Instead, when the festival gates opened each morning, visitors rushed to be first in line at the gold mining pavilion. The festival crowds showed much interest in the human showcases as well, particularly in the bushmen at the South-West Africa pavilion. Not only did crowds want to see and touch the bushmen, they were also interested in what the bushmen thought and had to say. Thus, instead of simply asserting the "benefits" of "civilization," the human showcases raised the issue of what constituted modernity and progress in South Africa in the 1950s. Was it "civilized" to put humans on display?[48]

The statistics of crowd sizes at the various exhibits indicate that the three major attractions were the gold pavilion, the diamond pavilion, and the bushmen display.[49] People spent hours in line to see gold smelted, to experience going down a gold mine, to be bedazzled by the array of valuable items on display in the Jewel Box in the Diamond Pavilion, and to gaze at the bushmen making bows and arrows. Let us follow the crowds to two of these pavilions, those of the gold mining industry and South-West Africa (where the bushmen were on display), take a look at what they saw, and examine some of their responses.

The Gold Mine at the Seaside

From nearly all entrances to the festival fair, the direct path led to plot 98, where, next to Van Riebeeck's birthplace, Culemborg, stood the largest and most imposing display at the festival fair: the gold pavilion presented by the Transvaal Chamber of Mines. Yet this pavilion, which became such a huge drawing card, had almost been withdrawn from the fair initially because, as noted in chapter 2, the Chamber of Mines saw the Van Riebeeck festival as a possible "political manoeuvre" designed to enhance the election chances of the National Party. Only after items in the pageant were revised and floats altered did the Chamber agree to set up its pavilion and to "take the chance of being involved in a political demonstration."[50]

If the decision to set up the mining pavilion was taking a chance, then the odds in the Chamber's favor were very low. However, the Van Riebeeck festival fair presented the Chamber with an ideal opportunity—some might say a golden one—to continue the massive publicity campaign it had embarked on after the Second World War. In the face of the phenomenal growth of secondary industry, the government's attempts to impose higher taxes and to regulate the mining industry, and the increased militancy among the African workforce, culminating in the 1946 mine workers' strike, the Chamber moved from a private dialogue, which kept its technological and labor practices confined, to a discourse in which the knowledge of mining and all its operations were open to a wider public. Once the public had acquired "self-knowledge" about mining, they would come to the "self-realization" of the "damaging effect that apparently innocuous legislation, ill-considered regulations and ill-advised taxation can have—and are having—upon the industry from which the community draws so much of its current income." By sharing knowledge and facts with the public, the mining industry identified itself as sharing "common interests ... [with] ... the nation."[51]

The knowledge the public received was carefully regulated through various media. The Chamber of Mines publication, *The Mining Survey*, launched in 1946, contained detailed, illustrated articles about living and working conditions on the mines, the contribution of mines to the South African economy, and technical aspects of mining operations. An additional way to open up the mining industry and to control the knowledge of its operations, the Chamber arranged for people to see the mines "for themselves." Underground mine tours had been in operation since 1926, but from 1946 they were extended and regularized, with the Chamber transporting visitors to and from the mine. When visitors arrived at the mine shaft, they were fitted out in protective clothing before entering the cage to begin their descent. The feeling one had standing at the top of the shaft was "a mixture of nervousness and excitement, very like the feeling one gets waiting for one's first plane to take off." Then the cage lurched and headed downward at "breakneck speed," past "brilliantly lit stations," to reach the underground workings. Although some visitors experienced a "sick feeling in the stomach," the *Mining Survey* assured its readers that there was "no unpleasant sinking feeling."[52] Once the visitors had crawled along the dark, narrow corridors, they could witness the miners at work:

> See, there they are, a white miner and his black assistants! See how their bodies shine, how the sweat pours down face and neck and arms! One of the black men is lying under the drill, guiding it with his foot, and drilling holes in the rock wall. In these holes will be placed charges of dynamite, and when all of us have retired to a safe distance, the charges will be detonated. Then the rock will come tumbling down, and the whole mine will seem to shake and tremble, filling us again with that feeling that is a compound of excitement and fear.[53]

Safely returned to the surface, and imbued with the confidence of "seasoned mineworkers," visitors were invited to visit selected "native quarters," which, almost inevitably, they found to be "scrupulously clean and pleasant" where "great attention" was paid to the "health and recreation" of the workers. Even a "Zulu chief," Bhekizizwe Zondi, was invited to see how "his people" lived on the mines. He "was well pleased with what he saw" and concluded that "his people" were "very well cared for and contented." By making knowledge public, and carefully selecting and representing it, the Chamber not only asserted its centrality but deflected growing criticism, especially internationally, "that Natives are taken by the scruff of the neck and flung down a mine where they stay until they die."[54]

By the early 1950s thirty-five hundred visitors per year were taking underground tours. Although the tours were invaluable in terms of "increasing the public knowledge" about the industry, the small numbers on these tours limited their impact. Fairs and exhibitions, which were "for the many," were an occasion to allow even more people to become aware of "the high prestige the gold mining industry enjoys in South African affairs." Between March 1952 and September 1953 the Chamber of Mines spent vast sums in setting up pavilions at exhibitions. In addition to the £120,000-pavilion at the Van Riebeeck festival fair, massive exhibits were constructed at the Central African Rhodes Centenary Exhibition in Bulawayo and at the Rand Easter Show in Johannesburg. Almost a million people visited these exhibits, an indication that the Chamber was broadening its campaign of increasing "public knowledge and appreciation" of the gold mining industry.[55]

At the Van Riebeeck festival fair, not only did the Chamber allocate a large budget for the gold mining pavilion, but much time and planning went into ensuring that the pavilion would attract the crowds through "ingenious" models, presentations, and displays. The pavilion, the first on which construction was begun at the fair, contained five central features: a scaled-down model of surface operations; a smelting house where gold was poured every half hour; a visual display of twenty-eight exhibits containing models, charts, photographs, and goldware depicting the history of the industry and its value to South Africans; an information desk, where special Van Riebeeck festival information packages about the mining industry were handed out and where "young [white] men" could inquire "about entering this great industry which pays its European employees . . . an average wage of £750 a year"; and, finally, the highlight for many festival goers, a simulated trip underground in a gold mine which was constructed meters away from "where the waves of the Atlantic break over the sands of Table Bay."[56]

The emphasis at the mining pavilion was on participation, enjoyment, and excitement. As a result, crowds were drawn to the pavilion as to a "magnet." According to one official, the 469,024 visitors at the pavilion, a little more than half the total attendance at the fair, was probably the biggest for any exhibit or show in South Africa. Of these, 104,021 experienced the thrill of "the underground." The only other area of the festival where one could possibly have experienced more excitement was by being "swung end over end, faster and faster" in the "flying jets, looping cars and a moon rocket" at the amusement park. But that cost more money, which many of the festivalgoers were reluctant to pay. "I went into the mine quite a few times. And the things were all free. No entrance fee for this and that."[57]

The Chamber of Mines clearly believed that the large numbers at the pavilion at the Van Riebeeck festival contributed to establishing gold mining as a "national" enterprise for all white South Africans. By bringing "fathers," "mothers," "schoolboys," "Boy Scouts," and burly farmers" together to go "underground" and gaze on the "Native mineworkers using jackhammers in the stopes," the Chamber, it hoped, had established a sense of common white South African identity. The "platteland [had] taken the gold-mining industry to its bosom," and the nation, united by gold, could gaze on the "natives," who were "foreigners," not part of the South African nation but labor for the "nation."[58]

While "the mining industry was contending it was a modern day Van Riebeeck,"[59] for festival goers, the chance of "going down" a gold mine, even a simulated one, was, like the mine tours on the Witwatersrand, an experience of excitement tinged with an element of danger.

> At the entrance was a notice to the effect that everyone using this shaft did so at his own risk. This made me feel a little apprehensive, but as there were hundreds of people in the queue behind me it was too late to turn back. Our party entered the "lift."[60]

Upon entering the lift, the visitor was "filled with the . . . awful feeling of claustrophobia." As one "descended" into the "depths of the earth," it really "felt like going down." On reaching the workings, there was a moment of darkness and "there was a feeling that we were deep underground." Then a cacophony of sounds erupted, "roar[ing] . . . jackhammers, rumbl[ing] . . . loaders and the hiss of compressed air." This was all a "wonderful" experience for the crowds, not only for the excitement it generated but because it had an "atmosphere of realism" and "authenticity."[61]

Since festival goers did not have the opportunity to visit the "native compounds" after their experience "underground," 150,000 information packs were distributed, containing a mini-edition of the *Mining Survey*, some "facts" about the industry, and a picture booklet entitled *African Contrast*. The booklet comprised a series of photographs, with very little text, comparing "kraal" and "compound," with the latter cast in a progressive light. The "modern" features of the "native single quarters" were contrasted to the "stilt huts of a kraal," the dark, "disorganized" "interior of a Native hut" with a bright, "clean" kitchen and the "primitive practice" of "crude surgery in the kraal" with "modern science" in a "mine Native hospital." These photographic images, laid out next to one another, were not only provided as carefully selected visual "evidence" of labor practices on the mines but also depicted the Chamber and the industry as contributing "to the healthy advancement of the native" man. It was this "native," trained by the white men on the mines to meet their requirements, who, when he went home to "his wife" bearing "presents for his family," was, according to the Chamber, automatically bestowing development on "South Africa" and "his people." In this way, like the Native Affairs Department, the Chamber of Mines associated itself with the modernizing project that was claiming to provide "Betterment for the Bantu."[62]

But visitors to the Van Riebeeck festival fair had neither the experience of seeing the actual "native compound" nor of going underground. The fairgoers did not work eight- to ten-hour shifts nor did they experience the heat, darkness, dirt, and danger of the underground. This particular image of the mining industry had come to feature more prominently in the press in the few years before the Van Riebeeck festival, particularly with the opening of Free State goldfields in 1946. Accidents in these mines were reported regularly. There was a growing sense of disquiet about the safety standards on these mines, especially when the managers of the mine seemed to shift the onus of responsibility to the workers without considering mechanical and structural problems. Indeed, as a schoolboy from Salt River in Cape Town wrote, "The fate of a mine worker" was often "a lonely grave."[63]

Visitors to the gold mining pavilion at the Van Riebeeck festival did not experience the daily fear that they might never emerge alive from the depths of the earth. They remained very much on the surface, far from the danger of rockfalls and explosions. Although the Chamber's "danger sign" at the entrance to the "lift shaft" claimed an element of risk, visitors were assured that they would remain unscathed upon emerging from their thirty minutes "underground" with their memories, photographs, and a sense of knowing "what it really was like" to work in a gold mine. Their knowledge, like their journey, barely scratched the surface.

"This Terrible Thing"

While the gold mining pavilion commanded a central position and drew a large crowd, lines were also long outside plot 50 in the southwest corner of the fairgrounds at an entrance gate near Marine Drive (Figure 15). This plot, across the pathway from Culemborg, accommodated the pavilion of the South-West African administration, a low-lying "modern" £20,000-building displaying color photographs of the scenery of South-West Africa, an exhibition of developments in the territory, and housing a Bavarian beer garden that served "the famous South-West African beer." A booklet illustrated with photographs of government buildings, Karakul sheep, diamond mining operations, and fish factories was distributed to interested visitors. But this is not what the fifteen hundred people, who, on some days, passed through the pavilion every hour, came to see. They were far more interested in the "native section" of the pavilion, where there were "members of South-West African tribes in tribal dress." In particular, they wanted to gaze on the "full-blooded" bushmen, "the last remnants of this almost extinct aboriginal people."[64]

At the time of the Van Riebeeck festival, most bushmen in South-West Africa had been "tamed" into becoming "useful workers," an "invisible proletariat" living and working on white settler farms. The seventeen Kung bushmen who came to Cape Town, however, were defined as "a pure tribe," coming from northeastern South-West Africa, beyond the white farming areas. Labeled by the settler population of Namibia as "dishonest" and "wild bushmen," they did not work for the white farmers who were moving into the Kaukaveld in increasing numbers but frequently stole their cattle. This "problem" had to be "solved" and, in the grand South African tradition, a commission of enquiry was set up in 1949: the Commission for the Preservation of the Bushmen. The chair of this commission was none other than P. J. Schoeman, game ranger, anthropologist, and writer of hunting tales for children.[65]

As the name of the commission indicates, the "problem" was turned on its head from one dealing with the interests of white farmers to one concerned with the "preservation of the bushmen." This inversion enabled the commissioners to speak on behalf of the bushmen while still catering to the farming lobby's concerns for greater control of the "wild bushman." Central to this process was the role of Schoeman, who, as a "trained anthropologist," could claim to speak for the interests of the bushman. Schoeman's major concern as a *volkekundige* [anthropologist] at Stellenbosch University in the 1940s had been to find a "solution" to the "native problem" which would serve to maintain "the racial purity of the Afrikaners." Using a notion of "racial differentiation"— "that race was linked to the level of civilization, and the nature of life, and that these differences were inherent"—he, along with other anthropologists at Pretoria and Stellenbosch, had proposed the territorial segregation of races in South Africa. By isolating blacks and giving them their own areas with which they could identify, Schoeman maintained, the problem of the miscegenation of the Afrikaners would disappear.[66]

This formed the basis of knowledge Schoeman carried with him into South-West Africa in the 1950s. In speaking for the bushmen, he constantly asserted that they wanted to have a piece of land for themselves where they could live

and thereby perpetuate the race. His novel, *Jagters van die Woestynland* [Hunters of the desert land], which tells of the lives of the "wild bushmen," describes the way they hunt, and relates bushman stories, ends with a plea to the "*Wit Vader*" [White Father]:[67]

> The Ovambo's have their own land. . . . its name is Ovamboland. Kwangerri have their own land. . . . it is called Okavango. The Herero's have land. The Bastard people of Rehoboth have land. They all have land where the white man's law looks after them. Only the Bushmen have no land. And we, the Bushmen people, were in this country first. Then, all the land belonged to us. . . . now we have nothing. . . . Aau. . . . Father. . . . White Father. . . . baas Naude. . . . baas Hoogenhout. . . . baas Neser. . . . ask them to listen to the weeping of a race which is very tired of running away. Give us a piece of land too.[68]

This was all part of the change in official discourse in the 1940s and 1950s from seeing "natives" as a "homogeneous" group to regarding them as "heterogeneous population categories." It was this newly discovered "reality" which had to be taken into account when "solving" the "native problem." When Schoeman tabled the commissioner's interim report in September 1951, the "solution" he thus recommended was that two bushman reserves be set up in land that the white farmers did not require, one for the Kung and another for the Heikom. In this way the "wild bushmen" could be controlled and their "race preserved."[69]

A few months after the tabling of the interim report, Schoeman and R. F. Morris, the chief Native Commissioner in Okavango, set about selecting a group of bushmen to take to the Van Riebeeck festival. Although, in the preliminary arrangements for the fair, the bushmen were included in discussions over the NAD Bantu pavilion, it was decided that they would form an "independent exhibit of primitive cultures in S.W.A." Here there would be no displays of education and progress, "as the other provinces were so much ahead of them." Instead, the aim was to show the bushmen in "natural surroundings" and thereby to "depict a phase in the history of Africa that is fast fading." The only way this phase could ultimately be retained, "for themselves and for prosperity," according to Schoeman, was that the bushmen be placed in a reserve when they returned home from the festival in Cape Town. The bushmen were to be shown as a "dying race," and he, Schoeman, was to be both their protector and the guarantor of their survival through the setting up of reserves.[70]

An ahistorical history such as this appealed to officials in the NAD and the Department of the Interior, who had initially expressed reservations that the bushman display was contravening the 1939 principle of prohibiting "such performances" in other countries where the issue of maintaining control had been paramount. In this case, though, it was felt that the purpose of the display was not to make a monetary profit but to give the "correct historical background." This, according to the Secretary for Native Affairs, was similar to the other "native exhibits" in "our pavilion." Moreover, it coincided with government plans to incorporate South-West Africa into South Africa. These plans, which attempted to counter the mounting international criticism for the discriminatory racial policies of the South Africans in the territory and their violation of the terms of the UN mandate, based their claims for extended authority on the assertion that, like in South Africa, the South African government was "preserving," "protecting," and "bettering" the "natives" of South-West Africa. The Native Affairs Department, portrayed in the government's proposals as the "special Department of State to look after Native interests," therefore had no objections to the bushmen being exhibited, under the auspices of their "protector," P. J. Schoeman, in the South-West Africa pavilion at the Van Riebeeck festival fair.[71]

A meeting was arranged with 140 bushmen at Caudum, sixty miles south of the Okavango River and twenty miles from the Botswana border. How this group came together at Caudum is not known. There was initially no clamoring to make the trip to the festival, but then material incentives such as money, blankets, food, and tobacco were offered. "Volunteers" came forward and, from the larger group, seventeen were chosen to go to Cape Town. Schoeman claimed he had chosen these bushmen because, as an anthropologist, he knew they were racially closest to the Cape bushmen Van Riebeeck had encountered—"small yellow ones." The anthropological evidence on which Schoeman was able to make this claim is unknown. But by presenting his choice as being based on "knowledge," rather than on a random selection of those who were either prepared to go to Cape Town or cajoled into it, he validated the trip to the Van Riebeeck festival as "scientific," "historic," and in the best interest of "preserving the bushman race."[72]

Soon the bushmen were on their eighteen-hundred-mile journey to Cape Town. Upon clambering into a three-ton truck, they were driven to the headquarters of the Native Commissioner in Runtu. There a medical inspection by Dr. Werner Kuschke revealed a vitamin C deficiency, as evidenced by the state of their teeth. It was then back into the truck for the drive to Windhoek, then a long train journey, and ultimately arrival at Cape Town Station on 7 March. P. J. Schoeman led the bushmen onto the platform and introduced them to the press. He announced that the leader of the group, whom he had chosen, was a man called Cin Cau. The eldest member of the group was a woman of seventy, and the youngest was a baby named Non Ca. He said they had been well cared for on the trip down and fed with mealie meal [cornmeal] and meat. They had also tasted black coffee, which they liked, claimed Schoeman, as well as grapes, which "they love[d]."[73]

In the following four weeks Schoeman strode on the Cape Town stage as "preserver," "protector," and "father" of his group of "little men and women." He represented himself as their "security," the man they could "love and trust.'" The seventeen bushmen lived in a single room behind the South-West Africa pavilion, where they were provided with mattresses. At times, weather permitting, they chose to sleep outdoors around a fire. They were fed on a diet of meat, vegetables, mealie meal, bread, and milk, which, although it was not their usual food, had been "scientifically" approved by Professor Brock of the University of Cape Town's medical school. The white officials also had rooms at the back of the pavilion, which enabled them to watch over the bushmen. In an inversion of meaning distinctly similar to the appointment of the Commission for the Preservation of Bushmen in 1949, the whites were not there to oversee the bushman but to give them "a greater sense of security in their strange surroundings." If they were not there to watch over them, the officials maintained, "the Natives would feel abandoned and become unhappy."[74]

But Schoeman was much more than merely a preserver and protector of the bushmen in Cape Town. He almost totally controlled what they did, what they experienced, what they felt, and what they said. He wrote in *Die Huisgenoot* that although they were wary of making the trip to Cape Town in what, according to Schoeman, they called the "black millipede thing that smokes and eats stones," they were later very enthusiastic, acting like a bunch of teenagers going on a picnic. In Cape Town he arranged regular excursions for the bushmen into the countryside, in order, he said, for them to feel much more at home.[75] Later, when he took them to the University of Cape Town's medical school for blood tests, he said they were very brave and "even the children never flinched." They were taken to see a movie and "were particularly delighted with a sequence of a tortoise." Correspondents from local newspapers were invited into the "bushman enclosure" for private viewings. On the basis of his "scientific" knowledge, Schoeman would, in his "quiet voice," tell the reporters all about the history and legends of the bushmen. Then he asked the bushmen certain questions, after which he would report their replies. For someone who did not understand the bushmen's language and had to rely on an interpreter, Schoeman's knowledge of what the bushmen said and felt was remarkable. Yet his authority was never questioned by the reporters, who left the enclosure feeling they had developed a "new understanding" and now yearned for a return to the days of "pure and ancient Africa."[76]

The "protection" Schoeman thus gave to "his bushmen" in Cape Town enabled him to exercise power over the knowledge the public received about the bushmen. This knowledge only concerned the "ancient history," "folklore," "religion," and "legends," which were, like the people, dying out, almost "naturally." Nothing was said about how the bushman had become a "dying race" through a process of extermination carried out by settlers in Namibia in the late nineteenth and early twentieth centuries. Nor was anything said about how most bushmen in Namibia were, in the 1950s, barely managing to survive on settler farms. By silencing the process of genocide, and casting the knowledge of the bushmen in the mold of a curious, unchanging society in danger of extinction, and therefore one needing to be saved, Schoeman situated the bushmen in a discourse of nationing. In these terms, the "solution" to the "problem" of the "wild bushmen" of Namibia was to maintain their "purity"—and the "purity of Africa"—by setting up reserves. Schoeman therefore became the knight in shining armor who had "the cause of the tiny men" at heart and was constantly on patrol against "lurking serpents," or "wounded elephants," in order to "preserve their [the bushmen's] rapidly diminishing numbers."[77]

Although Schoeman could largely control the images that were emerging from these private viewings of the bushmen, his power was considerably lessened when it came to the public showings at the festival fair. Starting on 14 March the bushmen would sit for hour after hour patiently crafting bows and arrows, and making necklaces from ostrich shells, while thousands of visitors gazed on them. Yet, in this silence, the voices of the bushmen began to be heard. First, to the disappointment of thousands of onlookers, and despite prior assurances that the bushmen were so eager that they would even "dance on the station" if allowed, they did not dance for the spectators, because, according to their overseers, "it might tax their strength." Then, after a few days of sitting endlessly, doing very little, they became "tired of sitting" and only appeared at specific hours: from 10:00 in the morning to 12:30, and then from 3:00 (or sometimes as late as 4:30) in the afternoon to 5:30. Some days the bushmen were not on view at all because they were "feeling the strain." The result was that lines two hundred to three hundred yards long would form for hours before the "compound" opened. Frustration levels reached the breaking point, people jumped in line and pushed others out of the way, and the police were called in to keep control. When the bushmen were supposed to be taken to the sea for a swim, they refused to go, leaving the waiting press in the howling wind, getting their "eyes, ears and mouths [filled] with sand." Finally, to Schoeman's chagrin, the bushmen started accepting gifts of food and money from the spectators. Feeling his authority as "protector of the bushman" being undermined, he issued a statement calling on the public to stop offering them presents. "The Bushmen were being well fed and well paid," he maintained, and, moreover, "it was unfair that one should receive a gift and not the others."[78]

If he had problems controlling the bushmen, Schoeman had even more difficulties with the spectators. Despite the presence of Lochline Louw, whose role was to inform the public about the bushmen and to intervene when visitors "annoyed them too much when taking photographs," the crowds stared for hours, touched their "olive skins," lifted up their clothes, pulled their hair, and persisted in feeding them. Schoeman became so frustrated that he wondered who was the more civilized, the bushmen or the spectators. "The Bushmen are acting one hundred percent in a civilised way towards the festival goers, but some festival goers are showing that they are certainly not civilised."[79]

A sense of outrage began to filter through sections of the press. One individual, identifying himself only as "Scandalized" from Milnerton, found the display of "non-European men and women . . . as exhibits in a human zoo" repulsive and called for the immediate closure of these "kraals." The *Cape Times* gave space to a statement by the Franchise Action Committee, which labeled the bushman display "an insult and an affront to the dignity and self-respect of the 10,000,000 non-European people." *The Torch*, newspaper of the Non-European Unity Movement, reported on how the bushmen were deeply shocked at the way the crowds were treating them. A letter in the *Cape Argus* questioned whether the bushman display was progressive:

> At the Festival one may be able to see a lot of progress as far as machinery and industry are concerned, but from a humanitarian point of view I failed to see any progress when I looked at the little group of unhappy Bushmen huddled together while thousands walked closely past and stared at them as if they were monkeys in a zoo.[80]

The bushman display, instead of highlighting the "progress of the nation," or indeed the need to "preserve the bushman," was thus raising questions about the fundamental assumptions of the "white nation's" claim to modernity. In the words of *The Torch*, when it was heard that fellow human beings were to be displayed like wild animals, "the blood of truly civilised people throughout the world began to boil."[81]

The bushmen also began to "speak out." Not only were they "deeply shocked" at the way festivalgoers were treating them, but they were also finding the "white man's curiosity amazing." They asked their interpreter, "Why are the White people like baboons?" The resistance press, picking up on this, began to portray the bushmen within a tradition of resistance. *The Torch* called the bushmen—whom they labeled the Batwa—the world's "greatest hunters," who never surrendered, and "not once did they negotiate for peace." The *Guardian*, using the report from the *Cape Argus* on how the bushmen saw their onlookers, produced a cartoon which "depicted the bushmen gazing at the long-necked, short-limbed, white 'baboons,' clamouring for attention, while the bushmen re-

17. A cartoon in *The Guardian* reversed the gaze on the bushmen displayed in the South-West Africa pavilion at the Van Riebeeck festival fair. "I Believe if You Annoy Baboons They're Quite Dangerous," *The Guardian*, 27 March 1952. Courtesy of National Library of South Africa, Cape Town.

marked, 'I believe that if you annoy Baboons they're quite dangerous.'" The colonial gaze had been reversed, and the bushmen turned into heroes of resistance (Figure 17).[82]

By the beginning of April the bushmen were bored with the festival and did not want to stay on for the extra week the fair was extended. Moreover, they were unable to sell any more bows and arrows or beads to the public, as they had run out of the necessary materials. On 7 April, after almost 170,000 people had seen them at the festival fair, they packed their bags for the return trip home. The disgruntled expectant visitors were informed that the bushmen had grown scared of Table Mountain's tablecloth, the "big white cloud that came down the mountain and then stopped and then suddenly went away." The bushmen were none too sorry to say good-bye to all those "monkeys who did nothing but stare at them." Schoeman reserved an entire third-class coach for them, and together they bade farewell to what the bushmen labeled "'that terrible thing,'" the Van Riebeeck festival fair.[83]

"History! Van Riebeeck! Forget It!"

Even before the doors to the Van Riebeeck festival fair had been shut, the pavilions torn down, and the railway sheds restored to their intended function, the exhibitors, who had spent vast amounts of money on their pavilions, were "more than satisfied" with the number of visitors and the interest shown in their displays. By 15 April, when the fair was over, there was even more enthusiasm. Governor General E. G. Jansen thought it had showed "the rest of the world the progress made in South Africa." A Cape Town clothing manufacturer was pleased that thousands of people had "seen and handled our clothes." Above all, the Van Riebeeck festival was proclaimed a "sweeping success" and an "example of national unity."[84]

Yet the carefully constructed national project had often assumed a very different character from the one the festival organizers had attempted to sustain in 1952. On Cape Town's foreshore Van Riebeeck was often in danger of being subsumed by the "fun of the fair." "We didn't go to the festival with the idea of celebrating the landing of Jan van Riebeeck," said one festival visitor. "The furthest thing from our minds was Jan van Riebeeck. We were there to enjoy ourselves."[85] "I didn't feel, 'Whoopee! He's a hero,'" claimed another. "History! Van Riebeeck! Forget it! Who's that? No, that didn't matter to me."[86]

Moreover, the exhibits at the fair, from the gold mining pavilion to the bushman enclosure, which sometimes were quite unsystematically conceptualized as part of a "national project," often took on different meanings. At times the gold mining pavilion turned into little more than a fun-filled ride at which some "knowledge" was acquired, while some viewed the visit to the bushmen as "comic." Overall, according to a schoolgirl from Cape Town, the fair "did not contribute very much to the development of South Africa, but it was the biggest spectacle displayed by human hands in our country."[87]

The "*fees vir die oog*" [feast/festival for the eye] was a "producerly text" where, in order to widen the audience and seemingly loosen the bounds of social control, the sensual activities of the body, rather than "the mind and its sense," became the central focus. It was the "bodily pleasures" that offered "carnivalesque, evasive, liberating practices," and, in so doing, occasioned the "parody, subversion, or inversion" of the displays by festival visitors and participants. The Van Riebeeck festival fair was seen through a multitude of eyes, as spectators, participants, and organizers all surveyed different vistas and created a multiplicity of meanings for the activities which took place on the fore-shore between mid-March and mid-April 1952. To impute total social control from the construction of these images of the "nation" would be to fall into the very same trap as befell the *Cape Times* which confidently asserted that "All Loved the [Van Riebeeck festival] Fair."[88]

5 Local and National Pasts
The Journey of the Mail Coach "Settlers" through the Eastern Cape

The displays of the tercentenary festival of 1952 were centered on the figure of Van Riebeeck as the founder of a nation based on racial exclusivity with Cape Town as its place of origin. To make this Van Riebeeck spatially national, the organizers of the tercentenary of founding perceived it necessary to move beyond the geographical limits of Cape Town and its immediate environs and to ensure the participation of other locales in his festival. On the one hand, this involved inducing groups to relocate temporarily to the Cape in order to assume various roles. For example, the festival organizers approached those who controlled and managed larger towns and cities in South Africa, requesting that they stage exhibits at the festival fair. Others were asked if they would be willing to sponsor and construct floats for the pageants on Adderley Street. For most, though, this invitation meant taking up residence in one of the three tent villages providing temporary accommodations, Goodwood, Rosebank, and Belville, in order to perform in the mass displays or to witness the events of the festival. On the other hand, plans were afoot to take Van Riebeeck to various towns in South Africa prior to his landing in April 1952. The white inhabitants of these locales were encouraged to establish their own Van Riebeeck committees, to organize local pageants, and to write histories of the towns and cities. These local commemorations which selected moments of origin to designate "own founding," within the larger framework of "national beginning," were intended to provide these towns with the opportunity to become part of the festival and to show that "the rest of South Africa . . . ha[d] an interest in the fact that Van Riebeeck landed in 1652." Moreover, with the Cape Town City Council displaying, at times, a somewhat lukewarm response to Van Riebeeck, these local celebrations were vital to ensuring that the festival gathered and sustained its momentum.[1]

Linking the movement toward Cape Town and Van Riebeeck's excursions throughout South Africa were the journeys of the mail coaches organized by the Afrikaans Taal en Kultuur Vereneging [ATKV; Afrikaans Language and Cultural Association]. From the beginning of January 1952 seven mail coaches departed from their respective starting points—Ohrigstad, Windhoek, Beit Bridge, Groblersdal, Sabie, Amsterdam, and Umtata—to travel through nearly sixty major towns in South Africa, covering some eleven thousand miles and arriving in Cape Town on 30 March to usher in the festival week (Figure 18).

As the mail coaches passed through the towns en route to Cape Town, "great and impressive festivals" were to be organized by "all sections of the European population." The arrival of the mail coach provided a "tangible copulative incentive" for a frenzy of local festivities. The coach would enter the town, the mayor would welcome it in front of the town hall, and a local history written by "local experts"—usually schoolteachers or members of the local clergy—would be presented to the "*ritmeester*" [journey master] for "conveyance" to Cape Town to be deposited in the South African library. A float procession and a local pageant organized to coincide with the coach's arrival would take place. In the evening the town council would hold a banquet "in honour of the mail coach personnel" at which "the proverbial hospitality of our nation [would be] strikingly evinced." After spending the night, the coach, refreshed by the evening's proceedings, would continue on its way, not to deliver the mail but to gather the nation and revitalize its local history.[2]

The journeys of the mail coaches began on 4 January in a remote corner of the northeastern Transvaal, some two thousand kilometers from the scene of Van Riebeeck's landing at Granger Bay, at the "ruined Voortrekker town" of Ohrigstad (Figure 18). Before the journey began, twenty-three speeches were made and a historical pageant consisting of the *Dromedaris*, President Kruger of the Boer Republic of the Transvaal in the late nineteenth century in exile in Switzerland, Boer War generals, and a group of farmers paraded around the town's stadium. On center stage was D. F. Malan, the prime minister, who entered the town's arena "comfortably seated" aboard a replica of the *Dromedaris*.[3] As the light faded he gave the signal for the Van Riebeeck festival to begin: "Here, in the historical town of Ohrigstad, we are standing at the start of our nation-wide festival celebrations, which will reach its zenith on 6 April in Cape Town, our mother city."[4] A girl and boy from the Voortrekker youth organization then lit their torches from a huge bonfire, the coach horn sounded, the *Lied Van Jong Suid-Afrika* [Song of Young South Africa] was sung and the long journey to the beaches of Table Bay and "Darkest Africa full of Lions" started.[5]

As the coaches "started rolling southwards," local festivities were organized. Durban presented a cavalcade which followed a historical narrative from "barbarity" to "civilisation," "conforming to the procedure which . . . [was] being adopted throughout the Union" and in the streets of Cape Town. In Johannesburg there was a "Grand Procession" where Van Riebeeck was paraded alongside a "Group of diggers," representing the early days of mining, and a "Tribute to South African Womanhood." At the Border Rugby Union grounds in East London, more than 250 people acted in a pageant celebrating the founding of the town, with Lt. Col. John Baillie playing the part of his great grandfather "who hoisted the British flag on Signal Hill and proclaimed the annexation of

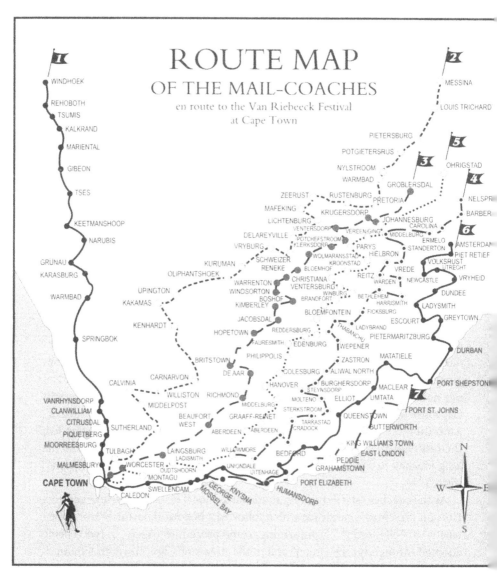

18. Route Map of the Mail Coaches en route to the Van Riebeeck festival at Cape Town. James Whitelaw, Design Matters, based on map in *The Star*, 11 July 1951.

Port Rex." Through these local Van Riebeeck festivals, from Ohrigstad to Cape Town, "throughout the length and breadth of the country," a "golden chain of unity and friendship" was to bind the country together through the festival slogan, "We Build a Nation." The organizers were confident that, as the coaches covered "nearly every part of the country," the festival would assume "a national character," the localities would find their place within the bounds of the nation, and "there will not be many who will again go and search for Ohrigstad somewhere in South West Africa."[6]

At the start of the journey in Ohrigstad, the radio commentator enthused over how the festivities were "all organised locally" and that, except for a few "visiting celebrities," those in attendance were mostly "local people from the district roundabout." But from the moment the journey of the mail coaches began, and Ohrigstad was criticized for eulogizing a past which featured a history of the "Great Trek" and Voortrekker leaders and thereby placed too much emphasis on an Afrikaner past, the contents of these local pasts was as heavily disputed as were the scenes of the national past in Cape Town. They had to be negotiated and ordered to take into account the discord of particular locales, as each area was meant to make its contribution to the festivities. Concerns and questions over how a "composite representation of a few of the highlights of the early history . . . of [localities] could also be depicted" emerged. How much local content should be included? What was a local event? What was a national event? Who determined the spatial boundaries of the past? What happened if the local past did not fit the national one? Just as the content and form of the People's Pageant had to be mediated carefully, so the mail coaches had to negotiate many hazardous roads on their journeys to these local/national pasts. It was through their excursion to the towns en route that the past was bounded into local and national narratives as communities participated (or did not participate) in the journey of settler history.[7]

By examining the production of local history through these dangerous journeys this chapter approaches places, their identities, and their pasts not as being characterized by some sort of internal essence. Instead, the chapter addresses how places cohere, how they are defined, named, bounded, identified with, and historicized, and how all these elements are always shifting, "temporary, uncertain and in process." In the constant construction and re-construction of these spatial identities, the making of histories becomes crucial as they seek to fix time, locating the individual in the present of a particular place that has a defined past and a future. Of these histories, those that become dominant are able to assert and maintain themselves through "the exercise of power relations"—political, legal, and physical forces—often on a national or a global level or both. Clearly these forms of power are important in shaping the contours of locales and their pasts, categorizing people into class/racial/ethnic/

national groups in specifically named and bounded places. But to see national or global history as mere impositions on the locality fails to recognize the contested nature of historical productions. Undoubtedly powerful interest groups can and do create pasts but they are not always easily accepted, and the changing forms they take are often dependent on conflicts over identities, which are often articulated and defended through reference to notions of timeless traditions. More than an imposition or indoctrination, the boundaries of the local pasts are mapped out in contest with national and global pasts.[8]

To try to establish some of the workings of local historical productions this chapter examines how the journeys to Cape Town and to Van Riebeeck sought to establish local/national places and their pasts, particularly in the geographical context of the eastern Cape. This region was spatially defined by the organizers of the Van Riebeeck festival as stretching from Umtata to Port Elizabeth but excluding Port St. Johns "because no festival committee could be formed" there (Figure 18). It was this route the mail coach "Settlers" traversed before joining up with the six others to arrive at the festival stadium on Cape Town's foreshore at the end of March. This was a particularly troublesome journey, where constituting and fitting the local and the national proved to be immensely difficult. By following this route as the mail coach brought "history and pageantry . . . together," the aim is to examine how spatial definition was, somewhat uneasily and always tenuously, settled.[9]

Mapping the Routes of the Mail Coaches to Cape Town

The journey of the mail coaches in 1952 was consciously planned as an attempt to re-create what was claimed to be the "tradition of large and countrywide Afrikaner volk festivals." The model that immediately came to the fore was the one used in the 1938 Voortrekker centenary festival where the movement of ox-wagons through towns and cities from Cape Town to Pretoria had provided the direction for and means to establish a history whose prime purpose was the mobilization of a white Afrikaner *volk*. A key aspect of this movement was to create local and national identities in which individuals embarked on their own travels, associating the space of the trek with personal journeys of identification with people and events in an Afrikaner past. The "Festival of the Ox-wagon Trek" of 1938 self-consciously traversed a "historical road of South Africa." From Cape Town, where the trek began, northward through Stellenbosch, Graaff-Reinet, Bloemfontein, in an "endless tableau," "Afrikaner history was distributed to the Afrikaner." Through commemorations held en route, local events and individuals were placed into an Afrikaner national past. This was a past that told the story of a journey away from British imperial control and toward the conquest of the southern African interior, "across the space of the landscape, obedient to the unfolding telos of racial advance and the rational mapping of measurable space."[10]

The response to the trek of 1938 was overwhelmingly positive, especially among recently urbanized Afrikaans speakers. Many of these were either employed or seeking employment in industries where wages were low, work hours long, and unsanitary working conditions often the norm. An increasing number of Africans entering the job market, especially toward the end of the 1930s, made the situation even more vulnerable for these workers. Afrikaner nationalist organizations presented themselves as champions of the workers' struggles for better conditions and job security against what was represented as "foreign" or "English" capitalists, who often controlled these industries. These capitalists were depicted as being concerned merely with profit, whereas the nationalists maintained that their interests lay with protecting the workers through networks of cultural filiation. Similarly, the Afrikaans-speaking petit-bourgeoisie of lawyers, teachers, and civil servants were having difficulty securing positions in an administrative apparatus seen to be under English control. An anti-imperial narrative of colonial conquest that was being presented, through the 1938 trek, as Afrikaner history, was therefore able to provide the basis for a "unique moment of cross-class mobilisation."[11]

The success of mobilizing support and enthusiastic participation in the events of 1938 enabled the organizers to assert that they had made a breakthrough in arranging festivals. It defined the method of journeys through local towns and histories toward a central place as an "Afrikaner festival technique." This technique was used again in 1949, when the moment arrived for the opening of the Voortrekker Monument. A group of *rapportryers* [dispatch riders] was sent to cover fifteen routes and collect messages from the "entire white population" to carry in their knapsacks to Pretoria. Under the auspices of a joint committee of representatives from the ATKV and the FAK, the dispatch riders conveyed messages "from all centres to their destination, the monument." Localities were urged to establish their own committees that would compile the messages to be taken to Pretoria. As in 1938, the directive indicated that these messages had to be of meaning to the Afrikaner *volk*, fitting in with a narrative of the *volk* as the bearer of "white civilization" alongside "the desire to be free" of imperial control. But there was a major difference: With the National Party now in power, these messages had to focus on giving inspiration and courage for the future rather than dealing with the "heroics" and "triumphs" of the past. The *rapportryer* was seen as ideal for this task. Not only would he convey these messages for the future but he was also depicted as an icon of tradition in the life of the Afrikaner *volk*.[12]

The journey of the mail coaches of 1952 was able to draw on symbolic and organizational associations with the treks of 1938 and 1949. Utilizing similar ATKV structures, the journeys were organized around the idea of "treks throughout the country to a central point."[13] Through the pageantry and the writing of local pasts, these journeys, across the South African landscape, as in 1938 and 1949, were intended to gather history together under their ambit, localize the nation, and nationalize the local. The organizing secretary for the journey of the mail coaches was M. C. Botha, the organizer of the 1949 inauguration of the Voortrekker Monument, who many had automatically presumed would be in charge of the entire Van Riebeeck festival and who had expressed reservations that the festival was losing its association with an Afrikaner past. Indeed, the emphasis on an Afrikaner nationalist past at Ohrigstad and in some of the local pageants point to the greater role of the Afrikaner nationalist organizations, with their experience and structures from 1938 and 1949, in creating the local pasts for the Van Riebeeck festival than the one they had in the streets of Cape Town.

But the mail coaches could not branch off by themselves and establish a national route that did not lead to Cape Town and Van Riebeeck. Those who presented local pasts for the mail coaches were warned early on by the organizing committee that they had to adhere strictly to the theme of the festival, "South Africa After 300 Years—The Building of a Nation." The major problem was that while journeys through locales might have been an appropriate method in attempting to make the festival national, the narrative where white Afrikaners were cast as the anti-imperial bearers of "civilization" did not fit into the national framework being established for Van Riebeeck. The national past being negotiated in 1952, on the one hand, denied race. It was not explicitly about colonial conquest but about European founding and settlement in what was largely depicted as an empty land. On the other hand, the Van Riebeeck festival was about re-constituting race as English speakers and Afrikaans speakers, the settlers, whose roads were to converge in Cape Town in April 1952. At the most obvious level, this meant reversing the route of anti-imperial colonial conquest to the interior that the Great Trek celebrations of 1938 and 1949 had traversed. With the mail coaches returning to Cape Town as the place of national settler founding, they had to associate themselves with a very different type of history, where the time of colonial conquest had to be reversed. Given the impossibility of reversing physical time, the mail coaches, the medium of nationing, focused back on a moment of timelessness, a moment situated between 1952 and 1652. The mail coaches became symbols evoking a nebulous "golden" "romantic" age, the "good old days," and were not likely to generate controversy over historical representation. Emphasis was placed on the appearance and construction of the mail coaches, the type of wood used, and the craftwork required. In "quality, lighting and composition," they moved as if part of "a Constable painting." It was the blast of the bugles, the "sprightly teams of horses," and the "dappled roans" which made a "man's heart feel good."[14]

In this moment of timelessness it was not history as personality and event that linked the "heart of the Tercentenary Festival" with the "remotest corners of South Africa" but the development of communication in the making of modern South Africa. In the days when the mail coaches had traversed the country—and there was some uncertainty as to when this precisely was—the interior was "not yet on a map." It was the history of white settlement which was seen as having brought people onto a map, a grid that was "able to say of anything that it was this, not that; it belonged here, not there." The mail coaches signified the process of the demarcation of boundaries in South Africa. In 1952 the mail coaches were seen to represent a bridge between "the century of the ox-wagon and the century of the machine." They were signifiers of the era of modern communication, the national roads, the modern harbors, the extended rail networks, and the emergent air routes, all of which mapped South Africa as a modern nation.[15]

To define the locality's position and participation in this discovered and re-covered exclusive modern South Africa, each specific place was to acquire moments of founding and then show how "events of great importance" in "the development" of the settler nation occurred there "for the first time." Local committees were directed to devise their own programs, "provided they adhere strictly to the theme of the Festival as set out in the memorandum which has been accepted as the basis of the celebrations."[16] There were guidelines for producing the local history that the coach would convey to Cape Town. It could not exceed fifty foolscap pages and had to contain the following:

1. Founding and early history
2. Development of local government
3. Religious, social, educational and cultural development, historic buildings, architecture, museums, art galleries, monuments, hospital services, etc.
4. Development of agriculture, commerce, industries and mining, railways, bridges, roads, irrigation schemes, etc.
5. Local heroes, battles, inventors and other local figures who became well-known, famous, or even notorious.[17]

The sense of notoriety was not specified but, in terms of the requirement to produce a shared interpretation of a settler past, it could not upset the "primary" purpose of festival as "the constructive growth of South Africa." Where there was conflict between elements of the settler population, the general instruction was that "little need be said in a work of this type." Famous local heroes could either appear on stage in this "general history of the country" or add a brief, but not upsetting, touch of color through their "notoriety." In this way the organizers sought to ensure that the local history did not "degenerate into a dry summary of insignificant, purely local events."[18] If that history did not conform to these requirements, then its past lost meaning and history.

The journey of the mail coaches was also to include, at times, "due consideration for the non-Europeans." Following the guidelines for "non-European" participation in the Van Riebeeck festival, "natives" who could not use the "national road as the main highway" into town, and who had to live in a fenced "location" separated by at least two hundred to five hundred yards from the "European" area, had to enter another past. The daily progress of the coach on its route into towns was to emphasize these boundaries within each locality, separating out "the presence of the Native population" as "non-Europeans." In some towns, the coach bearing the transported past would first make a short stop at "the location" before progressing to the white settlement. Schoolchildren from the location would sometimes be allowed to ride in the coach, provided they took their place at the back in the special area reserved for "non-European servants" who would look after the teams of horses. Typically, the radio commentator described "the natives" thronging together to welcome the coach in "one great mass." The mayor would deliver a brief address, the "famous native national song/anthem Sokielolo Afrika" would be sung, and the coach would move on. The brief, almost hurried passage through the "location" served to distinguish the space of the "native people" from that of colonial territory. In a powerful spatial reversal, the coach routinely emphasized that behind the perilous native frontier lay the " 'made' roads" and "events" of civilization.[19]

Women were not permitted on board the coaches in their journeys between towns because the trip was regarded as "tiring." This was in marked contrast to the trek of 1938 when women had traveled alongside the men and played a central role as stoic and suffering women on the much more arduous route of the ox-wagons, taking their place in the colonial conquest of the interior. In 1952 the women did not traverse the timeless road of modernity but would, as Maria van Riebeecks, welcome the men to their home at the place of founding. Dressed in seventeenth-century costume, the wives of cabinet ministers and members of the festival committee and the wife of the leader of the United Party would act as hostesses at an "old fashioned garden party" on the foreshore to greet the men in Cape Town after their strenuous travels. Women were to build and prepare the home at the place of founding so that their men could settle, with relative ease, once they had discovered and recovered.[20]

But the journeys to discover and recover local histories so they would become a part of Van Riebeeck's nation were far from settling. A local history, to become significant, had to be placed "against the background—or in conjunction"[21] with the given national context of founding and envelopment. The vagueness of how this was to be constituted in the time of the mail coaches created the potential for a conspicuous difference to emerge between the requirements of the festival organizers and the productions of local history. Moreover, the contradictions between 1952 replaying the journeys of 1938 and 1949, and the need of the mail coaches to restructure the narrative route of South Africa so as to return to the place of settler founding, made it likely that, as the national past had been contested and negotiated in Cape Town, more disputes would emerge over how the groundwork for local pasts was to be laid.

Taking the Local to Cape Town

The difficulties in ensuring local participation in Van Riebeeck's national festival were evident before the journeys of the mail coaches had even begun. Towns and cities were encouraged to participate in the float processions and the festival fair in Cape Town. It appears that, in the arrangements for these events, the towns and cities defined as "coastal" by the organizers of the tercentenary showed a marked lack of enthusiasm for the festival. Not only was the Cape Town City Council unwilling to provide a large sponsorship, but the local authorities in major port cities like Durban, Port Elizabeth, and East London were all, in different ways, erecting obstacles to participation in the manner the organizers required. Major issues raised by the councils in these coastal cities were the expenses involved and a deep suspicion, based on the involvement of Afrikaner nationalist organizations, that the festival in Cape Town could easily become a eulogy for Afrikaner nationalism. "Coastal," in this instance, was therefore not simply a geographical reference but a metaphoric one as well, signifying exclusion from the central activities of the soon-to-be-born settler nation. Jacques Pauw, the organizing secretary, and Anna Neethling-Pohl, the pageant mistress, had to make special visits to these "towns and ports to arouse interest" and to allay fears over the content of the festival.[22]

Many of the problems emerged in the region of South Africa's eastern seaboard and its immediate interior, an area generally known as the eastern Cape. Here, a narrative that stressed colonial battles, mostly fought by British imperial forces against the indigenous inhabitants, dominated the local settler histories. This was a history that had been taught at many schools in South Africa since the end of the nineteenth century, characterized by "the one to the sixth Kaffir War that you had to remember," the causes, the consequences, and the causes again.[23] In Wilmot's *History of the Cape Colony for Use in Schools*, chapters were bracketed by the beginning and termination of each of these wars, while in-between colonial officials are appointed, recalled, and re-appointed to deal with the people who are called "Kaffirs." On this frontier past, the key figure was not Van Riebeeck but the colonel and later governor Harry Smith. Smith was recalled as the man who had "driven" the "Kaffirs . . . from their fastness," one of the "Founders and Builders" of "South African History in Stories."[24] Dorothy Fairbridge gave Sir Harry Smith a very high rating in her imperial world of the Union of South Africa, almost, but not quite, equaling the ratings of Cecil Rhodes and Jan van Riebeeck. He was praised for "civilizing the Kaffirs, forbidding witchcraft, organizing agriculture and commerce, establishing a police drawn from the Kaffirs themselves, [and] bringing the chiefs Macomo and Tyali to swear allegiance."[25] This eulogy for Smith and the imperial project was not present in all textbooks. Significantly, in Afrikaans school history textbooks the frontier wars were portrayed in an anti-imperial aura. They were depicted as a clear indication of British "misrule of the eastern frontier" and a "main cause of the Great Trek." Harry Smith, as an imperial agent, was cast in a somewhat dubious light, labeled as someone "too hasty in wanting to change the life of the Kaffirs." Moreover, he was also seen as being responsible for attempting to bring the trekkers into the area between the Orange and Vaal Rivers under imperial control, defeating, in the process, one of the key icons of the Afrikaner past, the trek leader Andries Pretorius.[26]

When the organizers of the Van Riebeeck festival asked the City of East London to depict two of the seventy events in the historical pageants in the streets of Cape Town on 3 and 4 April, they chose to avoid the frontier wars and Harry Smith. Instead, East London was asked to depict "The Statute of Westminster," a piece of legislation that gave South Africa more autonomy within the ambit of the British Empire, and "The German Legionaries Become Immigrants in 1857," which referred to the Germans who had settled in the eastern Cape after initially having been brought in as soldiers.[27] The East London City Council was not altogether happy with this request and pushed for a series of floats the council claimed expressed the foundations of the region as part of "South Africa's common history":

> It would be led by a float representing the Brig "Knysna" with John Bailie, the founder of East London, and Captain John Findlay on the bridge, a sailor in the shrouds taking soundings as the "Knysna" enters the Buffalo Mouth. . . . This would be followed at a short distance by Sir Benjamin D'Urban, his staff and Andries Stockenstrom with a small escort of mounted burghers. All would have to be mounted. . . . Next could come Sir Harry Smith and [his Spanish Bride] lady Juanna Smith with staff, preceded by an imbongi [praise poet] shouting Smith's praises and followed immediately by a small group of mounted native chiefs distinguished by karosses of leopard skin and blue crane feathers as head-dresses. Sir Harry

Smith would be at the head of a body of Redcoated Soldiers.... This would be followed by a squad of German Legionaries ... with Baron van Ling-sengen and Sir George Grey and Staff mounted in the van. These would be followed by a group of "Lady Kennaway" girls who fraternise with the Legionaries to the grave concern of a duenna who endeavours to control them.[28]

This "common history" of South Africa which the East London City Council wanted to portray made reference to founding and settlement, the "sailor in the shrouds" and the "Lady Kennaway girls." But the central focus of events and actions represented was a history of colonization and conquest, a history where "the lives of blacks and whites ... had become inextricably—and inequitably —intertwined," where Harry Smith, as the "Great [British] Chief" who ordered the Xhosa chief Makoma "to kneel and set his foot on the chief's neck" was "cheer[ed]" by "[f]riendly Kaffirs" and had his praises sung by a "native" *im-bongi* [praise poet]. Not only would this assert a local and colonial history as part of a national history, but it would cost little in time, effort, and money to depict these "real historical characters," as they had already taken the stage at East London's Border Rugby Union grounds in 1948 during the city's cente-nary celebrations. The only additions required would be the costumes for "Sir Benjamin D'urban and Staff and the Native chiefs."[29]

These previous pasts, which the East London City Council was attempting, in part, to portray, were clearly at odds with the national history that the or-ganizers of the Van Riebeeck festival had in mind. Founding and settlement were to form the basis of the national past to be depicted in Cape Town's streets. As was seen in chapter 2, it was in terms of this settler past that the meeting between the frontier trader and settler representative, William Rowland Thompson, and the trek leader, Jacobus Uys, outside Grahamstown on 27 April 1837, was turned into a national event and the individuals elevated to the status of historical figures. Harry Smith, the British imperial figure, who was at times at odds with the trekkers, was hardly an appropriate individual to take the stage in a settler past that was devoid of conflict. He also had difficulty being re-cast as a Rhodes-type Van Riebeeck figure—as a builder of the nation—because his past continually crossed the racial frontiers. The sense of a commonality to be achieved for Van Riebeeck, even if it was cast in terms of conquest and colo-nization, hardly encountered blacks. The eight "Kaffir Wars" between 1779 and 1853, which "SOONER OR LATER you have to know about," were sidelined to the coastal road of the settler past. They were left out of the *Van Riebeeck Festival Pictorial Souvenir*, a collection of illustrations from South Africa's past distrib-uted to schools at the time, and were reduced in the pageant in Cape Town to "THE CLASH WITH THE BORDER TRIBES" typified by an "abandoned burnt-down [settler] homestead" that represented "the destruction which the eight border wars caused on the Eastern frontier." They became an event without history, a "long story, which you can cut short" to insert into a settler past.[30]

The organizers of the Van Riebeeck festival pageant were therefore taken aback somewhat by the suggestion from the East London City Council to constitute its participation in the float procession in terms of colonial conquest rather in the context of the "convergence of the [settler] roads" in the twentieth century. Hurriedly a meeting of the pageant committee was convened and it was decided that, "from a national point of view the pageant would be unwisely affected" by "bringing in those episodes which were [not] of national importance." The anticipated foundations of a national history would be disturbed, Harry Smith's *imbongi* would add a jarring note, and "the whole balance of the pageant" and the past would be "upset."[31]

But on 3 April 1952 the past was not entirely upset and two East London floats paraded through the streets of Cape Town, taking their place alongside the other national events in South Africa's designated settler history. The disagreement between the organizers of the Van Riebeeck festival pageant and the members of the East London City Council, however, had not merely been over the representation and content of South Africa's national past. It was also about the definition of race in South Africa, how the nation was constituted, the demarcation of race within the nation, and the assignation of space to all. The contests came into sharper focus as the journeys of the mail coaches began to take shape.

The Mail Coach Settlers Depart

Similar problems to those that had surfaced in persuading localities to partake in the People's Pageant emerged when plans involving the mail coaches began. It was initially decided that there would be twelve mail coaches, each financed by a local authority, with the Rembrandt Tobacco Corporation providing motor cars "painted in the Van Riebeeck colours" and covering "all expenses incurred in connection with the personnel . . . en route." Although Rembrandt's "great and esteemed help" was forthcoming—the corporation also agreed to provide loudspeakers and, as a gesture to indicate the historical nature of the proceedings, not to distribute free samples or pamphlets advertising its products—the local authorities were not so willing to paint themselves as Van Riebeeck and spend £800 sponsoring a coach. Some members of the Johannesburg City Council, for instance, considered the mail coaches to be of no historical significance and a total waste of money. One member even jokingly remarked that they may as well be sending flying boats from the Vaal Dam in the north to Table Bay in Cape Town. In the end only seven mail coaches were donated, and many towns found themselves excluded from the itinerary and "off the [nation's] route."[32]

There were coaches from the Cape, Pretoria, Johannesburg, Bloemfontein, Germiston, and Durban, all named after the respective town or district councils that had provided the sponsorship. The eastern Cape, however, was particularly troublesome. Not only did the East London City Council want Sir Harry Smith and his *imbongi* in the People's Pageant in Cape Town, but the eastern Cape showed little enthusiasm for grasping the "historical opportunity" and riding the mail coaches out of the "mists" of time. Not one town council between Port St. Johns and Knysna was prepared to assume financial responsibility, and it seemed, by mid-1951, that the eastern Cape would be "eliminated from the national festival." This, the organizers of the festival claimed, "we cannot allow." From Idutywa to Blue Lillies, from Blaaukrantz to Witteklip, the chief organizer of the Van Riebeeck festival called on "the goodwill of the Eastern Cape communities." The Afrikaans daily newspaper in the eastern Cape, *Die Oosterlig*, urged the "Eastern Cape people" to find a way to raise money for the mail coach. If the East London and Port Elizabeth city councils were not prepared to pay for the coach, the momentum, the editor of *Die Oosterlig* suggested, should be started "somewhere in the interior." The physical and metaphoric coast was clearly perceived as unwilling to "connect with the rest of the Union." At one stage it was even suggested that if these coastal locales did not participate, then the coach "Durban" should pass through those towns in the eastern Cape that did want to join the journey of the timeless past to Cape Town and Van Riebeeck. Passing the hat around, though, eventually raised enough money, and a separate eastern Cape coach was "borne" by city councils of Port Elizabeth, East London, King William's Town, Umtata, Hankey, Fort Beaufort, Mossel Bay, Humansdorp, Knysna, and Komgha.[33]

Naming the coach required agreement among its many parents. A name that would encompass this mixed and contested heritage did not immediately spring to mind. The directive from the mail coach organizing committee instructed that coaches not be given "historical names" but take the name of a single town or city that provided the sponsorship. In this way these centers would become markers of national progress, linked to the place of founding by the movement of mail coaches that suppressed regional, provincial, and historical differences on their timeless journeys into the past. In the case of the eastern Cape, naming the coach after one town presented a problem; not only was there joint sponsorship but so naming the coach would have accentuated the disputed historical marking of locales: the clashes over origins, traditions, boundaries, and capitals. Some "regional name . . . [had] to be devised" and even this was contentious as the boundaries of the region were not clear. Towns and villages incorporated into Route 7 complained that since they were nearer to the western Cape they did not fall into the "Eastern Cape" and did not want to be considered part of the latter. Ultimately a name was found that reflected both a settlement on the historical patterns and a fit with the national festival of founder nations. The coach on Route 7 was given the special name of "Settlers," defining the region as that which "Afrikaner Boers . . . British settlers . . . and German immigrants" inhabited after Van Riebeeck had landed.[34]

On 14 February 1952 the coach "Settlers" departed from the "thriving town" of Umtata, hooves ringing on "its formed and macadamised streets," toward the past of Cape Town's "bright future."[35] In the evening, prior to departure, the local branch of the ATKV performed a tableau of historical events at the Recreation Ground, and the African schoolchildren rendered a series of choral verses and dances in their own section. The following morning the mayor and his wife, together with the chief magistrate, the deputy commissioner of police, and ministers of various churches made a short journey, on board the mail coach, through the streets of Umtata. They were escorted to the city hall by members of the public who used all means of transportation, from horses to bicycles to cars. After they alighted, a copy of the history of Umtata, which contained an account of the male white fathers of the town who could scarcely believe the "metamorphosis that ha[d] actually taken place" since they had founded, was handed over to the *ritmeester* [journey master]. This Umtata, as conceived and given life by the Historic Committee of the Umtata Van Riebeeck festival, aroused the imagination and

> the feelings and aspirations of those pioneers of Umtata, through whose proud lot it fell to be the town's first "Fathers." [E]merging from the hut where the first meeting of the Municipal Council was held, they gazed over the expanse of veld and at the struggling, ugly village, and were filled with the ambition to turn the scattered native huts and unsightly wood and iron structures into a well-ordered town with . . . up-to-date buildings.[36]

The "clean wide streets" of Umtata held great promise, "in retrospect and prospect," for the unfettered progress of the "Settler" coach. They provided the orderly center from which routes radiated "to [and from] every district."[37]

Umtata's ordered past fit in with the criteria the organizers of the Van Riebeeck festival had established for local celebrations. The narrative of the history was required to extract a shared interpretation of a settler past, leaving the local history as a series of virtues and vices, of great men and historic scenes, each distinct from the other but all repeating the founding event. Umtata was so sure that it had secured its past within these categories that it was "destined to take a prominent place amongst the towns of South Africa." The future held out the promise of "progress, a bright commercial welfare, modernity and prosperity." While the new founding fathers rode the coach out of town, the servants—the "native" men—took their place at the back of the coach.[38]

East London, Sir Harry Smith's Town

Once "Settlers" had departed from Umtata, on its daily journeys through parts of the eastern Cape to Cape Town, in areas where the temperature sometimes reached 102 degrees, the ordering, clarity, and definition Umtata had formulated began to fade. "Shadows" began to fall over "a large portion of the large festival road where thousands of people from all parts of the country will converge on Cape Town."[39]

Down the Buffalo River, at the terminal of "a chain of forts," was East London, originally given the name Port Rex by the colonial authorities. On Christmas Day, 1847, it was re-born and baptized "London" by Harry Smith, and the following year was christened East London to distinguish it from its namesake. Just over one hundred years later, in 1948, at the "close of an industrially spent century," East London threw a lavish birthday party to celebrate not its founding but its naming as part of the "workshop of the world." For more than one hundred years "of municipal development," the garrison had progressed into a town and then a city, which had become a modern commercial center through the "busy cranes" of its "British port."[40]

This process of modernization, through municipal and economic development between 1870 and 1948, was given history through backward linkages with Britain and claiming East London as the "fighting port" of the colonial frontier. These "past accomplishments" provided a foundation to assert East London's "future prospects" and becoming part of a nation "spreading East London's name and fame." It had "local firms with national reputations" and, although great men did not live here, "nationally known products [were] made here."[41]

When Mayor Fox wrote the introduction to East London's local history in 1952, he re-called its tradition of two great white races defending the eastern "frontier" of Western civilization. It was this "human principle," derived from the colonial heritage of empire and appropriated by East London, that he wanted Van Riebeeck to convey to Cape Town. This endowment would demonstrate "one people" united in the face of the challenges confronting "our country" and the "Western world," from the "East." In the actual history, written by schoolteacher Mark Taylor, the theme of East London's supposed colonial frontier antecedents was further developed and linked to notions of pioneering industrial and municipal development. Drawing on the histories written for 1948, Taylor told a story of "East London and the tribes," followed by lengthy descriptions of the home front of "Municipal Enterprises," "The

Municipal Market," "Electricity," "Municipal Transport," and "Fire Protection," concluding with "Cultural Growth" and "Industrial Progress." As in 1948, through municipal process and industrial development, East London was set for an expansion that would "compare with the boom periods experienced by the Rand and Port Elizabeth," and thereby make its contribution to the nation and become part of national economic history.[42]

Van Riebeeck received this offering with some trepidation. He was pleased at the content of racial unity but not so certain about the civilizing tradition derived from the British colonial frontier. But there were two further processes at play in East London's public arena at the time, one that would ease the journey of the mail coach "Settlers," the other placing more obstacles in its way. The first was the growth of a young generation of white workers who had been drawn into skilled and supervisory roles in East London's industries during the Second World War. To retain their positions in industry after the war they increasingly asserted a nationalism of South Africa first against a "British" craft tradition. "Apprenticed without artisan control, skilled without craft," they "contested the narrative of the 'old country,' its primordial nature, the inventiveness of its traditions of labour and the . . . foundational representations of community." This group of white workers increasingly found their political home in the National Party. Almost simultaneously a young, much more militant group of political activists was emerging in East London's African townships. Extreme poverty, insufficient housing, overcrowding, unemployment, and low wages had created feelings of deep resentment toward the white inhabitants of the city, who were seen, in comparison, to be pursuing an affluent lifestyle. These material conditions, combined with the influence of intellectuals at nearby Fort Hare University, led to the establishment of a branch of the African National Congress Youth League (ANCYL) in East London in 1949. Embracing a discourse of Africanism, members of this branch broke with the "conventions of the conservative patriarchs and of the educated, cautious old guard" who had practiced a much more moderate form of politics. Instead, members of the ANCYL were "defiant of authority" and asserted an "invented Africanist past and present, of which they were an integral part." "Salvation of the African people," they claimed, "would not come from foreign nations, but as a result of their own efforts—from themselves."[43]

Thus, when "Settlers" mail coach crossed the Nahoon Bridge in East London on 22 February 1952 and "clopped clopped" up Oxford Street, it found not only that the city was officially promoting itself as the commercial port of the colonial frontier, but it also had to face these "doubly politicized nationalisms of race." On the one hand, the journey was made easier by the emergence of an anti-imperial white working-class movement. So it was Robbie de Lange, the "young East Londoner, who worked on the S.A. Railways," "with no special prospects" and who had come "a very long way from humble beginnings" to become the youngest and only Afrikaans-speaking city councilor among the "colonial chaps," who led the coach into town. On the other hand, the militant youth who associated themselves with an Africanist tradition were placing obstacles in the path of the mail coach. The young Miss K. Vitzthum, who took a group of students from the Duncan Village Teachers' Training and Practical School to the pageant in East London as the mail coach arrived as part of "their training in civic responsibilities," was stopped by "young men brandishing sticks and claiming to be members of the African Youth League."[44]

Faced with these contests on its public stages, East London was somewhat undecided over its mature parentage when Van Riebeeck arrived in 1952. Was it still on the racial or the commercial frontier or both? Or was it "Finding a Future! Forgetting the Past!" As Councilor Robbie de Lange led the Eastern Province and Border mail coach "Settlers" into town, and members of the ANCYL "barred" "Native students" from attending the pageant at the Border Rugby Union ground, the answer to this question began to take shape. It was the young South African men who were starting to define what the national future would be and were finding a national past. Some of these young men would bear Van Riebeeck to Granger Bay and beyond to the Castle and the settler nation, while others would attempt to ensure that his progress was brought to an abrupt halt. For the moment of the tercentenary it was the former who were able to assert an elevated status for themselves and assist the coach on its way to the landing of the settlers in Cape Town.[45]

On to King William's Town

If Umtata was molding itself into Van Riebeeck's nation(s) and East London was desperately seeking the nation(s), then King William's Town showed little interest in forfeiting its status on the colonial frontier. When "Settlers" arrived in town on 26 February 1952, it was presented with a local history that was not the type of history the organizers of the Van Riebeeck festival demanded. It was merely a 1911 souvenir production of the Coronation and Jubilee celebrations, but with a few photocopied pages included to show additional events up to 1952.[46]

This history of King William's Town that was carried to Cape Town aboard "Settlers" was largely one of royal patronage and presence in the eastern Cape, of Queen Victoria's second son, Prince Alfred, visiting the area in 1860 and being welcomed by the local indigenous inhabitants with wild yells of "'Bota Nkosi' (Welcome Prince)," "son of our great Queen," and "*Daars my Prins!*" [There's my Prince!]. This framework was carried into the photocopied section of the work in which King William's Town was brought up to date, affirming the colonial basis of the town, with the royal family visit in 1947 acting as a metaphor for the continuous "triumph" over the "barbarians."[47]

Van Riebeeck, in King William's Town's history, was not the founder of the nation but, instead, was situated on the frontier as "The Man Who Founded S.A.'s First Colony at the Age of 33." This fitted in more with nineteenth-century images of Van Riebeeck that had been propounded by the settlers in the eastern Cape and later by Cecil John Rhodes. Van Riebeeck was not the mere "instrument of policy" but its shaper, the man on the spot who, as the British would have done and later did, left "no stone unturned to ensure the healthy development of the colony." When the mail coach arrived at the Victoria Grounds in King William's Town, there to welcome it was the town's mayor, the choir from the Charles Morgan School singing "the Bantu National Anthem," and a pageant that recalled South Africa's history in a "series of graphic tableaux."[48] The highlight of this dramatization was "The Kaffir Wars (19th Century)" performed by Excelsior School:

> A dozen British Redcoats in their brilliant uniforms faced an equal number of black warriors with weapons poised for action. In a brief moment of action, one soldier fell "dead" on each side. . . . Afterwards, the "black" warriors caused a diversion on the grounds when they pursued some Native spectators with their mock spears.[49]

White warriors in black masks had thus diverted the road to the modern nation "of cars, trains and aeroplanes." But "the tumult was quickly quelled," allowing the mail coach to progress on its somewhat troubled journey along the coastal road and beyond to greet Van Riebeeck.[50]

Settlers Arrive in Grahamstown

As the coach moved toward Grahamstown, the town named in 1812 by the British Colonial Secretary after Lieutenant Colonel John Graham, the man who fancied himself as a black chief, there seemed little enthusiasm for "this great day" when the mail coach was scheduled to arrive. The editor of the local newspaper, the *Grocott's Daily Mail,* had to put in a special plea that this was "the only real [day] where all races stand an equal chance of paying tribute to those who have made the history of South Africa."[51]

The problem was that Grahamstown found it had very little history to contribute to Jan van Riebeeck and the national past. A large proportion of its presented past dealt with the period before the 1840s when, as a frontier town of European settlement, it perceived itself to be faced with constant threats from the Xhosa-speaking inhabitants of the region. This history of colonial conflict on the frontier was not the sort of narrative that interested the organizers of the Van Riebeeck Festival, who were more concerned with the coming together of the "European races." The second and generally less detailed part of Grahamstown's history was from the 1840s when, after the killing of the Xhosa king, Hintsa, by the forces of Harry Smith, Grahamstown no longer considered itself under threat. According to D. H. Thomson, the senior history master at Kingswood College, and author of the history of Grahamstown written for the Van Riebeeck festival, the "efficient and exuberant" Colonel Harry Smith displaced the Xhosa chief Hintsa from "the steep and rocky hills where he sat in his tiger-skin kaross," and Grahamstown "set her house in order." With the "Native chiefs" now acknowledging that "the kraal of Grahamstown was too large to be attempted," the process of reconstruction and development began apace. "Houses were rebuilt, rusty businesses' locks removed and fields cultivated afresh." In this moment, "relieved of the burden of self-preservation," a new Grahamstown was born, a place of colleges, schools, and cathedrals, the "City of Saints," the sleepy hollow, the "resting place of Rip Van Winkle." A future "younger generation of settlers" now took up the pen rather than the plough and the rifle. Under their guidance the history of the City of Saints, from 1840 to 1952, became an antiquarian curiosity, which was "interesting to observe." Located and labeled as the "western window" of the "most progressive town" on the frontier, the "enigma" of its future history followed the path of the new railway line that passed it by. There was very little history of Grahamstown after 1840 for the mail coach to take to Cape Town.[52]

To extricate itself from the "burden of this short history" and become part of the modern South African nation, the settlers of Grahamstown had to create a local history that moved beyond the days of the colonial frontier. Harry Smith, although not written out of the past, was changed from the "swash-buckling cavalier" to the "sturdy Sir Harry Smith on his proud steed," the man who united the "men and women," who enabled the "frontier Boer and British settler" of Grahamstown to fight "side by side." Instead of "calling a halt to the westward trek of the Natives," Grahamstown was presented as the Athenian defender of civilization, "education," and "achievement," playing a "vital role in the building of a strong, virile and enlightened nation." Onto the tableaux of Grahamstown's past strode the English settlers who had arrived in the 1820s, the English Jan van Riebeecks, each with his own contribution to the building of the nation and its settler traditions. Grahamstown also discovered a lengthy list of firsts. It was "the centre of the first telegraphic experiment" in South Africa, the "first town in South Africa" that applied to be part of the "first democratic institutions in South Africa" and become a municipality, where the first woolen cloth factory was established, and where "the identification of the first South African diamond" occurred. And pride of place went to . . . "CURTAIN UP. Pause for preliminary action. WATCH STAGE until Dr. Atherstone commences cutting" "the first surgical operation in South Africa performed under a general anaesthetic."[53]

To become modern and take its place on the mail coach, Grahamstown also had to be remodeled so that it did not become a "stagnant hollow." This entailed "more imagination," the "establishment of secondary industries," and "creating regular employment" for the "natives" who, claimed the local newspaper, "do not want to work." Its workforce, the newspaper went on to assert, was neither industrious nor modern, preferring to "squat" in the location called Fingo Village on the outskirts of the town, "collect unemployment benefits," and generally cause a lot of trouble. These troubles were largely attributed to outside agitators. Beyond the authorities' knowledge, maintained the newspaper, "natives from rural areas slip[ped] into the Fingo village" and became known only upon seeking employment. As at the national level, the system of apartheid was establishing the administrative and legal mechanisms to control and regulate the urban African proletariat, and in Grahamstown concerted attempts were being made to "bring the Fingo village under the Urban Areas Act" and to make all "Native employees carry a Stupa—a 'Record of Service certificate.'"[54]

The mail coach's arrival in Grahamstown provided a different moment on which to elaborate this project of modernizing and controlling the "troublesome natives" in Fingo Village. The coach was to be welcomed by a mounted commando at the top of Makana's Kop, the point from where "the treacherous attack on Grahamstown was made by the Kaffir Chief Makana," and escorted into town. On the way the coach would stop at the "location" to ensure that "the natives participated in the festivities." This was "an opportunity that must not be allowed to go by." The *ritmeester's* enthusiasm for this project, echoed by the Grahamstown Van Riebeeck Festival Committee, was somewhat dampened when the "leaders of the Natives and Coloureds" turned down this invitation to the "people." These leaders, the festival committee lamented, had "denied their own people the opportunity to see a unique spectacle and themselves the chance to offer it a welcome." On the "fine, sunny day" when the coach found its way down Raglan Road to the city, there was no brief stopover in the "location" and the "natives" did not come out to render their national anthem. The coach passed through onto the city's "main streets," "thronging" with people. The event, however, was "somewhat spoiled for the European audience" when its spectacle in front of the City Hall was obstructed "by large numbers of Native and Coloured children." The "Europeans" had to vacate their seats, which had been reserved for them "on either side of the dais." Only in this way could they could see above the heads of the "children who crowded in the area in front of the onlookers" and witness the arrival of "Settlers."[55]

Settlers Land in Port Elizabeth

On 4 March, at 9:30 A.M., the mail coach "Settlers," having traveled through much of the Eastern Cape, reached the Zwartkops Bridge on the outskirts of Port Elizabeth where "the early settlers had crossed the first river on their way into the interior." Welcoming the coach was the principal of the local school who called for more festivals to be held in South Africa. Carnivals, he believed, would help resolve conflict because people would develop political amnesia and "work together." The *ritmeester*, in response, echoed these sentiments and reiterated the message he had been carrying on his journey throughout the eastern Cape: "I say to you don't talk about race and racialism." [56]

The call of the *ritmeester*, A. Snyman, to avoid conflict was a bit insincere since a major confrontation had developed between him and the coachman, J. P. S. Botha, on the journey from East London to Port Elizabeth. At stake was who was really in charge of the mail coach, expressed, in the Afrikaans idiom, as who was "*baas*" [boss] and who was "*Klaas*" [roughly, underling]. The latter felt he was being relegated to the menial tasks of looking after the coach and the horses, while Snyman was basking in glory, being feted and wined and dined by all the local authorities. M. C. Botha had to intervene in an effort to clear up the dispute. He urged the *ritmeester* and the coachman to act in the same manner that they and others were encouraging the locals to do, to cooperate and share the tasks and organization equally, and, like "enthusiastic Afrikaners," to bury their differences for the sake of their participation in "one of the very biggest festival plans in the life of our volk." Although the missive from Botha seemed to have quieted things down—"It is going well or at least better," telegrammed Snyman to Botha nearly a week later—the tensions on "Settlers" were still discernible as it progressed along Route 7 on its troublesome journey to Cape Town. [57]

Unaware of the conflict aboard the mail coach, the organizers of the local Van Riebeeck celebrations in Port Elizabeth were attempting their utmost to heed Snyman's words for racial cooperation when "Settlers" crossed the Zwartkops Bridge. There was even talk of omitting one of the city's major local/national historical events, the landing of the British settlers in 1820, from Port Elizabeth's representations because "it would be a slap in the face for Afrikaners." Yet, as other speakers in a City Council meeting pointed out, seeing the Van Riebeeck festival in these terms was a fundamental misunderstanding of its design. The festival was primarily about European settlement, where modernization was cast as an alibi for race. "We are dealing with the civilised forces which came to this barbarian country," claimed B. Laubscher, who planned Port Elizabeth's stand at the festival fair. It was therefore crucial to depict the 1820 settlers, because they, along with Van Riebeeck, were represented as the bearers of "civilization" from Europe and provided a crucial component as the "English" "builders of the nation." Port Elizabeth, as one of the "only two cities on the coast of South Africa where settlers landed," therefore saw it almost as its duty to ensure that the settlers were present to greet Van Riebeeck when he arrived aboard the mail coach.[58]

The local festivities that had been arranged to coincide with the arrival of "Settlers" in Port Elizabeth took on extravagant proportions. "History" was "brought to life" as the "City turn[ed] back the clock" for the 1820 settlers to welcome the mail coach onto the "crowded, bunting-flanked streets." The mayor greeted the *ritmeester,* presented him with an illustrated brochure on Port Elizabeth's industries, and then accompanied him to the Crusader grounds for an evening of speeches, song, dances, and pageantry. The day's proceedings closed with a torchlight tableau where the landing of the 1820 settlers and that of Van Riebeeck were cast on the same stage, both leading to the moment of proclaimed settler nationhood in 1952.[59] On the following day, this process of situating Port Elizabeth and the 1820 landings on this settled national chart was extended. A somewhat hodgepodge procession of twenty-two floats, representing organizations from the South African Railways to the Red Cross and the Snake Park but excluding all industrial concerns in the city, paraded through the streets in the morning. The highlight of the proceedings came in the afternoon, when, in a ceremony which paralleled Van Riebeeck's landing at Granger Bay a month later, a group of 1820 settlers attired in period costume came ashore at King's Beach. Those who managed to make it from their rowboats onto the beach in a dry state—one of the boats overturned and its occupants had to be "hurried off to cars and homes to dry themselves"—were met by their "founding father," the acting governor of the Cape, Sir Rufane Donkin (played by Archdeacon T. B. Powell), who had renamed the bay Port Elizabeth as his own personal memorial to his wife. As the settlers "brought nineteenth century civilization by the shipful" onto the beach, "roads [were] constructed, permanent buildings erected, the rule of law expanded, organized education introduced," the Baakens Nature Reserve was renamed "Settlers Park," and the city adopted a coat of arms to reflect its newly established "Settlers' heritage."[60]

It would be incorrect to assume that the ceremonial landing at King's Beach to greet the Van Riebeeck mail coach as it "roll[ed] on westward to [the] Cape" had settled Port Elizabeth's local past into a national context where race found itself outside History. The editor of the *Port Elizabeth Evening Post,* for instance, raised questions about the vast expenditure on the local pageantry, particularly if one took into account the exclusion of "educated . . . non-Europeans" from the events in the streets, in the stadium, and on the beach. He asserted

19. The mail coaches from different parts of the country arrive for the tea party at the festival stadium, 30 March 1952. Manuscripts and Archives Division, University of Cape Town Libraries. Photo: *Cape Times.*

that the eastern Cape, with its 150 years of experience, had evolved a superior form of racial control, which was now being neglected by those who were organizing the festivities. The eastern Cape system, he maintained, was one where "the best elements among the Cape Bantu and Cape Coloured communities shar[ed] in some of the benefits of Western civilisation, accept[ed] a trusting white leadership." Without the "non-European groups . . . proudly taking part in the . . . festivities," this concept of "Western civilization," where "good natives" learned and accepted colonial control, was in "grave danger." Not surprisingly, therefore, although the eastern Cape, and Port Elizabeth in particular, was portrayed as the breeding ground of the "talented" 1820 settlers and not the "battlefield" of the past, its public history was a constant reminder of the "Kaffir Wars," military reinforcements landing at Algoa Bay, "marauding blacks," and "routing" the "rascally" Xhosa.[61]

The Commonwealth of Nations

On Monday afternoon, 31 March 1952, the mail coaches finally reached Cape Town. The bugles sounded, the bells rang out, and at exactly 3:50 P.M., "perfectly as planned," "in spite of detours," the mail coaches from all the different corners of the land entered the fifty-thousand-seater Van Riebeeck stadium on Cape Town's reclaimed foreshore. At the "unexcelled culmination of a long series of glorious episodes," there to welcome the men's nation home were their "mothers and housewives," all dressed up and waiting to perform their roles as Maria van Riebeecks at the tea party in the middle of the festival stadium (Figure 19).[62]

In the mail coach processions across the country and through the towns, space had been found through history, sometimes invented, sometimes reshaped, marked out and emptied, figures drawn on it, and ways made through it. In the time and space of the mail coach "Settlers," Harry Smith's public domain began to shift its identity until he lost his *imbongi* and started to sing Van Riebeeck's praises. The land of the colonial racial frontier was changing into "Settler Country," and the archivists were discovering "the contribution of British immigrants to the development of South Africa." They "built," "brought," "salvaged," "linked," "put up," "freed," "pioneered," "applied," "spread," "improved," and "produced" South Africa.[63]

But the journey of the mail coaches and its culmination on 30 March 1952 did not complete the job of bringing about the birth of the whole Settler nation at once. Many conflicts yet remained over the production of local/national pasts and the "fit" that was required. Still unresolved was East London's participation in the float procession that was to constitute the People's Pageant in Cape Town on 3 April 1952. East London responded in different ways to the contested images of its colonial/commercial/racial/settler past. In keeping with its newly found settler tradition, it started discovering its own group of settlers that would form part of the nation. Along with Berlin, Komgha, Stutterheim, and Keiskamahoek, it presented "the German Soldier Immigrants" to the nation in Cape Town. These soldiers and immigrants had "come out to reinforce the white settlement" and "although about a thousand men were later sent to India," the organizers of this historic float were sure that the "immigrants left their mark on our way of life."[64]

East London's other float was still a matter of deep dispute. Even though the directive had arrived from Cape Town to ban Sir Harry Smith and build the Statute of Westminster float, a great deal of dissatisfaction lingered.

> Why has the Cape Town Festival Committee not invited us to send a float depicting the history of "British Kaffraria" rather than a political Statute which led to so much strife on the Border. . . . A British Kaffrarian Float would have been appreciated; it would have provided an opportunity of fitting into the Pageant a representation of the progressive expansion and development of the frontier of the Cape Colony. . . . I am of the opinion that if East London makes an effort to depict a political statute which turned

South Africa into a sovereign independent State we shall be depicting something that reflects dishonour on the pioneers of British Kaffraria whose loyalty (European and non-European) was ever profound and sincere.[65]

The result was that, with Cape Town "passing the buck from West to East" and not showing East London's "real contribution to the building up of South Africa," the Statute of Westminster took on a decidedly different form from that envisaged by the pageant mistress Anna Neethling-Pohl and her committee. The float, as scripted in the program, was intended to highlight the events, negotiations, parliamentary activities, and personalities related to the publication of the Statute that "gave independent status to the [British] dominions." The prime minister at the time, General Hertzog, who "played an important role in framing the declaration" that led to the statute was expected to feature prominently. Instead, the East London float became the Commonwealth of Nations. It consisted of "a little sailing vessel manned by five young ladies of the City": "Miss Britannia," "Miss Canada," "Miss New Zealand," "Miss Australia," and "Miss South Africa." This emphasis on the British Commonwealth was not in keeping with the symbolic float of South Africa on the constitutional road to nationhood that the festival organizers had ordered. While Harry Smith was kept off the streets of Cape Town, it was still abundantly clear that from the "Frontier Land of Myth and Majesty" it was still a very "long road to the Cape." Shaping, mapping, naming, and historicizing locales into the places of the settler nation derived from Van Riebeeck was, indeed, a most unsettling experience.[66]

Conclusion

Post Van Riebeeck

In the years following the tercentenary festival, as attempts to maintain racially exclusive power in South Africa intensified, Jan van Riebeeck and Maria de la Quellerie found themselves increasingly cast as the lead characters in the first chapter of a "story of White Civilisation in South Africa." The date of 6 April became an official public holiday, with the intention of commemorating the "founder of white South Africa" as the bearer of "Christian civilization." Every year, on 6 April, wreath-laying ceremonies took place at the base of their statues on Adderley Street, Cape Town. A likeness to Jan van Riebeeck appeared on all bank notes and coins. In school textbooks extensive accounts were given of Jan's tenure at the Cape, and his capabilities as the founder of a white nation were extolled. These accounts were placed at the beginning of the South African History portion of the textbook, immediately after the General History section that provided a saga of the development of "Western civilization to which we belong." In one instance, Van Riebeeck followed immediately after the exploits of that "great explorer," Christopher Columbus, and in another he made his appearance after the European renaissance of the fifteenth century, which, according to Van Jaarsveld, "*placed the Whites of Western civilisation in a position of supremacy over the nations of America, the East and Africa.*" The latter were relegated by the same writer to a state of nature and "huts of mud and grass." Alongside Jan, at the moment of what was proclaimed "THE BIRTH OF WHITE SOUTH AFRICA" was Maria de la Quellerie. Students were required to learn her name by heart and recall it for test purposes. In addition, Jan Van Riebeeck now found himself accompanied by an extended list of family members and officials: "soldiers . . . craftsmen . . . his son Lambertus, two of his nieces, and the wife of Boom the gardener." Through this extended notion of family relations, the moment of landing in 1652 was turned into the arrival of a South Africa based on a form of racial exclusivity which simultaneously proclaimed itself to be nationally inclusive. This was the "*ONE* nation," heralded as the bearer of civilization at "the most southern point of Africa," including people who were said to be "of mostly Dutch, English, French and German extract" but excluding most of the local inhabitants of the region. These were the facts that school pupils in South Africa had to recite and regurgitate in order to pass their exams.[1]

During the last decade of the twentieth century aspirations to preserve a racial elite in South Africa were abandoned, and a new government, headed by the African National Congress, assumed power, proclaiming its commitment to a national state with a non-racial future. Although the meaning and the content of this non-racialism remain the subject of much discussion, debate, and ambiguity, the notion of racial exclusivity (and whiteness, in particular) has not explicitly served as a determinant of power in post-apartheid South Africa. In similar postcolonial contexts, it is often the liberation struggle against the colonial regime that is in the foreground in the creation of new national histories and identities. "Origin myths" of postcolonial states are located in this narrative, which glorifies "the individuality of great heroes of the nation" in the struggle for de-colonization. Another important marker is the assertion of a cultural difference from the world of the colonizer, giving the postcolonial nation its distinctive character. This is the paradox of nationalist discourse, always striving to achieve the status of a nation categorized in all its trappings as essentially modern while at the same time sustaining and building on the idea of "an ancient community of sacred identity," the nation that was always already there in form and situation from precolonial or precapitalist times. Significance is almost invariably accorded to a narrative of indigenousness that is prior to the moments of colonization.[2]

In asserting a past for a nation no longer derived from European founding and settlement, when there is "a movement against a version of history that underwrote white supremacy toward one that celebrates its downfall,"[3] what then happens to Jan van Riebeeck and Maria de la Quellerie? Some forty-four years after the massive tercentenary festival, 6 April 1996 coincided with Easter Saturday. For Capetonians, it seemed that it marked the beginning of winter. After days of glorious sunshine, it was a dull, overcast day with intermittent rain. At about 10:00 in the morning I put on my raincoat and went down to the statues on Adderley Street to see whether anyone was attempting to observe the day. The area surrounding the statues was almost entirely deserted. I sat in a coffee shop across the way to watch for any activity. After about two hours, sensing that nothing was going to happen, I approached the statues to see if anyone had left some mark of recognition of the landing some 344 years ago. The only sign was a small wreath that had been laid earlier in the morning by a group calling itself "Afrikaners, Gardens." A card attached to the wreath read: "In honour of JAN AND MARIA VAN RIEBEECK, who brought Christian religion and Western civilisation to South Africa, this country's two largest assets."

The large crowds that had gathered to pay homage to Jan and Maria van Riebeeck and those who had fought so vigorously to contest their settled past in 1952 seemed little more than a distant happening on that cold Cape autumn morning. Apart from that one, small, insignificant group, no one seemed to be paying the couple much attention at all. Indeed, since 1992, when the mayor of Cape Town, and occupant of the Van Riebeeck Chair, Frank van der Velde, announced that the Cape Town City Council would no longer organize proceedings in front of the statues because it would be "divisive to focus on a one-sided Eurocentric founding of Cape Town," the wreath-laying ceremony had attracted little public attendance. The following year, 1993, when the Jan van Riebeeck Foundation had organized the commemorations, the guest of honor, Frank van der Velde, caused a stir by referring to Van Riebeeck as one of the originators of racism in South Africa through instituting slavery and denuding the local Khoi inhabitants of land and cattle. Deeply upset by this outburst, the Jan van Riebeeck Foundation, in 1994, called on the administrator of the Cape, the National Party's Kobus Meiring, to make the keynote address. In his speech, delivered three weeks before South Africa's "first democratic elections," he refuted allegations that Van Riebeeck was a "racist, merciless, slave driver." Instead, he constructed Van Riebeeck as an example of a sensitive team worker and called on the "new South Africa" to face up to its future in a similar manner. A few months later, a newly elected Government of National Unity, led by the ANC and headed by Nelson Mandela, announced a new list of public holidays. Van Riebeeck Day (which had subsequently been re-named Founders Day and later Settlers Day) was dropped from the calendar along with Republic Day, Ascension Day, and Kruger Day. In their place came Human Rights Day (21 March), Constitution Day (27 April, when the elections were held), Youth Day (16 June), National Women's Day (9 August), and Heritage Day (24 September). There was also some talk, in the wake of the removal of the statue of H. F. Verwoerd—the prime minister who acquired the appellation "Architect of Apartheid"—from public display in Bloemfontein, that Jan and Maria might suffer the same fate and be moved to a less prominent place in the city. Nothing, as yet, has come of this suggestion, and it seems that not much has been discussed further in this regard. The overwhelming impression gained at the statues on that overcast morning of 6 April 1996 was that Jan and Maria van Riebeeck have been virtually forgotten in South Africa's public past. Nowadays they find themselves being used mainly in promotional campaigns. One instance of this occurred when a clothing manufacturer, in the middle of the night, furtively dressed Jan up in the company's latest designs in order to draw attention to the company, which had just been listed on the Johannesburg Stock Exchange. Another time an environmental awareness group draped Jan in a shroud to protest the planned shipment of plutonium from France to Japan, possibly via the Cape. Linking Van Riebeeck to the shipment of plutonium as the bearers of real and metaphoric pollution to South Africa, one of the protestors, wearing a mask and snorkel, affixed a sign to the statue calling for "No Shit on Our Shore" (Figure 20).[4]

The seeming withdrawal of Jan and Maria from the public gaze and the lack of reverence for their landing would seem to indicate that the ANC-led gov-

20. An environmental awareness group uses the Van Riebeeck statue to protest
against the shipment of plutonium around the Cape of Good Hope.
"No Shit on Our Shore," *Cape Argus,* 10 July 1992. Photo: Obed Zilwa.

ernment has "conquered the past." From its position of power it seemingly has "the freedom to ignore or display indifference to that which they might have found offensive in the past." This argument tends to see the historical images in the public domain as easily malleable instruments that can be twisted and turned to suit contemporary political circumstances. The argument of this book is that the production of public pasts is never quite so straightforward and easily adaptable to suit the political requirements of the day. The ability to configure public pasts is always limited by previous historical depictions and the ever-present conflicts that accompany any form of commemorative activity. As has been pointed out in relation to images of the American Civil War and the altercations over the making of General Robert E. Lee into an icon, these disputes "remind us that there is no single or unified experience of a commemorative image, and conflict often centers on whose experience the image tacitly recognizes and legitimates."[5] In chapter 1, which dealt with the period before the festival, it was apparent that no single unilinear effort had been made to establish Van Riebeeck as a central figure in South Africa's public past. He had only begun to acquire a more prominent position in the late nineteenth and early twentieth centuries through the endeavors of proponents of British imperialism, Dutch and Afrikaans cultural organizations, the institution of standardized textbooks in schools, and the publication of his diary as an authoritative text. Clearly, in all these spheres a form of organized activity was involved in promoting a memory of Van Riebeeck, and some of this activity was associated with governing authorities at different levels. But in these organizations and through a variety of forms different meanings were ascribed to founding. Among others, there was Van Riebeeck the *volksplanter* or the bearer of Christianity or the colonial governor or all three. All these identities depended largely on the history that was produced to follow in his wake. Although one can hypothetically raise the question as to which of these memories would have become dominant had the tercentenary festival not been staged, what the government-sponsored festival did in 1952 was to select elements from these various pasts in an attempt to construct a Van Riebeeck that would indicate the founding of a settler nation, whose history took different roads, at times, but converged on the sands of Granger Bay on 5 April.

A substantial portion of this book has dealt with how the government, festival committees, and particular individuals sought to establish this Van Riebeeck with an associated past that followed his landing through the mechanism of the festival. What is immediately apparent, however, particularly in chapter 2, is that there were immense problems in constructing a national settler past for Van Riebeeck in 1952 and that the resultant history was often the outcome of contests and negotiations over which events should be included and how they should be represented. Sometimes it was the response to the opposition of the conceptualization of the festival and its specific events that shaped the actual displays. These tensions, although they were either negotiated out of the past or censored, continually bubbled under the surface of the festival and did not create the settled Van Riebeeck that had been planned.

When this negotiated national past was then taken to locales expected to establish local pasts that accorded with this festival of settler founding, the fit became even more precarious. Specific guidelines were established for the type of history that had to be produced, which the mail coaches that traversed the country in 1952 would carry with them on their journeys to Cape Town and to Van Riebeeck. Framing and bounding spaces into places for the settler nation was much more difficult than simply following a set of criteria, particularly when local pasts were out of sync with the identity of national progress the festival sought to convey. As indicated in chapter 5, this lack of correspondence was particularly notable in the eastern Cape, where the effort to place race on the colonial frontier dominated local versions of national pasts. Even though many towns took part in the journey of the mail coach on Route 7, there was a general reluctance to participate with enthusiasm in the settler past. The gloss that was put on the local histories for Van Riebeeck in the region often subverted the intent of the national organizers. On both the national level, as displayed in the streets and theaters of Cape Town, and locally, through the 417 daily journeys of the mail coaches from town to town, it was immensely difficult to construct a singular national past of European settlement that flowed from the beach of Granger Bay. The Van Riebeecks, who took center stage in 1952 as the founders of these three hundred years, were clearly viewed as icons. But despite all the financial, organizational, and structural support, much of it emanating from the government, the festival was unable to completely suppress, select, and direct other memories into this racially exclusive past.

It was not only in the production of Van Riebeeck for the festival that difficulties arose in creating a national settler past as History. Crucial to the conceptualization and execution of the festival, and the bringing of its symbols into memory, was the emphasis on the visual content of the festival. From the pageantry in the streets and on the beaches to the parades in the festival stadium, the plays in the theaters, the displays in museums, the documentary newsreels, and radio commentators' imaginative descriptions, it was intended that the festival be visualized. Yet although this visual content was generally planned and performed with care, how it was received and seen was at times beyond the organizers' control. With such a plethora of visual symbols, often confusing and contradictory messages emerged, particularly for the eight hundred thousand people who visited the festival fair on the foreshore (see chapter 4). There was just so much to see and do that many interpreted the displays in their own individual ways and, forgetting the essence of the festival, left Jan and Maria van Riebeeck (André Huguenet and Frances Holland) to their own memories at their new home in the Castle.

The area where the festival most demonstrably floundered in its bid to attract a following for the Van Riebeecks and their national past was in its efforts to lure people designated as "non-Europeans" to view the proceedings and to participate in separate events (chapter 3). Very few of these "non-Europeans" turned up at the festival fair, even on cheap days that had been specifically set aside to inflate the number of visitors. For the Native Affairs Department display at the fair, the Griqua performances, and the Malay pageant in the stadium, the organizers had to search far and wide to find people willing to partake of these offerings. Sometimes they had to entice participants by promising material incentives from the government in the future. Indeed, in one such instance, one group of Malays was incensed after the festival. After they had agreed to participate in I. D. du Plessis's pageant, the government had "rewarded" them by offering, within the ambit of the Group Areas Act, what the Malays saw as small, barren, pieces of property in Surrey Estate, whereas the areas reserved for people designated as "coloured," the Malays claimed, were larger and generally in more preferable locations.[6]

Many "non-Europeans" decided not to attend the festival for a variety of reasons. Some showed no interest in the proceedings on the foreshore; others argued that they were "too educated" to sing and dance for Van Riebeeck; and still others claimed status as a "coloured" racial elite. There was also a massive political campaign, primarily orchestrated by affiliates of the Non-European Unity Movement, which called for a boycott of what they termed the "Festival of Hate." One of the notable aspects of this boycott campaign was that it inverted the symbols of the festival, turning Sheik Yusuf and the bushmen into heroes of resistance and Jan van Riebeeck into the initiator of racial oppression in South Africa. This mirroring of the festival's icons, instead of subverting them as was intended, played a large role in reinforcing and perpetuating their images as key markers in the South African past.

The Struggle to Liberate the Rainbow Nation

More than the actual designs and activities of the festival organizers, it was these conflicts over the past that enabled Jan and Maria van Riebeeck to reach their positions of prominence as the bearers of apartheid to the shores of a place that was always South Africa. And, in a postcolonial scenario, where attempts are being made to construct a singular new nation, the divisions and fractures may become even more apparent, with the potential to subvert the "state-sanctioned idea of one indivisible nation." Key questions revolve around who can be a part of the new nation, what positions and roles are constituted for those who are bounded by the nation, and how are different memories brought into, or excluded from, a new national past.[7] Despite the lack of activity in front of the statues on 6 April 1996, it is these continuing contests over the course and content of South African pasts that assists Jan and Maria in maintaining their conspicuous role, defining the moment of their inauspicious arrival in 1652 as pivotal in South African history.

One way Jan and Maria assert themselves in the new South Africa is that they now confidently insert themselves as beginning "a 350-year struggle for national unity,"[8] which supposedly everyone fought together, leading to the emergence of a multi-cultural South Africa constructed as "The Rainbow Nation." Jan and Maria bring to this rainbow a component which proclaims a European heritage in Africa. When tourism to the Cape as the "rainbow region" was promoted, actors dressed themselves in their seventeenth-century costumes and went on display at the tourist information center alongside the Bushmen from Kagga Kamma Nature Reserve, the Hermanus whale-crier, and the Cape Malay. For National Museum Day in May 1996, the "fun-packed programme" at the Castle, where Jan and Maria took up residence in 1952, included Scottish dancers, a military band and performances by the Muzzle Loaders Association, the University of Cape Town choir, and Jan van Riebeeck.[9] Similarly, the two-hour guided sightseeing tour of Cape Town on the open-top, double-decker bus—the Topless Tour as it is called—is a veritable journey through Van Riebeeckana. The script not only takes in the statues but points to the fountains in front of them as the precise place where Van Riebeeck landed, the palm trees on Cape Town's Grand Parade as the location where Van Riebeeck built his mud and wood fort, the state archives building in Roeland Street prison, which our guide told us "keeps documents dating back to 1652 and Van Riebeeck's day," and, finally, the Dutch East India Company Gardens, which point to the original reason Jan van Riebeeck was sent to the Cape, "to establish a replenishing station," and, where the guide maintained, we can still find trees he planted. All this accompanies a narrative that refers to apartheid as an unfortunate past, casts local inhabitants as thieves and a nuisance to the colonial enterprise, and celebrates the new nation and, in particular, Nelson Mandela. If we look to the right from the palm trees on the Parade (where you will remember Van Riebeeck built his fort), across the street is the balcony of the Cape Town City Hall where "Mandela gave his famous freedom speech" when he was released from prison.

Many of the new school textbooks also approach history as if it is a racial scale that has been unfairly weighted in the past and now has to balance "white and black history." In *Enjoying History*, which is part of the Rainbow series, the San, Khoi-Khoi, Black Peoples of Southern Africa, and "White Settlers" are all part of a section entitled "Indigenous History." In this framework Jan van Riebeeck becomes one of the key founders of the rainbow nation. Witness how his encounter with the local inhabitants is related: "Jan van Riebeeck got to know a Khoi-Khoi man named Harry who could speak Dutch. Harry became very important to Jan van Riebeeck because he could speak to the Khoi-Khoi people and tell Jan van Riebeeck what they said. He was an interpreter." Here the Khoi act as mediators of race from the beginning of the "indigenous settlement" by Europeans. Yet it is not so easy to construct this moment of Van Riebeeck's arrival as a moment of the creation of the Rainbow nation, since there were conflicts with local inhabitants and the system of slavery was instituted at the Cape. What must be ensured is that a delicate balance is maintained. Any conflict that might occur is depicted as the result of a "lack of understanding" or something that must be understood "'in context." Thus, "although it sounds terrible" that "Jan van Riebeeck decided to ask the DEIC [Dutch East India Company] to send him some slaves," students are told that they "must remember that, in those days, many countries traded in and used slaves." When conflict does occur and is mentioned it is easily, almost hurriedly, passed over to make way for the present time of "national unity."[10]

The 1952 tercentenary festival is re-called to memory in a similar multicultural milieu. In May 1996 a "Cape Malay Dance Musical," entitled *Rosa,* was presented by Bo-Kaap Productions. The musical takes place in the imaginative early 1800s when the Cape is under Dutch rule (presumably the Batavian Republic) and the governor, having made more than a hundred-year leap in time, is Simon van der Stel. The story line revolves around a nobleman who falls in love with a Malay slave girl. The story is secondary to the musical items, which glorify the essentials of a "Malay culture" constructed and promoted by I. D. du Plessis, with the "exotica" of *krans* and cushion dances encompassing "strange mystical powers." One of the "exclusive" items it presents is the lingo dance. Completely overlooking the struggles over Malay participation in the pageant Du Plessis organized in 1952, the promotional material for the musical proudly proclaims that this dance is being performed "for the first time on the professional stage since the Van Riebeeck Festival."[11]

The narrative of a "new national cultural heritage" was also proclaimed in the exhibition "300 Years: The Making of Cape Muslim Culture", which ran at the Good Hope gallery in the Castle in April 1994. Giving this exhibition its impetus was the tricentenary event that, instead of elevating Sheik Yusuf into a Malay Van Riebeeck, venerated him as the bearer of Islam to the Cape. Promotional material for the exhibition labeled it as according Muslims "a place" in South African history. A constant tension in the exhibition was this attempt to advance a Muslim identity and past in South Africa while not re-producing the static, essentialist, and ethnic categories of "Malay culture." In this vein, the historian Kerry Ward devised historical panels for the exhibition, one containing details about the Van Riebeeck festival and the Sheik Yusuf presentation in 1952. Unlike the musical *Rosa,* which had recalled the festival in positive terms, this display made a self-conscious effort to show visitors how the Malay and Muslim cultures had been manipulated in the tercentenary (as opposed to the tricentenary) festival to further the interests of the apartheid government and its emerging program of separate ethnic nations. It is debatable whether, in the context of the overwhelming dominance of the "living displays" of "Muslim craft traditions," such distinctions were even noted by the thousands who flocked to the Castle in April 1994 to visit the exhibition.[12]

It is this discourse of South Africa as a rainbow nation, where multi-culturalism reigns supreme, which enabled Nelson Mandela to affirm Jan van Riebeeck as a founder of a component of the new South African nation. On the evening of 15 May 1996 Nelson Mandela was present at the launch, in the parliamentary dining room, of a book by his ANC comrade, Govan Mbeki. The book, *Sunset at Midday,* relates the final years of resistance to the apartheid regime, the various internal and external pressures that led to its demise, and highlights the role of the armed wing of the ANC, Umkonto We Sizwe. But Mandela arrived at the function late. He had spent part of the day as the guest of honor at the seventy-fifth anniversary of Jan van Riebeeck Primary School in Cape Town. There the school had presented him with a donation to the Mandela Children's Fund. They also gave him a Jan van Riebeeck cap, which he then donned for his appearance before the television cameras. Not only has Jan van Riebeeck not been ostracized from the rainbow nation, he has found a niche for himself as the conveyor of "European influences" to the new nation.[13]

An Inverted Van Riebeeck

But it is not only in this multicultural struggle that Van Riebeeck appears as a marker of the South African national past. In the District Six Museum in Cape Town, a museum that provides a memory and experience of the apartheid policy of removals to assigned areas designated by the racial ordering of society, on one of the large quilted banners is the inverted, defaced image of Jan van Riebeeck, the very one that was on the podium at the Parade in 1952. This image of Van Riebeeck as a signifier of racial domination/oppression and a resultant 350-year liberation struggle on the "road to true democracy and empowerment"[14] is a national historical narrative that runs parallel to, and at times contradicts, the narrative that revolves around the rainbow nation.

It was this guise of Jan van Riebeeck as the initiator of oppression that was produced by those opposing the festival and the one that dominated the anti-festival histories that were published. Yet the festival boycott itself is hardly recalled in South Africa's emerging national pasts; instead, the defiance campaign, launched on 6 April 1952, becomes a pivotal moment of "significance" in histories built around the emergence and triumph of the African National Congress in the face of repeated surges of repression. In the face of this dominant, new "national" past, the boycott of the Van Riebeeck festival has become relegated to a forgotten historic realm, celebrated mainly in the ranks of the Unity Movement as a "massive nation-wide" "achievement" of united opposition to "the state and all its supporting classes."[15]

Nonetheless, at a time when South Africa is reconstituting itself and its history, the inverted Van Riebeeck has emerged as a key image in which to situate a longer history for a post-apartheid past. This was no more evident than in the reaction to the contents of the report of probably the major historical work of the South African government in constructing a new nation: the Truth and Reconciliation Commission (TRC). Established in 1995, the TRC was premised on the notion that racial reconciliation could only be built by recovering the apartheid past. Amnesty from prosecution was offered to those who came forward and were prepared to give a "full disclosure" of their role in "gross violations of human rights" under apartheid. The dates legally defined as constituting the apartheid period by the Promotion of National Unity and Reconciliation Act—the act under which the TRC operated—were 1960 to 1994, and nearly all the submissions by individuals and organizations kept within these parameters. But when Thabo Mbeki, ANC president and then deputy president of South Africa, presented the TRC report in February 1999 to the South African parliament, a much lengthier genealogy for apartheid was delivered. Members of the ANC were dissatisfied that, in their understanding, the TRC report had equated the human rights violations of the apartheid regime with those committed by the ANC, with perpetrators being identified on both sides of apartheid's violence. Mbeki was at pains to point out a fundamental difference between the acts of violence that members of the ANC committed in fighting for liberation and those perpetrated by the agents of the apartheid regime in defending and promoting an essentially unjust system. He therefore began his speech by asserting that "the great racial divides which continue to separate our communities" all started when the first commander of the Dutch East India Company's revictualing station at the Cape of Good Hope, Jan van Riebeeck, planted a hedge of "almond and thornbush . . . to ensure the safety of the newly arrived white European settlers by keeping the menacing black African hordes of pagan primitives at bay." This "Great Wall of China" was, according to Mbeki, the genesis of apartheid, where "Black and White had to be kept apart, circumscribed by an equation which described each as the enemy of the other, each the antithesis of the other." In Thabo Mbeki's history lesson, it is the actions of the commander of the Dutch East India Company's revictualing station at the Cape of Good Hope, established in 1652, which marks the onset of colonial and racial oppression in South Africa. Thus the ANC's at times excessive acts of violence had to be seen in the context of a legitimate struggle against apartheid and Van Riebeeck.[16]

This marking of 1652 as the moment of colonial/racial oppression and its personification in the image Van Riebeeck is evident in a variety of post-apartheid historical productions, from films to exhibitions, from school text-books to public commemorations. In the remake of the movie *Cry the Beloved Country*, released in 1996, the conservative white farmer, Jarvis, flies to Johannesburg, after hearing about the murder of his son, aboard an aircraft point-edly named Jan van Riebeeck. This self-same Jan also found himself part of a traveling exhibition, "Our Struggle for Land," presented in the lodge for slaves of the Dutch East India Company, which later became the South African Cultural History Museum, on Adderley Street. The exhibition narrative followed a chronological sequence starting with Jan van Riebeeck, who was depicted as carrying out "possibly the first recorded displacement of indigenous people by white settlers in South Africa." In asserting a past for a nation no longer derived from European founding and settlement, large portions of school textbooks are now devoted to people who lived in a country called South Africa that is seen to have existed since time immemorial. In this framework the categories of race are defined through settlement. In this land situated in an already de-fined and bounded space the "first real inhabitants" are called San, who in turn are distinguished from "the Black Peoples" who "originally came from the area known as Central Africa." "Strangers from across the sea" and "settlers," who arrive (in 1652) in a land named South Africa, are called "white." In this textbook past, in which categories of race (and sometimes ethnicity) are all-important, the arrival of the relatively obscure, if not ignominious, Dutch com-mander at the Cape of Good Hope in 1652 remains a key signifier. Charles Davidson Bell's nineteenth-century painting of the landing is once again re-produced, and on tests pupils are asked to recall the date when "the white settlement was founded." His image still adorns the cover of some textbooks, although it is usually placed in a much less prominent position. The moment of arrival in 1652 is being re-cast as the onset of racial conquest and Jan van Riebeeck installed as the initiator of dispossession.[17]

If Jan's image has changed from the one the festival organizers ascribed to him into the very mirror image of a racial oppressor promoted by his oppo-nents, then indeed a most remarkable transformation has been reserved for Maria who has actually altered her race. In the festival of 1952 it was Maria's increased prominence that enabled the organizers to bring the "white race" from Europe onto the beach at Granger Bay. Her statue, which the Dutch gov-ernment promised in 1952, arrived three years later and was placed not next to Jan but in front of the South African National Gallery in the Company Gardens. In 1967 the Cape Town City Council decided to move Maria to Adderley Street so she could be alongside Jan. There followed an immediate uproar, particularly from within Afrikaner nationalist circles, which claimed that the statues did not belong together. The statues were distinctly different in style, represented different epochs in the lives of Jan and Maria, a time when the two were not even married, and, most important, the darkness and heaviness of Maria's statue did not fit alongside the much lighter image of Jan. According to F. L. Alexander, writing in *Die Burger*, what was required was either a new Jan to fit in with Maria or a "new, lighter and more elegant Maria, to match Jan." The City Council preferred to ignore these warnings, and on 27 November 1968 Maria's "long wait" was over as she joined Jan at the top of Adderley Street.[18] But indeed the *Die Burger* reporter's worst fears have been realized. When Ciraj Rassool and I visited the statues on Adderley Street, someone crossing the center island where the statues are situated happened to notice we were eyeing Maria with interest and called out to us: "*Hulle lieg man*" [They are lying to you, man]. "*Sy's mos'n bruin vrou*" [She's really a brown woman]. The bearers of white civilization, proclaimed in the people's pageant, the festival fair, the journey of the mail coaches, and the landing at Granger Bay in 1952, had undergone a racial metamorphosis that would have horrified the promoters of the tercentenary festival. This was a future past they neither contemplated nor envisaged as they sought to build a racially exclusive white nation that would last for another three hundred years.

A Final Note: 350 Years

> Monuments are nothing if not selective aids to memory: they encourage us to remember some things and to forget others. The process of creating monuments, especially where it is openly contested . . . shapes public memory and collective identity.[19]

These words, written in relation to the construction of monuments in Berlin, resonate with the ways in which Jan and Maria van Riebeeck were inscribed into South African history. Through conflicts over the past in 1952, Jan and Maria became the founders of apartheid for those in power and for their political opponents. The historical depictions that came to the fore in 1952 retain a vigor derived from the continuing conflicts over the representation of the past, so that in post-apartheid South Africa the pair have become both the initiators of apartheid and colonialism and the founders of the rainbow nation.

When thoughts began to turn to the 350th anniversary of the landing in 2002, talk of what might be done to celebrate was met with a hushed silence. Apart from a few barely audible murmurings about exhibitions and conferences (and hints of a festival), no one seemed to be paying much attention in South Africa to the twin anniversaries of the establishment of a revictualing station by the Dutch East India Company at the Cape of Good Hope in 1652 and the founding of the Company itself in 1602. But, as the date approached, the conflicts again bubbled up from beneath the surface. Some wanted to commemorate the anniversary with an emphasis on multi-culturalism. In a bizarre twist, advocates of this idea claimed that, in so doing, "the heritage of the country as a whole would be taken into account." Others were less enthusiastic. Patricia de Lille, a Member of Parliament, was adamant: "We don't want to celebrate the myth that Van Riebeeck founded this country." And another political activist proclaimed: "Only clowns would celebrate their oppression." The ANC, which in 1952 condemned Van Riebeeck, is much more ambiguous. At the end of 2001 it formed a coalition with the descendants of the very party that instituted apartheid and celebrated Van Riebeeck, the New National Party, to govern the province of the Western Cape. The ANC has given its support to the commemorations as "an opportunity to celebrate and acknowledge our diversity and build unity and understanding as equal South Africans."[20]

Plans were put in place by the Cape Town City Council to hold a wreath-laying ceremony at the statues on Adderley Street and to fire a twenty-one-gun salute on 6 April 2002. The mayor of Cape Town, Gerald Morkel, in lending support for the ceremony, maintained that to "seek to obliterate or erase that history is to turn our back on our own biographies." The purpose of the ceremony, he claimed, would be to "commemorate the city's founding as a permanent settlement" and the "contributions of all who came to these shores to settle." Banners appeared around Cape Town with the number 350 inscribed on a blue background, together with images of Table Mountain and the sun. But on 6 April 2002 neither a wreath-laying ceremony nor a twenty-one-gun salute were held. No explanation for the lack of activity was forthcoming except that "military command in Pretoria denied permission for the salute." Some indications came from the Western Cape government that festivities would be held later in the year to "celebrate the country's long journey from subjugation to liberation." A publicity company, Blue Cape Media, was hired to promote these activities under the title "Cape Town 350." In a brochure produced by Blue Cape Media, various activities that had already been planned for 2002 were inserted into the program. But the brochure does not indicate what 350 refers to, completely ignores any idea of founding or settlement, and makes no mention of Jan Van Riebeeck or Maria de la Quellerie. Instead, a competition is announced in which Capetonians are asked to nominate their own heroes. By the end of June 2002 the most popular choice was Mark Shuttleworth, a space tourist, who has been described as an "Afronaut," "the first African in space."[21]

The non-celebrations on 6 April 2002 and the excision of Jan and Maria from the commemorative activities for their 350th anniversary would seem to indicate that these characters and the events surrounding them have been "consigned to the rubbish dump of history."[22] Such an assertion does not claim that these events did not occur; rather, in the postcolonial context, these events have been relegated to a past that is not to be recalled. Yet in the light of speeches in parliament, the statues retaining their positions on Cape Town's main thoroughfare, numerous school textbooks, and the decision to publicize "Cape Town 350," it appears that the date of 6 April 1652 and the arrival of Jan and Maria remain key moments and explanatory devices to narrate stories of South Africa's pasts. As the futures envisaged in these stories shift and are contested, so, too, do the roles of Jan and Maria, as contributors or subjugators or both, but always, in some guise, as founders. Through these contests Jan van Riebeeck and Maria de la Quellerie keep their vigil over the past, with their arrival in 1652 marking the onset of white rule as a key constituting moment of a nation that has always been South Africa.

Notes

Introduction

1. State Information Service, *South Africa's Heritage (1652–1952)* (Pretoria: State Information Service, 1952), 5; *Cape Times,* 29 October 1992; *Die Burger,* 29 October 1992.

2. *The Argus,* 6 April 1971; *Die Burger,* 12 November 1986; *Culemborgse Courant,* 5 November 1992.

3. *Culemborgse Courant,* 5 November 1992.

4. Ibid.; "Message from the Honourable the Prime Minister," *Official Programme of the Van Riebeeck Festival,* 7; *African Mirror,* no. 605 (31 January 1951), National Film and Video Archives (hereafter NFA), FA 2477; "Notes and News," *Quarterly Bulletin of the South African Library* 6, no. 4 (June 1952): 108; van Luttervelt, "Het uiterlijk van Jan van Riebeeck," 2–4; *Official Festival Programme,* 87; "Script for the Symbolic Landing of Van Riebeeck at Granger Bay, 5 April 1952," minutes, meeting of pageant subcommittee of the Van Riebeeck Festival, 17 January 1952, University of Cape Town, African Studies Library, McMillan Local History Collection, Van Riebeeck Festival folders (hereafter McM VR).

5. Telephone conversation between André Huguenet and the mayor of Culemborg, 12 April 1952, South African Broadcasting Corporation Sound Archives (hereafter SABC), 18/92–93 (52).

6. *Nederlandse Post,* 15 June 1952; "Nederlandsch Zuid-Afrikaansche Vereeeniging, Verslag over het jaar 1952," 7; Minutes of the mayor of Cape Town for the year ended 5 September 1952, CA, 3/CT 1/7/1/49; *Programma Jan van Riebeeck Herdenking Culemborg,* 10 May–2 June 1952; Minutes, meeting of Cape Town City Council, 26 June 1952, noting letter from the Secretary, South African Embassy, Holland, to the Council, 26 June 1952, CA, 3/CT 1/1/1/113; State Information Service, *South Africa's Heritage,* 10. As the latter publication (9) pointed out, one thing that this Hollander did do at the Cape was to arrange for the importation of slaves "from the west and east coast of Africa and from the East." In her attempt to assist in establishing cordial relations between Holland and the new South Africa of the 1990s, Mayor Bloemendaal seems to have overlooked this knowledge about the early importation of slaves to the Cape by the Dutch East India Company.

7. Elphick and Malherbe, "The Khoisan to 1828," 10; South African Broadcasting Corporation advertisement, *Cape Times,* 22 April 1994; ANC advertisement, *Cape Times,* 27 April 1994; *Cape Times,* 28 April 1994. The way that Van Riebeeck remains a central marker in South Africa's past can also be seen in Reader's Digest, *Illustrated History of South Africa: The Real Story,* a book designed to challenge apartheid history. Here the "pre-white past" is presented in "'flashback' form," and "1652, the date of the arrival of Jan van Riebeeck, the first 'settler,' remains pivotal to the text." See Witz and Hamilton, "Reaping the Whirlwind," 199.

8. I have borrowed the term "endocentricity" from Robinson, "Apartheid Subjects and Post-Colonialism," 4; *Daily News Learn Supplement,* produced in association with the Sached Trust, 4 July 1994; *Time Magazine,* 23 May 1994; *Ulibambe Lingashone* [Hold up the sun] is a television series on the history of the ANC, produced by Afravision and directed by Laurence Dworkin (June 1993). Parts of it were originally shown on the South Africa's pay channel, M-Net, and later on national television, SATV. Of course the ANC was only

formed in 1912 (then called the South African Native National Congress), but it portrays itself as the bearer of the tradition of resistance in South Africa.

9. Maylam, *A History of the African People of South Africa*, 2; *Time*, 23 May 1994.

10. Bonner, Delius, and Posel, "The Shaping of Apartheid," 1.

11. *The Torch*, 8 January 1952; 13 and 24 December 1951; 29 January 1952; *Cape Times*, 7 April 1952; *The Guardian*, 10 April 1952.

12. Tunbridge and Ashworth, *Dissonant Heritage*, 47–50.

13. Darnton, *The Great Cat Massacre*, 253, 12–14; Darnton, "The Symbolic Element in History," 228, 231; Geertz, *Local Knowledge*, 59. Darnton's work relies heavily on his reading of Geertz's *Interpretation of Cultures*.

14. Geertz, *Local Knowledge*, 3; Lalu, "The Grammar of Domination," 67; Biersack, "Local Knowledge," 80.

15. Burawoy, "The Extended Case Method," 10, 5; Biersack, "Local Knowledge," 80–81.

16. Biersack, "Local Knowledge," 81; Cohen, *The Combing of History*, 4–5; Hayes, Silvester, and Hartman, "Photographs, History, and Memory," 6; Ndlovu, "'He did what any other person in his position would have done,'" 100; Rassool, "The Rise of Heritage," 5; Witz, Minkley, and Rassool, "Who Speaks?" 17.

17. Cohen, *The Combing of History*, 4–5; Darnton, "The Symbolic Element," 231.

18. I am drawing here on Carolyn Hamilton's *Terrific Majesty*, 25–32, critique of Ranger and Hobsbawm, *The Invention of Tradition*.

19. Hein, *Learning in the Museum*, chap. 7; see also Hooper-Greenhill, *The Educational Role of the Museum*.

20. Kratz, *The Ones That Are Wanted*, 220.

21. Ibid., 213.

22. Hunt, "Foreword," xi; Falassi, "Festival," "2; Kirshenblatt-Gimblett, *Destination Culture*, 57; Chartier, "Texts," "690; Burawoy, "The Extended Case Method," 5, 17. I am drawing rather liberally here on Patrick Harries's review article, "Histories New and Old," 128, in order to make this point about festivals.

23. Ozouf, *Festivals*, 25, 31; Guss, *The Festive State*, 9–18; Karp, "Festivals," 282–283.

24. Bennett, *Birth of the Museum*, 130–153. Bennett is drawing here on the work of Bommes and Wright. See Bommes and Wright, "'Charms of Residence'"; and Wright, *On Living in an Old Country*.

25. Bennett, *Birth of the Museum*, 146, 141; Hunt, "Introduction," 12–13; Chartier, "Texts, Symbols and Frenchness," 689; Guss, *The Festive State*, 9, 13.

26. Bennett, *Birth of the Museum*, 141; Nkasawe, "Curating the Nation," 21–22.

27. Mostert, *Gedenkboek*, 59.

28. Posel, *The Making of Apartheid*, 1–5; see also Bonner, Delius, and Posel, "The Shaping of Apartheid," 1. On the internal political machinations of the National Party, see O'Meara, *Forty Lost Years*.

29. Chatterjee, *The Nation*, 109.

30. Ibid., 6; Hofmeyr, "Building a Nation," 105; Krebs, *Gender, Race and the Writing of Empire*, chaps. 5, 6.

31. Norval, *Deconstructing Apartheid*, 19–20; Dubow, "Afrikaner Nationalism," 215–216, 224–228.

32. Posel, *The Making of Apartheid*, 270.

33. Bonner, Delius, and Posel, "The Shaping of Apartheid," 1.

34. Summerhill and Williams, *Sinking Columbus*, 20–21.

35. Cochrane and Goodman, "The Great Australian Journey," 24; Souter, "Skeleton at the Feast," 14; Carter, *Botany Bay*, 34-35.

36. Eco, *Misreadings*, 136.

37. Cochrane and Goodman, "The Great Australian Journey," 24; Carter, *Botany Bay*, 1-2; Inglis, "Australia Day," 20-41; Souter, "Skeleton at the Feast," 14; Spearritt, "Celebration of a Nation," 8-15.

38. Florida Museum of Natural History, "First Encounters"; *Newsweek*, Columbus Special Issue, fall/winter 1991; *Time*, 7 October 1991. The outline of the development of the image of Columbus from the seventeenth to the nineteenth centuries draws on Sale, *Conquest of Paradise*, chap. 13; and Bushman, *America Discovers Columbus*, chaps. 5, 8. The concept of creating a public citizenry is based on Bennett's discussion of the development of the museum. See Bennett, *Birth of the Museum*, chaps. 2, 3.

39. Jenkins, *Re-Thinking History*, 47.

40. Hulme uses the term "beginning text" to indicate the way that certain words entered the English language for the first time via Columbus's journal. I am borrowing it rather freely to adapt to an examination of festivals of first settlement/discovery/encounter and their historical authentication (*Colonial Encounters*, 17). The claim of authenticity for and widespread knowledge of Columbus comes from Summerhill and Williams, *Sinking Columbus*, 32.

41. Pratt, *Imperial Eyes*, xi; Souter, "Skeleton at the Feast," 16-19; Thomas, "1938: Past and Present," 78-79; Ransby, "Columbus," 83; Healy, "History," 184; H. Davies, "Don't Spoil the Birthday Party with Modern Value Judgement," *Independent on Sunday*, 14 July 1991; Sale, *Conquest of Paradise*, 333; Murray, "Columbus and the USA," 50.

42. Cochrane and Goodman, "The Great Australian Journey," 21, 23, 26; Spearritt, "Celebration of a Nation," 15-16.

43. Ladurie, *Carnival*, xx; Ozouf, *Festivals*, 3-4, 10.

44. Thomas, "1938: Past and Present," 82-84.

45. "The visit of the 3 Caravels to Miami, February 15, 1992," postcard, Antonio Carbajo, Language Research Press, Miami Springs, Florida; Florida Museum of Natural History, "First Encounters"; Miami Space Transit Planetarium, "Showtime Schedule," December 1992; Cochrane and Goodman, "The Great Australian Journey," 36.

46. Spearritt, "Making the Bicentenary," 17, 18, 20.

47. Speeches and resolution quoted in Horner and Langton, "The Day of Mourning," 29-30; Treaty 88 Campaign, "Aboriginal Sovereignty," 1-2.

48. *Time*, 26 November 1992; Suzan Shown Harjo interview in *Rethinking Schools* Special Edition, *Rethinking Columbus*, Milwaukee, September 1991, 4; *Newsweek*, 24 June 1991; *Newsweek*, Special Columbus Issue, fall/winter 1991; quoted in Meade and Hunt, "Editors' Introduction," 1; *Latinamerica Press*, 23, 38, 17 October 1991; "Why Harold Hates Christopher . . . ," *Central America Report*, autumn 1991; Lister, "Why Harold Hates Christopher," *Independent on Sunday*, 14 July 1991; Damien Gregory, "A Red Light Day for Columbus," *History Today* 41 (December 1991): 5-6. Because of a heavy schedule the following year and the scaling down of the Columbus festival, Mandela did not fulfill his promise. For an extensive account of the failed attempts made to organize Columbus quincentennial commemorations, see Summerhill and Williams, *Sinking Columbus*.

49. Thomas, "The Untold Story," 32. Once again, this is a very simplistic and crude depiction in a popular history written explicitly for schoolchildren, but I would argue that it reflects the essential elements of the pre-conquest narrative that appears in anti-celebratory histories, such as Sale's *Conquest of Paradise*.

50. Thomas, "The Untold Story," 32; "Columbus 500—The Facts," *New Internationalist* 226 (December 1991): 18–19.

51. Pratt, *Imperial Eyes,* xi; H. Davies, "Don't Spoil the Birthday Party . . . ," *Independent on Sunday,* 14 July 1991; Seed, "On Caribbean Shores," 10; Aveling, "Not the Bicentennial History," 162. Isabel Hofmeyr makes a similar point about the interaction between indigenous and imported narratives in her study of oral historical narrative in a chiefdom in the Northern Transvaal. She argues that the "two traditions of chief and settler were by no means separate entities and they influenced each other in significant ways so that a neat distinction between chiefly/oral and settler/written is not possible" (Hofmeyr, "*We Spend Our Years,*" 14).

52. *Newsweek,* Columbus Special Issue, fall/winter 1991.

53. Welch, *Europe's Discovery of South Africa,* 1.

54. Carter, *Botany Bay,* xiv.

55. *Eastern Province Herald,* 11 August 1951; *Daily Dispatch,* 11 August 1951; *Queenstown Daily Representative,* 11 August 1951; *The Star,* 10 August 1951.

56. Bhabha, "DissemiNation," 300.

57. Hunt, "Introduction," 14. For further discussion on how oral evidence is used in an almost documentary style and mined for evidence, see Hofmeyr, "Reading Oral Texts"; Minkley and Rassool, "Orality, Memory and Social History."

58. Pratt, *Imperial Eyes,* 30; *Official Festival Programme,* 100.

59. Grundlingh and Sapire, "From Feverish Festival to Repetitive Ritual?" 19–20; Mostert, *Gedenkboek,* 59.

60. Mostert, *Frontiers,* xvii; South African Railways, 1; State Information Service, *South Africa's Heritage,* 56; *Die Jongspan,* 28 March 1952.

1. Van Riebeeck's Pasts

1. See, for example, Molsbergen, *Die Stichter;* Leipoldt, *Jan Van Riebeeck;* Thom, "Introduction," *Journal of Jan van Riebeeck,* vol. 1, 1651–1655, ed. Hendrik B. Thom (Cape Town: A. A. Balkema, 1952); Barker, *Jan van Riebeeck.*

2. Thom, "Introduction," xxvi.

3. Leipoldt, *Jan Van Riebeeck,* vii–viii, 20–22; Braun, "The Holocaust," 181.

4. Theal, *History of South Africa before 1795,* 6, 129; Leipoldt, *Jan Van Riebeeck,* 13; Thom, "Introduction," xvi–xxvi; J. Naidoo, *Tracking Down Historical Myths,* 20; Cohen, *The Combing of History,* 54.

5. Carr, *What Is History?* 11–13; Frisch, *A Shared Authority,* xxi. This concept of a "shared author-ity" extends Cohen's argument that the production of history does not merely occur within the academy (Cohen, *The Combing of History*). Here, it is being argued that the authenticity of history (both academic and public) is also tested and derived from the public domain. By doing this I am, quite liberally, extending Frisch's argument that tends to see the power derived from the oral record (community histories, in particular) as constituting a challenge to dominant versions of the past. I do not accept Frisch's limited view of a shared authority (with the emphasis on shared), as it seemingly neglects the multiple and differing layers of power that are present in the production of history.

6. Jenkins, *Re-Thinking History,* 9; Anderson, *Imagined Communities,* 46; Anne McClintock, in her critique of Benedict Anderson's location of the origins of national consciousness in the "convergence of capitalism and print technology," argues that print capital has had very limited appeal in the nineteenth and twentieth centuries, given the low levels of

literacy. Instead, she maintains that it was through the "mass national community spectacle" that collective unity was effectively mobilized. Undeniably McClintock is correct in pointing to the appeal of these spectacles, but by setting up her point as an argument against Anderson she fails to look at how and where different types of history operate (*Imperial Leather*, 374).

7. Braun, "The Holocaust," 176–177; Young, *Texture of Memory*, 7.

8. Braun, "The Holocaust," 177; Cohen, *The Combing of History*, 242.

9. *Journal of Jan van Riebeeck*, 1:19–20; Pagden, *European Encounters*, 34. Exactly who is the author of this document, known as the *Journal of Jan van Riebeeck*, is not entirely clear. See the discussion on this issue later in this chapter. The version used here is the 1952 edition, edited by H. B. Thom.

10. Barker, *Jan van Riebeeck*, 6–7; *Journal of Jan van Riebeeck*, 6 April 1652, 1:20; 7 April 1652, 1:25; 24 April 1652, 1:34.

11. Pagden, *European Encounters*, 34; Coetzee, "Visions," "40–41; *Journal of Jan van Riebeeck*, 12 and 15 May 1652, 1:39. The sermon on 12 May was later to be inscribed into the history of the Dutch Reformed Church as the first *nagmaal* (Holy Communion) to be held in South Africa (Olivier, *Ons Gemeentlike Feesalbum*, 28).

12. *Journal of Jan van Riebeeck*, 6 April 1654, 1:226.

13. Leipoldt, *Jan van Riebeeck*, 142; *Journal of Jan van Riebeeck*, 6 April 1654, 1:225, 226.

14. *Journal of Jan van Riebeeck*, 6 April 1655, 1:306; 6 April 1656, 2:27; 9 April 1656, 2:146; 10 June 1657, 2:28, 124; 6 April 1959, 3:30; 8 April 1660, 3:199; Thom, *Journal of Jan van Riebeeck*, 1:149 n.; Leipoldt, *Jan van Riebeeck*, 142.

15. Boeseken, *Drie Eeue*, 169, 210; Journal of Cape Governors (*Dag Register*), 8 April 1752, CA, VC 27. Boeseken does not indicate what her sources are, but her narrative is almost the same as that in the journal with some descriptive additions. I am grateful to Wayne Dooling for assistance with the translation of the eighteenth-century Dutch documents.

16. Theal, *History of South Africa, 1691–1795*, 143; Resolusies van die Politieke Raad, 21 March 1752, CA, C 130.

17. Du Toit and Giliomee, *Afrikaner Political Thought*, 10; Bank, "Liberals and Their Enemies," 56; Gerstner, *The Thousand Generation Covenant*, 242–243; Trapido, "Van Riebeeck Day and the New Jerusalem," 12–14. The identification between colonial settler society and ancient Israel was not peculiar to the Cape. At the centennial celebrations across the United States in 1876, where orations were the centerpiece of the occasion, speaker after speaker made allusions to the United States carrying out its biblical mission and compared the "sacred destiny of America with that of Ancient Israel" (Glassberg, *American Historical Pageantry*, 10). For discussions of the emergence of racial identities in South Africa, see Ross, *Beyond the Pale*; Worden, *Slavery in Dutch South Africa*; Crais, *The Making of the Colonial Order*; and Greenstein, *Genealogies of Conflict*. I am grateful to John Mason for discussions on this point.

18. Resolusies van die Politieke Raad, 21 March 1752, CA, C 130; *Journal of Cape Governors (Dag Register)*, 8 April 1752, CA, VC 27; Petrus van der Spuy, *Dank-Altaar Gode Ter Eere Opgericht*, 20, 25; Boeseken, *Drie Eeue*, 188.

19. *Het Nederduitsch Zuid-Afrikaansche Tydschrift* 2, no. 2 (March–April 1825): 120; *Kaapsche Courant*, 7 July 1804; *Het Nederduitsch Zuid-Afrikansche Tydschrift* 2, no. 2 (March–April 1825): 118–123.

20. *Kaapsche Courant*, 7 July 1804; *Het Nederduitsch Zuid-Afrikansche Tydschrift* 2, no. 2 (March–April 1825): 122.

21. Bank, "Liberals and Their Enemies," 244–248; Ross, *Beyond the Pale*, 91; *South Afri-*

can Commercial Advertiser, 3 April 1852; *Het Nederduitsch Zuid-Afrikaansch Tydschrift* 2, no. 7 (1825): iv.

22. Letter from Rev. A. Faure requesting that 6 April 1852 be declared a public holiday (Schapera, *David Livingstone Papers*, appendix 3, 178; *South African Commercial Advertiser*, 3 April 1852.

23. *South African Commercial Advertiser*, 7 April 1852.

24. Bank, "Liberals and Their Enemies," 258; Ross, *Status and Respectability*, 66–69; *South African Commercial Advertiser*, 3 April 1852.

25. John Phillip, *Researches in South Africa*, vols. 1, 2, quoted in Bank, "Liberals and Their Enemies," 240; Ross, *Beyond the Pale*, 197–199; Bank, "Liberals and Their Enemies," 241; Schapera, *David Livingstone Papers*, 73.

26. Schapera, *David Livingstone Papers*, 73.

27. Ibid.

28. Ibid., 73–74.

29. Crais, *The Making of the Colonial Order*, 87–90, 129; "Discourse delivered by the Rev. W. M. Shaw, in St. George's Church, Grahamstown, 10 April 1844," in Godlonton, *Memorials of the British Settlers*, 12; "Mr. Chase's address on proposing 'the memory of those Settlers whom it has pleased Providence to remove,' at Dinner in Port Elizabeth, 10 April 1844," in Godlonton, *Memorials of the British Settlers*, 67; Ross, *Status and Respectability*, 63–66; "Address by Mr. J. C. Chase on proposing the 'memory of Johan Van Riebeeck,' " in Godlonton, *Memorials of the British Settlers*, 60–62. As Ross (64) points out, this image of a glorious, triumphalist settler past by Godlonton and Chase did not go unchallenged within the settler communities of the eastern Cape, even though Godlonton assiduously tried to project, through *The Graham's Town Journal*, a singular, unified settler voice.

30. A.H.S., "Charles Davidson Bell," 81–82; Bank, "Liberals and Their Enemies," 286; Bradlow and Bradlow, "The English Vision," 7–8; Bunn, "Relocations," 45; Coetzee, *White Writing*, 39; van Luttervelt, "Het Uiterlijk van Jan van Riebeeck," 2–4; *Quarterly Bulletin of the South African Library* 6, no. 4 (June 1952): 108.

31. Van Luttervelt, "Het uiterlijk van Jan van Riebeeck," 4; Crump, van Niekerk, and Grundlingh, *Public Sculptures and Reliefs*, 22. Robert Ross speculates that the reason Harry Smith did not accord Van Riebeeck a public holiday in 1852 was the fear that the Dutch intelligentsia would utilize the day as a way to mobilize political support (*Status and Respectability*, 67). In relation to the statue on Adderley Street, an account of the Russian captain, Vasilii Mikhailovich Golovin, whose ship *Diana* was detained by the British authorities in Simon's Town between 1808 and 1809, also mentions a statue of Van Riebeeck at the Town House in Cape Town. This, however, appears to be an incorrect translation and presumably refers to a portrait of Van Riebeeck that was displayed in the Town House (Golovnin, *Detained in Simon's Bay*, 37). The sculptor who was engaged to create the statue at the end of the nineteenth century, Tweed, was also engaged by Rhodes to do a bronze statue of the poet Burns at Groote Schuur and brass reliefs for the Wilson memorial in Zimbabwe, *Cape Times*, 13 May 1899; 19 May 1899. Vivian Bickford-Smith suggests that the statue was donated by Rhodes as a token of rapprochement between English and Dutch speakers (*Ethnic Pride*, 139). What Bickford-Smith ignores are the British imperial associations that the image of Van Riebeeck had begun to assume in the nineteenth century, and therefore one cannot assume that Van Riebeeck was a symbol of reverence for Dutch speakers. The association between Rhodes and Van Riebeeck was again highlighted in 1902 when Rhodes died. Suggestions were made that a statue of Rhodes be built at the entrance to the Company Gardens, at the opposite end of Adderley Street, so that he could directly face "the statue of Mr. Van

Riebeeck, the last gift of Mr. Rhodes" (*Cape Times*, 1 April 1902). See also the editorial in the *Cape Times*, 5 April 1902.

32. *Cape Argus Union Jubilee Supplement*, 28 May 1960, 3, 13; Wilson, *Gone Down the Years*, 205; *The Pageant of South Africa*, October 1910 (Brochure), National Library of South Africa (hereafter SAL), EMC Loopuyt Collection (hereafter EMC), MSB 573; *Cape Times*, 29 October 1910.

33. *Cape Times*, 31 October 1910; 29 October 1910; *The Pageant of South Africa*, October 1910 (Brochure); *Cape Argus Union Jubilee Supplement*, 28 May 1960, 13; Ino, "Veertigduisend Toeskouers by Eerste Uniedag-Fees," *Die Burger*, 3 June 1950; *Cape Argus*, Weekly Edition, 2 November 1910.

34. *Cape Argus*, 1 November 1910; Parliamentary Hansard: Debates of the First Session of the First Parliament of the House of Assembly, 31 October 1910–25 April 1911, 67, 71, 131–132. In addition to Union Day and Victoria Day there were Good Friday, Easter Monday, and Ascension Day; House of Assembly Debates, 31 October 1910–25 April 1911, 67, 132. Dingaan's Day had first become a public holiday in the Transvaal in the 1860s but had been specifically promoted by the Afrikaner nationalist historian, Gustav Preller, in the period after the South African War of 1899–1902. See Hofmeyr, "Popularizing History," 527.

35. *Cape Times*, 8 April 1921.

36. Dentz, *Geschiedenis Van het Algemeen Nederlands Verbond*, 3–5, 24; Molsbergen, *De Stichter;* 3. Presumably Molsbergen had little hope that, by this time, either North America or the East Indies could be incorporated into this greater Dutch cultural world (*Cape Argus*, 8 April 1921).

37. Hofmeyr, "Building a Nation," 95–123; du Toit, "Hendrik Bibault," 17–18 October 1991; Dentz, *Geschiedenis Van het Algemeen Nederlands Verbond*, 6, 24.

38. *Cape Times*, 7 and 8 April 1921; Bradlow, *The Van Riebeeck Society*, 4; *Cape Argus*, 6 and 8 April 1921; *Die Burger*, 8 April 1921.

39. *Die Burger*, 7 April 1922.

40. Select Committee on Amendment of Public Holidays Act, 1925, SC. 10-'25; Grundlingh, "Politics, Principles and Problems," 9; Gie, *Geskiedenis Van Suid Afrika*, i–ii, 51–52; Dentz, *Geschiedenis Van het Algemeen Nederlands Verbond*, 25–26.

41. Select Committee on Amendment of Public Holidays Act, 1925, SC. 10-'25; Mostert, *Gedenkboek Van Die Ossewaens*, 110–117; *Cape Argus*, 8 August 1938; O'Meara, *Volkskapitalisme*, 76; Grundlingh and Sapire, "From Feverish Festival," 20.

42. Minutes, meeting of the ANV, 13 November 1939; see also Minutes of 16 October and 4 December 1939, ANV Library (hereafter ANV), Van Riebeeck Day (hereafter VRD), 1938–1960 file; Thom, *Van Riebeeck Day*, 12; "Van Riebeeck Day: Origins of Council participation," ANV, VRD file; O'Meara, *Volkskapitalisme*, 61, 75. Programme, Jan van Riebeeck Day Wreath Laying Ceremony, 7 April 1941, ANV, VRD file.

43. *Die Huisgenoot*, 17 March 1944.

44. Letter to the Editor of *Die Huisgenoot*, 27 March 1944, ANV, VRD file.

45. Letter to Mr. J. H. Viljoen, 20 February 1948; Afskrif van brief D. P. De Klerk, 21 December 1943; letter from Principal of Jan van Riebeeck High School to Secretary of the ANV, 30 March 1944, ANV, VRD file; *Die Huisgenoot*, 17 March 1944; "Van Riebeeck Day: Origins of Council Participation," ANV, VRD file.

46. Berghahn and Schlisser, "Introduction: History Textbooks," 1, 14.

47. Olson, "On the Language and Authority of Textbooks," 189–190; Altbach and Kelly, *Textbooks in the Third World*, 3, x; Barthes, *S/Z*, 4–6. Of course, not all textbooks can be categorized in this way, especially more recent ones which invite the reader to search for a

variety of interpretations. Yet, even in these texts, there is still a very strong tendency to remain bounded within a discourse of making simple declarations and marking essential points.

48. De Lima, *Geschiedenis;* Bosman, "Joseph Suasso De Lima," 219–220; *Het Nederduits Zuid-Afrikaansch Tydschrift,* December 1825, 453–454.

49. Bank, "The Great Debate," 2; Smith, *The Changing Past,* 15; John C. Kannemeyer, *Geskiedenis van die Afrikaanse Literatuur,* 26; D. E. Smit, introduction to De Lima, *Geschiedenis* (1975); *South African Library Reprint Bulletin* 35, no. 2 (1980); De Lima, *Geschiedenis,* 1, 8, 9, 14, 18; Mulholland, "The Evolution of History Teaching," 83. I am borrowing the phrase "sacred to secular history" from Samuel, *Theatres of Memory,* 6.

50. De Lima, *Geschiedenis,* 6–9.

51. George M. Theal, *History of South Africa since September 1795,* vol. 3 (London, 1908), 402, quoted in Smith, *The Changing Past,* 15; Samuel, *Theatres of Memory,* 6; Mulholland, "The Evolution of History Teaching," 159; Naipaul, *A Way in the World,* 104; Smith, *The Changing Past,* 15.

52. Mulholland, "The Evolution of History Teaching," 161; Du Toit and Hoogenhout, *Die Geskiedenis,* ii.

53. Wilmot, *History of the Cape Colony,* 5.

54. Ibid., 7, 9.

55. Kannemeyer, *Geskiedenis Van Die Afrikaanse Literatuur,* 59; See Hofmeyr, "Building a Nation," 96–99; "Manifesto of the Genootskap Van Regte Afrikaners," quoted in Kannemeyer, *Geskiedenis Van Die Afrikaanse Literatuur,* 52; *Die Patriot,* 30 March 1877, quoted in Mulholland, "The Evolution of History Teaching," 111; S. J. du Toit, quoted in Smith, *The Changing Past,* 60.

56. Du Toit, *Die Geskiedenis,* 146.

57. Theal and Young, *Korte Geskiedednis van Suid Afrika,* frontispiece.

58. Mulholland, "Evolution of History Teaching," 169; Saunders, *The Making of the South African Past,* 18.

59. Edgar, "The Teaching of History," 9.

60. Theal, *Primer,* 1–3.

61. Ibid., 1; Theal, *Short History,* Map 1, between 12–13; Theal and Young, *Korte Geskiedenis van Suid Afrika,* 1; Saunders, *The Making of the South African Past,* 39.

62. Theal, *Primer,* chaps. 2, 8.

63. Ibid., 8, 13, 16; Theal, *Short History,* 30, 31, 233.

64. Fairbridge, *A History of South Africa;* Mulholland, "The Evolution of History Teaching," 211; Merrington, "Pageantry and Primitivism," 643, 654.

65. Fairbridge, *A History of South Africa,* 133, 312.

66. The discussion on the writing of Fairbridge which follows is derived and adapted from Merrington, "Pageantry and Primitivism," 647–649.

67. Fairbridge, *A History of South Africa,* 263–265, 297.

68. Ibid., 297, 35–39. The association between Van Riebeeck, gardens, and imperial unity is more fully developed in Fairbridge, *Gardens of South Africa.* Fairbridge presents the scene of Jan van Riebeeck plucking the first oranges planted in the Company gardens and then comments, wistfully: "If he could but stand in Covent Garden market [London] to-day and see the place lighted up with the golden oranges and naartjes of South Africa. Perhaps he does see them. Who knows?" (7). For a similar association, but with the emphasis placed on a European past, see the foreword by R. H. Compton, director of the National Botanic Gardens, Kirstenbosch, to Karstens, *The Old Company's Garden,* ix. The opening sentence of

the foreword reads: "The history of the Europeans in South Africa begins with a Garden." The frontispiece of this book is a portrait of Van Riebeeck.

69. Fairbridge, *A History of South Africa*, 40, vii.

70. Du Toit, *Die Geskiedenis*, 6; Theal, *Primer*, 8; Elliot and Theal, *Our History in Picture*, 16.

71. Fairbridge, *A History of South Africa*, 25.

72. Fairbridge, *Lady Anne Barnard*, 1; Fairbridge, *A History of South Africa*, 135. Dorothy Driver has suggested that Lady Anne Barnard, like many women in the 1790s, held contradictory gender self-perceptions, often vacillating "between subject positions conventionally identified with 'activity' and 'passivity,' 'masculinity' and 'femininity,' 'intellect' and 'emotion,' 'culture and emotion.' " Fairbridge's modeling of Lady Anne Barnard seems to be based on this contradictory positioning. See Driver, "A Literary Appraisal," 8–9.

73. Mulholland, "The Evolution of History Teaching," 201–202; Howes, *Juta's History;* Fowler and Smit, *New History.*

74. Hofmeyr, *Kykies vir Kinders*, i; Howes, *Juta's History,* preface; Skinner, *Geskiedenisleesboeke vir die Laer Skool*, foreword; Stockenstrom, *Beknopte Handboek,* foreword.

75. Stockenstrom, *The New Matriculation History*, preface, 28–29; Lewis, *Juta's History and Civics*, 1–10.

76. Howes, *Juta's History,* preface; Hofmeyr, *Kykies vir Kinders*, ii.

77. "Introduction to Transvaal Education Department syllabus, Std 1-V111," Pretoria (1940), quoted in Mulholland, "The Evolution of History Teaching," 228; Hope, *Our Place in History,* 1.

78. Gie, *Geskiedenis van Suid-Afrika*, ii; Kammeijer and Van Rooyen, *Sketse Uit Die Vaderlandse Geskiedenis*, v.

79. Theal, *Primer*, 1; Fairbridge, *A History of South Africa*, 7; Lewis, *Juta's History and Civics*, 1; Skinner, *Geskiedenisleesboeke*, 7.

80. Hofmeyr, *Kykies vir Kinders*, 1:36; Lewis, *Founders and Builders*, 31; Fouche, *Groot Mannen;* Kammeijer and Van Rooyen, *Sketse.*

81. Lewis, *Founders and Builders*, 39–41; Howes, *Juta's History,* 12; Gie, *Geskiedenis van Suid-Afrika*, 77.

82. Gie, *Geskiedenis van Suid-Afrika*, 77.

83. Lewis, *Founders and Builders*, 40.

84. Gie, *Geskiedenis van Suid-Afrika*, 50; Hofmeyr, *Kykies Vir Kinders*, 37.

85. Freund, "Past Imperfect," 9.

86. Hofmeyr, *Kykies vir Kinders*, i–vi, 36.

87. Ibid., 36.

88. Ross, *Beyond the Pale*, 203.

89. Ibid., 193.

90. Premesh Lalu makes a similar point in relation to the way that Eddie Roux's *S. P. Bunting: A Political Biography* is used as a primary source for information on the early history of the Communist Party of South Africa, with almost total disregard for the changing contexts of its production. See Lalu, "Lived Texts," 84.

91. Based on the Company directive that copies are forwarded to its offices, H. B. Thom argues that the original, from which handwritten facsimiles were made, was the one kept in Cape Town (Thom, "Introduction," xxvii–xxviii).

92. Beyers, "Die Huisvesting," 46; Thom, "Introduction," xxxiii. The Resolutions of the Council of Policy found their way into a private collection and were later donated to the Cape archives. The slave lodge was a two-story building which housed the slaves directly

in the employ of the Dutch East India Company and was also used as a prison and an asylum. See Shell, *Children of Bondage*, 172–177, 248–251. The slave lodge today houses the part of Iziko Museums of Cape Town that was called the South African Cultural History Museum. The gravestones of Jan van Riebeeck and Maria de la Quellerie are displayed in the courtyard of this building. Thanks to Michele Pickover, the Curator of Historical Papers at William Cullen Library, University of the Witwatersrand, for sharing with me her knowledge relating to the collection of documents prior to the establishment of an official archive.

93. *Het Nederduitsch Zuid-Afrikaansch Tydschrift* 1, no. 2 (May/June 1824): 105; Kannemeyer, *Geskiedenis van die Afrikaanse Literatuur*, 30; Bank, "Liberals and Their Enemies," 248; *Het Nederduitsch Zuid-Afrikaansch Tydschrift* 7, no. 3: 222–223; quoted in Bank, "Liberals and Their Enemies," 248.

94. *Het Nederduitsch Zuid-Afrikaansch Tydschrift* 1, no. 2 (May/June 1824): 103; 4, no. 5 (September/October 1827): 353.

95. Ibid., vol. 1, no. 1 (March/April 1824): 4; vol. 1, no. 2 (May/June 1824): 104, 107.

96. Ross, *Beyond the Pale*, 194, 195. These events are referred to as either Hintsa's War or the Fourth Frontier War (Smith, "Introduction," viii).

97. Ross, *Beyond the Pale*, 203, 206–207; Bank, "Liberals and Their Enemies," 264–266; Moodie, *The Record*, 10.

98. Moodie, *The Record*, 10; Thom, *Journal of Jan van Riebeeck*, 1:30.

99. Historisch Genootskap Gevesitgd te Utrecht, *Dagverhaal*, v; Thom, "Introduction," xxxiii; D. B. Bosman, "Van Riebeeck Se Dagregister," *Die Huisgenoot*, 9 April 1948.

100. Historisch Genootskap, *Dagverhaal*, xii, ix; Thom, "Introduction," xxxiv; Bosman, "Van Riebeeck Se Dagregister."

101. Samuel, *Theatres of Memory*, 269; Preller, "Archival Development in South Africa," 43–44; Davies, "Organisational Development," 7–9. The archives were moved in 1883 to the South African Public Library and, in 1884, to a cellar below Parliament, where they were housed for the next fifty years. See Beyers, "Die Huisvesting," 47; Saunders, *The Making of the South African Past*, 13; Davies, "Hendrik Carel Vos Leibrandt," 385–387.

102. Davies, "Hendrik Carel Vos Leibrandt," 386; Boeseken, "Theal as Baanbreker," 37.

103. Thom, "Introduction," xl. See also Rossouw, "Die Werk van Hendrik Carel Vos Leibrandt," 71, who makes the point of expanding the audience for the archive.

104. Cohen, *The Combing of History*, 52.

105. Hofmeyr, "Building a Nation," 113.

106. This very brief synopsis of the origins and aims of the Van Riebeeck Society is derived from Bradlow, *The Van Riebeeck Society*. The back page of every publication of the society lists the laws of the society and its publications; H. Varley, "The Van Riebeeck Diary: Progress Report on the Tercentenary Edition, 1940–1952," 1 September 1952, US, Thom, Box 49; Minutes of Council Meeting of Van Riebeeck Society, 15 June 1940, SAL, Van Riebeeck Society (hereafter VRS), Minute Book, MSB 633, 1 (1); H. Thom, "Van Riebeeck Se Dagverhaal, *Die Huisgenoot*, 28 January 1944.

107. Thom, "Van Riebeeck Se Dagverhaal."

108. D. B. Bosman, "Van Riebeeck Se Dagverhaal," *Die Huisgenoot*, 3 March 1944.

109. H. B. Thom, "Van Riebeeck se Dagverhaal Nogeens," *Die Huisgenoot*, 10 March 1944.

110. Ibid.; Bosman, "Van Riebeeck Se Dagverhaal"; Thom, "Introduction," xvi.

111. Hofmeyr, *Kykies vir Kinders*, 36.

112. See Jeppie, "Aspects of Popular Culture," 147–150; Albert Grundlingh, "Die Mite van die Volksvader," *Vrye Weekblad*, 5 April 1991.

2. "We Build a Nation"

The title of this chapter is derived from a paper by Sperber, "Festivals of National Unity," 114–138.

1. See Worden and Van Heyningen, "Signs of the Times," 215–236; Bickford-Smith and Van Heyningen, *The Waterfront*, 7; *Official Festival Programme*, 7.

2. Interview with Joe Almond; A. Neethling-Pohl, "Verslag Oor Die Landing Van Die Dromedaris," 5 May 1952, CA, K. Jeffreys Collection, A1657, vol. 322.

3. "Script for Symbolic Landing of Van Riebeeck at Granger Bay," Minutes, Meeting of Pageant Sub-Committee, 17 January 1952, UCT (ASL), McM: Van Riebeeck Festival. For a description of the landing from the perspective of a marine cadet, see Bole, "The Landing," 31–32.

4. This account of events on the beach of Granger Bay on 5 April 1952 is based on A. Neethling-Pohl, "Verslag Oor Die Landing"; "Script for Symbolic Landing of Van Riebeeck"; "Order of Stage Directions for the Landing of the *Dromedaris*," CA, A 1657, vol. 322; "Landing van Van Riebeeck te Granger Bay," SABC, 19/31–35 (52).

5. *Official Festival Programme*, 87.

6. Ibid., 11; De Kock, *Our Three Centuries*, 31; State Information Service, *South Africa's Heritage*, frontispiece.

7. Minutes of Annual General Meeting Van Riebeeck Society, 24 March 1945, SAL, VRS, MSB 633, 1 (1); "The Van Riebeeck Diary: Progress Report on the Tercentenary Edition," US, Thom, Box 49.

8. Jeeves, "Arthur Keppel-Jones," 24; interview with Arthur Keppel-Jones, conducted by Alan Jeeves, 15.

9. Keppel-Jones, *When Smuts Goes*, 3–4.

10. Ibid., 4.

11. Jeeves, "Arthur Keppel-Jones," 25; interview with Arthur Keppel-Jones, conducted by Alan Jeeves, 15; *Die Burger*, 9 April 1952.

12. Institute for Contemporary History, University of the Orange Free State [hereafter INCH], ATKV Collection, PV 379: A 11/13; Minutes of Meeting of Commission for the Volksfees (1952), 24 August 1945, INCH, FAK Collection, PV 202: 1/8/3/5/1; Minutes, Jan van Riebeeck Feeskomitee (1952), 1 April 1946, INCH, PV 202: 1/8/3/5/1.

13. Letter from Chair *Jan van Riebeeck-Feeskomitee* (1952) to T. E. Donges, Member of Parliament, 5 April 1946, INCH, PV 202: 2/10/1/3/1; letter from Chair, *Jan Van Riebeeck-Feeskomitee* (1952) to J. C. Smuts, 5 April 1946, INCH, PV 202: 1/8/3/5/1.

14. Letter from Private Secretary of the Prime Minister to Chair of *Jan van Riebeeck Feeskomitee* (1952), 10 April 1946, INCH, PV 202: 1/8/3/5/1; Minutes of First Representative Meeting of the *Jan van Riebeeck Feeskomitee*, 23 August 1946; Executive Committee of *JVR Feeskomitee*, 21 January 1947; 9 August 1947; 28 January 1948, INCH, PV 202: 1/8/3/5/1; Minutes, Executive Committee of *JVR Feeskomitee*, 28 January 1948; letter from Chair *Jan Van Riebeeck-Feeskomitee* (1952) to J. C. Smuts, 5 April 1946; Minutes, Executive Committee of *JVR Feeskomitee*, 21 January 1947, INCH, PV 202: 1/8/3/5/1; letters to editors of Afrikaans newspapers from *Van Riebeeck Fees Komitee;* letters to Dutch Reformed Mission Churches from *Van Riebeeck Fees Komitee*, 19 February 1947; letter from J. G. Strijdom, General Secretary Dutch Reformed Mission Church, OFS, to A. F. Weich, Secretary, FAK, 22 February 1947, INCH, PV 202: 2/10/1/3/1; Dutch Reformed Church, *Die Koms van Jan van Riebeeck: Ramp of Redding?* (Cape Town, 1952), 5.

15. *Cape Times,* 4 January 1946; 7 February 1946; 11 February 1946; 27 February 1946; 21 March 1946.

16. Ibid., 11 February 1946; 21 March 1946; 15 April 1947.

17. "The Van Riebeeck Diary: Progress Report"; *Cape Times,* 15 April, 17 June 1947; 7 February 1948. These descriptions of the 1947 royal tour are mainly from *African Mirror* newsreels which were re-broadcast on South African television several months before Queen Elizabeth II and Prince Philip visited South Africa in 1995. They are labeled "Royal Tour— Episode 1" and "Royal Tour—Episode 5." See also the *Cape Times,* 22, 28 February, 3, 20 March 1947.

18. African Mirror: "The Royal Tour," Episode 5; *Cape Times,* 24 April 1947.

19. African Mirror, "The Royal Tour," Episode 1; *Cape Times,* 20 February 1947. This is not to deny that many other factors contributed to the National Party election victory in 1948. Much has been written on these issues, but, apart from focusing on the 1938 centenary celebrations, little has been said on the contested nature of the imagery. It is almost as if there is a presumed straight line between 1938 and 1948 with no sense of how the *voortrekker* past had to compete with other pasts, especially with the royal visit being such a recent occurrence. The analysis presented here is similar to the point Raphael Samuel makes in his critique of the concept of the "invention of tradition." He argues that changes in public attitudes are not inventions but are underpinned by a "great mass of pre-existing public sentiment" (*Theatres of Memory,* 307). It would appear that, in this specific instance, the mass of public sentiment around the royal visit was not in any way sufficient to alter local identities, which had been assembled in the past half-century and more. For differing conceptions of apartheid in Afrikaner nationalist circles, see Posel, *The Making of Apartheid,* 49–60.

20. "Voortrekkermonument Byvoegsel," *Die Burger,* 10 December 1949; Rapportryers-Reelingskomitee, *Die Rapportboek van die Rapportryers* (Johannesburg, 1949), 3; *Official Programme for the Inauguration,* 14–15; M. C. Botha, "The Inauguration," in Board of Control of the Voortrekker Monument, *The Voortrekker Monument Pretoria: Official Guide,* Pretoria, n.d., 71.

21. G. Moerdijk, "The Historical Frieze," and G. Moerdijk, "Design and Symbolism of the Afrikaner Monument," in *The Voortrekker Monument Pretoria: Official Guide,* 51, 34.

22. Delmont, "The Voortrekker Monument," 101; Posel, *The Making of Apartheid,* 270; Thompson, *The Story of a House,* 132–133; *The Star,* 16 December 1949; *Cape Times,* 17 December 1949. Posel's book, as the title indicates, deals with the contests over the formulation of apartheid policy, focusing on influx control. She does not look, however, at how establishing a white identity and a past were also central to the conception and maintenance of apartheid.

23. *Cape Times,* 17 and 15 December 1949; *The Star,* 14 December 1949; Bond, *The Saga of The Great Trek,* 40; Etherington, "Old Wine in New Bottles," 37; Bond, *The Saga of the Great Trek,* 40.

24. Minutes of Meeting of Executive Committee of Jan van Riebeeck-Feeskomitee, 9 February 1949, INCH, PV 202: 1/8/3/5/1.

25. Ibid.; letter from E. G. Jansen, Minister of Native Affairs, to T. E. Donges, Minister of Interior, 29 June 1949; letter from C. F. Albertyn to T. E. Donges, 15 September 1949, CA, Donges collection, A1646, vol. 338; Minutes of the first meeting of the Breë Kommittee van die Van Riebeeck Feeskommittee, 10 March 1950, CA, A1646, vol. 338.

26. *Cape Times,* 6 April 1950.

27. Ibid., 6 and 7 April 1950; *Die Burger,* 6 April 1950; *Die Suiderstem,* 6 April 1950; Glassberg, *American Historical Pageantry,* 65.

28. *Die Burger,* 6 April 1950; M. C. Botha to E. G. Jansen, Minister of Native Affairs, 13 June 1950, INCH, PV 202: 2/10/1/3/3. See introduction for a discussion on the trend which emerged in the twentieth century to give Afrikaners a specific European ancestry.

29. Minutes, Meeting of Cape Town Tercentenary Committee, 28 June 1950, CA, A1646, vol. 338; Minutes of Tercentenary Action Committee, 17 July 1950, INCH, PV 202: 2/10/1/3/3.

30. M. C. Botha to E. G. Jansen, Minister of Native Affairs, 13 June 1950, INCH, PV 202: 2/10/1/3/3; *Cape Times,* 7 August 1950; *Die Burger,* 7 August 1950; *Cape Argus,* 7 August 1950. A. J. van der Merwe, the moderator of the Dutch Reformed Church, later replaced Jansen.

31. Minutes, Tercentenary Action Committee, 17 August 1950 and 26 September 1950, INCH, PV 202, 1/8/3/5/2; radio talk by T. E. Donges in connection with the Van Riebeeck Festival, 28 September 1951, SABC, 28/93(51). See full script of talk in CA, A1646, vol. 339; Minutes of the first meeting of Central Committee, Van Riebeeck Festival, 8 September 1950, INCH, PV 202, 1/8/3/5/1.

32. Letter from Chair of Cape Town Committee to Secretary, Central Committee, Van Riebeeck Festival, 4 October 1950, INCH, PV 202, 2/10/1/3/4.

33. Ibid.; Minutes, Meeting of Executive Committee of Van Riebeeck Festival, 16 October 1950, US, Thom, Box 49.

34. Keppel-Jones, *When Smuts Goes,* 3; M. C. Botha to E. G. Jansen, Minister of Native Affairs, 13 June 1950, INCH, PV 202: 2/10/1/3/3; Minutes of Meetings of Executive Committee of Van Riebeeck Festival, 16 October 1950, 3 November 1950, US, Thom, Box 49; *Cape Times,* 7 November 1950.

35. Minutes of Meetings of Executive Committee of Van Riebeeck Festival, 3 November 1950, US, Thom, Box 49; *Official Festival Programme,* 7.

36. Minutes of Meetings of Executive Committee of Van Riebeeck Festival, 3 November 1950, US, Thom, Box 49; *Official Festival Programme,* 11, 23, 68. The festival fair is discussed in detail in chapter 4 and the journey of the mail coaches in chapter 5.

37. Parliamentary Hansard, House of Assembly Debates, 8 February 1951, 908; Merrington, "Masques, Monuments and Masons," 3; "Schedule of suggestions submitted for consideration by Action Committee arising out of public appeal," Annexure to Minutes Tercentenary Action Committee, 17 July 1950, INCH, PV 202: 2/10/1/3/3; Parliamentary Hansard, House of Assembly Debates, 8 February 1951, 913, 917; Glassberg, *American Historical Pageantry,* 40; A. Neethling-Pohl to M. Pienaar and S. Hunter, Chairs of the Pageant Sub-Committee, Van Riebeeck Festival, 5 May 1952, CA, A 1657, vol. 322. The linear and spatial imagery of pageants is discussed in relation to American pageants in Glassberg, *American Historical Pageantry,* 1.

38. J. C. Pauw, Organising Secretary, Van Riebeeck festival to Secretary, SABC, 9 February 1951, US, Thom, Box 49; A. Neethling-Pohl to M. Pienaar and S. Hunter, 5 May 1952. See Moodie, *The Rise of Afrikanerdom.*

39. A. Neethling-Pohl to Gladstone and Rosa, 29 May 1951, US, WEG Louw collection, 158, k.u.24 (142).

40. Reply to criticisms of the pageant made at the meeting of the Cape Town Committee for the Van Riebeeck Festival (1952) held on Friday, 24 August 1951, by a City Council Deputation, US, 158.ku.1.Va (12). On the stated function of the hospital rag, see message from T. B. Davie, Principal and Vice-Chancellor of UCT, *Sax Appeal: University of Cape Town Rag Mag,* March 1952, 13.

41. Minutes of Meeting of historical presentations sub-committee, 16 November 1950,

UCT (ASL), McM: Van Riebeeck Festival; J. C. Pauw to Head, Department of History, University of Stellenbosch, 18 November 1950, US, Thom, Box 49; Kotze, *Professor H. B. Thom,* 17; Grundlingh, "Politics, Principles and Problems," 2; A. Neethling-Pohl to H. Thom, 7 January 1952; A. Neethling-Pohl to H. Thom, 21 January 1952, US, Thom, Box 49. See also the debate on the Public Holidays Bill in the House of Assembly, 18 February 1952, where the Minister of the Interior refers to Thom as "pre-eminently an expert on Van Riebeeck's period" (Hansard, 18 February 1952, 1362).

42. Minutes, Council meeting Van Riebeeck Society, 20 March 1948, SAL, VRS, MSB 633, 1 (4); 8 Dec 1945, SAL, VRS, MSB 633, 1 (1); Van Riebeeck Society Progress Report on the Tercentenary Edition, 1952, SAL, VRS, MSB 633 1 (5); Minutes, Daghregister Editorial Committee, 24 January 1952, SAL, VRS, MSB 633, 1 (4). This included publication, transcription, and translation costs.

43. Minutes, Council Meeting, VRS, 29 March 1952, SAL, VRS, MSB 633, 1 (4); VRS, 12 September 1952, SAL, VRS, MSB 633, 1 (4); Van der Watt, "Art, Gender, Ideology and Afrikaner Nationalism," 12. With the agreement of the publisher, A. A. Balkema, it was decided that the best way for the government to recover some of the money it had spent was for the Education Department to take over 1,500 copies and distribute them for free in schools, while the publisher would sell the remaining 248 copies at R2.50 to buyers from overseas who had specialized interests (J. Du P. Scholtz, Chair VRS to Secretary of Education, 1964[?], SAL, VRS, MSB 633, 3 [1]).

44. Coetzee, *White Writing,* 162; Proposals for Honours Degrees to be conferred at the summer Graduation Ceremony, March 1952, University of the Witwatersrand archives [hereafter Wits (A)] Misc.Hons DS/375/51; Minutes of a Meeting of the Honorary Degrees Committee held at the Principal's residence, 31 August 1951, Wits (A), Hons. D.S./310/51; Minutes of Council of University of the Witwatersrand, 30 November 1951, Wits (A); *Die Vaderland,* 19 March 1952; Botha, *Our South Africa;* De Kock, *Our Three Centuries.* Coetzee points out that Millin's writings were very much in tune with many of the racial theories dominant at the time.

45. *Zionist Record,* 28 March 1952; *Natal Daily News,* 24 March 1952; *Sunday Times,* 25 March 1952; *Die Transvaler,* 24 March 1952.

46. "Opsomming Van Die Historiese Volksoptog Soos Goedgekeur Deur Die Optogkomitee," attached to letter from J. C. Pauw to H. B. Thom, 11 July 1951, US, Thom, Box 49.

47. "Report for the Festival Fair Committee on the Political Aspect in the Transvaal," 1951, CA, A1646, vol. 339; *Rand Daily Mail,* 10 July 1951. In the 1950s the Anglo-American Corporation was setting itself up to assume control of most of the mining operations in southern Africa. In 1952 it produced 25 percent of South Africa's gold and 24 percent of its uranium, 43 percent of southern Africa's coal, 51 percent of Northern Rhodesia's copper, and sold 41 percent of the world's diamonds (Innes, *Anglo American,* 157).

48. "Report for the Festival Fair Committee on the Political Aspect in the Transvaal." Report from *Die Transvaler,* quoted in *The Star,* 13 July 1951.

49. "Report for the Festival Fair Committee on the Political Aspect in the Transvaal"; *Benoni City Times,* 13 July 1951; Lodge, *Black Politics,* 131–134.

50. "Report for the Festival Fair Committee on the Political Aspect in the Transvaal."

51. *The Star,* 11 July and 19 July 1952; *Cape Times,* 11, 18 and 19 July 1951; *Die Transvaler,* 18 July 1951; *Rand Daily Mail,* 18 July 1951; Thom to Pauw, 16 July 1951, US, Thom, Box 49; *Official Festival Programme,* 109, 119–123; Script for *"Historiese Optog—Streng Vertroulik"* [Historical procession—strictly confidential] containing alterations made in pen to typescript, UCT (ASL), McM: Van Riebeeck Festival.

52. *The Star,* 19 July 1951, 12 September 1951; *Rand Daily Mail,* 20 July 1951, 19 September 1951. *Cape Times,* 19 July 1951; *Die Burger,* 24 August 1951. For an account of the festival fair and the Chamber of Mines exhibit, see chapter 4.

53. *Die Burger,* 19 July 1951; *Die Vaderland,* 20 July 1951. *The Forum,* 27 July 1951 (quoting excerpts from *Die Transvaler); Die Transvaler,* 20 and 25 July 1951; For the different structural bases of Afrikaner nationalism in the Cape and the Transvaal, and early struggles between *Die Transvaler* and *Die Burger,* see O'Meara, *Volkskapitalisme.*

54. "Bedenkinge in verband met die historiese volksoptog: Van Riebeeck-fees (1952)," 4 August 1951, INCH, ATKV collection, PV 379, A11/13.

55. *Official Festival Programme,* 112–115, 132; Anna Neethling-Pohl to the Chairs, Pageant Sub-Committee, 5 May 1952, CA, A1657, vol. 322; *Die Transvaler,* 20 July 1951; *The Star,* 20 July 1951; *Souvenir Programme Johannesburg Van Riebeeck Festival and Mail Coach Celebrations* (Johannesburg: 1952); *African Mirror,* 28 January 1952, NFA, AM 657, FA 2442; Minutes, meeting pageant sub-committee, 13 December 1951, UCT (ASL), McM: Van Riebeeck Festival; "Die Optog van die Hede," SABC, 19/60–61 (52), 3 April 1952; *Daily Dispatch,* 9 September 1948. See chapter 5 for an account of local Van Riebeeck festivals and the journeys of the mail coaches.

56. *The Woman and Her Home,* 4, 39 (1952), 5, 50, 51, 53 and 74; *Cape Times,* 27 July 1951; *Nederlandse Post,* 15 April and 15 June 1952; Mees, *Maria Quevellerius,* 124; *Sarie Marais,* 26 September 1951; *Die Volksblad,* 20 September 1951. The other stamps in the set were a portrait of Jan van Riebeeck, the official seal of the Dutch East India Company, the arrival of Van Riebeeck's ships in Table Bay, and the painting of the landing by Bell (Supplement to *The South African Philatelist,* December 1951). Thanks to Andrew Bank for showing me the Exhibition Commemorative Cover that the post office issued with these stamps and a Van Riebeeck festival postmark dated 6.4.52.

57. Du Toit, "Women, Welfare and the Nurturing," 103–107, 201–203; personal visit to the Vrouemonument, Bloemfontein, April 1995; Kruger, "Gender, Community and Identity," 142–143; Van der Watt, "Art, Gender Ideology," 47–48; McClintock, *Imperial Leather,* 378; McClintock, "Family Feuds," 72; Hyslop, "White Working-Class Women," 60–65. For an account of images of male supremacy in the commemorative publications of the *Vrouemonument,* see Cloete, "The National Women's Monument Brochures." Kruger provides an extensive discussion of the emergence and the meaning of the *volksmoeder* discourse in the 1920s. Du Toit makes the very important point that this *volksmoeder* discourse was not merely a male imposition but was shaped by Dutch-Afrikaans–speaking women.

58. Kruger, "Gender, Community and Identity," 300–308; Hyslop, "White Working-Class Women," 63; Du Toit, "Women, Welfare and the Nurturing," 276–277; *Official Programme for the Inauguration,* 46–47. See also Delmont, "The Voortrekker Monument," 100. McClintock (*Imperial Leather,* 377–378) also argues that the *Gedenkboek* of the *Ossewatrek* (Commemorative Album of the Ox Wagon Trek) of 1938 presents, through its photographs, a similar imagery. Women in immaculate white bonnets and dresses "serve as boundary markers visibly upholding the fetish signs of national difference and visibly embodying the iconography of race and gender purity." For an account of the Afrikaner nationalist campaigns against the Garment Workers Union, see Witz, "Servant of the Workers," chap. 5.

59. "Bedenkinge in verband met die historiese volksoptog," 4 August 1951, INCH, PV 379, A11/13; *The Woman and Her Home,* March 1952, 61–62.

60. Mills, *First Ladies of the Cape,* 1, 2, 9, 16; A. de Villiers, "Ook Maria Van Riebeeck Moet Geeer Word," *Die Huisgenoot,* 7 March 1952; Leipoldt, *Jan Van Riebeeck,* 244; E. M. Berman, "City Will Honour Cape's First Lady," *Cape Times,* 27 July 1951; Wilson, *They*

Founded for the Future, 14, 16; A. de Villiers, "Eerste Vroue aan die Kaap," *Sarie Marais*, 26 September 1951; *Official Festival Programme*, 108.

61. *Sarie Marais*, 23 January 1952; 26 December 1951; Kruger, "Gender, Community and Identity," 244–247; O' Meara, *Volkskapitalisme*, 204; "Round the Tea-Table," *The Woman and Her Home*, March 1952, 51. O'Meara gives a brief and fascinating account of the emergence of the Rembrandt Corporation and its employment policies, 201–205.

62. Wilson, *They Founded for the Future*, 14; *Cape Times*, 18 August 1951; *Sarie Marais*, 20 February 1952; Mills, *First Ladies of the Cape*, 6.

63. *Cape Times*, 18 August 1951; Minutes of Meeting of Cape Town City Council, 27 September 1951, CA, 3/CT, 1/1/1/112; *Cape Times* and *Die Burger*, 21 July 1951; *Die Burger, The Star, Cape Argus*, 28 September 1951.

64. *Cape Times*, 12 January 1948.

65. *Cape Argus*, 12 October 1951; Thompson, "William Rowland Thompson," 144–145; Thompson, *The Story of a House*, 138–139; *Cape Times*, 5 and 11 October 1951; 21 July 1951.

66. "Reply to Criticisms of the Pageant," 24 August 1951; *Cape Times*, 11 October 1951, *Cape Argus*, 12 October 1951; *The Friend*, 18 August 1951.

67. "Reply to Criticisms of the Pageant"; *Cape Argus*, 1 August 1951; *The Friend*, 18 August 1951. For a brief biography of Kahn and an account of some of his speeches, see Saks, "Sam Kahn," 25–29.

68. *Cape Argus*, 25 August 1951; "Reply to Criticisms of the Pageant."

69. "Reply to Criticisms of the Pageant"; *Cape Times*, 20 September 1951.

70. "Reply to Criticisms of the Pageant"; W. E. G. Louw, "We Build a Nation," speech given at Humansdorp, 10 March 1952, US, 158.L.1.T. 12 (7).

71. *Cape Argus*, 24 August 1951; Agenda of meeting of the Central Organising Committee, Van Riebeeck Festival, 29 November 1951, US, Thom, Box 49.

72. Minutes of Meeting of Executive Committee of Van Riebeeck Festival, 3 November 1950, US, Thom, Box 49; *Cape Times*, 3 December 1951; *Natal Daily News*, 5 December 1951; Agenda van Vergadering van Sentrale Kommittee, 29 November 1951, US, Thom, Box 49; Rassool and Witz, "Constructing and Contesting," 450; *Daily Dispatch*, 9 September 1948; *Cape Times*, 11 October 1951; State Information Service, *South Africa's Heritage*, 66; *Rand Daily Mail*, 10 July 1951. This argument relies on Posel's analysis in *The Making of Apartheid* that there was no grand master plan for apartheid when the Nationalists took power in 1948 but that over the next ten years it was formulated through struggles over its different elements.

73. Agenda of meeting of the Central Organising Committee, Van Riebeeck Festival, 29 Nov 1951, US, Thom, Box 49; *Cape Times*, 11 October 1951; *Daily Dispatch*, 9 September 1948; Jeppie, "Historical Processes," 9; Du Plessis, *The Cape Malays*, 3, 37, 71–76, 3–7, 47–48; Van Riebeeck Festival Arts Committee, Catalogue, *Historical Exhibition of Arts, The Castle, Cape Town*, 9; Catalogue, *Exhibition of Malay Arts and Crafts*, 3; M. Masson, "Festival 'Merry-Go-Round,'" *Cape Times*, 20 March 1952; Agenda of meeting of the Central Organising Committee, Van Riebeeck Festival, 29 November 1951, US, Thom, Box 49. For the beginnings of the construction of a separate Malay identity, see Jeppie, "Historical Processes," 17–28.

74. Minutes, Meeting Cape Town City Council, 27 September 1951, CA, 3/CT, 1/1/1/112; *Die Burger, The Star, Cape Argus*, 28 September 1951; *Die Burger*, 28 September 1951; *Cape Times*, 3 October 1951; *Cape Argus*, 12 October 1951.

75. *Cape Argus*, 12 October 1951.

76. Ibid.; Minutes, Meeting Cape Town City Council, 12 October 1951, CA, 3/CT 1/1/1/112; *Cape Times,* 27 February 1951.

77. *Cape Times,* 27, 28, 29 February, 12 March and 9 April 1952; Minutes, Cape Town City Council, 30 October 1951, 29 November 1951, 24 December 1951, CA, 3/CT 1/1/1/112; 28 August 1952, CA, 3/CT 1/1/1/113; Mayor's Minute for the year ended 4 September 1953, including Report of the City Engineer for year ended 31 December 1952, CA, 3/CT 1/7/1/50; Muthien, "Pass Control and Resistance," 189; House of Assembly Debates, Hansard, 13 June 1951, 9397–9398, 9482–9483; *Cape Argus,* 28 September 1951.

78. *Die Burger,* 20 March 1952; *Cape Times,* 25 March, 17 April 1952. For a detailed account of all the controversies and issues surrounding the judgment, see Scher, "The Disenfranchisement," chap. 7.

79. *Cape Times,* 5 April 1952.

80. *Cape Argus,* 29 March 1952.

81. NFA, *Ons Nuus,* no. 38, 9 April 1952.

82. For an account of the boycott of the festival, see chapter 3.

83. *The Festival in Pictures,* 38–39; *Official Festival Programme,* 76–77; *Die Burger,* 3 April 1952, 10 April 1952; *Cape Times,* 3 April 1952; "Opnames van die Griekwas by die Van Riebeeckfees," 2 April 1952, SABC, 18/88–91.

84. *The Festival in Pictures,* 38–39; *Official Festival Programme,* 76–77; *Die Burger,* 3 April 1952; M. Masson, "Festival 'Merry Go-Round,'" *Cape Times,* 20 March 1952.

85. *Cape Times,* 3 April 1952; *Die Burger,* 3 and 10 April 1952.

86. *Cape Times,* 3 April 1952; *Die Burger,* 3 and 10 April 1952.

87. *Cape Times,* 29 March 1952; "Verslag oor die Optogte," 5 May 1952, CA, A 1657, vol. 322; *Die Burger,* 3 April 1952.

88. *Die Burger,* 5 April 1952; *Official Festival Programme,* 79, 100, 123.

89. "Volksoptog," 3 April 1952, SABC, 20/14/52.

90. *Official Festival Programme,* 122–123; *Cape Times,* 4 April 1952.

91. *Official Festival Programme,* 105–121; Millin, "Pioneers in Africa," 28.

92. *Official Festival Programme,* 116–117.

93. *Die Burger,* 7 April 1952.

94. Interview with Joe Almond; "*Die Transvaler se Van Riebeeck Bylaag,*" 4 April 1952.

95. *Cape Times,* 4 and 15 April 1952; *Cape Argus,* 4 and 7 April 1952; *Die Burger,* 7 April 1952; "Verslag oor die Optogte," 5 May 1952, CA, A 1657, vol. 322.

96. *Die Burger,* 10 and 11 April 1952; *Cape Times,* 12 April 1952; *Cape Argus,* 7 April 1952.

3. Contesting Van Riebeeck's Nation

1. Karis and Carter, *From Protest to Challenge,* Document 89: "Opening Address" at Annual Conference of the South African Indian Congress, by Dr. S. M. Molema, January 25, 1952, 477–478.

2. Ibid.

3. Ibid., Document 91: "April 6: People's Protest Day," flyer issued by the ANC (Transvaal) and the Transvaal Indian Congress, 482–483.

4. *The Torch,* 1 April 1952; Ntantala, *A Life's Mosaic,* 151–252.

5. Schrire, *Digging through Darkness,* 32.

6. Mamdani, *Citizen and Subject,* 96.

7. *The Festival in Pictures,* 38–39; *Official Festival Programme,* 76–77; *Die Burger,* 3 and

4 April 1952; *Cape Times,* 3 April 1952. The different ethnic events designed for the festival fair are elaborated in chapters 2 and 4.

8. Dutch Reformed Church, *Die Koms van Jan van Riebeeck,* 5–7; Duminy, *Twilight over the Tygerberg,* 108–109; *Cape Times,* 15 March 1952. See chapter 4 for a discussion of the fair, the costs involved, and the expectations relating to the size of the crowds.

9. *Cape Times,* 2 April 1952; Director, South African Mint, to Secretary for Education, Arts and Sciences, 27 August 1951, CAD, UOD 2229, Part 5, vol. E 357/11; *Cape Argus,* 12 September 1951; *Port Elizabeth Evening Post,* 12 September 1951; *The Torch,* 18 September 1951; *The Star,* 11 September 1951. For schools deciding not to accept the medallions because of the costs involved, see the various letters to the Secretary of Education from school principals between July and October 1951, CAD, UOD 2229, Part 5, E357/1.

10. Lewis, *Between the Wire and the Wall,* chap. 8, gives an extensive account of the events leading to the radicalization of the TLSA and the emergence of the Unity Movement. On the principles of the Unity Movement, see also Nasson, "The Unity Movement Tradition," 147–148. The ten-point program called for a full franchise for all, free and equal education, freedom of speech, freedom of movement, complete equality for all, inviolability of person, and a revision of the land question, the civil code, taxation and labor legislation in accordance with these rights. Rassool, "Going Back to Our Roots," 16; Lewis, *Between the Wire and the Wall,* 221; Rassool and Witz, "The 1952 Jan van Riebeeck Tercentenary Festival," 460; Alexander, "Non-collaboration in the Western Cape," 184–186; *The Guardian,* 10 April 1952. After the Van Riebeeck festival it was planned to extend the boycott to the segregated stands at Newlands rugby ground (*Eastern Province Herald,* 31 March 1952).

11. *The Torch,* 29 April 1952.

12. Quoted in Rassool, "Going Back to Our Roots," 29; *The Torch,* 9, 16, and 23 January 1950.

13. Quoted in *The Educational Journal* 13, no. 6 (March 1952); interview with G. H., a retired nurse, quoted in Nasson, "The Unity Movement," 160.

14. *The Educational Journal,* March, April, and May/June 1951.

15. *Oudtshoorn Courant,* 13 October 1951. See also *The Educational Journal,* October 1951, and *Diamond Fields Advertiser* and *Die Vaderland,* 9 October 1951, for reports on the regional conference. *The Torch,* 2 and 9 October 1951; 12 February 1952. For a discussion over the wage disparity between white and coloured teachers and its political ramifications, see Lewis, *Between the Wire and the Wall,* 234–235.

16. Lewis, *Between the Wire and the Wall,* 266–268; Lodge, *Black Politics,* 40; Karis and Carter, *From Protest to Challenge,* Document 97: "A Declaration to the People of South Africa from the Non-European Unity Movement"; Statement by the NEUM, April 1951, 497; *The Guardian,* 3 May 1951.

17. Quoted in Musson, *Johny Gomas,* 108; *The Guardian,* 11 October 1951. See also *Die Volksblad,* 5 October 1951; and *Die Burger* and *Natal Witness,* 6 October 1951.

18. *The Torch,* 9 October 1951.

19. Ibid.

20. Jeppie, "Historical Processes," 9, 62; *The Torch,* 9 October 1951.

21. Native Affairs Department Memo, c. 9 October 1951; "NAD Exhibition on Van Riebeeck Festival Fair," CAD, NTS 987/400; *Diocesan College Magazine* 37, no. 1 (March 1952); *The Guardian,* 27 September 1951. See chapter 4 for the costs involved in staging the NAD display at the festival fair and details of its contents. For populations statistics of Langa in the early 1950s, see Molapo, "Sports, Festivals and Popular Politics," 6; Musemwa, "History of Langa Township," 29–30.

22. "NAD Exhibition on Van Riebeeck Festival Fair," CAD, NTS 987/400; *The Guardian*, 27 September 1951; *The Torch*, 9 October 1951.

23. Musemwa, "History of Langa Township," 133–142; reply to I. D. Mkhize's circular letter by teachers belonging to the WPBTL, n.d., quoted in Molapo, "Sports, Festivals and Popular Politics," 128–129.

24. *The Guardian*, 10 April 1952; 27 September 1952. See Karis and Carter, *From Protest to Challenge*, Document 67: letter from I. B. Tabata to Nelson Mandela, 16 June 1948, 362–368.

25. *The Torch*, 9 October 1951.

26. Ibid.

27. Native Commissioner, Salt River, to Wyatt Sampson, 15 October 1951, CAD, NTS 9787 987/400; *The Torch*, 9 October 1951.

28. Mandela, *Long Walk to Freedom*, 142.

29. "Report of the Joint Planning Council of the African National Congress and the South African Indian Congress," submitted to the National Congress of the ANC, 15–17 December 1951, Wits (HP), ANC Collection, Ba2.

30. *The Guardian*, 27 December 1951; "Report of the Joint Planning Council."

31. *Natal Daily News*, 17 March 1952; *The Guardian*, 27 December 1951; Karis and Carter, *From Protest to Challenge*, "Opening Address" by S. M. Molema, Document 89, 477.

32. Department of Afrikaans Kultuurgeskiedenis, US, no. 214; *Official Festival Programme*, 99–123.

33. *Varsity*, 17 September 1951; *Grocott's Daily Mail*, 14 August 1951; *Official Festival Programme*, 122; The Wits University SRC turned the invitation from the festival committee on its head and agreed to participate "subject to their having full right to send a delegation representative of the University." Knowing full well that this delegation would include black students, and that the festival organizers wanted to place "native education" in a separate enclosure of the "tribal village," this effectively meant that the students from Wits would not participate (Minutes of SRC Executive Meeting, 23 November 1951; Minutes SRC Meeting, University of Witwatersrand, 29 November 1951, Wits [A]).

34. Correspondence between T. B. Davie and the Secretary for Education, October–December 1951, CAD, UOD 2227, E357, Part 2; *Festival Programme*, 122, 45; De Kock, *Our Three Centuries*, 5; *Varsity*, 17 September 1951;

35. *Varsity*, 9 August and 17 September 1951; UCT SRC Minutes, 12 September 1951, UCT (MA).

36. Interview with Ronald Segal; *Varsity*, 9 August 1951.

37. *Varsity*, 17 September 1951.

38. Interview with Leonard Thompson, conducted by Lynn Berat, 17–19; UCT Faculty of Arts, Board Minutes, 4 September 1950; 12 April 1951, UCT (MA); Minutes, UCT SRC meeting, 12 September 1951, UCT (MA); *Varsity*, 17 September 1951; *The Star*, 13 September 1951. South African history from 1788 was taught to about fifty students who chose to take the subject in their second year, following an introductory-level course in the first year of study which gave an "Outline of the History of Western Civilization," UCT Calendar, 1952.

39. Segal, *Into Exile*, 93.

40. Ibid.

41. Ibid., 93–94; *Die Volksblad*, 18 September 1951; Minutes, UCT SRC Executive, 3 October 1951; Minutes, UCT SRC, 21 September and 19 November 1951, UCT (MA). The following year Segal and Benjamin Pogrund, the Day Students Councilor, attempted to revive this anti-Van Riebeeck festival campaign by advocating a boycott of the university rag magazine, *Sax Appeal*, which had brought out a special festival issue. On the front cover, accom-

panying a pinup of a woman in a swimsuit, the festival logo was emblazoned. Among its contents were a message from the festival chair, cartoons on "*Die Volksplanting*" and "Van Riebeeck Revisits the Cape," and a mock replica of "Ye Olde Dutch Times." The SRC severely reprimanded Segal and Pogrund for their actions and at the same time reaffirmed its previous decision to support the festival. *Sax Appeal; Varsity,* 21, 28 March, 24 April 1952; Minutes, UCT SRC, 24 March 1952, UCT (MA).

42. *The Torch,* 9 October and 24 December 1951; 8 January 1952.

43. *Spark,* 11 April 1952.

44. Molapo, "Sports, Festivals and Popular Politics," chap. 2; *The Guardian,* 2 August 1951; *Varsity,* 24 April 1952; *The Guardian,* 4 October 1951. See also *The Guardian,* 4 January 1951, and *The Torch,* 18 March 1952, for critiques of the "coon carnival."

45. Joan Naidoo, "A Review of the Year," and Zubeida Moosa, "Social Club," *Durban Indian Girls High School Magazine* 9 (December 1952): 6, 21.

46. Samuel, *Theatres of Memory,* 5; *The Guardian,* 4 October 1951.

47. Edgar, "Festivals of the Oppressed," 19–30; *The Guardian,* 11 October 1951; 25 January 1951; Karis and Carter, *From Protest to Challenge,* Document 89, 480. *Cape Argus,* 4 October 1951; *Die Volksblad,* 5 October 1951; *Natal Witness,* 6 October 1951; *Die Burger,* 6 October 1951; Lewis, *Between the Wire and the Wall,* 267–268. A year later Eddie Roux, the author of *Time Longer Than Rope: A History of the Black Man's Struggle for Freedom in South Africa,* first published in 1948, suggested other individuals to be added to this list of historically significant figures: John Philip, Tengo Jabavu, the Schreiners, Bishop Colenso, John Dube, Johannes Nkosi, and Clements Kadalie (*The Guardian,* 14 February 1952).

48. Karis and Carter, *From Protest to Challenge,* Document 90: "Letter Replying to Letter from the Prime Minister's Office and Statement of Intention to Launch Defiance Campaign, from Dr. J S Moroka and W M Sisulu to Prime Minister D F Malan, February 11, 1952," 480–482.

49. "Catalogue of Oppressive Laws Made against Africans by the Union Government since 1910," speech delivered at the Elite Hall, Mafikeng, 21 February 1952, Wits (HP) ANC, Fb22. Who the speaker was is unclear from the notes for the speech that was delivered, but, given that Molema lived in Mafikeng, his extensive historical knowledge, and a tone similar to his SAIC address, it seems reasonable to assume that he was the speaker.

50. Molema, *Chief Moroka,* 191, 198–199.

51. Karis and Carter, *From Protest to Challenge,* Document 89, 478.

52. Ibid.

53. "Catalogue of Oppressive Laws: Resolution of the Non-European National Organisations," February 1952; "Africans of All Classes and Tribes Unite," Mafikeng, February 1952, Wits (HP), ANC, Fb22.

54. "Africans of All Classes and Tribes Unite," Mafikeng, February 1952.

55. *The Spark,* 11 April 1952; *The Guardian,* 10 April 1952.

56. *Eastern Province Herald,* 7 April 1952; *Alice Times,* 10 April 1952. See also *Daily Dispatch,* 8 April 1952.

57. *Official Festival Programme,* 89–90; *Die Burger,* 11 April 1952.

58. *Daily Dispatch,* 7 April 1952; *The Guardian,* 10 April 1952.

59. *Port Elizabeth Evening Post,* 7 April 1952; *Alice Times,* 10 April 1952; Lodge, *Black Politics,* 34; interview with Vuma Nkosinkulu; interview with Sipho Makalima; letter from N. B. Lukashe, *Evening Post,* 15 February 1952; *Rand Daily Mail,* 7 April 1952.

60. *The Torch,* 18 September 1951; 2, 9 and 16 October 1951; 5 and 19 February 1952; 18 March 1952.

61. Ibid., 5 February 1952; *The Educational Journal,* April 1952.

62. *Umthunywa,* 12 January 1952; *Eastern Province Herald,* 31 March 1952; The *Torch,* 5 February 1952.

63. *Umthunywa,* 12 January 1952; *The Guardian,* 27 December 1951. For further reports on Tsotsi's speech, see *Natal Witness,* 17 December 1951, and *The Torch,* 24 December 1951.

64. *Umthunywa,* 12 January 1952.

65. *The Torch,* 9 October 1951; 11 December 1951; 12 and 26 February 1952; 18 March 1952; *Cape Times,* 29 and 31 March 1952; Ntantala, *A Life's Mosaic,* 151. Secretary for Native Affairs to Secretary to the Treasury, 21 February 1952, CAD, TES 3973, F20/999/1; Memo to Under-Secretary Administration, NAD, from Wyatt Sampson, Liaison Officer, 12 November 1951, CAD, NTS 9787, 987/400.

66. Taylor, *The Role of the Missionaries; The Torch,* 29 April 1952.

67. Taylor, *The Role of the Missionaries;* Jaffe, *Three Hundred Years; The Torch,* 29 January–18 March 1952; 1 April 1952; *The Educational Journal,* February/March–May/June 1951; Jordaan, "Jan van Riebeeck"; Eddie Roux, "1652 and All That," *The Guardian,* 14 February to 17 April 1952; Melanchthon, "Three Centuries of Wrong"; For extended discussion on the Forum Club, see Rassool, "Going Back to Our Roots," 25–28.

68. *The Guardian,* 17 and 28 February 1952; *The Torch,* 29 January, 5 and 19 February 1952; Rassool and Witz, "Constructing and Contesting," 465–466.

69. Rassool and Witz, "Constructing and Contesting," 466.

70. Roux, "1652"; *The Guardian,* 14, 21, 28 February and 17 April 1952; Saunders, *The Making of the South African Past,* 134; Lalu, "Lived Texts," 148–149.

71. *The Torch,* 5, 12, 19 February and 18 March 1952; Young, *Colonial Desire,* 5. From the similarity between the series in *The Torch* and *Three Hundred Years,* it would seem that "Boycott" was a nom de plume for Hosea Jaffe.

72. Nasson, "The Unity Movement Tradition," 160; Molema, *The Bantu Past and Present,* 220; *Official Festival Programme,* 108–109; *Cape Times,* 4 August 1951. I do not go into the content of these books in detail as they have already been extensively dealt with by Saunders, *The Making of the South African Past,* chap.13; Rassool, "Going Back to Our Roots"; and Nasson, "The Unity Movement Tradition."

73. Nasson, "The Unity Movement Tradition," 161; Saunders, *The Making of the South African Past,* 137; A.F.S., "Book Review of 300 Years," *The Educational Journal,* April 1952, 8; quoted in letter from I. B. Tabata to Dora Taylor, 1 August 1953, quoted in Rassool, "Notes on Gender"; Taylor, *Role of Missionaries,* introduction; Jaffe, *Three Hundred Years,* introduction; *Cape Times,* 5 April 1952. Thanks to Ciraj Rassool for permission to use material from his conference paper.

74. Jordaan, "Jan van Riebeeck," 162, 158, 137.

75. *The Herschelian* 27 (December 1952): 12; Book Exhibition Committee Van Riebeeck Festival, *South Africa in Print,* front cover.

76. Nasson, "The Unity Movement," 157–159.

77. *Die Huisgenoot,* 11 April 1952.

78. Interview with M. S. "Cappy" Ndlumbini, conducted by Rochidi Molapo. Thanks to Rochidi Molapo for giving me access to his interviews. For attendance at the festival fair, see chapter 4.

79. *Die Huisgenoot,* 11 April 1952.

80. Ibid.; Jaffe, *Three Hundred Years,* 176; *The Torch,* 8 April 1952; Ntantala, *Life's Mosaic,* 152.

81. Jaffe, *Three Hundred Years,* 176.

82. Tabata, "Boycott as Weapon of Struggle," 197–198.

83. *The Guardian,* 10 April 1952; *The Torch,* 15 April 1952; interviews with Thami Mgijima, Langa and Constance Macozoma, Langa, conducted by Rochidi Molapo.

84. *Drum,* June 1952.

85. Ibid.; *Die Burger,* 10 April 1952.

4. "'*n Fees vir die Oog*"

1. Kapp, *Ons Volksfeeste,* 121; *African Mirror,* no. 647, 19 November 1951, NFA, FA 2511; *Die Burger,* 9 April 1952.

2. *Cape Times,* 5 March 1952; Nichols, *Representing Reality,* 12–13. A small selection of these newsreels dealing with the Van Riebeeck festival are *Ons Nuus,* no. 5, 22 August 1951; no. 16, 7 November 1951; no. 31, 20 February 1952; no. 35, 19 March 1952; no. 38, 9 April 1952; *African Mirror,* no. 637, 10 September 1951, FA 2558; no. 647, 19 November 1951, FA 2511; no. 658, 4 February 1952, FA 2580; 24 March 1952, FA 2624; *British Movietone News,* April 1952, FA 747, all in National Film Archives, Pretoria.

3. De Kock, *Our Three Centuries,* 23–24; *British Movietone News,* April 1952, NFA, FA 747; *Cape Times,* 4 August 1951.

4. Julian Sandler, "The Festival," *Rondebosch Boys' High School Magazine,* June 1952, 38.

5. *Byvoegsel tot Die Burger,* 8 March 1952.

6. Fiske, *Understanding Popular Culture,* 103–104. Barthes's dichotomy of readerly and writerly texts (*S/Z,* 3–6) is paralleled by Umberto Eco's use of closed and open texts. In a closed text "the reader supplies little to organize the text," whereas an open text "makes more complex demands upon the reader . . . [and] is seen differently by different readers at different times"; Smith, "Semiotics and Communication Theory," 205.

7. Fiske, *Understanding Popular Culture,* 104.

8. Ibid., 105; Fiske, "The Cultural Economy of Fandom," 37–39; Basie Hanekom interviews W. A. de Klerk about the Festival Fair, Feesplakboek II, SABC, 19/5–7 (52).

9. Opening of Van Riebeeck Festival Fair by E. G. Jansen, 13 March 1952, SABC, 19/62–5 (52); *Official Guide Book and Catalogue of the Van Riebeeck Festival Fair,* 25.

10. *Official Festival Programme,* 41, 23, 51, 81–89; *Het Kasteel De Goede Hoop,* guidebook for visitors to the Castle (Cape Town, n.d.), 5.

11. Ley and Olds, "Landscape as Spectacle," 194: Davison, "Material Culture, Context and Meaning," 171–172; Bourdieu and Darbel, *The Love of Art,* 112; Karp, "Festivals," 281–282; Ozouf, *Festivals and the French Revolution,* 11; Report of the General Manager of Railways and Harbours for the Year Ended 31 March 1952, UG 51/1952, 22.

12. This is based on reports and cartoons in the *Cape Times* and *Die Burger* on 6 and 7 March 1952.

13. This is based on reports in the *Cape Argus* on 7 March 1952 and the *Cape Times* on 8 March 1952. A great deal of debate exists over the nomenclature to use when referring to people who claim to be or are made out to be living descendants of the original huntergather communities of southern Africa. I do not intend to take a position in this difficult and sometimes heated discussion. Instead, in this book I opt to use the term "bushman," not because I think this is the correct terminology but because this is how the people who were taken from Namibia to be on display at the Van Riebeeck Festival Fair were named and stereotyped.

14. Based on an essay by T. Hughes and E. Atkinson (Std 5), "Beautiful Models at the

Van Riebeeck Festival," *The Beehive, Selborne Primary School Magazine* 2, no. 1 (East London, 1952): 7.

15. *Cape Times*, 10 April 1952; Goodwin, "The Van Riebeeck Festival Fair," 53; Karp, "Festivals," 282; *Cape Argus*, 12 April 1952; Kapp, *Ons Volksfeeste*, 122; Hughes and Atkinson, "Beautiful Models," 7; in Committee Minutes, Cape Town City Council, 27 March 1952, CA, 3/CT 1/1/1/113.

16. *Die Burger*, 9 April 1952; *Cape Times*, 7 April 1952.

17. *Die Burger*, 11 April 1952; *Cape Times*, 15 April 1952; Hughes and Atkinson, "Beautiful Models," 7. It seems that *Die Burger*'s correspondent was referring to the speech by Eric Louw, Minister of Economic Affairs, at the opening of the festival fair on 13 March 1952, SABC, 19/62–65 (52). These numbers are based on attendance figures that appeared in *Die Burger*, 15–31 March 1952; *Cape Times*, 17 March–15 April 1952; and *Cape Argus*, 31 March–8 April 1952. Of course, many people went to the fair more than once (such as the schoolchildren from East London), but it is impossible to tell how many. According to the *Cape Argus* (9 April 1952), "thousands of people had visited the Fair more than once."

18. *Cape Times*, 19 March 1952; *Cape Argus*, 19 March 1952; interview with Yvonne Taylor, visitor to festival fair; interview with Shirley Broomberg, visitor to festival fair; *Die Burger*, 3 and 5 March 1952. On organized school visits to the fair, see, for example, the *Wynberg Girls' High School Magazine*, no. 37 (1952); *Sea Point Magazine* 118 (1952); and *Rustenburg High School for Girls' Magazine* (1952). *Die Burger*, 3 April 1952, comments on the large numbers of children in attendance, and the *Cape Argus*, 14 April 1952, provides statistics of receipts.

19. *Cape Argus*, 14 April 1952; Financial Statement of the Van Riebeeck Fees, tot 30 Junie 1952, CA, A1646, vol. 339.

20. An account of these various plans can be found in Pinnock, "Ideology and Urban Planning," 150–168; *The Cape Town Foreshore Plan*, v, 39–41; Pinnock, "Ideology and Urban Planning," 152.

21. *The Cape Town Foreshore Plan*, 19, 12, 16, 19, 40; Pinnock, "Ideology and Urban Planning," 163; "Almal se Mikrofoon: Inlywing van die droogleggebde gebied by die stadsgebied van Kaapstad," 15 January 1951, SABC 21/49(51); Barnett, "The Planned Destruction of District Six in 1940," 17, 13; Minutes, Railway and Foreshore Special Committee, 27 June 1950, CA, 3/CT 1/5/19/1/3; Pinnock, "Ideology and Urban Planning," 152; Annual Report of Town Clerk for year ended 31 December 1951, in Minute of Mayor of Cape Town for year ended 5 September 1952, CA, 3/CT 1/7/1/49.

22. Memorandum to be submitted to the Minister of the Interior by the Cape Town Committee of the Van Riebeeck festival, 22 January 1951, A 1646, vol. 339; "Inlywing van die droogleggebde gebied," SABC 21/49(51); Report by City Engineer, Solly Morris, to members of the Van Riebeeck Committee, 19 January 1951, appendix C, memo to Minister of Interior from Cape Town Committee, A1646, vol. 339. Presumably the international situation referred to here is the Korean War.

23. *The Cape Town Foreshore Plan*, 1; Report by City Engineer, Solly Morris, to members of the Van Riebeeck Committee, 19 January 1951; *African Mirror*, no. 637, 10 September 1951, NFA, FA 253; *Ons Nuus*, no. 21, 12 December 1951, NFA; interview with C. Cilliers, assistant organizer, Van Riebeeck festival fair; Memorandum from Cape Town Committee to the Minister of the Interior, 22 January 1951, A 1646, vol. 339.

24. Financial Statement of the Van Riebeeck Festival, up to 30 June 1952, CA, A1646, vol. 339; *Cape Times*, 7 April 1952; *Guide Book Festival Fair*, 81.

25. *Guide Book Festival Fair*, 31; Minutes of Meeting of the Executive Committee of the

Van Riebeeck Festival, 3 November 1950, US, Thom, Box 49; Allwood, *The Great Exhibitions,* 152–153; Howell, "The Festival of Britain"; Cox, *The South Bank Exhibition,* 8; *Cape Times,* 5 April 1952.

26. *Guide Book Festival Fair,* 170, 59, 73.

27. Greenhalgh, *Ephemeral Vistas;* Breckenridge, "The Aesthetics and Politics of Colonial Collecting," 197; Bennett, "The Exhibitionary Complex," 76–80; Foucault, *Discipline and Punish,* 210; Davison, "Festivals of Nationhood," 16; Greenhalgh, *Ephemeral Vistas,* 89, 113. Bennett ("The Exhibitionary Complex," 78–81) argues that these exhibitions sometimes functioned both as spectacle and surveillance, citing the Eiffel Tower at the Paris exhibition of 1889 as a prime example of this.

28. Greenhalgh, *Ephemeral Vistas,* 88–89.

29. Hinsley, "The World as Marketplace," 351, 356; Mitchell, *Colonizing Egypt,* 1; Greenhalgh, *Ephemeral Vistas,* 97; Greenstein, "South African Studies and the Politics of Theory," 9; Bennett, "The Exhibitionary Complex," 92.

30. Greenhalgh, *Ephemeral Vistas,* 91; Corbey, "Ethnographic Showcases," 358, 342; Coombes, *Reinventing Africa,* 86, 89, 90; Memo by D. L. Smit, Secretary for Native Affairs, to the Minister of Native Affairs, RE: Application by Captain F. A. van der Loo for permission to take Natives to Holland, 8 May 1939, CAD, NTS 9629, 505/400; Capt F. A. van der Loo to D. L. Smit, Secretary for Native Affairs, 24 April 1939, CAD, NTS 9629 505/400; Memo by D. L. Smit to the Minister of Native Affairs, 8 May 1939, CAD, NTS 9629, 505/400.

31. *Empire Exhibition Souvenir Catalogue,* 129; Gordon, *The Bushman Myth,* 148; *Rykstentoonstelling Suid Afrika/Empire Exhibition South Africa,* 4–5; *Liberty Cavalcade,* front cover and 24; *Western Province Liberty Cavalcade,* map of Liberty Cavalcade, 41, 19. For accounts of the bushman display at the Empire Exhibition in Johannesburg, see Gordon, " 'Bain's Bushmen,' " and Hayes and Rassool, "Science and the Spectacle," 117–161.

32. *Western Province Liberty Cavalcade,* March 1944, Programme, 9, 7; *Liberty Cavalcade: Cape Midlands,* July–August 1943, 24.

33. Netherlands Van Riebeeck Committee, Cape Town, *Culemborg 1952* (Cape Town, 1952), 11. For a discussion on the distinction between nation/citizen, on the one hand, and country/residents, on the other, see Kratz and Karp, "Islands of 'Authenticity.' "

34. Opening of Festival Fair, 13 March 1952, Commentary by Pieter Naude, SABC 19/62–65(52); Begroting Bantoe Paviljoen: Van Riebeeckfees, n.d., CAD, NTS 9787 987/400, Part 1; Memorandum on Native Affairs Exhibit at Van Riebeeck Festival Fair, 2 November 1951, CAD, NTS 9787 987/400, Part 1; NAD statement to SAPA on the Bantu Pavilion, November 1951, NTS 9787 987/400, Part 1; Report and Proposals on Agenda Items, Pamphlet Collection, CAD, 448; *Cape Argus,* 22 March 1952; *Cape Times,* 19 March 1952.

35. Blaut, *The Colonizer's Model of the World,* 28; Roberts and Coleman, *Betterment for the Bantu,* 13–14, 4–6, 15, 11; Yawitch, *Betterment,* 10; Hofmeyr, "We Spend Our Years," 11; Thom, "Introduction," xxxix; Memorandum on Native Affairs Exhibit at Van Riebeeck Festival Fair, 2 November 1951, CAD, NTS 9787 987/400, Part 1.

36. Begroting Bantoe Paviljoen, n.d., CAD, NTS 9787 987/400, Part 1; *The Friend,* 23 November 1951; *Rand Daily Mail,* 23 November 1951; *Die Transvaler,* 12 September 1951; Secretary for Native Affairs, Memo, 19 February 1952, CAD, NTS 9787 987/400, Part 2; *Drum,* November 1951; Memo from Liaison Officer, Department of Native Affairs, W. A. Sampson, 4 August 1951, CAD NTS 9787 987/400, Part 1. The bushmen, as indicated earlier, were not displayed in the Bantu Pavilion. The reasons for this are discussed later in this chapter.

37. Note to the Accountant on the Departmental Exhibit, n.d., CAD, NTS 9787, 987/400, Part 1; Memorandum on Native Affairs Exhibit at Van Riebeeck Festival Fair Cape Town,

14 March–5 April 1952; 2 November 1951, CAD, NTS 9787, 987/400, Part 1; Liaison Officer, NAD, to Native Commissioner, Sibasa, n.d., CAD, NTS 9787, 987/400, Part 11; F. Rosdeth, Under-Secretary for Native Affairs, to Superintendent, Westfort Institution, 17 May 1952; F. Rosdeth to (a) Chief Native Commissioner, Pietersburg, 5 May 1952, (b) Chief Native Commissioner Pietermaritzburg, 1 May 1952 CAD, NTS 9787, 987/400, Part 11; Chief Native Commissioner Potchefstroom to Secretary for Native Affairs, 29 January 1952, CAD, NTS 9787, 987/400, Part 11; Onderhoud van Sekretaris van Naturellesake met kapteins en raadslede in diens by die Van Riebeeckfees, Woensdag 9 April 1952, NAD Memo, 28 April 1952, CAD, NTS 9788, 987/400, Part 111; NAD Statement to South African Press Association on Bantu Pavilion, November 1951, CAD, NTS 9787, 987/400, Part 1; Note on Demonstration of Operation of Bantu Authorities Act at Van Riebeeck Festival Fair, CAD, NTS 9787, 987/400, Part 11, 22 January 1952; Secretary for Native Affairs to Chief Inspector of Native Education, n.d., CAD, NTS 9787, 987/400, Part 11. F. Rosdeth, Under-Secretary for Native Affairs, to Sipho Mbete, Chairman Bensonvale School, 5 May 1952, CAD, NTS 9787, 987/400; *Guide Book Festival Fair,* 59; Secretary for Native Affairs to Organizer of Industrial Work, CAD, NTS 9787, NTS 987/400, Part 11, 31 January 1952; *Cape Times,* 20 March 1952.

38. G. M. Caine, Principal, Weaving School, St. Cuthberts, Tsolo, to A. W. Sampson, Liaison Officer, NAD, 12 February 1952, CAD, NTS 9787, 987/400, Part 11; Memo from A. W. Sampson, Liaison Officer, NAD to Secretary for Native Affairs, 19 February 1952; Telegram from Secretary for Native Affairs to Chief Native Commissioner, Kingwilliamstown, 3 March 1952, CAD, NTS 9787, 987/400, Part 11; P. S. Mbete, Principal, Bensonvale Institution, Herschel to A. W. Sampson, Liaison Officer, NAD, 25 February 1952, CAD, NTS 9787 987/400, Part 11; F. Rosdeth to Chief Magistrate Umtata, 15 March 1952, CAD, NTS 9787, 987/400, Part 11; NAD to Chief Magistrate, Somerset West, 22 March 1952, CAD, NTS 9788, 987/400, Part 111; Memo from Liaison Officer to Under-Secretary for Native Affairs, Staff for Van Riebeeck Festival Fair, 13 December 1951, CAD, NTS 9787, 987/400, Part 1; Secretary for Native Affairs to Secretary to the Treasury, 2 February 1953, CAD, TES 3973 F20/991/1; W. C. M. Smith to the Manager, Government garage, 22 March 1952, CAD, NTS 9788, 987/400, Part 111; F. Rosdeth to (a) Chief Native Commissioner, Pietersburg, 5 May 1952, (b) Chief Native Commissioner Pietermaritzburg, 1 May 1952, CAD, NTS 9787, 987/400, Part 11; Report and Proposals on Agenda Items, Pamphlet collection, CAD, 448; *Cape Times,* 19 March 1952.

39. *Guide Book Festival Fair,* 45–47; Donovan, *The Radio Companion,* 183; *Radio: Journal of the SABC* 1, no. 9 (23 June 1950): 7; *Radio* 1, no. 40 (26 June 1951): 23; Report and Proposals on Agenda Items, Pamphlet Collection, CAD, 448; interview with Rosalie Kleynhans; *African Mirror,* no. 622, 24 March 1952, NFA, FA 2624; M. Cresswell, "The Van Riebeeck Festival," *The Chronicle of Cambridge High School* (December 1952), 27.

40. NAD statement to SAPA on the Bantu Pavilion, November 1951, CAD, NTS 9787 987/400, Part 1; *Natal Daily News,* 5 December 1951; *The Diocesan College Magazine* 37, no. 1 (March 1952): 50; *Rand Daily Mail,* 13 March 1952; *Architect and Builder,* May 1952, 31.

41. *Guide Book Festival Fair,* 118; Netherlands Van Riebeeck Committee, *Culemborg 1952,* 6; *Architect and Builder,* 36; Begroting Bantoe Paviljoen: Van Riebeeckfees, n.d., CAD, NTS 9787 987/400, Part 1.

42. *Guide Book Festival Fair,* 185.

43. *Official Festival Programme,* 53; *Guide Book Festival Fair,* 41–42; *Architect and Builder,* 30; Netherlands Van Riebeeck Committee, *Culemborg 1952,* 12, 15, 16, 3; *Ons Nuus,* no 21, 12 December 1951, NFA FA 9623; Minutes of Meeting of Nederlands Van Riebeeck Commit-

tee 18 June 1951, ANV; Message from D. F. Malan to the Nederlandse Volk, 25 March 1952, SABC 28/52(52).

44. *Guide Book Festival Fair,* 41–43; Netherlands Van Riebeeck Committee, *Culemborg 1952,* 17; D. F. Malan's message to the Nederlandse Volk, 25 March 1952, SABC 28/52(52).

45. Roberts and Coleman, *Betterment for the Bantu,* 4; Begroting Bantoe Paviljoen: Van Riebeeckfees, n.d., CAD, NTS 9787 987/400, Part 1; *Guide Book Festival Fair,* 55.

46. Ashforth, *The Politics of Official Discourse,* 164; Eric Louw's opening speech, SABC 19/62–65 (52); *Guide Book Festival Fair,* 31; *Cape Times,* 5 April 1952.

47. Executive Committee Hall of Science, *Science Serves South Africa,* 59, v, vi, 44; Council for Scientific and Industrial Research, *Exhibit of the CSIR: Van Riebeeck Festival* (Pretoria: CSIR, 1952); Goodwin, "The Van Riebeeck Festival Fair," 53.

48. F. G. Holliman, Secretary to the Executive Committee, Liaison Officer, University of Cape Town, to Secretary, Department of Education, Arts and Science, 7 May 1952, CAD, UOD 2228 E357, vol. 4.

49. Crowd sizes at specific exhibits were reported, on an irregular basis, in the *Cape Times, Die Burger,* and *Cape Argus,* between 15 March and 14 April 1952.

50. *The Star,* 12 September 1951; Report for the Festival Fair Committee on the Political Aspect of the Transvaal, 1951, CA, A1646, vol. 339; *Rand Daily Mail,* 10 July 1951.

51. *The Mining Survey,* A Transvaal Chamber of Mines Publication, PRD series no. 2, 1, 1 (April 1946), inside front cover.

52. Paton, *South Africa,* 48; *The Mining Survey,* September 1953, 23.

53. Paton, *South Africa,* 49.

54. *The Mining Survey,* September 1953, 25, 20–22, 27; G. Rich (Form 111A) "Tribal Dances," *Athlone Girls' High School Magazine* (1952), 6; Paton, *South Africa,* 50; *Umteteli Wa Bantu,* 19 January 1952.

55. *The Mining Survey,* September 1953, 2, inside front cover, 1–2.The pavilion at the Rand Easter Show became a permanent exhibit at the Milner Park show grounds, which schools could visit to find out more about the mining industry.

56. *The London Magazine,* April 1952; Memo to the Under-Secretary for Native Affairs from E. W. Sampson, Liaison Officer, NAD, 21 September 1951, CAD, NTS 9787, 987/400 Part 1; *Cape Argus,* 13 March 1952; *The Mining Survey,* June 1952; *Transvaal Chamber of Mines, Van Riebeeck Festival Folder* (Johannesburg, 1952); *Cape Times Magazine,* 22 March 1952.

57. *The Mining Survey,* June 1952, 1–2; Perera, *A Guatemalan Boyhood,* 118; *Guide Book Festival Fair,* 81; interview with Rosalie Kleynhans.

58. *The Mining Survey,* June 1952, 4; *The London Magazine,* April 1952. This was part of the official discourse of "native policy" in the 1950s, which stressed the idea that "both black and white society are really composed of distinct (and emergent national) units"; Ashforth, *Official Discourse,* 153.

59. Rassool and Witz, "Constructing and Contesting," 455.

60. Creswell, "The Van Riebeeck Festival," 27.

61. Interview with Ronette Olivier; interview with Rosalie Kleynhans; *Die Burger,* 13 March 1952; J. Sandler, "The Festival," *Rondebosch Boys' High School Magazine* 46, no. 149 (June 1952): 38; *Cape Times Magazine,* 22 March 1952; Cresswell, "The Festival," 27; *The Mining Survey,* June 1952, 4.

62. *The Mining Survey,* June 1952, 1–2; *Cape Argus,* 14 March 1952; *Cape Times,* 7 April 1952; Transvaal Chamber of Mines, *Van Riebeeck Festival Brochure, African Contrasts,* 1–6, inside back cover. The Chamber, intensely aware of its public image, used an electronic eye

to keep an accurate count of the number of people who visited the pavilion (*Die Burger*, 13 March 1952).

63. Paton, *South Africa*, 49; *The Mining Survey*, September 1953, 25; *Cape Argus*, 5, 6, and 8 March 1952, 4 April 1952; *Cape Times*, 17 and 18 March 1952; W. Christians, "Die Lot Van Die Mynwerker," *Wesley Training School Magazine* (1952): 9; *Die Burger*, 5 and 18 March 1952. This is not to argue that the closer one comes to an essential experience the more real it becomes. Indeed, as Ciraj Rassool and I have argued elsewhere, it is this search for the experience of reality that forms the basis of one of the largest image-making productions, the tourist industry. See Rassool and Witz, "South Africa: A World in One Country," 335–371.

64. *Windhoek Advertiser*, 22 December 1951; *Van Riebeeck Festival South-West Africa, 1952*, Cape Town (1952); *Guide Book Festival Fair*, 55; *Cape Times*, 7 April 1952; *Die Burger*, 26 March 1952.

65. Gordon, *Bushman Myth*, 157, 161, 163; *Cape Times*, 29 March 1952; *Die Huisgenoot*, 21 March 1952; *Windhoek Advertiser*, 10 March 1952. (Thanks to Patricia Hayes for the last reference.) The concept of "a grand tradition of commissions" is borrowed from Ashforth, *Official Discourse*. Schoeman's hunting books for Afrikaans children, in particular his trilogy about Fanie who became the "*Grootwildjagter*" [Big Game Hunter] were reprinted almost every year between 1948 and 1960. See, for instance, *Fanie se Veldskooldae*, 7th printing (Johannesburg, 1960), and *Fanie Word Grootwildjagter*, 9th printing (Johannesburg, 1960).

66. Gordon, "Serving the Volk," 84–86. See also Sharp, "The Roots of and Development of Volkekunde," 19, who argues that the central notion in volkekunde is ethnos theory, "the proposition that mankind is divided into volke and that each volk has its own particular culture."

67. Schoeman, *Jagters van die Woestynland*, 190.

68. This quotation is from the translated version of Schoeman's *Jagters van die Woestynland*, 159. Col. P. I. Hoogenhout was administrator of South-West Africa; J. Neser, secretary of South-West Africa; and Major Naude, police commander of the territory. They had paved the way for Schoeman to enter the land of the "wild bushman" to do research for the book.

69. Ashforth, *Official Discourse*, 153; Gordon, *Bushman Myth*, 165.

70. Bruwer Blignaut, NAD Windhoek, to Wyatt Sampson, Liaison Officer, NAD, Pretoria, 12 September 1951, CAD, NTS 9787, 987/400, Part 1; summarized minutes of a committee meeting of provincial chief inspectors of Native education, 27 September 1951, CAD, NTS 9787, 987/400, Part 1; *Cape Times*, 29 March, 22 March 1952.

71. Memo from Minister of Native Affairs, H. F. Verwoerd, to Secretary of Native Affairs, W. M. Eiselen, 11 March 1952, CAD, NTS 9788, 987/400, Part 111; Secretary of Native Affairs to Secretary of Interior, c. 11 March 1952, CAD, NTS 9788, 987/400, Part 111; *South West Africa and the Union of South Africa*, 98.

72. *Cape Times*, 7 and 29 March 1952; *Die Huisgenoot*, 21 March 1952; *Die Burger*, 10 March 1952.

73. *Die Burger*, 8 and 10 March 1952; *Cape Argus*, 7 March 1952; *Die Huisgenoot*, 21 March 1952.

74. *Cape Times*, 27 March and 19 April 1952.

75. *Die Huisgenoot*, 21 March 1952.

76. *Die Huisgenoot*, 21 March 1952; *Cape Argus*, 12 March 1952; *Cape Times*, 19 March 1952; *Die Burger*, 8 March 1952; *Cape Times*, 27 March 1952.

77. *Cape Times*, 27 March 1952. The silencing of the processes of genocide in both popular representations and anthropological studies of the bushmen is a central point of Robert Gordon's study, *The Bushman Myth*.

78. *Cape Argus*, 8 April 1952; *Windhoek Advertiser*, 11 March 1952; *Cape Times*, 15, 18, 26 March and 1 April 1952; *Die Burger*, 17 March 1952; *Cape Argus*, 29 and 31 March 1952.

79. *Die Burger*, 15 March 1952; *The Torch*, 25 March 1952; *Cape Times*, 18 March 1952.

80. *Cape Argus*, 25 March 1952.

81. Ibid., 5 April, 21 March 1952; *Cape Times*, 20 March 1952; *The Torch*, 25 March 1952.

82. *Cape Argus*, 18 March 1952; *The Torch*, 18 and 25 March 1952; *The Guardian*, 27 March 1952; Rassool and Witz, "Constructing and Contesting," 465.

83. Interview with Yvonne Taylor; *Cape Times*, 3 April 1952; *Cape Argus*, 7 April 1952.

84. *Cape Times*, 7 and 15 April 1952.

85. Interview with Shirley Broomberg.

86. Interview with Yvonne Taylor.

87. D. Buxmann, "Die Jan van Riebeeck Feesskou," *The Wynberg Girls' High School Magazine* (1952), 33.

88. Fiske, *Reading the Popular*, 6; *Cape Times*, 7 and 12 April 1952. See also Ronald Walter's discussion on proposals by the Disney Corporation to build a history theme park, where he argues that the meanings audiences create for themselves must not be determined by "reading into" the images displayed (Walters, "In Our Backyard," 3–4).

5. Local and National Pasts

1. *The Star*, 11 July 1951; "Report of the Activities of the Mail Coach Organising Committee for the Van Riebeeck Festival," US, Thom, Box 49; letter to the *Rand Daily Mail*, 12 July 1951.

2. "Report, Mail Coach Organising Committee."

3. *Port Elizabeth Evening Post*, 8 January 1952; Departure of the Mail Coach from Ohrigstad, 4 January 1952, SABC 28/83-4(52).

4. Speech of D. F. Malan, at the start of the Van Riebeeck Festival, 4 January 1952, from Bloemrus Niewoudt, *Geskiedenis in Klank: Die Van Riebeeck Fees in Herennering Geroep*, 6 April 1976, SABC, T 76/54.

5. Departure of the Mail Coach from Ohrigstad, 4 January 1952, SABC 28/83-4(52); "Van Riebeeckfees Te Ohrigstad," memo issued by P. D. Rautenbach, Organising Secretary, Ohrigstad, 19 November 1951, CAD, BNS 1/1/741 342/73; Gwen Pritchard, "The Landing of Van Riebeeck," *Wynberg Girls' High School Magazine* (August 1952): 37.

6. "Report, Mail Coach Organising Committee"; Durban Festival Committee, *Van Riebeeck Tercentenary Celebrations Durban Festival*, 3, 13-21; *Souvenir Programme of the Johannesburg Van Riebeeck Festival and Mail Coach Celebrations*, Van Riebeeck Festival Committee (Johannesburg), 1952; *East London Daily Dispatch*, 23 February 1952; Speech of D. F. Malan, 4 January 1952, SABC, T 76/54; *Official Festival Programme*, 100, 88, 69; Suid-Afrikaanse Spoorwee en Hawens, "Verkeerswee: Die Verhaal van 300 Jaar van Vervoer in Suid Afrika" (1952); Speech of Dr. A. P. van der Merwe, Chair of the Van Riebeeck Festival Committee, at the start of the Van Riebeeck Festival, 4 January 1952, SABC, T 76/54.

7. The Departure of the Mail Coach from Ohrigstad, 4 January 1952, SABC 28/83-4(52); *Port Elizabeth Evening Post*, 8 and 9 January 1952; "Report, Mail Coach Organising Committee; notes from a meeting held in the Council Chamber, East London, 12 October 1951, to establish an East London Van Riebeeck Festival Committee, CA, 3 ELN, vol. 1439, Ref 50/2059.

8. Massey, "Places and Their Pasts," 186, 190; see also Driver and Samuel, "Rethinking the Idea of Place," v–vii.

9. "Report, Mail Coach Organising Committee"; *African Mirror*, no. 647, 19 November 1951, NFA, FA 2511. Another mail coach, "Durban," went through towns usually defined as being in the eastern Cape: Matatiele (although, somewhat controversially, in terms of the 1994 South African Constitution, it is placed in Kwazulu/Natal), Queenstown, Fort Beaufort, Alice, Uitenhage, and Uniondale. Because this chapter largely follows the route of the eastern Cape mail coach "Settlers," these towns have been excluded from the eastern Cape in this instance.

10. *Die Burger,* 9 April 1952; *Die Burger Voortrekkermonument-Byvoegsel,* 10 October 1949; "Die Pad Van Suid-Afrika: Ossewatrek van die Afrikaanse Taal en Kultuur Vereneging (SAS&H)," chart sponsored by Pegasus and Mobil Oil, on display in Cape Provincial Nature Conservation Museum, Cirtrusdal; McClintock, *Imperial Leather,* 377.

11. *Die Burger Voortrekkermonument-byvoegsel,* 10 December 1949; Witz, "Servant of the Workers," 268; McClintock, *Imperial Leather,* 376; Grundlingh and Sapire, "From Feverish Festival to Repetitive Ritual?" 20.

12. *Die Burger,* 9 April 1952; 10 December 1949; Rapportryers-Reelingskomitee, *Die Roeteboek Van Die Rapportryers,* v–3; *The Voortrekker Monument, Pretoria, Official Guide,* 69.

13. *Die Burger,* 9 April 1952.

14. Ibid., 4 April 1951; SAR&H "Verkeerswee: Die Verhaal van Vervoer"; *Die Burger,* 1 April 1952.; Van Riebeeckfees: Bou van die Poskoetse, 9 August 1951, SABC, 28/17–18 (51); *Pretoria News,* 18 August 1951; *Cape Times Week-end Magazine,* 19 April 1952; *Die Burger,* 1 March 1952; Arrival of the Mail Coaches in Cape Town, SABC, 18/76–83(52).

15. *Die Burger,* 1 April 1952; SAR&H, "Verkeerswee: Die verhaal van vervoer"; Anderson, *Imagined Communities,* 184; *Die Burger,* 1 April 1952.

16. Memorandum on Van Riebeeck Festival Local Committees, attached to letter from Pauw, Organising Secretary of the Van Riebeeck Festival, to Mayor of East London, 28 June 1951, General Purposes Committee Report, East London City Council, File 50/1756.

17. Ibid.

18. Minutes, Mail Coach Organising Committee, 2 April 1951, INCH, PV 379, A 11/13/1; De Kock, *Our Three Centuries,* 31; Memorandum on Van Riebeeck Festival Local Committees.

19. "Report, Mail Coach Organising Committee"; *Natal Mercury,* 31 January 1952; Minutes, Executive Committee Mail Coach Organising Committee, 21 January 1952, INCH, PV 379, A 11/13/1; Poskoetsfees Graaff-Reinet, 6 March 1952, SABC 28/80–82 (52); *Grocotts Daily Mail,* 21 February 1952; Script, "The Building of a Nation: Grahamtown's Contribution," Cory, MS 6442.

20. M. C. Botha to Mr. Gaum, 12 February 1952, INCH, PV 379, A 11/13/12; *Official Festival Programme,* 69.

21. Minutes, Mail Coach Organising Committee, 2 April 1951, INCH, PV 379, A 11/13/1.

22. *Daily Dispatch,* 17 April 1951; *Port Elizabeth Evening Post,* 6 July 1951.

23. Interview with Ronette Olivier, a visitor at the Van Riebeeck Festival.

24. Wilmot, *History of the Cape Colony,* vii; Lewis, *Founders and Builders,* 151.

25. Fairbridge, *A History of South Africa,* 203.

26. Skinner, *Geskiedenisleesboeke vir die Laer Skool,* 74, 104; Stockenstrom, *Handboek,* 182.

27. Notes on meeting to establish East London Van Riebeeck Committee, 12 October 1951, CA, 3 ELN, vol. 1439, Ref 50/2059.

28. Letter to pageant mistress, Anna Neethling-Pohl, from the Mayor of East London, E. H. Tiddy, 2 August 1951, CA, 3 ELN vol. 1439, Ref. no. 50/2059. The words in brackets are mine and are taken from the title of the novel by Georgette Heyer, published in 1940, about

Harry Smith, his fourteen-year-old "Spanish bride," Juanna, and the Peninsular Wars. See Hodge, *The Private World of Georgette Heyer*, 57–59.

29. Crais, *The Making of the Colonial Order*, 125; Lewis, *Founders and Builders*, 135, 153; letter from E. Tiddy to A. Neethling-Pohl, 2 August 1951, CA, 3 ELN, vol. 1439. Ref 50/2059.

30. *Van Riebeeck Festival Pictorial Souvenir; Official Festival Programme*, 110; Marquard and Mervis, *Blame It on Van Riebeeck*, 28. This satirical history of South Africa, which was originally produced for the Van Riebeeck Festival but came out later in the year, also ridicules the way the "Kaffir Wars" were depicted in South African history texts at the time. This satire highlighted the crude but at the same time legitimating imagery of colonial conquest pervasive in school history texts at the time of the festival.

31. *Official Festival Programme*, 120–122; A. Neethling-Pohl to E. Tiddy, 22 August 1951, CA, 3 ELN vol. 1439, Ref 50/2059.

32. "Report, Mail Coach Organising Committee"; letter from M. C. Botha to J. C. Pauw, 12 September 1951, INCH, PV 379, A 11/13/8; *Die Vaderland*, 28 March 1951.

33. SAR&H "Verkeerswee: Die verhaal van 300 Jaar van Vervoer"; Minute 8489 of the General Purposes Committee, East London City Council, 19 March 1951. The General Purposes Committee recommended to the Council that it resolve not to participate in the celebrations by providing a historic mail coach at an estimated cost of £800; letter from the General Organising Secretary of the Van Riebeeck Festival to the Mayor of East London, 28 June 1951, General Purposes Report Book, East London City Council, File 50/1756; *Die Oosterlig*, 1 June 1951; telegram from M. C. Botha to Paul Reyger, 5 June 1951, INCH, PV 379, A 11/13/8; letter from the Mayor of Port Elizabeth to the Mayor of East London, 19 June 1951, stating that his council has decided to donate £250 toward a stage coach and requesting East London Council to assist in raising the additional £550; General Purposes Committee Report Book, East London City Council, File 50/1756; Minute 9474 General Purposes Committee, East London City Council, 12 July 1951. The committee recommended to the council that it contribute £200 toward constructing a coach representing the eastern Cape; "Report, Mail Coach Organising Committee."

34. Minutes, Mail Coach Organising Committee, 25 May 1951, INCH, PV 379, A 11/13/1; letter from the mayor of Port Elizabeth to the mayor of East London, 19 June 1951, General Purposes Report Book, East London City Council, File 50/1756; letter from Pauw to M. C. Botha, 4 March 1952, INCH, PV 379, A 11/13/7(2).

35. "Report, Mail Coach Organising Committee"; *Umtata: Fragments of Its History and Growth*, comp. History Committee of the Umtata Van Riebeeck Festival Committee (1952), 9.

36. *Umtata: Fragments of Its History and Growth*, 9.

37. Ibid., 9, 8, 14.

38. Ibid., 15; Minutes of Meeting of Local Van Riebeeck Festival Committee, Umtata, 18 January and 7 February 1952, INCH, PV 379, A 11/13/7.

39. Letter from A. Snyman, *Ritmeester* on Routes 6 and 7 to the Secretary of the Native Affairs Dept., 3 December 1951, CAD, NTS 9787/400, Part 1; *Evening Post*, 5 March 1952; *Die Burger*, 8 March 1952.

40. Taylor, *A History of East London*, 5; Reader, *The Black Man's Portion*, 4. *Daily Dispatch East London Centenary Supplement* (1948), 66, 34, 4; *East London Centenary Official Souvenir Brochure and Programme* (East London, 1948), 154.

41. *Centenary Supplement*, 66, 42; *Centenary Programme*, 154

42. Taylor, *History of East London*, introductory message, 29.

43. Minkley, "Border Dialogues," 181–182, 179, 331, 325; Lodge, "Political Mobilisation," 320–323: *Daily Dispatch*, 5 April 1952.

44. *Daily Dispatch*, 1 March 1952; Minkley, "Border Dialogues," 356; Shingler, *Women of East London*, 47; interview with Robbie de Lange, Sr.; *Daily Dispatch*, 26 February 1952; *The Torch*, 11 March 1952.

45. "Finding a Future, Forgetting the Past" was the publicity caption for *Westward the Women*, a "gripping, outdoor drama" on circuit at the time, starring Robert Taylor and Denise Darcel, *Cape Times*, 5 March 1952; Mayor's Minute, 4 September 1952, Municipality of the City of East London, 36; *Daily Dispatch*, 26 February 1952.

46. *Souvenir of the Visit of the Settlers Mail Coach to King William's Town*, 26 February 1952.

47. Ibid., 6–7, 11.

48. *King William's Town Mercury*, 26 and 28 February 1952.

49. Ibid., 28 February 1952.

50. Ibid.

51. Maclennan, *A Proper Degree of Terror*, 23, 148; *Grocott's Daily Mail*, 26 February 1952.

52. Thomson, *A Short History of Grahamstown*, 15, 27–28, 30, 1, 32, 24.

53. South African Railways, "Grahamstown," 2; Thomson, *A Short History of Grahamstown*, 2, 23, 30; *Grocott's Daily Mail*, 27, 29 February and 3 March 1952; script of performance by Grahamstown Amateur Dramatic Society, "The Building of a Nation: Grahamstown's Contribution," 29 February 1952, Cory, MS 6442. As seen in chapter 1, this association between Van Riebeeck and the 1820 settlers was not a new one. The point I make here is that only in the 1950s did this idea firmly begin to take root, when the concept of a white settler nationalism was being broadly promoted through association with Van Riebeeck. This mutated tradition gained greater currency and definition in 1965 when the 1820 Settlers Memorial Museum was built and later in the 1970s with the establishment of the Settler Monument and the National Arts Festival (du Preez, *Museums of the Cape*, 18–22; Programme "Settlers Monument Festival," *Weekend Post*, 22 June 1974).

54. *Grocott's Daily Mail*, 17 and 14 January 1952; 9 April 1952.

55. Ibid., 21 February 1952, 3 March 1952; letter from A. Snyman, *Ritmeester* on Routes 6 and 7, to the Secretary of the Native Affairs Dept., 3 December 1951, CAD, NTS 9787/400, Part 1.

56. *Evening Post*, 5 March 1952.

57. Letter from M. C. Botha to A. Snyman and J. P. S. Botha, 5 March 1952; telegram from A. Snyman to M. C. Botha, 11 March 1952, INCH, PV 379, A 11/13/7(2).

58. *Evening Post*, 11 January 1952.

59. Ibid., 8 April 1952; *Eastern Province Herald*, 6 March 1952.

60. Ibid., 5 and 7 March 1952; *Evening Post*, 6 March 1952; Port Elizabeth Publicity Association, "Port Elizabeth: Your Passport to Sun, Fun and Friendliness," 1; Readers' Digest, *Illustrated Guides*, 30–31; Snook, *Eastern Province*, 3; *Eastern Province Herald*, 29 February 1952; Port Elizabeth and Grahamstown Publicity Associations, *Settlers Heritage* (pamphlet), n.d.

61. *Evening Post*, 7 March 1952, 5 March 1952; see also the editorial of the *Evening Post* on 12 December 1951; Snook, *Eastern Province*, 2–3.

62. "Report, Mail Coach Organising Committee"; *Official Festival Programme*, 69.

63. Ozouf, *Festivals and the French Revolution*, 127; *Lantern* 29, no. 3 (September 1980), Special Edition: Partners in Progress, 1820–1980, 1; see also Hockley, *The Settlers of 1820*.

64. *Official Festival Programme*, 113.

65. Letter from A. W. Burton to East London Town Clerk, 27 November 1951, CA, 3/ELN, vol. 1439, Ref 50/2059.

66. Ibid.; *Official Festival Programme*, 122; East London Mayor's Minute, 1952, 39; *Guide to Southern and Eastern Cape*, 46; *Ons Nuus*, no. 33, 5 March 1952, NFA.

Conclusion

1. Hansard, House of Assembly, 18 February 1952, 1350, 1353; 21 February 1952, 1586–87; Van Jaarsveld, *New Illustrated History*, 11, 104; Havinga, Robbertse, Roodt, and Stevens, *History for Std VI*, 66–72.

2. Webner, "Smoke from the Barrel of a Gun," 70–75; Chatterjee, *The Nation*, 6–7; Wade, "Introduction," xix.

3. Dwyer, "Interpreting the Civil Rights Movement," 661.

4. *Cape Argus*, 1 April 1992; *Cape Times*, 8, 28, and 30 April 1992; 7 April 1993; 7 April 1994; 8 September 1994; *Rapport*, 11 September 1994; *Cape Argus*, 30 September 1996; *Weekend Argus*, 5/6 October 1996; *Cape Times*, 15 October 1996; *Cape Argus*, 10 July 1992.

5. Grundlingh, "A Cultural Conundrum?" 103; Savage, "Life of Memorials," 18.

6. Letter from Mr. Gool to the Minister of Interior, 3 February 1953, CAD, BEP 321, G7/302. Thanks to Uma Mesthrie for this reference.

7. Werbner, "Smoke from the Barrel of a Gun," 73.

8. Speech delivered by Cyril Ramaphosa, Chairperson of the Constitutional Assembly, at Sharpeville, 10 December 1996, at the signing of the constitution. Thanks to the office of the Executive Director of the Constitutional Assembly for supplying me with a copy of this speech.

9. Gordon, Rassool, and Witz, "Fashioning the Bushman," 269. See also *Cape Argus*, 26 November 1993; and *Athlone News*, 15 May 1996.

10. Govender, Mynaka, and Pillay, *New Generation*, foreword; Stokes, *Enjoying History*, 36, 38, 48–49.

11. *Athlone News*, 15 May 1996; Programme for *Rosa*, presented by Bo-Kaap Productions at the Baxter Theater, University of Cape Town, May 1996.

12. Ward, "The '300 Years,' " 122, 101; *Cape Times*, 4 April 1994. See Ward, "The '300 Years,' " and Witz, Minkley, and Rassool, "Thresholds, Gateways and Spectacles," for the debate on the images constructed in this exhibition and how they were received.

13. SATV News, 15 May 1996; "Welcome to South Africa: A World in One Country," http://www.satour.org/TenReasons.html, accessed 11 May 2002.

14. C. Ramaphosa, speech delivered at the signing of the South African Constitution, Sharpeville, 10 December 1996.

15. Lodge, *Black Politics*, 43, 61; Pampallis, *Foundations of the New South Africa*, 197–198; Frederikse, *The Unbreakable Thread*, 52; Jaffe, *European Colonial Despotism*, 169.

16. Act No. 34 of 1995: Promotion of National Unity and Reconciliation Act, 1995, http://www.doj.gov.za/trc/legal/act9534.htm, accessed 11 December 2002; Statement of the President of the African National Congress, Thabo Mbeki, on the Report of the TRC at the joint sitting of the Houses of Parliament, Cape Town: 25 February 1999, http://www.gov.za/speeches, accessed 17 May 2002. See also Hendrik Coetzee, "Tirannie is nie verskoning vir apatie—Mbeki," *Die Burger*, 26 February 1999. Thanks to Brent Harris for this reference.

17. Text from traveling exhibition, "Our Struggle for Land," Cultural History Museum, April 1996; Clacherty and Ludlow, *Looking into the Past*, 126–129; Stokes, *Enjoying History*,

10–36; Grobler, Dhladhla, and Bagwandeen, *Fun and Facts*, 24; Marneweck, Sieborger, and Torr, *Making History*, 1, 91.

18. *Die Burger*, 19 October 1967. See also *Die Burger*, 1 and 6 September 1967, and *Cape Argus*, 27 November 1968.

19. Ladd, *The Ghosts of Berlin*, 11.

20. To Praise Him or to Bury Him?" *Cape Times*, 30 November 2001; "Van Riebeeck Gets His Day in Cape Town," *Cape Times*, 10 February 2002, IOL online, http://www.iol.co. za/index.php?set—id=1&click—id=13&art—id=ct20020210211223464M252562, accessed 17 May 2002; Müller, "Herdenkingsjaar 350."

21. M. Peters, "Van Riebeeck Celebrations Make a Small Bang," *Cape Argus*, 5 April 2002, IOL online, http://www.iol.co.za/index.php?set_id=1&click_id=13&art_ id=ct20020405210824361R120606, accessed 17 May 2002; D. Carew, "Not with a Bang, but a Whimper," *Cape Argus*, 6 April 2002, http://www.iol.co.za/index.php?set_id=1&click_ id=13&art_id=ct20020406193850710A510781, accessed 17 May 2002.

22. "To Praise Him or to Bury Him?" *Cape Times*, 30 November 2001.

Bibliography

Manuscript Sources

State Archives, Central Archives Depot (CAD), Pretoria

NATIVE AFFAIRS DEPARTMENT, NTS

Van Riebeeck Festival Fair, NTS 9787–88 987/400, Parts 1–3.
Application by Captain van der Loo for permission to take Natives to Holland, NTS 9629, 505/400.

DEPARTMENT OF PLANNING, BEP

Aaansoek om 'n groepsgebied in Distrik Kaapstad, Deel 3, BEP 321, G7/302.

PAMPHLET COLLECTION

Van Riebeeck Festival, P 448.

TREASURY DEPARTMENT, TES

Van Riebeeck Tercentenary Celebrations 1952: Participation by Government Departments in the Festival Exhibition, TES 3973, F20/999/1.

UNION EDUCATION DEPARTMENT, UOD

Driehonderdjaarige Herdenking van die landing van Jan Riebeeck, UOD 2227–9 E 357, Parts 1–5.

State Archives, Cape Archives Depot (CA), Cape Town

Journal of Cape Governors (Dag Register), VC 27.
K. Jeffreys Collection, A1657.
Minutes of Meetings of Cape Town City Council, 3/CT.
Minutes of Meetings of East London City Council, 3/ELN.
Resolusies van die Politieke Raad, C130.
T. E. Donges Collection, A1646.

University of Stellenbosch Document Centre (US)

Department of Afrikaans Kultuurgeskiedenis collection, 214.
H. B. Thom Collection, Box 49.

WEG Louw Collection, 158.

University of Bloemfontein, Institute for Contemporary History (INCH)

ATKV Collection, PV 379.
FAK Collection, PV 202.

University of the Witwatersrand, Historical Papers (Wits, HP)

ANC Collection.

University of the Witwatersrand Archives (Wits, A)

Minutes of University Council Meetings.
Minutes of Honorary Degrees Committee Meetings.

University of Cape Town Manuscripts and Archives (UCT (MA))

Bax collection, BC 1011.
Leo Marquard papers, BC 587.
UCT Faculty of Arts, Board Minutes.
UCT SRC Minutes.

University of Cape Town, African Studies Library (UCT [ASL])

McMillan Local History Collection, Van Riebeeck Festival (collection of material by
    Mrs. A. M. Preller—formerly Mrs. A. M. Viljoen—who was a member of the
    pageant sub-committee).

Algemeen Nederlands Verbond Library, Cape Town (ANV)

Minutes of meetings, ANV.
Nederlands Van Riebeeck Committee minutes.
Van Riebeeck Day 1938–1960 file.

Rhodes University, Cory Library (Cory)

Fort Hare SRC Minutes, MS 14788.
Minutes of Meetings of Rhodes University Senate, MS 17504.
Programme of entertainment at City Lords, Grahamstown, February 1952, PR 408.
Robert Henry Shepherd collection of papers on acceptance of invitation by Moderator
    of the Church of Scotland, MS 14,727.
Script of performance by the Grahamstown Amateur Dramatic Society, 29 February
    1952, MS 6442.

Durban Public Library (DPL)

Minutes of Durban City Council, Microfilm Collection.

East London City Council

General Purposes Committee Report Book File 50/1756.

National Library of South Africa, Cape Town (SAL)

EMC Loopuyt Collection, MSB 573.
Van Riebeeck Society Papers, MSB 633.
van der Spuy, P. *Dank-Altaar Gode Ter Eere Opgericht; Of Eene Plegtige Redenvoering Ter Gelegentheid Van's Ed Comp Hondert Jaarige Possessie des Gouvernements van Cabo de Goede Hoop, In eene Verklaaring en Toepassing van Pf. CXLVII; vers 12,13, en 14*, Gysb Tieme van Paddenburg and Abraham van Paddenburg, Utrecht (1753).

Printed Primary Sources

Official Records

The Cape Town Foreshore Plan: Final Report of the Cape Town Technical Committee, June 1947, Government Printer, Pretoria (1948).
Hansard: British House of Commons, 497 H.C. DEB. 5s, 3–21 March 1952.
Hansard: South African Parliament, House of Assembly, 31 October 1910–25 April 1911; 8 February 1951; 13 June 1951; 18 February 1952.
Leibrandt, Hendrik C. V. *Precis of the Archives of the Cape of Good Hope, December 1651– December 1653, Riebeeck's Journal & C*, Government Printers, Cape Town (1897).
Report of the General Manager of Railways and Harbours for the Year Ended 31 March 1952, UG 51/1952.
Roberts, H. R., and Coleman, K. G. *Betterment for the Bantu*, Native Affairs Department, Pretoria (1952).
Select Committee on Amendment of Public Holidays Act, 1925, SC.10–'25.
South West Africa and the Union of South Africa: The History of a Mandate, Government publication, Pretoria (ca. 1946).

Newspapers and Periodicals

Alice Times, Seymour and Peddie Gazette, 10 April 1952.
Athlone Girls High School Magazine, 1952.
Athlone News, 15 May 1996.
Benoni City Times, 13 July 1951.
Both Watches, 1952.
Byvoegesel tot Die Burger, 8 March 1952.
Cape Argus, 1 November 1910; 6 April 1921; 8 August 1938; 1, 24, 25 August 1951; 12, 18, 28 September 1951; 4, 12 October 1951; January–April 1952; 26 November 1968; 1 April 1992; 25 August 1992; 26 November 1993; 30 September 1996.
Cape Argus, Weekly Edition, 2 November 1910.
Cape Argus Union Jubilee Supplement, 28 May 1960.
Cape Times, 13, 19 May 1899; 1, 5 April 1902; 29, 31 October 1910; 7, 8 April 1921; 4, 5 January 1946; 7, 11, 27 February 1946; 21 March 1946; February–June 1947; 12 January 1948; 15, 17 December 1949; 6, 7 April 1950; 7 August 1950; 7 November 1950; 27 February 1951; 11, 18, 19, 21, 27 July 1951; 4, 18 August 1951; 20 September 1951; 3, 5, 11 October 1951; 3 December 1951; January–April 1952; 6 April 1971; 8, 28, 30 April 1992; 29 October 1992; 7 April 1993; 4, 7, 22, 27, 28 April 1994; 8 September 1994; 29 May 1996; 15 October 1996; 5 December 1996; 30 November 2001.

Cape Times Week-end Magazine, 19 April 1952.
Central America Report, Autumn 1991.
The Chronicle of Cambridge High School, December 1952.
The Coelacanth, April 1972.
Culemborgse Courant, 5 November 1992.
Diamond Fields Advertiser, 9 October 1951.
Die Burger, 8 April 1921; 7 April 1922; 9 August 1938; 10 December 1949; 6 April 1950;
        3 June 1950; 7 August 1950; 19, 21 July 1951; 24 August 1951; 28 September 1951;
        6, 16 October 1951; 1, 6 September 1967; 19 October 1967; January–April 1952;
        12 November 1986; 29 October 1992; 26 February 1999.
Die Huisgenoot, 28 January 1944; 3, 10, 17 March 1944; 9 April 1948; 7, 21 March 1952;
        11 April 1952; 4 October 1963; 26 February 1999.
Die Oosterlig, 1 June 1951.
Die Suiderstem, 6 April 1950.
Die Transvaler, 18, 20, 25 July 1951; 12 September 1941; 24 March 1952.
Die Transvaler se Van Riebeeck Bylaag, 4 April 1952.
Die Vaderland, 28 March 1951; 20 July 1951; 9 October 1951; 19 March 1952.
Die Volksblad, 15 December 1949; 18, 20 September 1951; 5 October 1951.
Diocesan College Magazine, March 1952.
Drum, November 1951, June 1952.
Durban Indian Girls High School Magazine, December 1952.
Eastern Province Herald, 11 August 1951; 21 December 1951; 5, 6, 7, 31 March 1952; 7 April
        1952.
East London Daily Dispatch, 9 September 1948; 17 April 1951; 11 August 1951; 23, 26 Feb-
        ruary 1952; 1, 24 March 1952; 4, 5, 7, 8 April 1952.
East London Daily Dispatch, Centenary Supplement, 1948.
The Educational Journal, 1951–52.
The Forum, 27 July 1951.
The Friend, 18 August 1951; 23 November 1951.
Grocott's Daily Mail, 13, 14 August 1951; 14, 17 January 1952; 21, 26, 27, 29 February 1952;
        3, 4 March 1952; 9 April 1952.
The Guardian, January 1951–April 1952.
The Herschelian, December 1952.
Het Nederduitsch Zuid-Afrikaansche Tydschrift, 1824–25, 1827.
Independent on Sunday, 14 July 1991.
Kaapsche Courant, 7 July 1804.
Kingswood College Magazine, 1952.
King William's Town Mercury, 26, 28 February 1952.
Lantern, September 1980.
Latinamerica Press, 17 October 1991.
The London Magazine, April 1952.
The Mining Survey, April 1946, June 1952, September 1953.
Natal Daily News, 28 August 1951; 13 November 1951; 5, 6, 8 December 1951; 17,
        24 March 1952.
Natal Daily News Learn Supplement, 5 July 1994.
Natal Mercury, 24 August 1951; 1, 7 November 1951; 14 December 1951; 31 January 1952.
Natal Witness, 6 October 1951; 17 December 1951.
Nederlandse Post, 15 April 1952; 15 June 1952.

New Internationalist, December 1991.
Newsweek, special Columbus issue (Fall/Winter 1991); 24 June 1991.
Oudtshoorn Courant, 13 October 1951.
Port Elizabeth Evening Post, 6 July 1951; 10, 11, August 1951; 12, 18 September 1951; 12 December 1951; 4, 8, 9, 11 January 1952; 1, 15 February 1952; 5, 6, 7, 29 March 1952; 2, 7, 8 April 1952.
Quarterly Bulletin of the South African Library, June 1952.
Queenstown Daily Representative, 11 August 1951.
Radio, 23 June 1950; 26 June 1951.
Rand Daily Mail, 10, 12, 18, 20 July 1951; 19 September 1951; 23 November 1951; 13 March 1952; 7 April 1952.
Rapport, 11 September 1994.
Rethinking Schools, Special Edition, September 1991.
The Rhodeo, 18 August 1951.
Rondebosch Boys' High School Magazine, June 1952.
Rustenburg High School for Girls Magazine, November 1952.
Sarie Marais, 1951–52.
Sax Appeal, March 1952.
The Scotsman, 4, 5, 17 March 1952.
Sea Point High Magazine, December 1952.
Selborne Primary School Magazine, The Beehive, 1952.
South African Commercial Advertiser, 3 April 1852.
The South African Outlook, 1 April 1952.
The South African Philatelist, December 1951.
Spark, 11 April 1952.
The Star, 14, 16 December 1949; 11, 13, 19, 20 July 1951; 10 August 1951; 11, 12, 13, 28 September 1951.
Sunday Times, 25 March 1952.
Time, 7 October 1991; 26 November 1992; 23 May 1994.
The Torch, January 1950–April 1952.
The Woman and Her Home, 1952.
The Wynberg Girls' High School Magazine, August 1952.
Umteteli Wa Bantu, 19 January 1952.
Umthunywa, 12 January 1952.
Varsity, 9 August 1951; 17 September 1951; 21, 28 March 1952; 24 April 1952.
Voortrekkermonument Byvoegsel, Die Burger, 10 December 1949.
Vrye Weekblad, 5 April 1991.
Weekend Post, 22 June 1974.
Weekend Argus, 11 September 1994, 5/6 October 1996.
Wesley Training School Magazine, 1952.
Windhoek Advertiser, 21, 22 December 1951; 10, 11 March 1952.
Zionist Record, 28 March 1952.

Electronic Sources

Act No. 34 of 1995: Promotion of National Unity and Reconciliation Act, 1995. http://www.doj.gov.za/trc/legal/act9534.htm, accessed 11 December 2002.
D. Carew, "Not with a Bang, but a Whimper," *Cape Argus* 6 April 2002,

http://www.iol.co.za/index.php?set_id=1&click_id=13&art_
id=ct20020406193850710A510781, accessed 17 May 2002.

M. Peters, "Van Riebeeck Celebrations Make a Small Bang," *Cape Argus* 5 April 2002,
IOL online, http://www.iol.co.za/index.php?set_id=1&click_id=13&art_
id=ct20020405210824361R120606, accessed 17 May 2002.

Statement of the President of the African National Congress, Thabo Mbeki, on the
Report of the TRC at the joint sitting of the Houses of Parliament, Cape
Town: 25 February 1999, http://www.gov.za/speeches, accessed 17 May 2002.

"Van Riebeeck Gets His Day in Cape Town," *Cape Times*, 10 February 2002, IOL
online, http://www.iol.co.za/index.php?set_id=1&click_id=13&art_
id=ct20020210211223464M252562, accessed 17 May 2002.

"Welcome to South Africa: A World in One Country," http://www.satour.org/
TenReasons.html, accessed 11 May 2002.

Audio-Visual Sources

National Film and Video Archives, Pretoria, NFA

AFRICAN MIRROR, A.M.

31 January 1951, FA 2477.
10 September 1951, FA 2558.
19 November 1951, FA 2511.
28 January 1952, FA 2442.
4 February 1952, FA 2580.
24 March 1952, FA 2624.

ONS NUUS

no. 5, 22 August 1951.
no. 16, 7 November 1951.
no. 21, 12 December 1951.
no. 31, 20 February 1952.
no. 33, 5 March 1952.
no. 35, 19 March 1952.
no. 38, 9 April 1952.

BRITISH MOVIETONE NEWS

April 1952, Part 3, including scenes from Van Riebeeck Festival in Cape Town, FA744.

UNTITLED "HOME MOVIES" ON THE VAN RIEBEECK FESTIVAL, FA 7495 AND FA 12291

South African Broadcasting Corporation, Sound Archives (SABC)

Almal se Mikrofoon: Inlywing van die droogleggebde gebied by die stadsgebied van
Kaapstad, 15 January 1951, 21/49(51).
Henry Howell, The Festival of Britain, 19 April 1951, T 51/16.
Van Riebeeckfees: Bou van die Poskoetse, 9 August 1951, 28/17–18(51).

Radio talk by T. E. Donges in connection with the Van Riebeeck Festival, 28 September 1951, 28/93(51).

The Departure of the mail coach from Ohrigstad, 4 January 1952, 28/83–84(52).

Basie Hanekom interviews W. A. de Klerk about the Festival Fair, Feesplakboek II, 19/5–7(52).

Opening of Van Riebeeck Festival Fair, 13 March 1952, 19/62–65(52).

Message from D. F. Malan to the Nederlandse Volk, 25 March 1952, 28/52(52).

Poskoetsfees Graaff-Reinet, 6 March 1952, 28/80–82 (52).

Arrival of the Mail Coaches in Cape Town, 31 March 1952, 18/76–83(52).

Opnames van die Griekwas by die Van Riebeeckfees, 2 April 1952, 18/88–91(52).

Volksoptog, 3 April 1952, 20/9–16(52).

Die Optog van die Hede, 3 April 1952, 19/60–61 (52).

Volksdanse van die stamlande, 3 April 1952, 20/7–8(52).

Massa vertoning van Volkspele, 3 April 1952, 19/51–52(52).

Landing van Van Riebeeck te Granger Bay, 5 April 1952 19/31–35(52).

Telephone conversation between André Huguenet (Van Riebeeck) and the mayor of Culemborg, 12 April 1952, 18/92–93(52).

Bloemrus Niewoudt, Geskiedenis in Klank: Die Van Riebeeck Fees in Herennering Geroep, 6 April 1976, T 76/54.

SATV Programs

"Royal Tour—Episode 1" and "Royal Tour—Episode 5," African Mirror Re-broadcasts, SATV, 1995.

SATV News, 15 May 1996.

TV1 religious program, *Koinonia,* 31 July 1994.

Ulibamba Lingashone, directed by Lesley Lawson; series director, Lawrence Dworkin; produced by Afravision, 1993.

Pamphlets and Brochures

Administrasie van die Suid-Afrikaanse Spoorwee en Hawens by Geleentheid van die Van Riebeeck Fees. *Verkeerswee: Die Verhaal van 300 Jaar van Vervoer in Suid Afrika Tesame met n Geillustrede Kaart.* N.p., 1952.

Barnard, E, ed. *Old Time Recipes.* Cape Town, 1952.

Board of Control of the Voortrekker Monument. *The Voortrekker Monument Pretoria: Official Guide,* Pretoria, n.d.

Bond, J. *The Saga of The Great Trek and Pictorial Record of Inaugural Celebrations at the Voortrekker Monument at Pretoria, December 1949. The Star,* Johannesburg, 1950.

Book Exhibition Committee Van Riebeeck Festival. *South Africa in Print.* Cape Town, 1952.

Bradlow, F. *The Van Riebeeck Society, 1918–1978.* Cape Town, 1978.

Cape Times. The Festival in Pictures. Cape Town, 1952.

Council for Scientific and Industrial Research. *Exhibit of the CSIR: Van Riebeeck Festival.* Pretoria, 1952.

Cox, I. *The South Bank Exhibition: A Guide to the Story It Tells.* London, 1951.

Dentz, O. *Geschiedenis Van het Algemeen Nederlands Verbond in Zuid-Afrika en in het Bijzonder van de Afdeling Kaapstad van 1908–1953.* Cape Town, 1953.

Durban Festival Committee. *Van Riebeeck Tercentenary Celebrations Durban Festival.* 1952.

Durban Visitors' and Tourists' Brochure. Durban: Godfrey-Alan, 1953(?).

Dutch Reformed Church. *Die Koms van Jan van Riebeeck: Ramp of Redding?* Cape Town, 1952.

East London Centenary Official Souvenir Brochure and Programme. East London, 1948.

Eastern Province Herald Historical Supplement to Commemorate Port Elizabeth Municipal Centenary, 16 July 1960.

Empire Exhibition Souvenir Catalogue. Johannesburg, 1936.

Executive Committee Hall of Science. *Science Serves South Africa: An Introduction to the Hall of Science Exhibition, Van Riebeeck Festival Fair.* Cape Town, 1952.

Exhibition of Malay Arts and Crafts. Catalogue. Cape Town: J. Ryan Pty, 1952.

Florida Museum of Natural History. *First Encounters: Spanish Explorations in the Caribbean and the United States.* Pamphlet for a traveling exhibit. Miami, 1992.

Grahamtown Publicity Association. *Grahamstown.* Pamphlet. Grahamstown, 1994.

Het Kasteel De Goede Hoop. Guidebook for visitors to the Castle. Cape Town, n.d.

History Committee of the Umtata Van Riebeeck Festival Committee. *Umtata: Fragments of Its History and Growth.* Umtata, 1952.

Liberty Cavalcade: Cape Midlands, July–August 1943—The Story of a Great War-time Achievement by the Home Front. Port Elizabeth, 1943.

Melanchthon. *Three Centuries of Wrong.* Karis and Carter Microfilm, Reel 15B, 2QV1:84/2, 1952.

Miami Space Transit Planetarium. "Showtime Schedule." December 1992.

Müller, Wilmer. "Herdenkingsjaar 350." Bylae by *Die Burger,* 22 June 2002. Cape Town: Blue Cape Media, 2002.

Netherlands Van Riebeeck Committee, Cape Town. *Culemborg 1952.* Cape Town, 1952.

Official Programme of the Van Riebeeck Festival. Cape Town, 1952.

Official Guide Book and Catalogue of the Van Riebeeck Festival Fair. Cape Town, 1952.

Port Elizabeth and Grahamstown Publicity Association. *Settlers Heritage.* Pamphlet, n.d.

Port Elizabeth Publicity Association. *Port Elizabeth South Africa Souvenir Brochure, 1860–1960.* Port Elizabeth, 1960.

Port Elizabeth Publicity Association. *Port Elizabeth: Your Passport to Sun, Fun and Friendliness.* Port Elizabeth: Image Marketing, 1993.

Programma Jan van Riebeeck Herdenking Culemborg, 10 May–2 June 1952.

Rapportryers-Reelingskomitee. *Die Rapportboek van die Rapportryers.* Johannesburg, 1949.

Readers' Digest. *Illustrated Guides to Southern and Eastern Cape, including the Garden Route, Country and the Wild Coast.* Cape Town, 1983.

Roux, M., and M. St. Leger. *Grahamstown: Fingo Village.* Johannesburg, 1971(?).

Rykstentoonstelling Suid Afrika/Empire Exhibition South Africa, Johannesburg September 1936–January 1937. Pamphlet. N.p., n.d.

Snook, J. *Eastern Province,* Cape Town (1975).

South Africa State Information Service. *South Africa's Heritage (1652–1952).* Pretoria, 1952.

South African Library Reprint Bulletin 35, no. 2 (1980).

South African Tourist Corporation. *South Africa's Transkei and East London: Information for the Visitor.* Johannesburg, n.d.
South African Railways and Municipality of Grahamstown. *Grahamstown: Eastern Province of the Republic of South Africa.* Johannesburg, 1963.
Souvenir of the Visit of the Settlers Mail Coach to King William's Town. 26 February 1952.
The Pageant of South Africa. October 1910 (Brochure).
Thom, H. B. *Van Riebeeck Day.* Cape Town, 1940/1941(?).
Thomson, D. H. *A Short History of Grahamstown.* Grahamstown, 1952.
Transvaal Chamber of Mines. *Van Riebeeck Festival Folder.* Johannesburg, 1952.
Van Riebeeckfeeskomitte van die N G Kerk. *Ons Bou 'n Nasie: Feesboodskap van ons Kerk en Volk.* Cape Town, 1952.
Van Riebeeck Festival South-West Africa 1952. Cape Town, 1952.
Van Riebeeck Festival—Fees (1952), Herdenkingsalbum—Pictorial Souvenir. Cape Town, 1952.
Van Riebeeck Festival Committee (Johannesburg). *Souvenir Programme of the Johannesburg Van Riebeeck Festival and Mail Coach Celebrations.* Johannesburg, 1952.
Van Riebeeck Festival Arts Committee. *Historical Exhibition of Arts, The Castle, Cape Town.* Catalogue. Cape Town, 1952.
Voortekker Monument Inauguration Committee. *Official Programme for the Inauguration of the Voortrekker Monument, 13 to 16 December 1949.* Pretoria, 1949.
Western Province Liberty Cavalcade, March 1944. Program. Cape Town, 1944.
Wilson, I. M. *They Founded for the Future.* Cape Town: Maskew Miller, 1952.
Yawitch, J. *Betterment: The Myth of Homeland Agriculture.* Johannesburg: South African Institute of Race Relations, 1982.

Secondary Sources

Selected Books

Aiken Hodge, Jane. *The Private World of Georgette Heyer.* London: Bodley Head, 1984.
Allwood, John. *The Great Exhibitions.* London: Studio Vista, 1977.
Altbach, Philip G., and Gail P. Kelly, eds. *Textbooks in the Third World: Policy, Content and Context.* New York: Garland, 1988.
Anderson, Benedict. *Imagined Communities.* London: Verso, 1993.
Appleby, Joyce, Lynn Hunt, and Margaret E. Jacob. *Telling the Truth about History.* New York: Norton, 1994.
Ashforth, Adam. *The Politics of Official Discourse in Twentieth Century South Africa.* Oxford: Oxford University Press, 1990.
Auerbach, Franz. *The Power of Prejudice in South African Education: An Enquiry into History Textbooks and Syllabuses in the Transvaal High Schools of South Africa.* Cape Town: Balkema, 1965.
Barker, Brian J. *Jan van Riebeeck: Die Nederlandse Vestiging Aan Die Kaap.* Cape Town: Struik, 1989.
Barthes, Roland. *S/Z.* Oxford: Basil Blackwell 1990.
Bennett, Tony. *The Birth of the Museum.* London: Routledge, 1995.
Bickford-Smith, Vivian. *Ethnic Pride and Racial Prejudice in Victorian Cape Town.* Johannesburg: Witwatersrand University Press, 1995.

Bickford-Smith, Vivian, and Elizabeth van Heyningen, eds. *The Waterfront.* Cape Town: Oxford University Press, 1994.

Blaut, James M. *The Colonizer's Model of the World: Geographical Diffusionism and Intellectual History.* New York: Guilford, 1993.

Boeseken, Anna. *Drie Eeue: Die Verhaal Van Ons Vaderland.* Volume 1. Cape Town: Nasionale Pers, 1952.

Bonner, Phil, Peter Delius, and Deborah Posel, eds. *Apartheid's Genesis, 1935–1962.* Johannesburg: Ravan/Witwatersrand University Press, 1994.

Botha, C. Graham. *Our South Africa: Past and Present.* Cape Town: United Tobacco, 1938.

Bourdieu, Pierre, and Darbel, Alain. *The Love of Art: European Art Museums and Their Public.* Cambridge: Polity, 1991.

Brown, Josh, et al., eds. *History from South Africa: Alternative Visions and Practices.* Philadelphia: Temple University Press, 1991.

Bulpin, Thomas V. *Discovering Southern Africa.* Cape Town: T. V. Bulpin, 1983.

Bushman, Claudia L. *America Discovers Columbus: How an Italian Hero Became an American Hero.* Hanover, N.H.: University Press of New England, 1992.

Callinicos, Luli. *Gold and Workers, 1886–1924.* Johannesburg: Ravan, 1980.

Carr, Edward H. *What Is History?* 2d ed. Harmondsworth: Penguin, 1987.

Carter, Paul. *The Road to Botany Bay: An Exploration of Landscape and History.* Chicago: University of Chicago Press, 1989.

Chatterjee, Partha. *The Nation and Its Fragments: Colonial and Postcolonial Histories.* Princeton, N.J.: Princeton University Press, 1993.

Clear, Dudley C. R. *Our Country: A Concise History of South Africa for Standard VI.* Cape Town: Juta, 1939(?).

Coetzee, James M. *White Writing: On the Culture of Letters in South Africa.* Johannesburg: Radix, 1988.

Cohen, David W. *The Combing of History.* Chicago: University of Chicago Press, 1994.

Comaroff, Jean, and John Comaroff, eds. *Modernity and Its Malcontents.* Chicago: University of Chicago Press, 1993.

Coombes, Annie. *Reinventing Africa: Museums, Material Culture and Popular Imagination in Late Victorian and Edwardian England,* New Haven, Conn.: Yale University Press, 1994.

Cory, George E. *The Rise of South Africa.* Vol. 3. London: Longman Green, 1919; Reprint, Cape Town: Struik, 1965.

Crais, Clifton. *The Making of the Colonial Order: White Supremacy and Black Resistance in the Eastern Cape, 1770–1865.* Johannesburg: Witwatersrand University Press, 1992.

Crump, Alan, Raymond van Niekerk, and Geoffrey Grundligh. *Public Sculptures and Reliefs in Cape Town.* Cape Town: Clifton, 1988.

Darnton, Robert. *The Great Cat Massacre and Other Episodes in French Cultural History.* Harmondsworth: Penguin, 1991.

de Kock, Victor. *Our Three Centuries.* Cape Town: Central Committee for the Van Riebeeck Festival, 1952.

de Lima, Joseph. *Geschiedenis van de Kaap de Goede Hoop.* Cape Town: South African Library Reprint, 1975 [orig. 1825].

Donovan, Paul. *The Radio Companion.* London: Harper Collins, 1991.

Duminy, Jacobus P. *Twilight over the Tygerberg.* Cape Town: J. F. Midgley, 1979.

du Plessis, Izak D. *The Cape Malays*. Cape Town: Maskew Miller, 1944.

du Preez, H. M. J., comp. *Museums of the Cape*. Cape Town: Department of Nature and Environmental Conservation, 1982.

du Toit, Andre, and Herman Giliomee. *Afrikaner Political Thought: Analysis and Documents, 1780–1850*. Cape Town: David Philip, 1983.

du Toit, S. J., and C. P. Hoogenhout. *Die Geskiedenis van Ons Land in die Taal van Ons Volk*. Pretoria: Human and Rousseau, 1975, facsimile edition of original, published in Cape Town: Die Genootskap van Regte Afrikaners, 1877.

Eco, Umberto. *Misreadings*. London: Picador, 1994.

Elliot, Arthur, and George Theal. *Our History in Picture*. Cape Town: Maskew Miller, ca. 1910.

Fairbridge, Dorothea. *A History of South Africa*. London: Oxford University Press, 1917.

———. *Gardens of South Africa*. Cape Town: Maskew Miller, 1924.

———. *Lady Anne Barnard at the Cape of Good Hope*. Oxford: Clarendon, 1924.

Fiske, John. *Understanding Popular Culture*. Boston: Unwin Hyman, 1989.

Foucault, Michel. *Discipline and Punish: The Birth of the Prison*. Harmondsworth: Penguin, 1987.

Fouche, W. *Groot Mannen Van Zuid-Afrika*. London: Longman Green, 1916.

Fowler, Cecil De K., and G. J. J. Smit. *New History for Senior Certificate and Matriculation*. Cape Town: Maskew Miller, ca. 1945.

Frederikse, Julie. *The Unbreakable Thread: Non-Racialism in South Africa*. Johannesburg: Ravan, 1990.

Freund, Bill. *The Making of Contemporary Africa*. London: Macmillan, 1984.

Frisch, Michael A. *A Shared Authority: Essays on the Craft and Meaning of Oral and Public History*. Albany: State University of New York Press, 1990.

Geertz, Clifford. *The Interpretation of Cultures*. New York: Basic Books, 1973.

———. *Local Knowledge: Further Essays in Interpretive Anthropology*. New York: Basic Books, 1983.

Gerstner, Jonathan N. *The Thousand Generation Covenant: Dutch Reformed Covenant Theology in Colonial South Africa, 1652–1814*. Leiden: E. J. Brill, 1991.

Gie, Stephanus F. *Geskiedenis Van Suid Afrika of Ons Verlede*. Stellenbosch: Pro Ecclesia, 1940.

Glassberg, David. *American Historical Pageantry: The Uses of Tradition in the Early Twentieth Century*. Chapel Hill: University of North Carolina Press, 1990.

Godlonton, Robert, comp. *Memorials of the British Settlers of South Africa, Being the Records of Public Services Held at Graham's Town and Port Elizabeth on the 10th of April and at Bathurst on the 10th of May, 1844, in Commemoration of the Landing in Algoa Bay and the Foundation of the Settlement of Albany, in the Year 1820*. Grahamstown, 1844; Cape Town: South African Library reprint series, 1971.

Golovnin, Vasilii M. *Detained in Simon's Bay: The Story of the Detention of the Imperial Sloop Diana, April 1808–May 1809*. Translated by L. Millner. Edited by O. H. Spohr. Cape Town: Friends of the South African Library, 1964.

Gordon, Robert. *The Bushman Myth: The Making of a Namibian Underclass*. Boulder, Colo.: Westview, 1992.

Govender, Suren P., Margaret Mynaka, and Gengs Pillay. *New Generation History Standard 10*. Durban: New Generation, 1997.

Greenhalgh, Paul. *Ephemeral Vistas: The Expositions Universelles, Great Exhibitions and World's Fairs, 1851–1939*. Manchester: Manchester University Press, 1988.

Greenstein, Ran. *Genealogies of Conflict: Class, Identity and State in Palestine/Israel and South Africa.* Hanover: Wesleyan University Press, 1995.

Grobler, J., Dhladhla, E. and D. R. Bagdwandeen. *Fun and Facts.* Pretoria: Via Afrika, 1996.

Guss, David M. *The Festive State: Race, Ethnicity, and Nationalism as Cultural Performance.* Berkeley: University of California Press, 2000.

Hamilton, Carolyn. *Terrific Majesty: The Powers of Shaka Zulu and the Limits of Historical Invention.* Cape Town: David Philip, 1998.

Havinga, J. F. E., G. F. Robbertse, A. G. Roodt, and T. W. Stevens. *History for Std VI.* Cape Town: Nasionale Boekhandel, n.d.

Hein George E. *Learning in the Museum.* London: Routledge, 1998.

Historisch Genootskap Gevesitgd te Utrecht. *Dagverhaal van Jan Van Riebeeck.* Utrecht: Keminck, 1884.

Hobsbawm, Eric, and Terence Ranger, eds. *The Invention of Tradition.* Cambridge: Canto, 1992.

Hockley, Harold E. *The Settlers of 1820: A Brief History for Use in Schools.* Cape Town: Juta, 1966.

Hofmeyr, Isabel. *"We Spend Our Years as a Tale That Is Told": Oral Historical Narrative in a South African Chiefdom.* Johannesburg: Witwatersrand University Press, 1993.

Hofmeyr, Nico. *Kykies vir Kinders Deel 1 (tot 1806): Leesboek oor Ons Geskiedenis vir Skool en Huis.* Cape Town: Nasionale Pers, 1921.

Hooper-Greenhill, Eilean, ed. *The Educational Role of the Museum.* 2d ed. London: Routledge, 1999.

Hope, C. D. *Our Place in History: A Comparative History of South Africa in Relation to Other Countries.* Cape Town: Juta, 1909.

Howes, Robert B. *Juta's History for Matriculation Students.* 4th ed. Cape Town: Juta, 1924.

Hulme, Peter. *Colonial Encounters: Europe and the Native Caribbean, 1492–1797.* London: Routledge, 1992.

Hunt, Lynn, ed. *The New Cultural History.* Berkeley: University of California Press, 1989.

Innes, Duncan. *Anglo American and the Rise of Modern South Africa.* Johannesburg: Ravan, 1984.

Jaffe, Hosea (Mnguni). *Three Hundred Years.* Cape Town, 1952. Reprint, Cumberwood: APDUSA, 1988.

———. *European Colonial Despotism: A History of Oppression and Resistance in South Africa.* London: Kamak House, 1994.

Jauss, Hans R. *Toward an Aesthetic of Reception.* Brighton: Harvester, 1982.

Jenkins, Keith. *Re-thinking History.* London: Routledge, 1991.

Johnstone, Frederick. *Class, Race and Gold.* London: Routledge, 1976.

Kammeijer, Heinrich W., and H. H. Van Rooyen. *Sketse Uit Die Vaderlandse Geskiedenis.* Part 2. Bloemfontein: Nasionale Pers, 1924.

Kannemeyer, John C. *Geskiedenis Van Die Afrikaanse Literatuur.* Pretoria: Academia, 1978.

Kapp, Pieter H. *Ons Volksfeeste.* Cape Town: Tafelberg, 1975.

Karis, Thomas, and Gwendolyn Carter, eds. *From Protest to Challenge: A Documentary*

History of African Politics in South Africa, 1882–1964, vol. 2. Paperback ed. Stanford, Calif.: Hoover, 1987.

Karstens, Mia C. *The Old Company's Garden at the Cape and Its Superintendents.* Cape Town: Maskew Miller, 1951.

Keppel-Jones, Arthur. *When Smuts Goes: A History of South Africa from 1952 to 2010.* Cape Town: The African Bookman, 2015, 1947.

Kirshenblatt-Gimblett, Barbara. *Destination Culture: Tourism, Museums, and Heritage.* Berkeley: University of California Press, 1998.

Kotze, Dirk J. *Professor H. B. Thom.* Stellenbosch: University of Stellenbosch, 1969.

Kratz, Corinne. *The Ones That Are Wanted: Communication and the Politics of Representation in a Photographic Exhibition.* Berkeley: University of California Press, 2002.

Krebs, Paula. *Gender, Race and the Writing of Empire: Public Discourse and the Boer War.* Cambridge: Cambridge University Press, 1999.

Ladd, Brian. *The Ghosts of Berlin: Confronting German History in the Urban Landscape.* Chicago: University of Chicago Press, 1997.

Le Roy Ladurie, Emmanuel. *Carnival: A People's Uprising at Romans, 1579–1580.* London: Scolar, 1979.

Leipoldt, C. Louis. *Jan Van Riebeeck: A Biographical Study.* London: Longman Green, 1935.

Lewis, Gavin. *Between the Wire and the Wall.* Cape Town: David Philip, 1987.

Lewis, Cecil. *Founders and Builders: South African History in Stories.* Part 1. London: Thomas Nelson, 1921.

———. *Juta's History and Civics for Junior Certificate (Departmental) Examination, Standards Vii and Viii.* Cape Town: Juta, 1922.

Lodge, Tom. *Black Politics in South Africa since 1945.* Johannesburg: Ravan, 1983.

Maclennan, Ben. *A Proper Degree of Terror: John Graham and the Cape's Eastern Frontier.* Johannesburg: Ravan, 1986.

Mamdani, Mahmood. *Citizen and Subject: Contemporary Africa and the Legacy of Late Colonialism.* Cape Town: David Philip, 1996.

Mandela, Nelson. *Long Walk to Freedom.* London: Abacus, 1995.

Marneweck, Lorraine, Rob Sieborger, and Louise Torr. *Making History.* Johannesburg: Heinemann, 1995.

Marquard, Leo, and Joel Mervis. *Blame It on Van Riebeeck.* Cape Town: Frederick Canon, 1952.

Maylam, Paul. *A History of the African People of South Africa: From the Early Iron Age to the 1970s.* Cape Town: David Philip, 1986.

McClintock, Anne. *Imperial Leather: Race, Gender and Sexuality in the Colonial Context.* New York: Routledge, 1995.

Mees, W. C. *Maria Quevellerius: Huisvrouw van Jan van Riebeeck.* Assen: Van Gorcum, 1952.

Mills, Gwen M. *First Ladies of the Cape.* Cape Town: Maskew Miller, 1952.

Mitchell, Timothy. *Colonizing Egypt.* Berkeley: University of California Press, 1991.

Molema, Silas M. *The Bantu Past and Present.* Edinburgh: W. M. Green, 1920.

———. *Chief Moroka: His Life, His Times, His Country and His People.* Cape Town: Methodist, 1951.

Molsbergen, Everhardus C. Godee. *De Stichter Van Hollands Zuid-Afrika Jan Van Riebeeck.* Amsterdam: S. L. Van Looy, 1912.

Moodie, Donald. *The Record; or, A Series of Official Papers Relative to the Condition and*

Treatment of the Native Tribes of South Africa. Amsterdam: A. A. Balkema reprint, 1960.

Moodie, Dunbar. *The Rise of Afrikanerdom: Power, Apartheid and the Afrikaner Civil Religion.* Berkeley: University of California Press, 1975.

Mostert, Dirk, comp. *Gedenkboek Van Die Ossewaens Op Die Pad Van Suid-Afrika.* Cape Town: Nasionale Pers, 1940.

Mostert, Noel. *Frontiers.* New York: Knopf, 1992.

Musson, Doreen. *Johnny Gomas: Voice of the Working Class.* Cape Town: Buchu Books, 1989.

Naidoo, Jay. *Tracking Down Historical Myths.* Johannesburg: Ad Donker, 1989.

Naipaul, Vidiadher S. *A Way in the World.* London: Minerva, 1994.

Newby, Eric. *The World Atlas of Exploration.* London: Artists House, 1975.

Newton Thompson, J. *The Story of a House.* Cape Town: Howard Timmins, 1968.

Nichols, Bill. *Representing Reality: Issues and Concepts in Documentary.* Bloomington: Indiana University Press, 1991.

Norval, Aletta J. *Deconstructing Apartheid Discourse.* London: Verso, 1996.

Ntantala, Phyllis. *A Life's Mosaic.* Cape Town: Mayibuye Books/David Philip, 1992.

O'Meara, Dan. *Volkskapitalisme: Class, Capital and Ideology in the Development of Afrikaner Nationalism, 1934–1948.* Johannesburg: Ravan, 1983.

———. *Forty Lost Years: The Apartheid State and the Politics of the National Party, 1948–1994.* Johannesburg: Ravan, 1996.

Olivier, Phillipus L., ed. *Ons Gemeentlike Feesalbum.* Cape Town: Nasionale Pers, 1952.

Opland, Jeff. *Xhosa Oral Poetry.* Johannesburg: Ravan, 1983.

Ozouf, Mona. *Festivals and the French Revolution.* Cambridge, Mass.: Harvard University Press, 1988.

Pagden, Anthony. *European Encounters with the New World: From Renaissance to Romanticism.* New Haven, Conn.: Yale University Press, 1993.

Pampallis, John. *Foundations of the New South Africa.* Cape Town: Maskew Miller Longman, 1991.

Paton, Alan. *South Africa and Her People.* London: Lutterworth, 1957.

Posel, Deborah. *The Making of Apartheid, 1948–1961: Conflict and Compromise.* Oxford: Oxford University Press, 1991.

Perera, V. *Rites: A Guatemalan Boyhood.* London: Fontana, 1987.

Pratt, Mary L. *Imperial Eyes: Travel Writing and Transculturation.* London: Routledge, 1992.

Reader, Desmond H. *The Black Man's Portion: History, Demography and Living Conditions in the Native Locations of East London, Cape Province.* Cape Town: Oxford University Press, 1961.

Reader's Digest. *Illustrated History of South Africa: The Real Story.* 2d ed. Cape Town: Reader's Digest, 1989.

Roodt, A. G., and T. W. Stevens, *History for Std VI.* Cape Town: Nasionale Boekhandel, n.d.

Rosenstone, Robert. *Visions of the Past: The Challenge of Film to Our Idea of History.* Cambridge, Mass: Harvard University Press, 1995.

Ross, Robert. *Beyond the Pale: Essays on the History of Colonial South Africa.* Johannesburg: Witwatersrand University Press, 1994.

———. *Status and Respectability in the Cape Colony, 1750–1870: A Tragedy of Manners.* Cambridge: Cambridge University Press, 1999.

Roux, Eddie. *S. P. Bunting: A Political Biography.* Cape Town: The African Bookman, 1944; Cape Town: Mayibuye Books, 1993.

———. *Time Longer Than Rope: The Struggle of the Black Man in South Africa.* London: Gollancz, 1948: Madison: University of Wisconsin Press, 1964.

Sale, Kirkpatrick. *The Conquest of Paradise: Christopher Columbus and the Colombian Legacy.* London: Hodder and Stoughton, 1991.

Samuel, Raphael. *Theatres of Memory.* London: Routledge, 1994.

Saunders, Christopher. *The Making of the South African Past: Major Historians on Race and Class.* Cape Town: David Philip, 1988.

Schapera, Isaac, ed. *David Livingstone South African Papers, 1849–1853.* Cape Town: Van Riebeeck Society Publications, 1974.

Schoeman, Pieter J. *Jagters van die Woestynland.* 4th impression. Cape Town, 1961. Translated as *Hunters of the Desert Land.* Cape Town: Howard Timmins, n.d.

Schrire, Carmel. *Digging through Darkness: Chronicles of an Archaeologist.* Johannesburg: Witwatersrand University Press, 1995.

Segal, Ronald. *Into Exile.* London: Jonathan Cape, 1993.

Sellar Walter C., and Robert J. Yeatman. *1066 and All That.* Harmondsworth: Penguin, 1967 [1930].

Shell, Robert. *Children of Bondage: A Social History of Slave Society at the Cape of Good Hope, 1652–1838.* Johannesburg: Witwatersrand University Press, 1994.

Shingler, J. P. *Women of East London, 1900–1979 (formerly Port Rex).* East London: J. P. Shingler, 1980.

Skinner, W. *Geskiedenisleesboeke vir die Laer Skool, Standerd V.* 2d ed. Cape Town: Juta, 1942.

Smith, Ken. *The Changing Past: Trends in South African Historical Writing.* Johannesburg: Southern Book Publishers, 1988.

Stockenstrom, Eric. *The New Matriculation History.* Stellenbosch: Pro Ecclesia, 1918.

———. *Beknopte Handboek in Aardrykskunde en Geskiedenis,* Standaard VIII. Stellenbosch: Pro Ecclesia, 1922.

———. *Handboek van Die Geskiedenis van Suid-Afrika.* Stellenbosch: Pro Ecclesia, 1922.

Stokes, J. *Enjoying History, Grade 5/Standard 3.* Pretoria: Kagiso, 1997.

Summerhill, Stephen J., and John A. Williams. *Sinking Columbus: Contested History, Cultural Politics, and Mythmaking during the Quincentenary.* Gainesville: University Press of Florida, 2000.

Taylor, Dora. *The Role of the Missionaries in Conquest.* Cumberwood: Unity Movement History series, 1986; first published, Johannesburg: SOYA, 1952.

Taylor, Mark H. *A History of East London.* East London, 1952.

Theal, George M. *History of South Africa, 1691–1795.* Vol. 2. London: Swan Sonneschein, 1888.

———. *Short History of South Africa (1486–1826) for the Use in Schools.* Cape Town: Darter Brothers and Walton, 1890.

———. *Primer of South African History.* London: T. Fisher Unwin, 1895.

———. *The Beginning of South African History.* London: T. Fisher Unwin, 1902.

———. *History of South Africa before 1795.* Vol. 3. Cape Town: C. Struik, 1964. Reprint from the 3d ed., London: George Allen and Unwin, 1922; 1st ed., 1907.

Theal, G., and Thomas Young. *Korte Geskiedenis van Suid Afrika.* Cape Town: Maskew Miller, 1909.

Theal, George M., and Arthur Elliot. *Our History in Picture.* Cape Town: Maskew Miller, ca. 1910.

Thom, Hendrik B., ed. *Journal of Jan Van Riebeeck*. Vol. 1 (for the Van Riebeeck Society). Cape Town/Amsterdam: A. A. Balkema, 1952.

Tunbridge, John E., and Gregory J. Ashworth. *Dissonant Heritage*. Chichester: Wiley, 1996.

Turner, Victor. *The Anthropology of Performance*. New York: Paj, 1987.

Unsworth, Barry. *Sacred Hunger*. Harmondsworth: Penguin, 1992.

Van Jaarsveld, Floris A. *New Illustrated History, Standard VI*. Translated by F. R. Metrowitch. Johannesburg: Voortrekkerpers, 1969.

Welch, Sidney R. *Europe's Discovery of South Africa*. Cape Town: Juta, 1953.

Wilmot, Alexander. *History of the Cape Colony for Use in Schools*. Cape Town: J. C. Juta, 1871.

Wilson, George H. *Gone Down the Years*. London: Allen Unwin, 1948.

Wolf, Eric. *Europe and the People without History*. Berkeley: University of California Press, 1982.

Worden, Nigel. *Slavery in Dutch South Africa*. Cambridge: Cambridge University Press, 1985.

Wright, Patrick. *On Living in an Old Country: The National Past in Contemporary Britain*. London: Verso, 1985.

Young, James E. *The Texture of Memory: Holocaust Memorials and Meaning*. New Haven, Conn.: Yale University Press, 1993.

Young, Robert. *Colonial Desire: Hybridity in Theory, Culture and Race*. London: Routledge, 1995.

Young, Thomas, and George Theal. *Short History of South Africa and Its People*. Cape Town: Maskew Miller, 1909.

Selected Articles and Book Chapters

A.H.S. "Charles Davidson Bell—Designer of the Cape Triangular Stamps." *Africana Notes and News* 11, no. 3 (June 1954): 81–87.

Alexander, Neville. "Non-collaboration in the Western Cape, 1943–1963." In *The Angry Divide*, ed. Wilmot James and Mary Simons, 180–191. Cape Town: David Philip, 1989.

Aveling, Marian. "Not the Bicentennial History." *Australian Historical Studies* 23, no. 91 (October 1988): 162–167.

———. "Writing History for Bicentenaries." *Australian Historical Studies* 23, no. 91 (October 1988): 103–113.

Bank, Andrew. "The Return of the Noble Savage: The Changing Images of Africans in Cape Colonial Art, 1800–1850." *South African Historical Journal* 39 (1998): 17–43.

Bennett, Tony. "The Exhibitionary Complex." *New Formations* 4 (spring 1988): 73–102.

Berghahn, Volker, and Hanna Schlisser. "Introduction: History Textbooks and Perceptions of the Past." In *Perceptions of History: International Textbook Research on Britain, Germany and the United States,* ed. Volker Berghahn and Hanna Schlisser, 1–16. Oxford: Berg, 1987.

Beyers, C. J. "Die Huisvesting van die Kaapse Argief." *South African Archives Journal* 1, no. 1 (1959): 46–54.

Bhabha, Homi K. "DissemiNation: Time, Narrative, and the Margins of the Modern Nation." In *Nation and Narration,* ed. Homi K. Bhabha, 291–322. London: Routledge, 1990.

Biersack, Aletta. "Local Knowledge, Local History: Geertz and Beyond." In *The New Cultural History,* ed. Lynne Hunt, 72–96. Berkeley: University of California Press, 1989.

Boeseken, Anna. "Theal as Baanbreker." *South African Archives Journal* 1, no. 1 (1959): 33–42.

Bole, I. V. "The Landing of Jan van Riebeeck." *Both Watches* (1952): 31–32.

Bommes, Michael, and Patrick Wright. "'Charms of Residence': The Public and the Past." In *Making Histories: Studies in History Writing and Politics,* ed. Centre for Contemporary Cultural Studies, 253–302. London: Hutchinson, 1982.

Bonner, Phil, Peter Delius, and Deborah Posel. "The Shaping of Apartheid: Contradiction, Continuity and Popular Struggle." In *Apartheid's Genesis 1935–1962,* ed. Phil Bonner, Peter Delius, and Deborah Posel, 1–41. Johannesburg: Ravan/ Witwatersrand University Press, 1994.

Bosman, F. C. L. "Joseph Suasso De Lima." In *Dictionary of South African Biography,* 1:219–220. Pretoria: HSRC, 1967.

———. "D. B. Bosman." In *Dictionary of South African Biography,* 3:83–84. Pretoria: HSRC, 1977.

Bourke, Paul. "Making Professional History." *Australian Historical Studies* 23, no. 91 (October 1988): 193–201.

Bozzoli, Belinda, and Peter Delius. "Radical History and South African History." In *History from South Africa: Alternative Visions and Practices,* ed. Josh Brown et al., 3–25. Philadelphia: Temple University Press, 1991.

Braun, Robert. "The Holocaust and Problems of Historical Representation." *History and Theory* 33, no. 2 (1994): 172–197.

Breckenridge, Carol. "The Aesthetics and Politics of Colonial Collecting: India at World Fairs." *Comparative Studies in Society and History* 31, no. 2 (April 1989): 195–216.

Bunn, David. "Relocations: Landscape Theory, South African Landscape Practice, and Transmission of Political Value." *Pretexts* 4, no. 2 (1993): 44–67.

Burgmann, Varity, and Jenny Lee. "Australia Deconstructed: Assembling *A People's History of Australia since 1788.*" *Australian Historical Studies* 23, no. 91 (October 1988): 153–161.

Burawoy, Michael. "The Extended Case Method." *Sociological Theory* 16, no. 1 (March 1998): 4–33.

Chartier, Roger. "Texts, Symbols and Frenchness." *Journal of Modern History* 57, no. 4 (December 1985): 682–695.

Clacherty, Glynnis, and Helen Ludlow, *Looking into the Past.* Standard 3/Grade 5. Cape Town: Maskew Millar Longman, 1995.

Clark, Charles Manning H. "Writing *A History of Australia.*" *Australian Historical Studies* 23, no. 91 (October 1988): 168–170.

Cochrane, Peter, and David Goodman. "The Great Australian Journey: Cultural Logic and Nationalism in the Postmodern Era." *Australian Historical Studies* 23, no. 91 (October 1988): 21–44.

Coetzee, Carli. "Visions of Disorder and Profit: The Khoikhoi and the First Years of the Dutch East India Company at the Cape." *Social Dynamics* 20, no. 2 (1994): 35–66.

Corbey, Raymond. "Ethnographic Showcases, 1870–1930." *Cultural Anthropology* 8, no. 3 (1993): 338–369.

Daniels, Kay. "Slicing the Past." *Australian Historical Studies* 23, no. 91 (October 1988): 130–140.

Darnton, Robert. "The Symbolic Element in History." *Journal of Modern History* 58, no. 1 (1986): 218–234.

Davies, J. H. "The Organisational Development of the Government Archives of the Union of South Africa." *South African Archives Journal* 2, no. 2 (1960): 7–19.

———. "Hendrik Carel Vos Leibrandt." In *Dictionary of South African Biography*, 2:385–387. Pretoria: HSRC, ca. 1972.

Davison, Graeme. "The Use and Abuse of Australian History." *Australian Historical Studies* 23, no. 91 (October 1988): 55–76.

———. "Festivals of Nationhood: The International Exhibitions." In *Australian Cultural History*, ed. S. L. Goldberg and F. B. Smith, 158–177. Cambridge: Cambridge University Press, 1988.

Delmont, Elizabeth. "The Voortrekker Monument: Monolith to Myth." *South African Historical Journal* 29 (November 1993): 76–101.

Driver, Dorothy. "A Literary Appraisal." In *The Cape Journals of Lady Anne Barnard, 1797–1798*, ed. Lewin Robinson A. M., 1–13. Cape Town: Van Riebeeck Society, 1994.

Driver, Felix, and Raphael Samuel. "Rethinking the Idea of Place." *History Workshop Journal* 39 (1995): v–vii.

Dubow, Saul. "Afrikaner Nationalism, Apartheid and the Conceptualization of 'Race.'" *Journal of African History* 33, no. 2 (1992): 209–237.

Dwyer, Owen. "Interpreting the Civil Rights Movement: Place, Memory, and Conflict." *Professional Geographer* 52, no. 4 (2000).

Edgar, D. "Festivals of the Oppressed." *New Formations* 3 (winter 1987): 19–30.

Edgar, J. "The Teaching of History by the Aid of Pictures." In A. Elliot and G. Theal, *Our History in Picture*, 9. Cape Town: Maskew Miller, ca. 1910.

Elphick, Richard, and Herman Giliomee. "The Origins and Entrenchment of European Dominance at the Cape, 1652–c. 1840." In *The Shaping of South African Society, 1652–1840*, 2d ed., ed. Richard Elphick and Herman Giliomee, 521–566. Cape Town: Maskew Miller Longman, 1989.

Elphick, Richard, and V. C. Malherbe. "The Khoisan to 1828." In *The Shaping of South African Society, 1652–1840*, 2d ed., ed. Richard Elphick and Herman Giliomee, 3–65. Cape Town: Maskew Miller Longman, 1989.

Etherington, Norman. "Old Wine in New Bottles: The Persistence of Narrative Structures in the Historiography of the Mfecane and the Great Trek." In *The Mfecane Aftermath*, ed. Carolyn Hamilton, 35–49. Johannesburg: Witwatersrand University Press, 1996.

Falassi, Alessandro. "Festival: Definition and Morphology." In *Time Out of Time: Essays on the Festival*, ed. Alesasandro Falassi, 1–10. Albuquerque: University of New Mexico Press, 1987.

Fiske, John. "The Cultural Economy of Fandom." In *The Adoring Audience: Fan Culture and Popular Media*, ed. Lisa A. Lewis, 30–99. London: Routledge, 1992.

Fitzpatrick, Peter. "'History—The Musical': A Review and a Retrospect." *Australian Historical Studies* 23, no. 91 (October 1988): 171–179.

Freund, Bill. "Past Imperfect." *Southern African Review of Books*, December 1988/January 1989, 9.

Goodwin, A. J. H. "The Van Riebeeck Festival Fair: Archaeology and Human Paleontology." *South African Archaeological Bulletin* 6, no. 25 (March 1952): 53–54.

Gordon, Robert J. "Serving the Volk with Volkekunde: On the Rise of South African

Anthropology." In *Knowledge and Power in South Africa*, ed. Jonathan Jansen, 79–97. Johannesburg: Skotaville, 1991.

Gordon, Robert J., Ciraj Rassool, and Leslie Witz. "Fashioning the Bushman in Van Riebeeck's Cape Town, 1952 and 1993." In *Miscast: Negotiating the Presence of the Bushmen*, ed. Pippa Skotness, 257–269. Cape Town: UCT, 1996.

Greenstein, Ran. "Racial Formation: Towards a Comparative Study of Collective Identities in South Africa and the United States." *Social Dynamics* 19, no. 2 (1993): 1–29.

Gregory, Damien. "A Red Light Day for Columbus." *History Today* 41 (December 1991): 5–6.

Grundlingh, Albert. "Politics, Principles and Problems of a Profession: Afrikaner Historians and Their Discipline, c. 1920–c. 1965." *Perspectives in Education* 12, no. 1 (1990–1991): 1–19.

Grundlingh, Albert. "A Cultural Conundrum? Old Monuments and New Regimes: The Voortrekker Monument as a Symbol of Afrikaner Power in a Postapartheid South Africa." *Radical History Review* 81 (fall 2001): 95–112.

Grundlingh, Albert, and Hilary Sapire. "From Feverish Festival to Repetitive Ritual? The Changing Fortunes of Great Trek Mythology in an Industrializing South Africa, 1938–1988." *South African Historical Journal* 21 (1989): 19–37.

Harries, Patrick. "Histories New and Old." *South African Historical Journal* 30 (May 1994): 121–134.

Hayes, Patricia, Jeremy Silvester, and Wolfram Hartman. "Photographs, History and Memory." In *The Colonising Camera: Photographs in the Making of Namibian History*, ed. Patricia Hayes, Jeremy Silvester, and Wolfram Hartman, 2–9. Cape Town: UCT, 1998.

Hayes, Patricia, and Ciraj Rassool, "Science and the Spectacle: Khanako's South Africa, 1936–1937." In *Deep hiStories: Gender and Colonialism in Southern Africa*, ed. Wendy Woodward, Patricia Hayes, and Gary Minkley, 117–161. Amsterdam: Rodopi, 2002.

Healy, Chris. "History, History, Everywhere but. . . . " *Australian Historical Studies* 23, no. 91 (October 1988): 180–192.

Hinsley, Curtis M. "The World as Marketplace: Commodification of the Exotic at the World's Columbian Exposition, Chicago, 1893." In *Exhibiting Cultures: The Poetics and Politics of Museum Displays*, ed. Ivan Karp and Steven D. Lavine, 344–365. Washington, D.C.: Smithsonian Institution, 1991.

Hofmeyr, Isabel. "Building a Nation from Words: Afrikaans Language, Literature and Ethnic Identity." In *The Politics of Race, Class and Nationalism in Twentieth Century South Africa*, ed. Shula Marks and Stanley Trapido, 95–123. London: Longman, 1987.

———. "Popularizing History: The Case of Gustav Preller." *Journal of African History* 29 (1988): 521–535.

Horner, Jack, and Marcia Langton. "The Day of Mourning." In *Australia 1938*, ed. Bill Gammage and Peter Spearritt, 28–35. Broadway: Fairfax, Syme, 1987.

Hunt, Lynn. "Introduction: History, Culture, and Text." In *The New Cultural History*, ed. Lynn Hunt, 1–22. Berkeley: University of California Press, 1989.

———. "Foreword." In *Festivals and the French Revolution* by Mona Ozouf, ix–xiii. Cambridge, Mass.: Harvard University Press, 1988.

Hyslop, Jonathan. "White Working-Class Women and the Invention of Apartheid: 'Purified' Afrikaner Nationalist Agitation for Legislation against 'Mixed' Marriages, 1934–1939." *Journal of African History* 36 (1995): 57–81.

Inglis, Ken S. "Australia Day." *Historical Studies Australia and New Zealand* 13, no. 49 (October 1967): 20–41.

James, Wilmot G., and Mary Simons. "Introduction." In *The Angry Divide*, ed. Wilmot G. James and Mary Simons, vii–xiii. Cape Town: David Philip, 1989.

Jeeves, Alan H. "Arthur Keppel-Jones: Scholar, Teacher, Liberal Intellectual." *South African Historical Journal* 32 (May 1995): 24–33.

Jordaan, Kenny. "Jan van Riebeeck: His Place in South African History." In *Contribution of Non-European Peoples to World Civilization*, ed. Maurice Hommel, 135–163. Johannesburg: Skotaville, 1988.

Karp, Ivan. "Festivals." In *Exhibiting Cultures: The Poetics and Politics of Museum Displays*, ed. Ivan Karp and Steven D. Lavine, 24–33. Washington, D.C.: Smithsonian Institution, 1991.

Kros, Cynthia. "Experiencing a Century in a Day? Making More of Gold Reef City." *South African Historical Journal* 29 (November 1993): 28–43.

Lalu, Premesh. "The Grammar of Domination and the Subjection of Agency: Colonial Texts and Modes of Evidence." *History and Theory* 39 (December 2000): 45–68.

Lee, Jenny. "Divers Observations on *Australians: A Historical Library*." *Australian Historical Studies* 23, no. 91 (October 1988): 141–152.

Ley, David, and Kris Olds. "Landscape as Spectacle: World's Fairs and the Culture of Heroic Consumption." *Society and Space* 6 (1988): 191–212.

———. "World's Fairs and the Culture of Consumption in the Contemporary City." In *Inventing Places*, ed. K. Anderson and F. Gale, 178–193. Melbourne: Longman Australia, 1992.

Lodge, Tom. "Political Mobilisation during the 1950s: An East London Case Study." In *The Politics of Race, Class and Nationalism in Twentieth Century South Africa*, ed. Shula Marks and Stanley Trapido, 310–335. London: Longman, 1987.

Mamdani, Mahmood. "Reconciliation without Justice." *Southern African Review of Books*, November/December 1996, 3–5.

Massey, Doreen. "Places and Their Pasts." *History Workshop Journal* 39 (1995): 182–192.

Matthews, Jill J. "'A Female of All Things': Women and the Bicentenary." *Australian Historical Studies* 23, no. 91 (October 1988): 90–102.

McClintock, Anne. "Family Feuds: Gender, Nationalism and the Family." *Feminist Review* 44 (summer 1993): 61–80.

McEwen, Ellen. "Australians 1888: A Very Personal View." *Australian Historical Studies* 23, no. 91 (October 1988): 114–120.

Meade, Theresa, and Margaret Hunt. "Editors' Introduction." Special Columbus issue, *Radical History Review* 53 (Spring 1992): 1–4.

Menso, H. S. N. "Van Riebeeck's Youth, Family and Medical Training." *South African Medical Journal* 26, no. 14 (5 April 1952): 273–278.

Merrington, Peter. "Pageantry and Primitivism: Dorothea Fairbridge and the 'Aesthetics of Union.'" *Journal of Southern African Studies* 21, no. 4 (December 1995): 643–656.

Millin, Sarah G. "Pioneers in Africa: Van Riebeeck and Rhodes." *Optima* 2, no. 1 (March 1952): 25–32.

Minkley, Gary, and Ciraj Rassool. "Orality, Memory and Social History in South Africa." In *Negotiating the Past*, ed. Sarah Nuttall and Carli Coetzee, 89–99. Cape Town: Oxford University Press, 1998.

Mintz, Steven. "Review of Robert A. Rosenstone, ed., *Revisioning History: Film and the Construction of a New Past*, Princeton: Princeton University Press, 1995." H-Net Book Review, 24 October 1995.

Murphy, John. "Conscripting the Past: The Bicentenary and Everyday Life." *Australian Historical Studies* 23, no. 91 (October 1988): 45–54.

Murray, Nancy. "Columbus and the USA: From Mythology to Ideology." *Race and Class* 33, no. 3 (1992): 50–65.

Nasson, Bill. "The Unity Movement Tradition: Its Legacy in Historical Consciousness." In *History from South Africa*, ed. Josh Brown et al., 144–164. Philadelphia: Temple University Press, 1991.

Ndlovu, Sifiso M. " 'He did what any other person in his position would have done to fight the forces of invasion and disruption': Africans, the Land and Contending Images of King Dingane ('the Patriot') in the Twentieth Century, 1916–1950s." *South African Historical Journal* 38 (May 1998): 99–143.

Newton, Thompson J. "William Rowland Thompson: Frontier Merchant." *Africana Notes and News* 17, no. 4 (December 1966): 139–166.

Olson, David R. "On the Language and Authority of Textbooks." *Journal of Communication* 30 (1980): 186–196.

Pinnock, Don. "Ideology and Urban Planning: Blueprints of a Garrison City." In *The Angry Divide*, ed. Wilmot G. James and Mary Simons, 150–168. Cape Town: David Philip, 1989.

Preller, J. F. "Archival Development in South Africa (1876–1922)." *SA Archives Journal* 3, no. 3 (1961): 43–47.

Ransby, Barbara. "Columbus and the Making of Historical Myth." *Race and Class* 33, no. 3 (1992): 79–86.

Rassool, Ciraj. "Foundations of a New Mythology." *South African Historical Journal* 26 (1992): 251–256.

———. "The Rise of Heritage and the Reconstitution of History in South Africa." *Kronos* 26 (August 2000): 1–21

Rassool, Ciraj, and Leslie Witz. "The 1952 Jan van Riebeeck Tercentenary Festival: Constructing and Contesting Public National History in South Africa." *Journal of African History* 34 (1993): 447–468.

Rassool, Ciraj, and Leslie Witz. " 'South Africa: A World in One Country': Moments in International Tourist Encounters with Wildlife, the Primitive and the Modern." *Cahiers d'Etudes africaines* 143, no. 36 (1996): 335–371.

Robinson, Jennifer. "(Dis)locating Historical Narrative: Writing, Space and Gender in South African Social History." *South African Historical Journal* 30 (May 1994): 144–157.

Rowse, Tim. " ' . . . Fallen among Gentlemen': A Memoir of the Bicentennial History Project." *Australian Historical Studies* 23, no. 91 (October 1988): 121–129.

Saks, David Y. "Sam Kahn and the Communist Party." *Jewish Affairs*, autumn 1996, 25–29.

Samuel, Raphael. "Local History and Oral History." *History Workshop* 1 (spring 1976): 191–207.

———. "Reading the Signs: II. Fact-Grubbers and Mind-Readers." *History Workshop Journal* 33 (1992): 220–251.

Savage, Kirk. "The Life of Memorials." *Harvard Design Magazine* (fall 1999): 14–19.

Searle, Richard. "Lewenskets van Mev. Cecile De Ridder, Leidster van ons eie Volkspele." Offprint from *Pretoriana* 103 (July 1993): 1–60.

Seed, Patricia. "On Caribbean Shores: Problems of Writing History of the First Contact." *Radical History Review* 53 (1992): 5–11.

Sharp, John. "The Roots of and Development of Volkekunde in South Africa." *Journal of Southern African Studies* 8, no. 1 (1981): 16–36.

Smit, D. E. "Introduction." In Joseph de Lima, *Geschiedenis van de Kaap de Goede Hoop*. Cape Town: South African Library Reprint, 1975.

Smith, Anna. "Introduction." In Donald Moodie, *The Record; or, A Series of Official Papers Relative to the Condition and Treatment of the Native Tribes of South Africa*, v–viii. Amsterdam: A. A. Balkema Reprint, 1960.

Smith, Robert R. "Semiotics and Communication Theory." *Journal of Communication* 30 (winter 1980): 205–210.

Souter, Gavin. "Skeleton at the Feast." In *Australians 1938*, ed. Bill Gammage and Peter Spearritt, 12–27. Broadway: Fairfax, Syme, 1987.

Spearritt, Peter. "Celebration of a Nation: The Triumph of Spectacle." *Australian Historical Studies* 23, no. 91 (October 1988): 3–20.

Sperber, Jonathan. "Festivals of National Unity in the German Revolution of 1848–1849." *Past and Present* 136 (August 1992): 114–138.

Tabata, Isaac B. (M. Temba). "Boycott as Weapon of Struggle." In *Contribution of Non-European Peoples to World Civilization*, ed. Maurice Hommel, 165–201. Johannesburg: Skotaville, 1988.

Thomas, Julian. "1938: Past and Present in an Elaborate Anniversary." *Australian Historical Studies* 23, no. 91 (October 1988): 77–89.

Treaty 88 Campaign. "Aboriginal Sovereignty—Never Ceded." *Australian Historical Studies* 23, no. 91 (October 1988): 1–2.

van Luttervelt, R. "Het Uiterlijk van Jan van Riebeeck in De Volksverbeelding." *Nederlandse Post*, 15 March 1952, 2–4.

Viola, Herman J. "Seeds of Change." In *Seeds of Change: Five Hundred Years since Columbus*, ed. Herman J. Viola and Carolyn Margolis, 11–15. Washington, D.C.: Smithsonian Institution, 1991.

Wade, Jean-Philippe. "Introduction." In Johan van Wyk, *Constructs of Identity and Difference in South African Literature*. Durban: CSSAL, 1995.

Walters, R. G. "In Our Backyard." *Perspectives: American Historical Association Newsletter* 33, no. 3 (March 1995): 3–4.

Ward, Kerry. "The '300 Years: The Making of Cape Muslim Culture' Exhibition Cape Town, April 1994: Liberating the Castle?" *Social Dynamics* 21, no. 1 (winter 1995): 96–131.

Webner, Richard. "Smoke from the Barrel of a Gun: Postwars of the Dead, Memory and Reinscription in Zimbabwe." In *Memory and the Postcolony: African Anthropology and the Critique of Power*, ed. Richard Webner, 71–102. London: Zed, 1998.

White, Jerry. "Beyond Autobiography." In *People's History and Socialist Theory*, ed. Raphael Samuel, 33–42. London: Routledge, 1981.

Witz, Leslie, and Carolyn Hamilton. "Reaping the Whirlwind: The Reader's Digest *Illustrated History of South Africa* and Changing Popular Perceptions of History." *South African Historical Journal* 24 (1991): 185–202.

Witz, Leslie. "'n Fees vir die Oog': Looking in on the 1952 Jan van Riebeeck Tercentenary Festival Fair in Cape Town." *South African Historical Journal* 29 (November 1993): 5–27.

———. "From Langa Market Hall and Rhodes' Estate to the Grand Parade and the Fore-shore: Contesting Van Riebeeck's Cape Town," *Kronos* 25 (1998/99): 187–206.

———. "Beyond Van Riebeeck." In *Senses of Culture*, ed. Sarah Nutall and Cheryl-Anne Michael, 318–343. Cape Town: Oxford University Press, 2000.

Worden, Nigel, and Elizabeth van Heyningen. "Signs of the Times: Tourism and Public History at Cape Town's Victoria and Alfred Waterfront." *Cahiers d'Etudes africaines* 36, nos. 1–2 (1996): 215–236.

Worpole, Ken. "A Ghostly Pavement: The Political Implications of Local Working-Class History." In *People's History and Socialist Theory*, ed. Raphael Samuel, 22–32. London: Routledge, 1981.

Yeo, Stephen. "The Politics of Community Publications." In *People's History and Socialist Theory*, ed. Raphael Samuel, 42–48. London: Routledge, 1981.

Unpublished Articles, Dissertations, and Theses

Bam, June. "The Development of a New History Curriculum For the Secondary Level in South Africa." M.Ed. thesis, University of Cape Town, 1990.

Bank, Andrew. "Liberals and Their Enemies: Racial Ideology at the Cape of Good Hope, 1820–1950." Ph.D. diss., Cambridge University, 1985.

———. "The Great Debate and the Origins of South African Historiography." Paper presented at *South African Historical Society Conference*, Grahamstown, July 1995.

Barnett, Naomi. "The Planned Destruction of District Six in 1940." Paper presented at University of Cape Town History Workshop, November 1991.

Bradlow, Frank, and Edna Bradlow. "The English Vision of the Cape Prior to 1875." Centre for Extra Mural Studies, mimeo, University of Cape Town, 1984.

Cloete, Elsie. "The National Women's Monument Brochures: A Rhetoric of Male Supremacy." Paper presented at *Myths, Monuments, Museums: New Premises?* Conference, University of Witwatersrand, 16–18 July 1992.

Comaroff, Jean. "The Empire's Old Clothes: Fashioning the Colonial Subject." Paper presented at the South African and Contemporary History Seminar, University of the Western Cape, 5 October 1993.

Davison, Patricia. "Material Culture, Context and Meaning: A Critical Investigation of Museum Practice, with Particular Reference to the South African Museum." Ph.D. diss., University of Cape Town, 1991.

———. "Reading Exhibitions: Towards an Understanding of Popular Responses to Museum Representations of Other Cultures." Paper presented at *Myths, Monuments, Museums: New Premises?* Conference, History Workshop, University of the Witwatersrand, 16–18 July 1992.

du Toit, Andre. "Hendrik Bibault *of* Die Raaisel van Prof. J. L.M Franken oftewel Enkele Filosofiese Vrae en Refleksies oor die Afrikaanse Geskiedskrywing." Paper presented at *Afrikaanse Geskiedskrywing en Leeterkunde—Verlede, Hede en Toekoms*, University of the Western Cape, 17–18 October 1991.

du Toit, Marijke. "Women, Welfare and the Nurturing of Afrikaner Nationalism: A Social History of the Afrikaanse Christelike Vroue Vereniging, c. 1870–1939." Ph.D. diss., University of Cape Town, 1996.

Gordon, Robert. "'Bain's Bushmen': Scenes at the Empire Exhibition, 1936." Paper presented at the African Studies Association Annual Meeting, Boston, November 1993.

Greenstein, Ran. "South African Studies and the Politics of Theory: Old Challenges and New Paradigms." *Paradigms Lost, Paradigms Regained*, Journal of Southern African Studies Conference, York, September 1994.

Hofmeyr, Isabel. "Reading Oral Texts: New Methodological Directions." Paper presented at the South African and Contemporary History Seminar, University of the Western Cape, 3 October 1995.

Jeppie, Shamil. "Historical Processes and the Constitution of Subjects: I. D. du Plessis and the Reinvention of the 'Malay.'" B.A. Honors long essay, University of Cape Town, 1987.

———. "Aspects of Popular Culture and Class Expression in Inner Cape Town, circa 1939–1959." M.A. thesis, University of Cape Town, 1990.

Kratz, Corrine A., and Ivan Karp. "Islands of 'Authenticity': Museums in Disney's World." Paper presented at the South African and Contemporary History Seminar, University of the Western Cape, 28 April 1999.

Kruger, Lou Marie. "Gender, Community and Identity: Women and Afrikaner Nationalism in the Volksmoeder Discourse of Die Boerevrou (1919–1931)." M.Soc.Sci. thesis, University of Cape Town, 1991.

Lalu, Premesh. "Lived Texts, Written Texts and Con-Texts: Eddie Roux and the Making of the South African Past." M.A. thesis, University of the Western Cape, 1994.

Merrington, Peter. "Masques, Monuments and Masons: The 1910 Pageant of the Union of South Africa." Paper presented at the South African and Contemporary History Seminar, University of the Western Cape, 21 May 1996.

Minkley, Gary. "Border Dialogues: Race, Class and Space in the Industrialisation of East London, circa 1902–1963." Ph.D. diss., University of Cape Town, 1994.

Minkley, Gary, and Ciraj Rassool. "Oral History in South Africa: Some Critical Questions." Paper presented at Centre for African Studies seminar, University of Cape Town, 22 March 1995.

Molapo, Rochidi. "Sports, Festivals and Popular Politics: Aspects of the Social and Popular Culture in Langa Township, 1945–70." M.A. thesis, University of Cape Town, 1994.

Mulholland, Rosemary. "The Evolution of History Teaching in South Africa: A Study of the Relationship between the Modes of Political Organization and History Taught in Schools." M.Ed. thesis, University of the Witwatersrand, 1981.

Musemwa, Muchaparara. "Aspects of Social and Political History of Langa Township, Cape Town, 1927–1948." M.A. thesis, University of Cape Town, 1993.

Muthien, Yvonne. "Pass Control and Resistance, Cape Town 1939–1965," Ph.D. diss., Oxford University, 1989.

Nkasawe, Monde. "Curating the Nation: Nation-Building, Public Iconography and the Production of History in Post-Apartheid South Africa." M.A. mini-thesis, University of the Western Cape, 1998.

Rassool, Ciraj. "Going Back to Our Roots: Aspects of Marxist and Radical Thought and Politics in South Africa, 1930–1960." M.A. thesis, Northwestern University, 1987.

———. "Notes on Gender in the Making of Isaac Bangani Tabata." Paper presented at the *Paradigms Lost, Paradigms Regained*, Journal of Southern African Studies Conference, York, September 1994.

Robinson, Jennifer. "Apartheid Subjects and Post-Colonialism: Native Administration in Port Elizabeth, 1945–1970." Paper presented at *Democracy: Popular Prece-*

dents, Practice, Culture, History Workshop Conference, University of the Witwatersrand, 13–15 July 1994.

Rossouw, Cornelis J. "Die Werk van H C v Leibrandt as Argivaris en Suid-Afrikaanse Geskiedskrywer." M.A. thesis, University of South Africa, 1944.

Scher, Dave M. "The Disenfranchisement of the Coloured Voters, 1948–1956." Ph.D. thesis, University of South Africa, 1983.

Trapido, Stanley. "Van Riebeeck Day and the New Jerusalem: Identity, Community and Violence in the Eighteenth and Nineteenth Century Cape." Institute of Commonwealth Studies, London, Postgraduate Seminar, 5 March 1993.

Van der Watt, Liese. "Art, Gender, Ideology, and Afrikaner Nationalism: A History of the Voortrekker Monument Tapestries." M.A. thesis, University of Cape Town, 1996.

Witz, Leslie. "Servant of the Workers: Solly Sachs and the Garment Workers' Union, 1928–1952." M.A. thesis, University of the Witwatersrand, 1984.

Witz, Leslie, and Gary Minkley. "Sir Harry Smith and His Imbongi: Local and National Identities, Eastern Cape, 1952." Paper presented at Democracy: Popular Precedents, Practice, Culture, History Workshop Conference, University of the Witwatersrand, 13–15 July 1994.

Witz, Leslie, Gary Minkley, and Ciraj Rassool. "Thresholds, Gateways and Spectacles: Journeying through South African Hidden Pasts and Histories in the Last Decade of the Twentieth Century." Paper presented at The Future of the Past conference, University of the Western Cape, July 1996.

———. "Who Speaks for South African Pasts?" Paper presented at the Biennial Conference of the South African Historical Society, University of the Western Cape, 11–14 July 1999.

Interviews

Conducted by Leslie Witz (Tape recordings of these interviews are in the possession of the author)

Albertyn, C. F., organizer of the Van Riebeeck festival, at his office in Stellenbosch, 25 August 1994.

Almond, Joe, participant in the Van Riebeeck festival, at his home in Fish Hoek, 23 September 1994.

Broomberg, Shirley, visitor to the Van Riebeeck festival, at her home in Kenilworth, Cape Town, 4 September 1994.

Cilliers, C., organizer of the Van Riebeeck festival, at his home in Fish Hoek, Cape Town, 15 September 1993.

de Lange, Sr., Robbie, participant in the Van Riebeeck festival, at his home in East London, 19 January 1994.

de Ridder, Cecile, organizer of the Van Riebeeck festival, at her home in Verwoerdburg, 10 December 1993.

de Wet, Sylvia, visitor to the Van Riebeeck festival, at her home in Stellenbosch, 23 September 1994.

Dudley, R. O., campaigner against the Van Riebeeck festival, at his home in Elfindale, Cape Town, 24 August 1994.

Halliday, Mr. and Mrs. K., participants in the Van Riebeeck festival, at their home in Pinelands, Cape Town, 9 September 1994.

Kleynhans, Rosalie, visitor to the Van Riebeeck festival, at her home in Pinelands, Cape Town, 7 September 1994.

Makalima, Sipho, campaigner against the Van Riebeeck festival, at his home in Alice, 20 January 1994.

Nkosinkulu, Vuma, campaigner against the Van Riebeeck festival, at his home in Grahamstown, 25 January 1994.

Olivier, Ronette, visitor to the Van Riebeeck festival, at her home in Rondebosch East, Cape Town, 2 September 1994.

Pheiffer, Roy, participant in the Van Riebeeck festival, in his office at the Dept. of Afrikaans and Nederlands, University of Cape Town, 7 August 1992.

Segal, Ronald, campaigner against the Van Riebeeck festival, at the Vineyard Hotel, Newlands, Cape Town, 14 August 1992.

Taylor, Yvonne, visitor to the Van Riebeeck festival, at her home in Sybrandt Park, Cape Town, 21 September 1994.

von Holdt, Sally, participant in the Van Riebeeck festival, at her home in Wynberg, 28 September 1994.

Conducted By Rochidi Molapo

Macozoma, Constance, Langa, Cape Town, 5 September 1993.

Mgijima, Thami, Langa, Cape Town, 23 January 1994.

Ndlumbini, M. S. "Cappy," Langa, Cape Town, 22 January 1994.

Conducted by Others

Keppel-Jones, Arthur, conducted by Alan Jeeves at Queens University, 14 June 1994, *South African Historical Journal* 32 (May 1995): 11–23.

Ntantala Jordan, Phyllis, conducted by Ciraj Rassool at the University of the Western Cape, 4 November 1993.

Thompson, Leonard, conducted by Lynn Berat, 14 August 1993, *South African Historical Journal* 30 (May 1994): 16–32.

Index

Livingstone, D., 40–41
Local Authorities Against Apartheid, 1
Locations Advisory Board, 155
London Missionary Society, 40, 113, 174
Louw, E., 182
Louw, L., 212
Lovedale mission, 93

Macomo, 226, 227
Mafikeng, 166, 170
Mail coaches, 27–28, 105, 144, *218*, 228–29, *239*, 239–40, 247; and ATKV, 119, 216–17, 221–22; Cape Town coach, 133; "Settlers" coach, 28, 230–39, 240
Makana, 164, 236
Malacca, 30, 77
Malan, D. F., 2, 89–90, 131, 134; and ANC, 157, 165; and Festival, 135, 144, 148, 217; and Voortrekker Monument, 96, 97, 126
Malan, Mrs. D. F., 139, 140
Malan, F. S., 51
Malan, W. de V., 128
Malangabi, J., 155–56
Malay history and culture, 130–31, 250–51
Malay Pageant, 26, 88, 130–31, *136*, 136–37, 147; and boycott, 135, 153, 177, 179, 248
Malherbe, D. F., 110
Malherbe, N., 1
Mandela, N., 4, 23, 157, 244, 249, 251
Mandelbrote, H. J., 158, 161
Marks, J. B., 167
Mashaba, O. A., 196
Matatiele, 285n9
Matthews, Z. K., 167–68
Maynardville, 152
Mbeki, G., 251
Mbeki, T., 4, 252
McKay, H., 111
Meiring, K., 244
Mfengu festival, 163
Millin, S. G., 110, 141
Missionaries, 25, 38–39, 40, 174; Pageant, 113, 115, 127
Mitchell, M. L., 161
Mkhize, I. D., 154
Moerdyk, G., 122
Mohale, A., 196
Molelekwa, Mr., 156
Molema, S. M., 144, 165–67, 170, 174
Molsbergen, E. C. Godee, 47
Moodie, D., 71, 74–76
Moore, H., 180
Morkel, G., 255

Moroka, J., 166
Moroka, Dr. J. S., 157, 167, 168, 178
Morris, R. F., 208
Morris, S. S., 188
Moshoeshoe, 164; festival, 163
Moslem Lads' Brigade, 147
Mossel Bay, 229
Much-Binding-in-the-Marsh Pavilion, 191, 194, 197–98, 199, 200. *See also* United Kingdom Pavilion
Muizenberg, 24
Museum exhibits, 8–9, 21, 182–83, 253; Malay history and culture, 131, 250–51. *See also* Bushmen

Namibia. *See* South-West Africa
National Council of African Women, 155
National Party, 2, 12, 89–90, 122, 133–34, 232; election victory, 4, 11, 14–15, 95, 96–97; and Festival 5, 89–90, 104, 115, 202, 350. *See also* New National Party
Nationalism, 13, 243; white settler, 200–201. *See also* Afrikaner nationalism; Settlers
Native Affairs Department, 165; Bantu Pavilion, 153–56, 191, 194–97, 198, 200, 208–209, 248; human showcases, 192–93; Langa festival, 129–30, 171
"Native policy": history, 74–76
Native Representatives Council, 155
Nazis, 89
Het Nederduitsch Zuid-Afrikaansche Tydschrift, 39, 71, 72–74, 75, 76, 77, 82
Neethling, D., 144, *145*
Neethling-Pohl, A., 84, 106–109, 124, 225; Pageant, 130, 138, 142; —, script, 86, 112–14, 119, 241
Netherlands, 2–3; Royal family, 120
Netherlands Van Riebeeck Committee, 198, 199
New National Party, 255
New South Wales, 17
New York, 101
Newfoundland, 17
Newton Thompson, J. C., 97, 126, 133
Newton Thompson, Joyce, 126, 132
Ngwevela, J., 156
Nkosi, J., 276n47
Non-European Unity Movement, 5, 148–49, 151–52, 160, 178; Festival boycott, 5, 144–45, 152–53, 155, 162, 248, 252; use of history, 169–72, 176
Nongauza, M., 156
Ntantala, P., *145*, 177
Ntloedibe, E. L., 177
Ntsikana, 93; festival, 163
Nuwedorp, 1
Nyanga, 169

South African Native National Congress. *See*
   African National Congress
South African Nautical College, 86
South African Police Band, 87
South African Railways and Harbours, 187, 189
South African Republic, 96
South African War, 25, 44, 48, 93, 96, 98; blacks
   and, 155; Pageant, 113, 115–16, *116*, 118, 140, 141;
   women in, 121
South-West Africa: pavilion, 191, 198, 202, 206–14
Southern Rhodesia, 191
Stamps, commemorative, 120
Standerton, 94
The Star, 98, 117
State: role in festivals, 9–11
The State, 62
Statute of Westminster, 226, 240–41
Stellenbosch, 36, 117, 220
Steyn, G., 133
Steyn, M. T., 51
Stockenstrom, E., 66
Strandlopers, 86, 179, 180, 248
Strauss, J. G. N., 142
Street processions, 107–108, 238; Cape Town, 93,
   112–13, 138–41, 180. *See also* Pageant, van Rie-
   beeck Festival
Strikes, 15, 151–52, 157; miners', 155, 203
Stuttaford, R., 193
Stutterheim, 240
Stuyvesant, P., 47
Surrey Estate, 248
Sydney Cove, 16, 17, 20
Sydney Harbor, 21–22
Symbolism, 9, 62–63, 93–94, 96–97

Tabata, I. B., 145, 169, 170, 177–78
Table Bay, 2, 3, 4, 33. *See also* Granger Bay
Table Mountain, 33; Festival focus, 103–104,
   105, 188
Taylor, D., 171–72, 174–75
Taylor, M., 231
Teachers Educational and Professional Associa-
   tion, 148, 151
Teachers League of South Africa, 148–50, 152
Textbooks, 53; history 25, 32, 53–70. *See also*
   van Riebeeck, J.: in history textbooks
Theal, G. M., 31, 77–78; *History of SA*, 36, 128,
   160, 161, 175; and history textbooks, 60–62, 63,
   64, 66, 67, 83
Thom, H. B., 30, 34, 50–51, 71, 72–73; and Festi-
   val, 90, 108–109, 115, 128, 158; and van Riebeeck
   diary, 79–82, 83, 89, 109–10, 175
Thompson, J. C. Newton, 97, 126, 133

Thompson, Joyce Newton, 126, 132
Thompson, L., 160–61
Thompson, M., 126, 140, 160
Thompson, W. R., 97, 126, 227
Thomson, D. H., 235
The Torch, 149, 152–53, 172, 173, 178, 212
Torch Commando, 107, 134
Tourism: and van Riebeeck, 249
Traders' Association, 155
Transvaal Chamber of Mines, 114, 117; Pavilion,
   117, 202–206
Die Transvaler, 114, 118, 119, 142
Treaty 88, 22
Truth and Reconciliation Commission, 252
Tsotsi, W., 170, 171
Tukwayo, Mr., 156
Tulbagh, R., 36, 37
Tweed, J., 43
Tyali, 226

Uitenhage, 285n9
Umkonto we Sizwe, 251
Umtata, 28, 216, 220, 229, 230–31, 233
Union of South Africa, 62, 63, 66, 155, 170; com-
   memorative pageant, 44; and public holidays,
   45; and van Riebeeck Festival Pageant, 113,
   116, 118
Uniondale, 285n9
United Kingdom Pavilion, 198–99, 200. *See also*
   Much-Binding-in-the-Marsh Pavilion
United Party, 89, 133–34; and Festival, 90, 91, 92–
   94, 115, 142
United States of America: founding festival, 16–
   18, 19, 21, 22–23, 261n17
Universities: and Festival, 157–58
University of Cape Town: and Festival, 158–62;
   hospital rag, 108, 163; Medical School, 210;
   Speech and Drama Dept., 138, *139*. *See also*
   Davie, Dr. T. B.
University of the Witwatersrand, 110–12, 275n33
Unlawful Organisations Bill, 157
Uys, J., 97, 126, 140, 227

Die Vaderland, 111, 118
Van den Berg, J., 199
Van der Lingen, Rev. G. W. A., 39
Van der Merwe, A. J., 134
Van der Poel, J., 160–61
Van der Spuy, Rev. P., 36–37
Van der Stel, S., 119, 129, 164
Van der Stel, W. A., 78, 113
Van der Velde, F., 243–44
Van Koningsbruggen, H. A. J. M., 2

Index 323

LESLIE WITZ is Associate Professor of History at the University of the Western Cape.

Lightning Source UK Ltd.
Milton Keynes UK
UKHW020345280422
402152UK00006B/384